W9-ATP-413

INSTRUMENTATION /ORCHESTRATION

Longman Music Series
Series Editor: Gerald Warfield

INSTRUMENTATION /ORCHESTRATION

ALFRED BLATTER

Drexel University

INSTRUMENTATION/*ORCHESTRATION*

Longman Inc., New York
Associated companies, branches, and representatives
throughout the world.

Developmental Editor: Gordon T.R. Anderson
Editorial and Design Supervisor: Joan Matthews
Interior Design: George Chien
Cover Design: Charles Fellows
Manufacturing and Production Supervisor: Louis Gaber
Composition: Melvin Wildberger
Printing: Crest Litho, Inc.
Binding: American-Book Stratford Press

Library of Congress Cataloging in Publication Data

Blatter, Alfred W
Instrumentation/*orchestration.*

(Longman music series)
Bibliography: p.
Includes index.
1. Instrumentation and orchestration.
I. Title. II. Series.
MT70.B56 781.6'4 79-17001
ISBN 0-582-28118-0

Manufactured in the United States of America

9 8 7 6 5 4 3 2 1

In memory of the man who first answered my questions and stimulated my interest in music and its instruments—my father

A. Oscar Blatter
1911 - 1977

Preface

INSTRUMENTATION/*ORCHESTRATION* is written to provide a text for beginning or intermediate students of instrumentation and orchestration and to serve as a reference for teachers and composers. For the student who may be encountering the problems of writing for instruments for the first time, this book provides practical information on score preparation and parts extraction, chapters on transcribing and arranging, in addition to the usual information on instrumental ranges and qualities. For the public school band or orchestra director having to prepare a special arrangement according to his students' more limited abilities, student ranges are included in addition to specific suggestions for transforming musical materials from one medium to another. The professional arranger will find the detailed information on less common instruments valuable and the articles on wind articulations and vocal limitations to be especially useful. The composer will find the book to be an indispensable reference work, as it provides thorough explanations of such diverse topics as percussion mallets, instrumental pictograms, and contemporary techniques and possibilities, and includes extensive fingering charts for all instruments and basic information on electronic modification of sound.

The books generally available on instrumentation caution the reader about those things one should *not* do and the possibilities that the instruments do *not* possess. While not ignoring the physical limitations of the instruments, the approach of this book is to advocate what an instrument *can* do. The reader is reminded that the list of instrumental possibilities is continually growing longer while the "impossibilities" list grows shorter.* No book, whose words and diagrams are frozen in time, can adequately reflect the evolving state of an art. It is therefore important that the reader remain in touch with the musicians who are both the creators and imparters of this knowledge.

It is not the purpose of this book to embrace or condemn any particular compositional or performance style. Therefore, many instruments and techniques often omitted or glossed over in other reference books are included here. The author has also attempted to minimize the insertion of his own tastes or preferences into the commentary; however, he is not so naïve as to believe that he has totally succeeded in the latter endeavor.

*For example, in 1972 a composition for solo tuba written by the author and containing multiphonics was thought to be performable by only a few, specially skilled professional tubists in the world. Four years later multiphonics had become so thoroughly assimilated into tuba performance techniques that the piece was performed by undergraduate tuba students at several schools of music.

Preface

Acknowledgments

Many debts are owed to many friends and colleagues who have provided so much help in this project. First and foremost among these is Gerald Warfield who first proposed the project and then did all the right things to make sure that is was completed. His experience as an editor and his knowledge as a musician made this job a pleasure. Next I must thank Robert Bays, who understood the demands upon my time that this task created and was more than understanding in providing the needed time and support.

A special group must be acknowledged: the musicians who, as excellent and imaginative performers, shared their insights with me by reading and commenting upon the information provided about their respective instruments. This includes Jan Bach, Sanford Berry, Robert Black, Paul Cox, Jeffrey Elliott, Frederick Fairchild, John Fonville, Thomas Fredrickson, David Hickman, Maria Merkelo, Daniel Perantoni, Guillermo Perich, G. David Peters, Leonard Rumery, David Shrader, Thomas Siwe, Scott Wyatt, and Wilma Zonn.

In addition to these, many other musicians provided innumerable bits and pieces of information and helped to clarify some of the knotty problems encountered. These include Thomas Albert, Richard Ashley, Shirley Blankenship, Patrick Castle, John Cranford, Eric Dalheim, Guy Duker, Robert Gray, Thomas Holden, Edward Krolick, Arthur Maddox, Harold and Peggy Rosenthal, Ray Sasaki, Stuart S. Smith, and Tom Ward.

The photographs in the book are the result, too, of many efforts. Locating the instruments, finding appropriate space in which to photograph them, and assisting with the task of setting up and taking down the objects required the efforts of the following people: Harry Begian, Robert Chamberlin, Michael Chunn, William DeMont, Ron DeVore, Guy Duker, John Ellis, David Hickman, Thomas Holden, Edward Krolick, Carl A. Landrum, Richard R. Lask, Austin McDowell, Jameson Marvin, Maria Merkelo, James Moffit, John O'Connor, Marshall Onofrio, Eldon Oyen, Daniel Perantoni, Thomas Siwe, Gary E. Smith, Hugh Soebbing, Russell Winterbottom, and Wilma Zonn. Special mention must go to Frederick Fairchild who spent hours locating and helping to arrange the percussion equipment; Skip Paul of the 1st National

Guitar Store in Urbana, Illinois, who lent both the space and the instruments for the fretted strings photographs; and David Hruby who was more than a photographer—he was a creative and imaginative artist who shaped the pictures he took.

I also wish to thank Mark Thomas of the W. T. Armstrong Company, Inc. who made available to me the photograph of the flute family.

M. William Karlins read an early draft and provided many valuable suggestions which have found their way into the book. A later draft was thoroughly read by James Eversole, who offered many suggestions and whose insights into the ordering of the material was of special value.

The information on scoring for student ensembles was enriched by the observations of Jerry Jordan and Daniel Kohut. The chart on page 326 was provided by Dr. Kohut from a handout for his instrumental methods course.

To Paul Vermel, Herbert Brun, and Alberto Segre I offer thanks for having read and corrected the portions of the manuscript in French, German, and Italian. Their efforts and encouraging comments have meant a lot to me.

Other contributors were typists Norma Runner and Ofelia Dawley; John Simpson, who helped locate and reproduce hundreds of examples; and many orchestration students, who by their questions and successes, helped to shape this book.

The project could never have been completed without the help of my wife Marilyn, who has proofread every page of every draft, has run countless errands, and has put up with outrageous demands upon her time, her housekeeping, and her patience. She, as much as anyone, has made it possible. Of great importance, too, has been the help and support of my mother.

The most special thanks of all is reserved for my friend, neighbor, and colleague Paul Zonn, who not only read portions of the book in various stages of evolution, but spent hours discussing raw ideas, helping me formulate into words some basic concepts. He freely offered his advice, criticism, information, library, and instruments as needed, and created both the oboe and clarinet fingering charts which he is allowing me to publish for the first time.

To all of the above, I am indebted. Without them, there would be no book.

Contents

List of Figures

Notes on the Use of This Book

INSTRUMENTATION/*ORCHESTRATION* is designed to serve a dual purpose: as a textbook in a one- or two-semester orchestration or arranging course, and as a reference work for students, teachers, and professionals.

AS A TEXTBOOK

By the ordering of the chapters, the student is first introduced to the coloristic and technical characteristics of the various instruments, and then to the practices and procedures of orchestration. The order of presentation of this material and the specific chapters to be included or excluded in a course of study would be determined by the nature of the course in which the book is used. In an advanced course, the students might skip over the chapters on instrumentation (2 through 7) and start immediately with Chapter 8, the first chapter to deal specifically with orchestration. A less experienced group would probably follow pretty closely the order in which the material is presented here; but a teacher might also have the students study the material on instrumentation concurrently with that on orchestrational techniques and devices. A course in band arranging would probably omit the chapter on strings, or assign it as extra reading. In a single-semester course on orchestration, it might be practical to limit the instruments discussed to those in Chapters 2 through 5 only. In any case, Chapter 1 is fundamental to whatever approach is decided on, providing guidelines and practical information necessary to complete the problem sets that are distributed throughout the text. The problem sets contain enough material to keep even an ambitious student very busy for two semesters. Because of the length and difficulty of these assignments, the instructor may want to limit or edit them to more closely match the time, resources, and personnel available to the students.

From the General to the Specific

The assignments found in Chapter 1 and Chapters 8 through 12 require more general problem-solving techniques directed at the actual approach to orchestration projects. The assignments found in the instrumental chapters are more specific, involve less creative effort, and deal with the specifics of the instruments under consideration. The instructor is encouraged to "mix and match" these tasks to the needs of his students and the goals of the course. It is not intended that a student would do all or even most of the assignments; they exist in quantity to provide alternatives and variety.

AS A REFERENCE

The placement of the instrumental chapters together, near the front of the book, is intended to aid the professional composer, arranger, or teacher who will need the book primarily as a reference. General information about the characteristics of the choir to which an instrument belongs comes first, followed by the more specific information about the instrument's family as well as its specific properties. (Throughout the book the term *choir* is used to refer to all instruments that produce a tone in a similar manner, such as the brass choir, while *family* is used to refer to instruments that are generically related, such as the clarinet family.) Specific information only rarely needed is collected in the Appendices.

THE DYNAMIC CURVE

Included with the description of most instruments is a dynamic curve which graphically represents the characteristic dynamic properties of the instrument in relation to its register. It is meant to assist the orchestrator in making reasonable demands on instrumentalists, but it certainly does not describe the exact limitations of every performer. To the contrary, most professional performers have spent a lifetime learning to minimize the effects illustrated by the dynamic curve. Nevertheless, even the most competent performer may have more limited flexibility in some registers that interferes with balance and control.

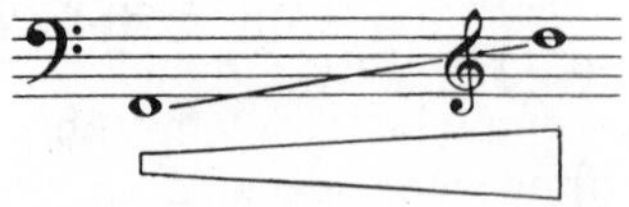

(Above) A typical dynamic curve showing that an instrument is capable of greater dynamic power in its highest register (may have difficulty playing softly) but is somewhat weaker (easily covered) in its lower register.

INSTRUMENTAL RANGES

Instrumental ranges are given according to the following diagram system:

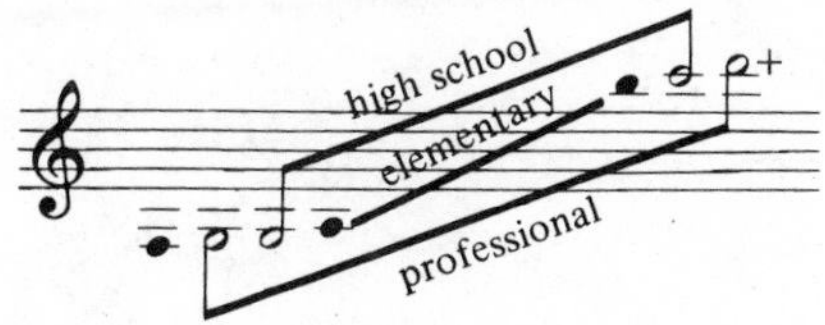

1. Large stemless black notes connected by a line within the diagram represent a typical junior high school performer's range.
2. Large white notes, beamed together, with stems up represent a typical high school or college performer's range.
3. Large white notes with stems down and beamed together, represent a professional performer's range.
4. Small stemless black notes outside of these ranges indicate pitches available on some specially equipped instrument or available to some performers who have developed special skills.
5. A plus sign (+) indicates that the possibility of extending the range beyond the indicated limits exists and is often encountered, though it represents a rather special situation at this time.
6. For rare instruments, only the professional range is given since nonprofessionals would seldom possess or play such an instrument.

One should remember that an exceptional junior high school performer might be capable of performing within a typical high school performer's range while an exceptional high school performer could be considered professional. Therefore, a college music major must be considered a professional within the above classification system.

IN CONCLUSION

No book can accurately describe the sound of an instrument and the peculiar qualities of its various registers. Only by listening to the instruments can the sound properties have meaning. A live hearing is best, but in lieu of this records will suffice. As instruments are studied, listening assignments designed to increase the student's exposure to both the timbre of a particular instrument and to some of its idiomatic usages, both in solo repertory and as a member of an ensemble, should be made. If possible, the student should have an opportunity to try to produce a few tones on the various instruments. This firsthand experience is extremely valuable.

1

The Basics: Preparing Scores and Parts

THE SCORE

The score is that copy of a piece of music in which all parts are displayed simultaneously and sequentially to show the nature of and the relationships among all the musical events that constitute a particular piece of music.

A score should effectively fulfill three requirements:

1. It should serve the composer or orchestrator by functioning as the workbench upon which he assembles his piece.
2. It should serve the conductor by effectively communicating the composition to him.
3. It should serve the performer by communicating to him, via the copyist, his individual performance instructions.

As long as the first requirement is the only one that needs to be met, the manner in which a score is prepared is only the concern of the individual composer or orchestrator. But when the second and third requirements, those involving communication, enter the picture, certain traditional practices need to be observed. Although these traditional practices may seem arbitrary (and at times are definitely not logical), it is always wise to attempt to conform to these procedures. Modifications should take place *only* if the musical conceptions of the composer or orchestrator cannot be expressed within the limits of traditional practice.

Instrumental Ordering and Vertical Spacing

The instruments or voices should be arranged in what is called *score order*. Traditional score order, by choirs, is, from top to bottom:

Woodwinds
Brasses
Percussion
Other Instruments
Strings

Within each choir, the traditional ordering is, again from top to bottom, the highest-pitched to the lowest-pitched *family.* (The determination of which is a higher- or lower-pitched family is based upon the lowest pitch of the most common member of the family. Thus flutes are traditionally above oboes in score order while clarinets are below the oboes.)

There are some notable exceptions to traditional score order, and these exceptions are also traditional. The horns, while certainly not the highest-pitched family among the brasses, are traditionally placed above the other brasses *in orchestra scores.* Vocal parts are usually placed below the percussion and above the strings, where one would place "other instruments," but sometimes below the violas and above the violoncellos. In commercial arrangements using voices, the vocal parts are often at the top of the page.

The following are some typical score orders for standard instrumental groups:

Brass Quintet

Trumpet I
Trumpet II
Horn
Trombone
Tuba

Woodwind Quintet

Flute
Oboe
Clarinet
Horn[1]
Bassoon[1]

Brass Sextet

Trumpet I
Trumpet II
Horn
Trombone
Euphonium
Tuba

Orchestra

Flutes
Oboes
Clarinets
Bassoons
Horns
Trumpets
Trombones
Tuba
Timpani
Percussion
Other instruments[2]
Violins I
Violins II
Viola
Violoncellos
Contrabasses

Concert Band

Flutes
Oboes
Bassoons
Clarinets
Saxophones
Cornets
Trumpets
Horns
Trombones
Euphoniums
Tubas
Timpani
Percussion

Jazz Band (Stage Band)

Saxophones
Trumpets
Trombones
Guitar
String Bass
Drums
Piano

[1]Sometimes these two are reversed.

[2]Other instruments include harp, piano, celesta, organ, voices, chorus, solo instruments (such as the solo violin part in a violin concerto), and sometimes saxophone(s). Since there is no traditional location for the saxophone in the orchestral score, one can find many variations; a logical choice would be below the bassoons and above the horns (or between clarinets and bassoons).

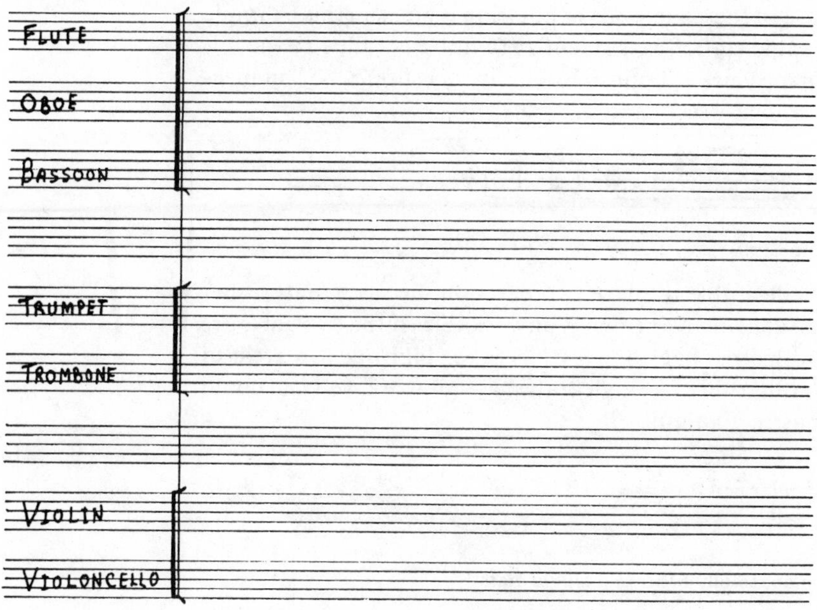

EXAMPLE 1 How a score page for a chamber piece might appear.

When there is enough space it is usually desirable to use a separate staff for each performer or separate part, and readability is improved by leaving extra space between choirs. In manuscript, this is accomplished by skipping a staff (as was done in Example 1).

Sometimes it is impractical to reserve a separate staff for each part, in which case one would then combine two different parts for the same instrument onto one staff. More than two parts on the same staff is not usually practical. It is essential that the instruments sharing a staff be alike, such as two oboes (Oboe I and Oboe II) and not two unlike instruments, even if they are from the same family (Oboe I and English horn.) So that a person reading the score may understand which of the instruments sharing a staff is to play, the following method is used: upward stems for one performer and downward stems for the other, sometimes in conjunction with the following symbols and abbreviations:

English	*French*	*German*	*Italian*	
1st	1er (or 1ère)	1ste	1°	first part only play
2nd	2e	2te	2°	second part only play
3rd	3e	3te	3°	third part only play
4th	4e	4te	4°	fourth part only play
both	à 2	zu 2	a 2	both parts play
all three	à 3	zu 3	a 3	all three parts play
all four	à 4	zu 4	a 4	all four parts play
all	tous	alle	tutti	all performers play
solo	seul	allein	solo	only one performer; an important line.

An illustration of the use of these methods of notation is given in this example of two flutes sharing the same staff. The student's attention is called to the following: the use of "a 2" in measure 1; opposite stems in measure 2; "2°" in measures 3 and 4; and "3°" in measures 4 and 5.

EXAMPLE 2 Two parts on one Staff.

Even when it would be desirable to place two parts on the same staff, other considerations may make such an arrangement unworkable. If the two parts are quite independent, or if both cross back and forth between high and low areas of the instrument's range, the sharing of a single staff may not work well and could create reading problems as in Example 3.

EXAMPLE 3 Two parts not successfully sharing a single staff.

At times it will improve clarity to allow extra space between two staves even if that would not ordinarily be done. Example 4-a illustrates a situation in which the low pitches of the clarinet interfere with the upper pitches of the bassoon. Example 4-b provides a suitable solution to the problem.

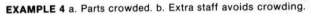

EXAMPLE 4 a. Parts crowded. b. Extra staff avoids crowding.

One is most likely to encounter this crowding problem in the ledger-line areas above the first violins, below the tuba, above the first trombone, above the bassoon, below the clarinet, and, on some occasions, above the flute.

Providing Necessary Information

There is a great variety of information that the composer or orchestrator may need to communicate to the performers and conductor. In the preparation of a score there are certain locations where this information is placed.

Cover (First or Title) Page

The following information should be placed on the cover page:

1. The title of the composition.
2. The name of the composer.
3. The name of the orchestrator (if any).
4. The name of the lyricist (if any).
5. The general instrumentation.

Most of these items are self-explanatory. The title would include any subtitle, for instance:

SYMPHONY NO. 103 IN E♭
"THE DRUM ROLL"

The composer's name should be as it would appear in a program: *W. A. Mozart,* not just *Mozart.*

The general instrumentation might be written as: *for Orchestra,* or *for String Quartet.* Usually, if it is not a standard group and consists of fewer than eight performers, then all should be listed: *for 2 flutes, oboe, guitar, soprano, and viola.* A larger group might be: *for soprano and 13 winds.* How detailed this listing is will depend upon the nature of the work and what the composer or orchestrator wishes to emphasize.

Inside Cover (Second) Page

This page would contain any explanations, special instructions, interpretation of special signs or symbols, or detailed information about the instruments to be used (such as a complete list of percussion instruments needed.) A translation of a text, if one is supplied, would also appear here. If the information of this nature is extensive, additional pages may be used. On the other hand, if no special information is required, the second page may be left blank.

First Page of Music

Traditionally, this is a right-hand page. On this first page of music all of the information of the cover page will appear plus the first system of music.[3] This system, with the instruments in score order and assigned to specific staves, as in Example 1, is indented so that the full name, part, and transposition of each instrument may appear on its staff line. In addition, clefs and tempo indications appear along with any needed key signatures or meter signatures.

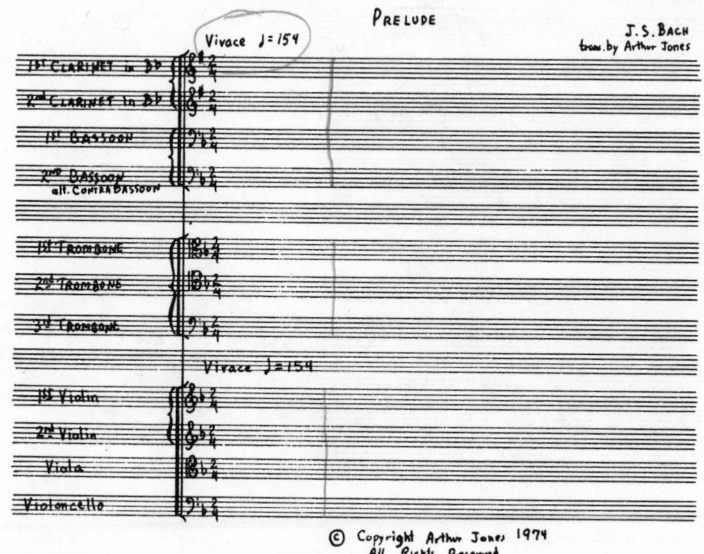

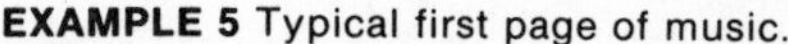

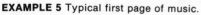

EXAMPLE 5 Typical first page of music.

[3]A *system* is a group of staves forming one complete portion of the score. In works for few instruments, several systems may appear on a single page.

In Example 5, note the placement of various items. Title is centered; composer's name is above the music on the right, orchestrator's name just below. The system is indented, choirs are connected by brackets [, groups of the same instrument are connected by braces { , and the names, parts, and transpositions are given on the left-hand side of the system. The key signatures are followed by the meter signature, and the tempo is given above the system on the left-hand side. (It is also commonly repeated above the strings.) If a lyricist's name were involved, it would be placed on the left above the tempo indication, at the same level as the composer's name.

If any of the performers are required to double on other instruments,[4] this information should be included on the first page of music. All instruments required anywhere throughout the composition, no matter how much later they may appear, should be accounted for on the first page of music, or, at least, on the inside cover page; even better, include the information at both locations.

Copyright Notice

The copyright notice may be placed either on the title page or on the first page of music or at both locations. Any notices regarding permission to use copyrighted material should be placed at these locations also. There is a prescribed form for a copyright notice. It must contain:

1. The word "copyright".
2. The name of the person(s) claiming copyright.
3. The year in which the work was created.

EXAMPLE 6 A later page from the same score as Example 5.

[4]When a performer plays two or more instruments within a composition, he is said to *double.* Typical examples are: 2nd Flute alt. Piccolo; 3rd Clarinet alt. Bass clarinet.

To claim international copyrights, the symbol ©, and the words "all rights reserved" should be added to the above notice.

Following Pages

Pages after the first page of music will usually not be indented, will use abbreviations for the instruments, and will repeat the organization of the system with respect to brackets, braces, blank staves, etc. Clefs and key signatures, if used, are also repeated on following pages and systems, but not meter signatures.

Problem Set No. 1

1. Prepare a cover or title page for this composition:

   Instrumentation: Violin, 2 Oboes, Bassoon, Violoncello.
   Composer: L. J. Oberschmitt
   Title: Sonata in B♭
   Arranged by: yourself

2. Prepare the first page of music for the composition given in the preceding exercise. The meter is $\frac{4}{4}$ and the tempo is Allegro.
3. Prepare the title page and the first page of score for a woodwind quintet transcription of this piece. The key signature for the clarinet will be one flat, and for the horn two flats. Do not attempt to assign any pitches to the instruments.

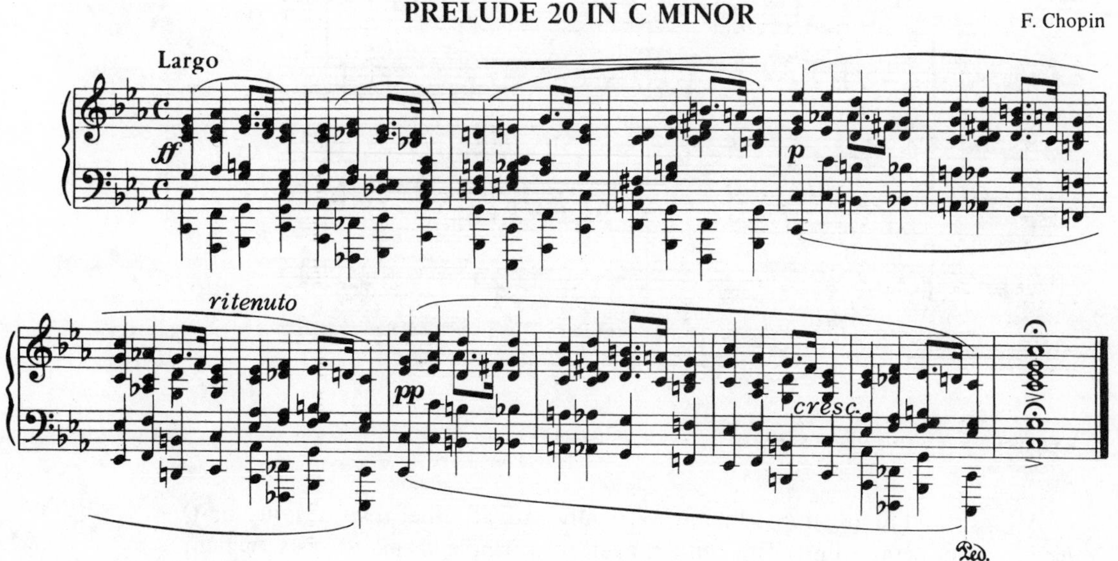

4. Prepare a second page of music for the piece assigned in either the first or the third exercise above (again, do not write any pitches).

Vertical Alignment

To facilitate reading a score, it is very important that the musical events that occur at the same time be aligned vertically. Examine Example 7.

EXAMPLE 7 A score showing poor vertical alignment.

In the above example it is difficult to tell what pitches will be sounded together. The trumpet note in the third measure appears to be on the third beat of the bar when in reality it is to be played on the first beat. Example 8, a well-aligned score, is much easier to read and understand.

EXAMPLE 8 A well-aligned score.

All rests and notes should line up vertically with all other rests or notes that occur at the same time. The only exception is whole measure rests, which should be centered in the measure or omitted.

In the actual process of preparing a score by hand, alignment is facilitated by first copying (in each measure) the musical line (part) with the most notes. There will then always be room for a half note or a whole note; trying to squeeze in a group of thirty-second notes—after the fact—is not always possible. After the line with the most notes has been copied, it will become much easier to align the other parts. Bar lines are placed after the notes are copied and should extend vertically from the top to the bottom of the system with gaps between the choirs. Do not try to draw bar lines freehand.

Problem Set No. 2

1. Redraw this score, correctly aligning the parts.

2. Here are the bass and treble lines for four contrapuntal measures. Prepare a piano staff showing these lines as they relate to one another. The first measure is done correctly for you.

Rehearsal Letters and Numbers

Rehearsal letters or numbers are necessary items and should be placed in the score (and parts.) They serve two purposes: the obvious one is that of providing a starting point within the piece when it is necessary to stop and restart the ensemble during rehearsals. They are also necessary for those performers who have long rests during the piece. For these performers the letters or numbers, assuming that they are placed at the beginnings of phrases or sections, serve as signposts with which they can keep track of the music.

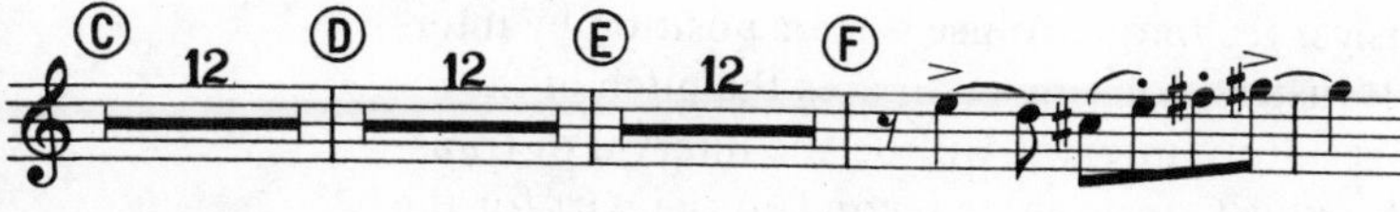

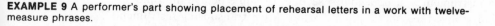

EXAMPLE 9 A performer's part showing placement of rehearsal letters in a work with twelve-measure phrases.

A performer who finds Example 9 in his part does not necessarily count 36 measures of rest. He is more likely to listen for three 12 measure phrases and then enter at the start of the fourth phrase. Thus, the placement of the letters by corresponding to phrases, reinforces the performer's certainty that he is indeed counting correctly.

An alternative to letters is cumulative numbers (measure numbers) placed in the score or parts at the beginning of phrases or at the beginning of each system. Whenever possible, the numbering of every measure in the score and parts will provide the quickest possible reference in a rehearsal.

Transposition

One basic skill that a composer or orchestrator must possess before he can write effectively for band or orchestra is the ability to transpose. Most instruments sound the written pitch when they play, but a few sound a pitch that is different from that which is written. These are called transposing instruments. A chart of them is given in Appendix I and they are discussed under their respective families in the body of this book.

Usually an instrument is written as a transposing instrument so that a performer may transfer eye-and-hand coordination skills learned on one family member to other family members. Thus when a clarinetist sees this written pitch: he covers the holes played by his thumb and first three fingers on the left hand *no matter what clarinet he may be playing*. However, the pitch that will be heard depends upon the physical size of the clarinet he is playing.

The names of these transposing instruments usually include the name of the *key* in which the instrument is pitched: B♭ clarinet, E♭ alto saxophone, etc. This name always identifies the concert pitch that will be heard when a written C is performed by the instrumentalist. Therefore, our clarinetist playing (i.e., fingering) the written C above, will, on a B♭ clarinet, produce a concert B♭, on an A clarinet, a concert A, or on an E♭ alto clarinet, an E♭. In terms of notation, these will be the results:

EXAMPLE 10 Written and sounding pitches for: a. B♭ clarinet. b. A clarinet. c. E♭ alto clarinet.

For most orchestrators the easiest technique to use is transposition by interval. To calculate the interval of transposition one compares the pitch of the instrument (B♭, F, etc.) to C; the resulting interval will be the interval of transposition. The interval between B♭ and C is a major second so the part for the transposing instrument will be a major second, or some octave multiple of a major second, above the concert pitch desired. Most transposing instruments sound *lower* than concert pitch and so are written *above* concert pitch. (Among the few common exceptions are the E♭ soprano clarinet and the D, E♭, and piccolo trumpets.)

EXAMPLE 11 Comparison of sounding or concert pitch and written or transposed notation for a B♭ trumpet.

Problem Set No. 3

1. Transpose the melody of the Chopin excerpt in the third exercise of Problem Set No. 1 (page 7) for an instrument in F (sounding a perfect 5th below concert pitch.)
2. Convert this transposed score into a concert pitch score. (All the instruments here *sound* lower than written.)

3. Transpose these two lines to concert pitch and place on a single staff. Use symbols given on page 3 if appropriate.

Transposed Versus Concert Pitch Score

There are two types of scores commonly found: the transposed score and the concert pitch score. The distinction has to do with the notation of pitch in each score. In the transposed score, the transposing instruments appear in the score exactly as they appear in the performers' parts. In the concert pitch scores, all parts are notated with the pitches that *sound,* regardless of the notation used in the individual parts. The only common exceptions in a concert pitch score are: the piccolos (which are written an octave lower than they will sound), the contrabasses (which are written an octave higher than they will sound), and certain percussion instruments such as the celesta and the xylophone.

Though the concert pitch score is apparently easier for the composer or orchestrator to use, there are at least four reasons to recommend the transposed score:

1. The copyist need not know how to transpose and can merely copy the parts directly from the score.
2. Conductors are familiar with reading from transposed scores; thus, reading from a concert pitch score usually requires an additional process for the conductor—to remember to forget to transpose.
3. Among several instruments from the same family, most have the same fingerings and response characteristics for the same notated pitch. Therefore, the orchestrator can transfer quickly his knowledge of one instrument to another of the same family, if the parts are transposed rather than concert pitch.
4. If the score and the parts are written in the same notation (i.e., transposed), the performer and conductor would be discussing any problems in the same terms and with respect to the same pitches during rehearsals, thereby saving time and minimizing confusion.

Since the transposed score is the norm, it is essential that a concert pitch score contain a prominently placed note to the conductor informing him of the fact that it is a concert pitch score.

Dynamics, Text, and Other Information

Dynamics, including crescendos and decrescendos, are usually placed below the staff in instrumental writing. The only exceptions are (1) when there is no room below the staff for dynamics; and (2) when two instrumental parts share the same staff and have separate dynamics, the dynamics for the instrument notated with stems pointing upward are placed above the staff while dynamics for the other instrument are placed below.

Indications of accelerando, rallentando, and other changes in speed are also usually placed below the staff, but indications to establish a new tempo or return to an old tempo are placed above.

In vocal music, the text is traditionally placed below the staff. However, if two voices share the same staff and have differing texts, the text for the upper voice is placed above the staff while the text for the lower voice is placed below. Because of the location of the text, dynamics and change of speed notations are all placed above the staff.

Score Preparation Shortcuts

Ideally, a well-prepared score will have every mark, note, and detail of every instrumental or vocal part indicated on its pages. Whenever time and energy allow, this is most desirable. However, there are some ways of lessening the chore of preparing the score as well as saving time.

One method of saving time is the use of the one-measure repeat sign: ⁒. As shown below, this means to play the material given in the first measure in each succeeding measure containing the sign.

EXAMPLE 12 The same measure to be played three times.

If the single-measure repeat sign is used in the score it must also be used at exactly the same point in the part, and vice versa. It is most appropriately employed in a composition where it may be used frequently, rather than only once or twice.

When a musical pattern of two measures in length is to be repeated, a two-bar repeat sign //. may be used. This sign is placed on the bar line to show clearly which two bars are to be repeated.

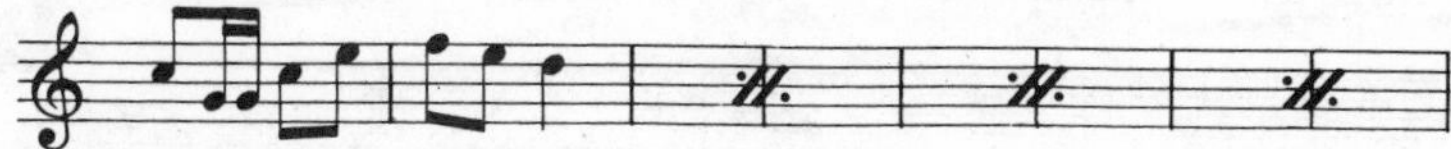

EXAMPLE 13 The two measure pattern is to be played four times.

In all other ways the two-bar repeat works like the one-bar repeat including the cautions given above.

In popular or commercial music one sometimes finds a notation indicating that the material written for one instrument (flute) is to be copied into another instrumental line (violin).

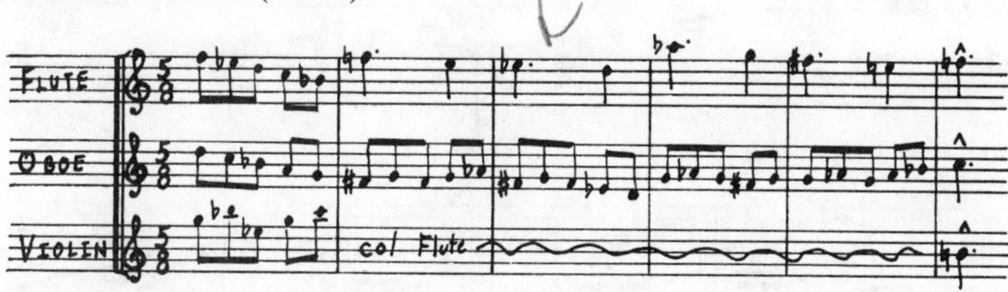

EXAMPLE 14 In measures 2 through 5 the violin part is to be identical to the flute part.

A related symbol is used when the staff directly below another is to contain the same material.

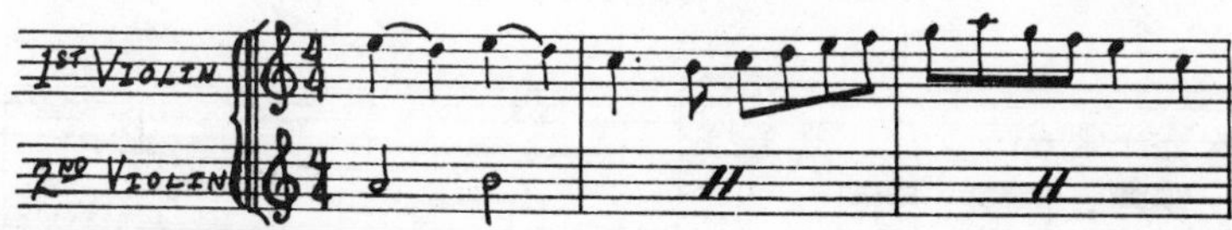

EXAMPLE 15 Second violin part is identical to the first in measures 2 and 3.

The short cuts shown in Examples 14 and 15 should be used only in situations where the instruments involved read the same clef, at the same octave, and use the same transposition.

Problem Set No. 4

1. Using the Bach choral prelude "Herzlich tut mich verlangen," given below, prepare a title page, the first page of music, and the second page of music for a transcription for the following instruments: violin, viola, bassoon, and tuba. Write out all the pitches. Assign the top (soprano) line to the violin in the treble clef; assign the second (alto) line to the viola in the alto clef; assign the third (tenor) line to the bassoon in the tenor clef; and assign the pedal (bass) line to the tuba in the bass clef. (This combination of instruments will require no transposition.) Be sure to place the instruments in score order and to align the events vertically. Include rehearsal letters and measure numbers.

2. Recopy the Bach chorale given below on four staves, assigning each voice part to a separate staff. Assume that the soprano and alto lines will be played by B♭ clarinets and copy the pitches accordingly (written one step higher than given.) Assume that the tenor and bass lines will be played by bassoons and copy these lines in tenor and bass clef respectively (no transposition is required). Follow all instructions given for good score preparation.

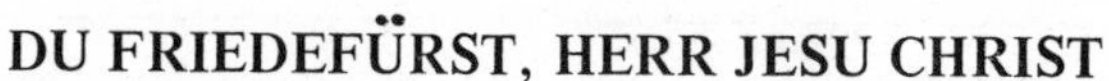

3. Rearrange this list of instruments in orchestral score order:

   viola, bass drum, tuba, horn, 1st violin, 2nd oboe, violoncello, 2nd flute, 1st clarinet, trumpet, 2nd violin, bassoon, 1st flute, contrabass, 1st oboe, 2nd clarinet.

4. Given the following information, prepare the first page of music for this composition:

   tempo: Allegro ♪ = 132; key signature: none; meter: $\frac{6}{8}$; composer: W. P. Greene; title: Sonata; instrumentation: 4 horns, 3 flutes, 2 clarinets in B♭, a bassoon, a violin, and a violoncello.

   Be sure to skip a staff between instrumental choirs.

5. Obtain a copy of the full score to Wagner's *Tristan und Isolde* or *Parsifal* for study. Note the many ways in which these scores differ from the score order given earlier in this book. Compare these to scores by Beethoven, Mozart, Brahms, etc. Why would Wagner's scores be set up differently? What are the advantages to Wagner's arrangement? What are the disadvantages?

THE PARTS

Once the score is completed, the next task is to extract the parts. A complete performance set of parts will contain at least one copy of each instrumental part found in the score. If some of the parts are to be performed by several performers, such as string parts (in an orchestra) or clarinet parts (in a band), then extra copies of the parts may be needed. Usually, one copy of a part for every two performers is desired.

The First Page

The information found on the first page of music in the score is also found on the first page of the part. (Title pages are uncommon for parts.) The first staff (or system) of the part is indented. An additional piece of information which must be added to a part page is the name of the instrument(s) and the part number, if any. See Example 16 below for a typical first page of a clarinet part.

EXAMPLE 16 First page of a clarinet part showing usual placement of information.

On following pages, one need not repeat any of the information written on the first page; but an abbreviation of the name and part number of the instrument along with a page number might be useful, should the pages ever become separated.

Except for the first staff of the part, the staves are not indented. The key signature, if one is used, is repeated on each staff, but the meter signature appears only at the beginning or at points of meter change.

Shared Versus Individual Parts

If a part is copied onto a page so that two different instrumental lines, such as first and second flutes, appear together on the same page, the result is what we will call a *shared* part. On the other hand, if a unique part is copied onto a page, such as 3rd bassoon by itself, the result is what we will call an *individual* part. There are advantages to both.

The shared part is practical because it only needs to be copied once and then photocopied, or otherwise reproduced, for the second performer. It is slower, more tedious to plan and prepare, but does allow the two performers to see each other's part which may be helpful in difficult music.

The individual part is quicker to prepare, less planning is necessary, and in many performance situations it is preferred by the musicians who are used to seeing this type of part. Extra copies for extra stands of players can be produced by photocopying. In the orchestra, only the percussionists regularly prefer a shared part. The trombone and tuba players, and to a lesser extent the trumpets and horns, sometimes see a shared part.

In a band, shared parts are usually used for the oboes and bassoons, horns, and percussion. Other sharings are occasionally seen, but are somewhat rare.

One method of preparing shared parts uses a separate staff for each instrumental line, connecting the two lines together into one system by use of brackets. This works well when the two parts sharing the same page are both very complex, or differ greatly from each other in terms of character, or where they use totally different portions of the range or different clefs. With this method one can have different instruments sharing the same page (clarinet and bass clarinet, trombone and tuba, etc.)

EXAMPLE 17 Two separate parts, each with its own staff, sharing a page.

Another method for shared parts utilizes a shared staff. This method is easier to prepare, since vertical alignments are not as difficult to maintain, but it only works well when both instrumental parts are rather simple and do not involve extensive voice crossings. The lines are kept visually separate by using upward stems for the higher part and downward stems for the lower, and the symbols found on page 3 whenever applicable. This does not work for two different instruments unless both use the same clef, transposition, etc. Even if it is possible, the use of this method for two different instruments is very unusual.

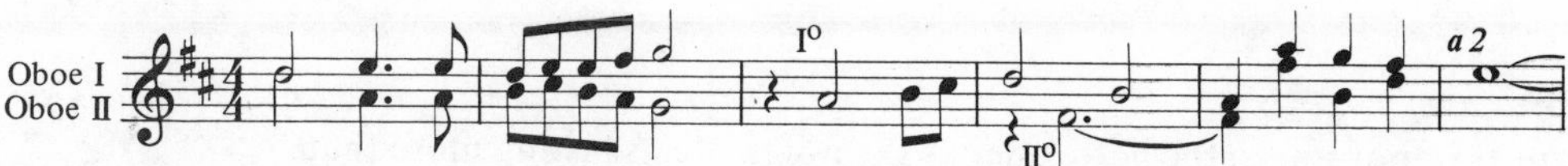

EXAMPLE 18 Two separate parts sharing the same staff.

A logical means of getting the most from the shared parts approach is to combine the two methods discussed above. Example 19 illustrates a combined approach.

EXAMPLE 19 Two separate parts sharing a staff, changing to each possessing its own staff.

Page Turns

Whenever an instrumental part consists of more than one page, a page turn may be required. When only one performer is playing from a single copy of the part, the performer must stop playing in order to make the page turn. There are few exceptions. A successful page turn will allow the performer enough time to remove the instrument from playing position and to turn the page *quietly*. Several measures in a moderate tempo are usually needed.

The best location for a page turn is in the middle of an extended rest—that is, several measures of rest before the page turn and several measures after. If for some reason it is necessary for the performer to turn the page especially quickly and then to play immediately after the page turn, the symbol V.S. is placed on the page before the turn to indicate *volti subito* (turn over quickly.) Do not use V.S. when there is plenty of time to turn the page. It will only lessen its impact when it really is needed.

EXAMPLE 20 The last staff before a page turn; the performer will expect to be required to play immediately after turning the page.

Avoid page turns at musically awkward moments such as in the middle of a general pause (G.P.) Also avoid having all of the strings make a fast page turn at the same time during a quiet passage or a similar turn during an expressive solo passage.

Rests

Rests are as important to the performer as the notes. Rests lasting more than a measure are placed into the performer's part differently than in the score. Example 21 shows how the rests should appear in the part; Example 22 is how these same rests appear in the score. Rests in an individual performer's part should *never* be copied as in Example 22; *always* as in Example 21.

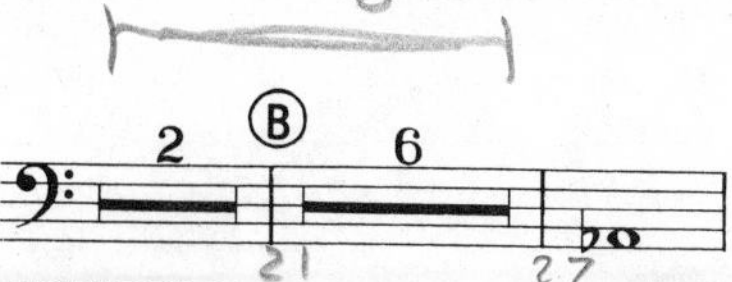

EXAMPLE 21 Rests in a performer's part placed in the correct manner.

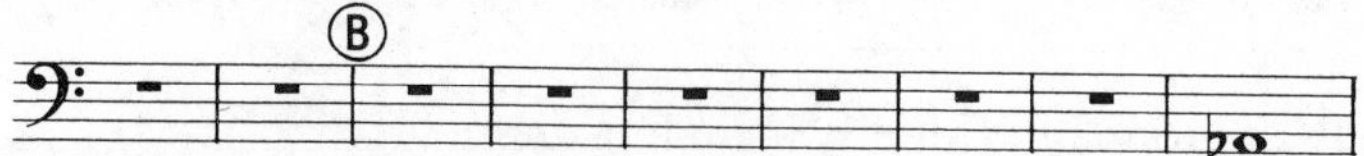

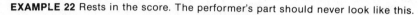

EXAMPLE 22 Rests in the score. The performer's part should never look like this.

Cues

There are three types of cues commonly used in performers' parts.

1. Landmark cues to assist the performer in locating or keeping his place in the music.
2. Performance cues intended to be performed in cases where the cue instrument is missing (or weak.)
3. Coordination cues used to assist a performer in the meshing of his part with another, very complex line.

The first type, or landmark cue, may simply be an indication in the part showing where a very easily heard event takes place.

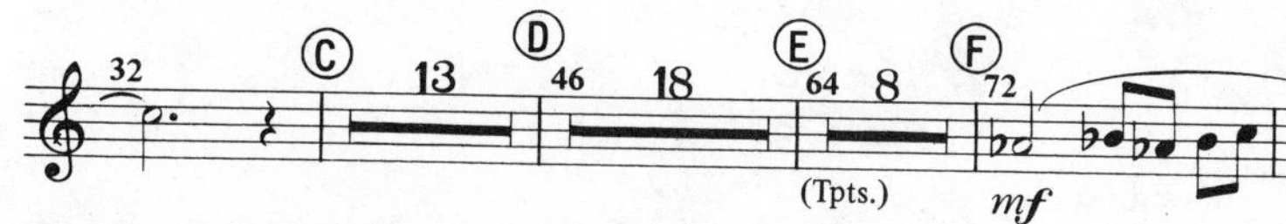

EXAMPLE 23 A landmark cue not using notes.

The performance cue would require the use of cue notes (smaller than normal notes with stems in the wrong direction) and an indication of the specific instrument being cued. These will be written in the key and range for the instrument in which part they appear.

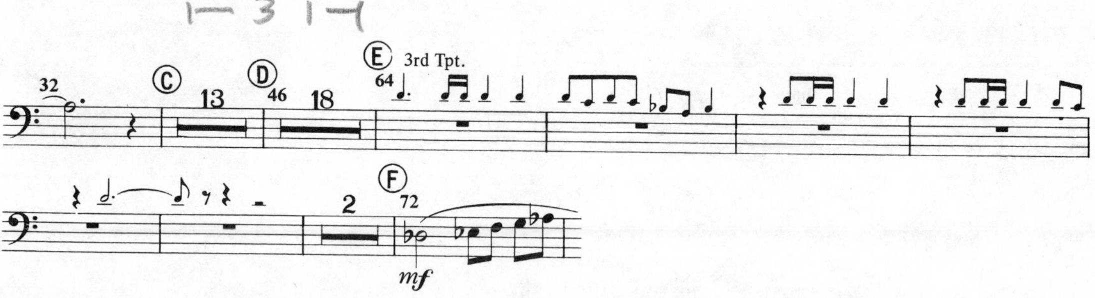

EXAMPLE 24 A performance cue in the trombone part showing the third trumpet passage at letter E. If the third trumpet is not available, a trombone could play the passage.

If a fermata occurs in the music and a performer who does not play notes leading into or out of the fermata must accurately rejoin the ensemble, coordination cues could help.

EXAMPLE 25 Coordination cues to assist the bassoonist in rejoining the flutist.

Often cue notes are not needed in this situation, and simply including enough details within the rests will serve as well.

EXAMPLE 26 Rests to enable the bassoonist in rejoining the flutist.

In complicated pieces a coordination cue, either on the staff or on a separate staff, will often clarify an otherwise awkward situation.

EXAMPLE 27 A coordination cue line on a separate staff.

After any extended series of rests, or after more than 12 measures, or whenever there is a danger of the performer losing his place, landmark cues, with or without special notes, should be used. Always use many cues in parts. It is also a good policy to number the first measure to be played after any extended rest.

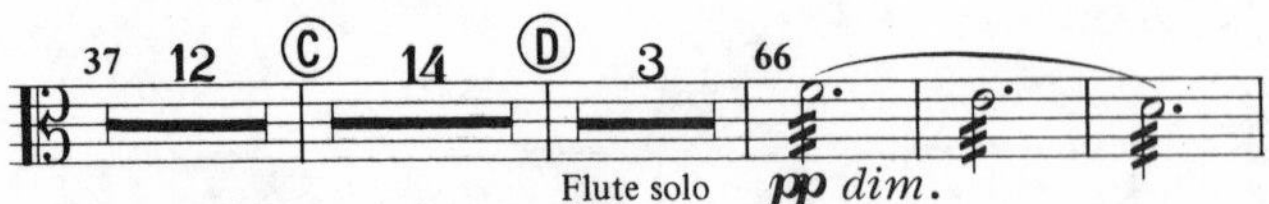

EXAMPLE 28 Placing a measure number on the first measure after an extended rest.

Fidelity to the Score and the Use of Tacet

One temptation that must be resisted during the preparation of the parts is the use of any shortcuts not found in the score. As a rule the parts must match the score note for note and item for item. This is especially crucial with respect to the use of repeats. The repeats in the parts *must* be the same as the repeats in the score and vice versa. (This caution does not apply to the single-measure or two-measure repeats discussed on page 13.)

It is obvious that measure numbers and rehearsal letters must also be faithfully replicated in the parts. Every staff should have the measure number over the first measure of each line. All dynamics from the score, along with tempo changes and similar information, must be included in the parts.

The major exception to this rule is use of the term *tacet*. The term means "it is silent" and is placed in a part to inform the performer that he is to remain silent. It is employed in two circumstances:

1. When a performer is to remain silent for an entire movement.
2. When a performer, having played in the composition, is to remain silent for the rest of the piece.

When the second situation is encountered, the indication *tacet* should be placed after a rehearsal letter or number. Never use *tacet* when a performer is expected to re-enter later in the movement.

Problem Set No. 5

1. Copy out separate parts for the instruments for which you prepared a score in exercise 1 from Problem Set No. 4 (page 14). Observe all the principles of good part preparation.
2. Copy out the clarinet parts from exercise 2 from Problem Set No. 4 (page 15) in two different ways: (a) two separate staves on the same page—watch the vertical alignment (b) sharing a single staff—watch stem directions.
3. Copy out the following measure as a coordination cue for a flutist who enters on the fourth quarter note with a pianissimo middle C.

4. Copy the measure given in exercise 3 above as it would appear in the tuba part if the tubist does not play during the measure. (Only rests will be required. See Example 26.)
5. Copy the 2nd clarinet part for these first 16 measures of the Minuet from Haydn's Symphony No. 104 in D Major. Include a performance cue of the 1st oboe part for the last 8 measures.
6. Copy a part for the 1st and 2nd oboes for the excerpt from the Haydn Minuet given in exercise 5, above. Place each instrument on a separate staff on the same page. For the last eight measures, give the 2nd oboe a performance cue of the viola line (watch the clef).

SYMPHONY NO. 104, IN D MAJOR

7. Copy these two trombone parts onto one page using *two* staves. Watch the vertical alignment.

8. Copy these two flute parts onto *one* staff. Watch vertical alignment, stem directions, and the use of 1°, a 2, etc.

9. Obtain scores and complete sets of parts to a string quartet, a woodwind quintet, a Beethoven symphony, a band piece, etc. In class, examine all of this material, discussing and comparing score and parts preparation. How clear are the passages in the quartet and quintet? Are there enough cues? Could you suggest ways of improving the parts for the symphony or the band piece?

BIBLIOGRAPHY

Donato, Anthony. *Preparing Music Manuscript.* Englewood Cliffs, N.J.: Prentice-Hall, 1963.

Karkoschka, Erhard. *Notation in New Music.* Translated from German by Ruth Koenig. New York: Praeger, 1972.

Myrow, Gerald. *Notography.* Chicago: G.I.A. Publications, 1976.

Read, Gardner. *Modern Rhythmic Notation.* Bloomington: Indiana University Press, 1978.

Risatti, Howard. *New Music Vocabulary.* Urbana: University of Illinois Press, 1975.

Sabbe, Herman, Kurt Stone, and Gerald Warfield, ed. "International Conference on New Musical Notation" *Interface,* Vol. 4, No. 1, 1975.

Warfield, Gerald. *How to Write Music Manuscript (with Pencil).* New York: Longman, 1977.

2

INSTRUMENTATION: *The Orchestral Strings*

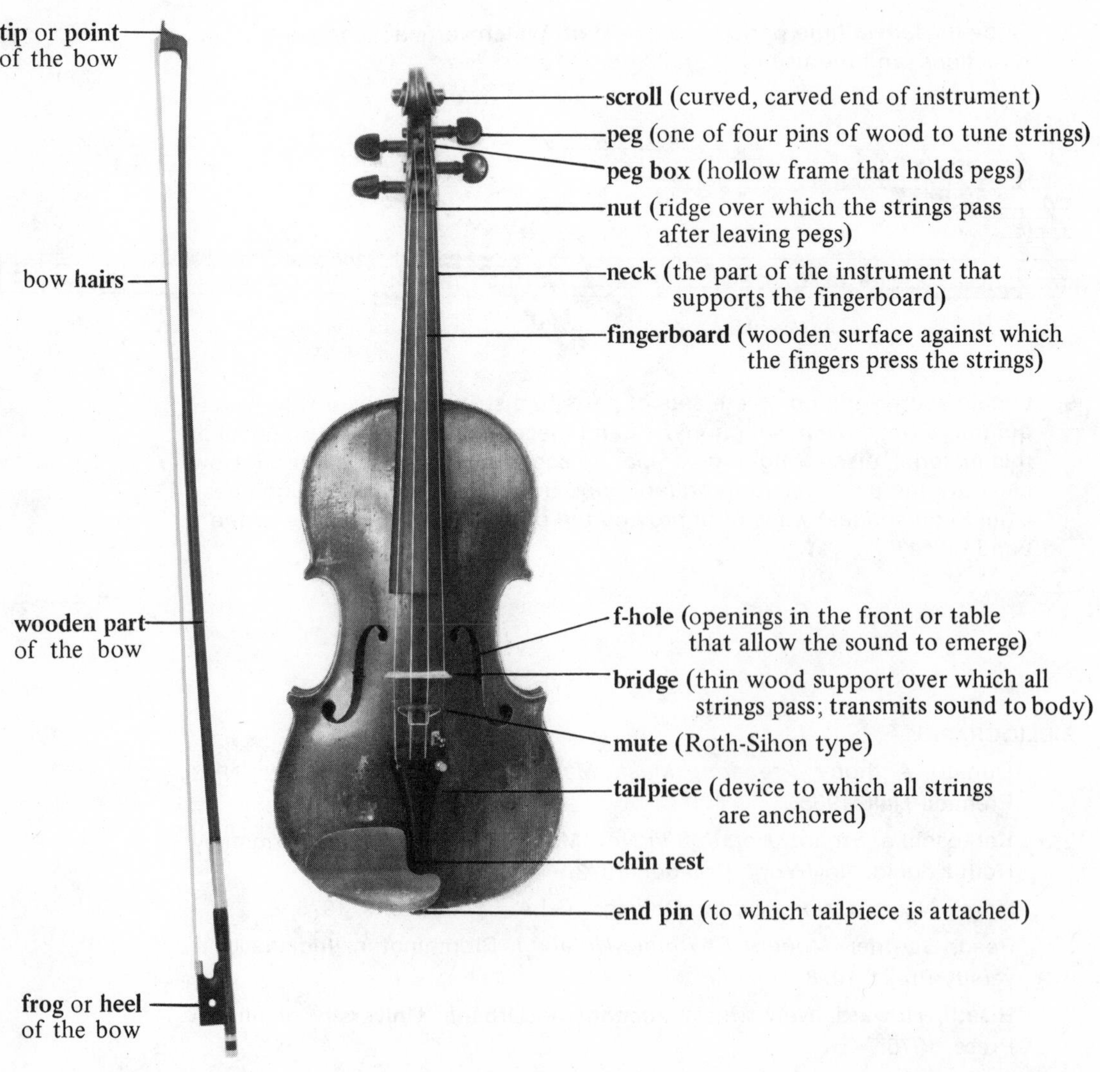

FIGURE 1 The parts of a string instrument and its bow.

GENERAL STRING INFORMATION

Although there are many musical instruments that produce sounds from vibrating strings, the violin, viola, violoncello, and contrabass are the only string instruments commonly associated with the symphony orchestra and are, therefore, often referred to as the orchestral strings.

The Parts of Orchestral String Instruments

Figure 1 shows a picture of a violin with the parts named. It would be of value to the student to learn the names of these parts of the instrument and bow since this knowledge will facilitate understanding of the ways in which string instruments are played and produce sounds.

The strings on the instruments are identified both by letter name and by number, usually expressed as Roman numerals. From high to low (right to left in Figure 1) the strings are numbered I, II, III, and IV. The vibration of the strings is transferred from the bridge to the front or table of the instrument. From there the sounds are transmitted to the back by means of the sound post, a small wooden rod inside the instrument and perpendicular to the front and back. It is located at the number I string end of the bridge.

The following table gives English, French, German, and Italian equivalents for the parts of the string instruments and bows.

English	*French*	*German*	*Italian*
tip or point of the bow	tête or pointe	Kopf *or* Spitze	testa *or* punta
scroll	volute	Schnecke	voluta *or* riccio
peg	cheville	Wirbel	cavicchi *or* bischeri *or* pirolo
peg box	chevillier	Wirbelkasten	cassetta
nut	sillet	Obersattel	capotasto
neck	manche	Hals	manico
fingerboard	touche	Griffbrett	tastiera
wooden part of the bow	le bois de l'archet	die Bogenstange	legno dell'arco
f-hole	ouïe	F-Loch	effe
bridge	chevalet	Steg	ponticello
tailpiece	cordier	Saitenhalter	cordiera
bow hair	crins de l'archet	Bogenhaare	crini dell'arco
frog or heel of bow	hausse *or* talon	Frosch	tallone
sound post	âme	Stimmstock	anima
string instrument	instrument à cordes	Saiteninstrument	strumento a corda
bowed string instruments	instruments à archets	Streichinstrumente	strumenti ad arco
bow	archet	Bogen	arco
front or table	table d'harmonie	Decke	piano armonico *or* tavola armonica
back	fond	Boden	fondo armonico

There are three ways in which a string is set into vibration: by plucking, striking, or bowing. When plucking is employed one usually uses the fingers, but for special effects a pick or plectrum may be used. When plucking is not an instrument's *usual* mode of tone production, as in the case of the orchestral strings, the instruction to pluck is *pizzicato,* which is usually written as *pizz.,* its abbreviated form. When striking the string, the wooden part of the bow may be used as well as percussion mallets (see p. 181) or the performer's hand. The latter method is especially typical of contrabass technique.

String Bowings

Bowing to produce the tone on a string instrument is a technique that is applied to the violins, violas, violoncellos, and contrabass (double bass) among our modern instruments. In addition, some non-Western stringed instruments are bowed, and one could conceive of bowing other stringed instruments as well.

The term *arco* indicates that the bow is to be used. However, the use of the bow is assumed in the case of modern orchestral strings, and therefore the instruction *arco* is used only when there may be some doubt as to how a particular passage should be played, or after a pizzicato passage when the composer wishes the performer to return to bowed playing.

The bow is made of horsehair or similar substance stretched on a very slightly curved wooden stick. One end of the stick is held in the player's hand and is larger than the opposite end, which is narrower and lighter. The end held in the player's hand is called the *frog* while the opposite end is called the *tip*.

There are basically two motions used to bow string instruments. In one motion, the player draws the bow across the string starting from the lowest third of the bow, near the frog, until a part of the bow nearer the tip is in contact with the string. This is called a *down-bow* and is indicated by this symbol: ⊓. By starting to draw the bow from the part nearest the tip and moving toward the frog, one produces an *up-bow;* the symbol for this is: V. (It is easily shown that the directions *down* and *up* have very little to do with these bow strokes, especially in the cases of the violoncello or contrabass.)

The down-bow, since it starts at a heavier portion of the bow and moves toward the lighter portion, has the basic effect of a decrescendo; while the up-bow, since the motion that produces it is just the opposite, has a natural crescendo effect. Good performers have spent years learning to minimize these differences, so that they are perfectly capable of executing up-bow decrescendos and down-bow crescendos. However, whenever it is possible to allow the bowing characteristics to reinforce the musical requirements of the passage, the passage will always seem well bowed. When the two requirements are working at cross-purposes for any extended amount of time, the passage will seem to be poorly bowed.

Because of the crescendo characteristics of the up-bow, the up-bow is traditionally associated with the upbeat (also called pickup or anacrusis). The ease with which one can accentuate notes begun with that portion of the bow close to the hand leads to the traditional association of the down-bow with the downbeat. Therefore, the following passages would be bowed as indicated:

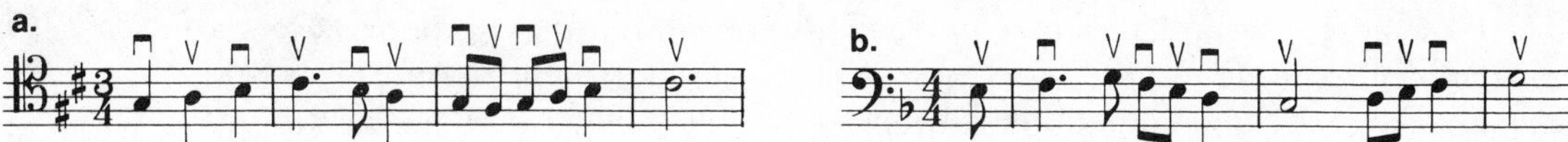

EXAMPLE 29 a. Alternate bowings beginning on a down-bow. b. Alternate bowings beginning with an up-bow.

The basic principle, stated above, is that upbeats are played up-bow and downbeats are played down-bow. The distribution of up-bows and down-bows throughout a piece of music is a concern of the composer, conductor, and performer, and is determined by various considerations. One of the most important is that several notes may be played during one bow-stroke. To indicate this, the following notation is used:

EXAMPLE 30 Four notes in each bow-stroke.

A violist playing the example above would play the first four notes with a down-bow, the next four with an up-bow, and so on, alternating groups of four per bow-stroke throughout the given passage. It is important for non-string players to understand that those arched lines are not merely slurs, but are bowing indicators which mean that all the notes under the mark are to be played within the same bow-stroke (that is, without any change in bow direction.) Bow direction changes when a new mark begins.

Assuming notes of equal length, a performer can play more notes during a single up-bow or down-bow stroke at softer dynamics than he can at louder dynamics. The corollary is, of course, that playing fewer notes during a single stroke will facilitate the production of louder dynamics. This is because the fullness of sound produced by a bowed instrument is a result of a combination of the pressure applied to the string by the bow and the speed at which the bow moves across the string. The greater the bow pressure, the more the bow tends to grab or dig into the string and the more attack the sound has. The faster the bow moves across the string, the louder the sound (steady state) is *but* the shorter it will last. The less pressure exerted, the more the bow may tend to bounce off of or skim over the string, producing a somewhat more wispy sound.

EXAMPLE 31 Using bowings to reinforce the dynamics of a passage.

The bowings in Example 31 work because they take advantage of the above principles—namely, that the *forte* passages also have fewer notes and the *pianissimo* passages have more. Notice too that the bowings match the musical figure so that at the repetition of the melodic material, the bowing pattern also repeats.

In actual practice one would not mark each up-bow and down-bow as was done in Example 31. The down-bow at the beginning might be marked, although it is the obvious bowing, and the arched lines will take care of the rest. Note that there are more *forte* up-bows than *forte* down-bows. The bowing works because of the *number of notes* per bow-stroke. When an even dynamic level is to be maintained, one should design the bowing so that the number of notes in each down-bow stroke is equal to (or nearly equal to) the number of notes in each up-bow stroke.

The bowings illustrated above do not provide any information relating to *articulation* (i.e. the manner in which a note begins and ends). It cannot be ascertained from the locations of up-bow or down-bow, nor from the note groupings within a bow-stroke, whether or not the notes are to be staccato or legato. Information providing more detailed descriptions of the articulations desired, must be added to the basic bowings that have been discussed.

We may sum up the basic concepts of bowing, to this point, as follows:

1. Upbeats are generally played up-bow and downbeats are played down-bow.
2. Louder passages require more frequent bow changes than softer passages.
3. Except for dynamic considerations, or for special effects, the durations of up-bows and down-bows within a given passage should be about equal.
4. Indications of bow direction and bow changes do not relate directly to articulation.

Bowed Articulations

Separate Bows

Separate bows, or *détaché,* is the term used for alternating up-bows and down-bows. It is the basic type of bowing, discussed above, and cannot be assumed to be either legato or non-legato. Therefore, since either articulation may be intended, it is wise to specify "legato" or "non-legato" in the part.

EXAMPLE 32 Notation for separate bows.

Legato Bowings

Legato is indicated by the use of the *slur,* or phrase mark. Whether a slur connects two notes, or many (as in Example 33), it is assumed to mean legato, unless dots or lines are placed over the notes. In Example 33, it is obviously impractical to attempt to use the slurs as bowing indications, but the performance style implied is clearly legato. Bow changes will be necessary in Example 33, and will be made as smoothly as possible within these phrase marks.

EXAMPLE 33 Legato bowing.

Brush Strokes

A series of notes (often on the same pitch) played within a single bow-stroke, each with a slight "push" and all slightly separated, is called *brush strokes* or *louré*. The effect is somewhat like a series of sighs. The proper notation for this articulation is as follows:

EXAMPLE 34 Brush strokes.

On-the-String Staccato

The use of staccato (····), staccatissimo (ꞌꞌꞌꞌ), or accents (∧∧∧ or>>>) placed on the notes, regardless of up-bow, down-bow, or the grouping of notes within single bow-stroke indications, usually calls for an *on-the-string staccato*, sometimes called *martelé*. Given these notations occur in music, the performer often *chooses* to play on-the-string, even though there are other options for interpreting them. To be sure that an on-the-string staccato is the choice, the word *martelé* or the words *on-the-string* should be added.

EXAMPLE 35 Several notations that may be understood to call for on-the-string staccato.

When several notes are marked staccato and placed under a slur (as in the second measure of Example 35), to be played on-the-string, a type of bowing sometimes called *slurred staccato* is achieved. In contrast to the more typical on-the-string staccato, which usually features a definite stopping and change of bow direction between notes, slurred staccato features the stopping without a direction change.

In the third and fourth measures of Example 35 is the notation for *hooked bowing*. Usually applied to all figures such as ♩ ♪, ♩. ♪, ♪. ♬, or ♪.. ♬, the notation for hooked bowing ♪. ♬ is actually the reverse of the performance technique which is to shorten the first, not the second, note. Both notes *are* played with the same bow stroke.

Off-the-String Staccato

If a very light, bouncy staccato is desired, one may ask the performer to take advantage of the natural stringiness of the limber bow and taut string combination. These bowings are called *off-the-string staccatos*, referring to the bounce off-of-the-string that takes place. As a general term, the off-the-string staccato is often called *spiccato*.

Spiccato is an alternative to on-the-string staccatos. Unless the orchestrator specifies one or the other, the choice between the two will be made by the performer or the conductor. At extremely fast or extremely slow tempi it may not be possible for the performer to produce an actual spiccato, that is, one caused by the *natural* bounce of the string and bow. However, performers can induce a spiccato-like bounce by using their wrist to produce the necessary hop of the bow off-the-string. At very slow tempi this becomes completely artificial. At very fast tempi, spiccato is impossible.

An up-bow spiccato in which several notes are played within a single up-bow stroke is sometimes called *staccato volante*. A down-bow spiccato in which from two to six notes are played in a single bow-stroke is called *saltando*. When this effect is desired it is necessary to specify the fact by placing the word *saltando* in the part.

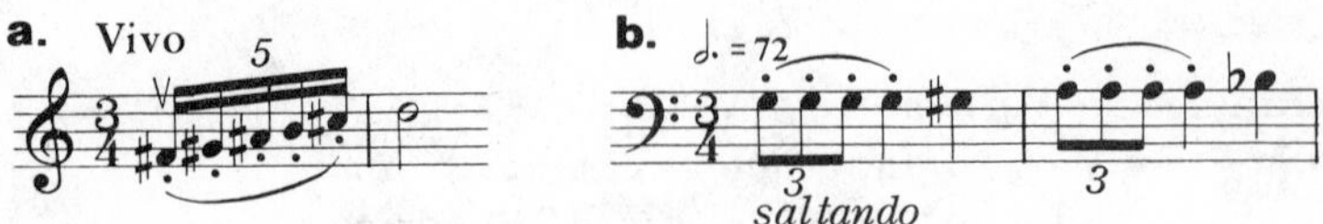

EXAMPLE 36 Notations for: a. Up-bow spiccato. b. Saltando.

Repeated Strokes

At most tempos, it is possible to produce a series of down-bow or up-bow notes. These would be accomplished by playing a note with a single down-bow stroke, for example, lifting the bow quickly, replacing it just as before, and then playing the next note. It provides a very clear separation between the notes. A series of successive down-bows has a very heavy, accented quality while a series of successive up-bows possess a light, delicate quality.

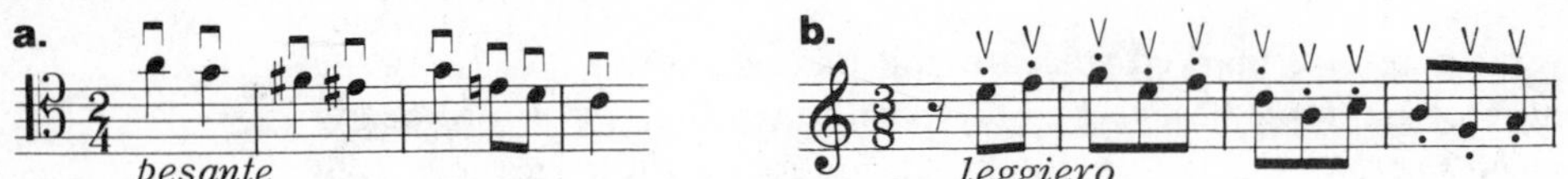

EXAMPLE 37 a. Successive down-bows. b. Successive up-bows.

Ricochet Bowing

Ricochet bowing is the technique of dropping or throwing the bow onto the string and then allowing the bow to bounce naturally (also called *jeté*). The number of unforced bounces that can be produced varies, but more bounces are possible with a combination of a light, loosely held bow and a heavier, taut string than with other combinations. A suggested notation is shown: ric.

As a word of caution to the composer or orchestrator: There is not universal agreement among string performers, conductors, authors, or dictionaries regarding the exact meanings of the terms, especially those of French and Italian origin, that are associated with the various bow-strokes. It is important for the composer of a piece of music to have heard enough examples of the bowings desired to be able to communicate to the performers just what is called for.

Bowed Tremolos

The *bowed tremolo* is merely the rapid alternation of up- and down-bows on a single pitch. It may be measured or unmeasured. It is important to note that at very slow tempos the unmeasured notation may be playable as a measured figure. Thus, an additional slash or two should be added to avoid confusion.

EXAMPLE 38 a. An unmeasured tremolo. b. An unmeasured tremolo at a slow tempo. c. A measured tremolo.

All bowed tremolos should be executed using as much of the bow as is necessary and using the portion of the bow that is convenient. If, in order to increase the heaviness and thickness of the effect, one wishes the bowing to take place in the lower third of the bow, the instructions "at the frog" or *al tallone* are added. If on the other hand, one wishes the lightness and transparency associated with the upper third of the bow, the instructions "at the tip" or *a punta d'arco* may be added.

Pizzicato Articulations

When changing from arco to pizzicato, the transition is quickest when the arco passage ends with an up-bow stroke. This is because at the end of an up-bow, the performer's right hand is almost at the bridge of the instrument and the change can be made within one beat at a moderate tempo. When changing from pizzicato to arco, the quickest change is when the pizzicato passage is followed by a down-bow. This takes a fraction longer than the opposite change.

The normal pizzicato is produced by plucking the string with the flesh of the finger. Usually, one does not need to specify "with the flesh." To obtain a more metallic effect, the orchestrator may ask the performer to produce the pizzicato with the fingernail. The usual instruction for this is "with the (finger)nail"; and if a return to a normal pizzicato is desired sometime after that, then "with the flesh" will be indicated.

The *snap pizzicato,* sometimes called a Bartók pizzicato and notated ♁, calls for the performer to pull the string hard enough to allow it to snap back against the fingerboard with a percussive thud. (In very rapid passages, this is not possible and in such cases, the performers could instead play the snap pizzicato notes as though they were heavy accents.)

The *left-hand pizzicato* is marked with a plus-sign + over the note. It is used to bring about a pizzicato when the right hand is not available. One must of course, consider the position in which the left hand is placed when planning a left-hand pizzicato, for it is not possible from every position.

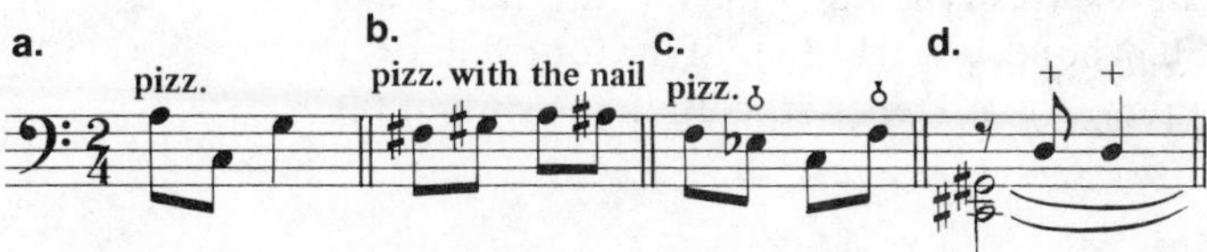

EXAMPLE 39 Types of pizzicatos: a. Normal. b. With the fingernail. c. Snap pizzicato. d. Left-hand pizzicato.

A *pizzicato roll* or *tremolo,* either measured or unmeasured, may be called for. The effect is achieved by plucking a string alternately with two or more fingers. Except for some jazz contrabass players who have developed this effect, most string performers find it tiring. Therefore, it should usually be used only for short periods of time.

EXAMPLE 40 a. Unmeasured pizzicato tremolo. b. Measured pizzicato tremolo.

STRING EFFECTS

String Selection

A subtle, but effective, means of altering the timbre of a string instrument is to specify that a passage be played on a particular string. Each string of an instrument has a unique tone quality and the orchestrator can take advantage of these characteristics by the notation "sul ____" where the name or number of the string is placed in the blank. The following table shows the English, French, and German, equivalents for the Italian *sul G* and the names of the strings found on orchestral strings in the four languages.

English	*French*	*German*	*Italian*
on G	4ᵉ corde (vln.)	auf der G Saite	sul G
C string	corde de ut	C Saite	corda di do
G string	corde de sol	G Saite	corda di sol
D string	corde de re	D Saite	corda di re
A string	corde de la	A Saite	corda di la
E string	corde de mi	E Saite	corda di mi

Harmonics

Harmonics may be used to produce timbral modification of string tone or to provide very high pitches relative to the normal range of the instrument. There are two types of harmonics generally called for: natural and artificial.

The sound of natural harmonics is very flutey and devoid of overtones. Natural harmonics are produced by lightly touching the string at one of its nodes[1], thus causing the string to produce one of its overtones rather than its fundamental. By touching the string, for example, at its midpoint, the pitch produced is that of the second partial, one octave higher than the open string. By touching a string at a point that is ¼ of the distance from the nut, or at a point that is ¼ of the distance from the bridge, the pitch produced will be that of the fourth partial, that is, two octaves higher than the open string. Depending upon the skill of the

[1]A node is a point on a vibrating string or body where the vibrating object is stationary or nearly stationary. The points or nodes are located at $1/2$, $1/3$, $2/3$, $1/4$, $3/4$, $1/5$, $2/5$, $3/5$, $4/5$, $1/6$, etc. of the length of the string.

performer and quality of the string and bow, the acoustical properties of the instrument, and the sound environment in the room of performance, it is possible to produce harmonics through the seventh, eighth, and even ninth partials. For situations where it is necessary to produce a specific, audible pitch, it would be wise to limit the natural harmonic to, at most, the fifth partial. When purely coloristic, filigree types of effects are desired, natural harmonics through the eighth partial may be called for.

The notation of natural harmonics is not consistant. Sometimes it is indicated merely by a small "o" over the desired pitch. This notation leaves it to the performer to solve the problem of how to play the pitch, i.e., which node on which string. Two alternative notations require a little less problem-solving on the part of the performer. These add to the first notation the identity of the string upon which the harmonic should be played.

EXAMPLE 41 a. Natural harmonics notation showing only the pitch to be heard. b. Natural harmonics notation showing the pitch to be heard and the string to be used. c. Natural harmonics notation showing the pitch to be heard and naming the string to be used.

All of the traditional notations for natural harmonics which are given above leave it to the performer to determine which node is to be touched to produce the required pitch. A recommended notation from the members of the string committee from the International Conference on New Musical Notation[2] suggests the use of open diamond-shaped notes showing the point on the string to be touched, with a small, black, stemless note in parentheses showing the pitch to be heard. To make this notation more clear, the addition of the name of the string is suggested.

EXAMPLE 42 A recommended notation for natural harmonics. The diamond-shaped notes indicate the point on the G string that should be touched; the pitch that will be produced is shown in small notes.

Artificial harmonics are really not artificial at all. These are produced by the performer simultaneously stopping a string with one finger and touching the same string, closer to the bridge, usually with the little finger.[3] The point touched

[2]The International Conference on New Musical Notation was held in Ghent, Belgium, October 22-25, 1974. It was sponsored by the Index of New Musical Notation, New York and the University of Ghent.

[3]In positions for playing higher pitches on the cello and contrabass, the string is stopped with the thumb and the node touched with the third finger.

is a node relative to the length of the stopped string. The most commonly called-for artificial harmonic is one produced by touching the string a perfect fourth above the pitch of the stopped string. This produces a harmonic that is two octaves above the stopped pitch.

Other nodes are also used for the production of artificial harmonics. These include touching the string lightly a major third above the stopped note, which produces a harmonic two octaves and a major third higher than the stopped note; touching the string lightly a minor third above the stopped note, which produces a harmonic two octaves and a perfect fifth above the stopped note; and, on the smaller string instruments (or on the higher pitches of the larger instruments), and if the performer has big enough hands, lightly touching the string a perfect fifth above the stopped note, which produces a harmonic that is an octave and a perfect fifth above the stopped note.

The notation for artificial harmonics is very straight forward. The note to be stopped is written in the normal fashion, the interval above this at which the finger is to touch the string is indicated by an open diamond-shaped note right above it, and the harmonic to be produced is either understood or given as a small note in parenthesis above the other two notes.

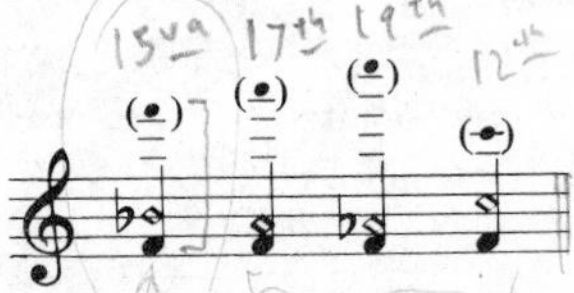

EXAMPLE 43 Generally accepted notation for artificial harmonics. Pitch stopped is indicated by normal note; point at which string is touched is indicated by diamond-shaped note; actual pitch produced is indicated by small notes in parentheses.

Mutes

The use of mutes on the string instruments is a common means of altering the tone quality. The mute is a device that attaches to the bridge of the instrument, reducing the amount of vibration that is transmitted to the body of the instrument. Due to the reduced amount of upper partials, the sound is darker than the open sound. The instructions for applying and removing mutes are:

English	*French*	*German*	*Italian*
muted *or* mute (s) on *or* with mute (s)	avec sourdine	mit Dämpfer	con sordina
mute(s) off	sans sourdine	ohne Dämpfer	senza sordina

The two types of mutes normally found in use are the wood, metal, leather, rubber, bone, or plastic clamp that must be placed upon the bridge, and the "Ma Sihon" or "Roth-Sihon" mute which is permanently attached to the strings below the bridge and which may be slid into place (see Fig. 1 on page 24). The traditional clamp type of mute requires five or more seconds to attach and three or more seconds to remove. When using a large section of strings, it is possible to ask the players to put on their mutes one or two at a time, causing the change from normal to muted tone to be gradual.

Col Legno

Since the bow is made up of both the hair and the wooden frame, there are two parts of the bow that can be used for setting the strings into vibration: the hair and the wood. The hair is the normal *(normale)* or ordinary *(ordinario)* way of producing tones. Bowing with the wood *(col legno)* is a special effect that is not popular among string players and yet is found in many pieces both old and new. (The reason that string players do not like *col legno* playing is that it tends to scratch off the varnish from the bow. Many players often have a cheaper bow which they use in *col legno* passages.) Bowing with the wood produces very little sound, so normally the performer "cheats" a bit and catches the string with both the wood and the very edge of the hairs. If one wishes to be sure that no hair is used, the instruction "wood only" or "no hair" should be added.

If one prefers the whisperish sound of the wood being *drawn* across the string, the instruction to be given is *col legno tratto.* If the arranger wishes to take advantage of the bouncing effect achieved by striking the strings with the wood and, by controlling the amount and speed of bounce, causing very clear rhythmic figures of a gentle, percussive nature, the instruction should be *col legno battuto.* To return to normal bowing (with the hair) the appropriate instruction is *modo ordinario* or *ordinario* or *ord.*

Sul Ponticello and Sul Tasto

As a means of changing timbre, the string performer may be instructed to play near the bridge or over the fingerboard. The terms used to indicate this are:

English	*French*	*German*	*Italian*
near the bridge	contre le chevalet	am Steg	sul ponticello
over the fingerboard	sur la touche	am Griffbrett	sul tasto *or* sulla tastiera
To cancel either of the above:			
natural *or* ordinary	naturel *or* ordinaire	natürlich *or* normal	naturale *or* normale

Playing near the bridge or over the fingerboard can be done either bowed or pizzicato. A *ponticello* sound is filled with dissonant overtones which give it an unearthly, glassy, metal-scratching quality. *Sul tasto* is a soft, unfocused type of sound with very little body. Often the word *flautando* (flutelike) is added to the instructions to play *sul tasto.* This especially calls the performer's attention to achieving the flutey quality that is characteristic of this effect.

Portamento and Glissando

These terms always create problems for the conductor, composer, performer, orchestrator, and scholar because the definitions given in the dictionaries and the day-to-day usage by most musicians no longer agree (if they ever did.)

According to the dictionaries, *portamento* signifies the sliding from one pitch to another by completely filling in *all* the intervening pitches—the entire pitch continuum between the two outside pitches. In contrast, *glissando* is defined as a very rapid scalelike passage connecting two pitches and itself containing a limited, countable number of pitches. One can produce a typical glissando on the piano or harp; a portamento is produced by a trombone or by sliding a finger along a string of an orchestral string instrument.

In practice these two definitions are often ignored or totally reversed. Glissando has become more all-inclusive, while portamento has been limited to a few special vocal and string effects. The use in this book will reflect the practice rather than the ideal. Therefore, glissando will be defined as the subsuming of all intervening pitches when connecting two pitches that form an interval, or attempting to do so. This applies to all performance media, not only strings.

The current notational practice for glissandos assumes that, except for an initial pause to establish the starting pich, the glissando will take up the entire value of the note. In older music, this may not be the case and the actual length of the glissando may be the subject of some debate, regardless of the notated duration. If one wishes to show the actual length the initial pitch is to be held and to indicate the glissando's duration, then a notation like that given in Example 44-b is used.

EXAMPLE 44 a. Usual glissando notation. The use of the term *glissando* or *gliss.* is optional, b. Glissando notation showing that the glissando begins on the second half of the second quarter of the first measure and ends on the second half of the first quarter of the second measure. The terms *glissando* or *gliss.* could be added.

The pizzicato glissandos are specially effective on the lower strings where the naturally slow decay (dying out of the sound) makes the glissando more audible.

EXAMPLE 45 Two pizzicato glissando notations.

Portamento is the sliding from one pitch to a second pitch. It is produced by the performer sliding the left hand finger that was used to stop the first pitch along the string to a point a tone or semitone above or below the second pitch. At the moment that the second pitch is to sound, the sliding finger is quickly lifted (or another finger is quickly pressed down) changing the vibrating length of the string to the length needed for the second pitch. The physical process is shown in Example 46-a and the usual notation used for portamento is shown in Example 46-b.

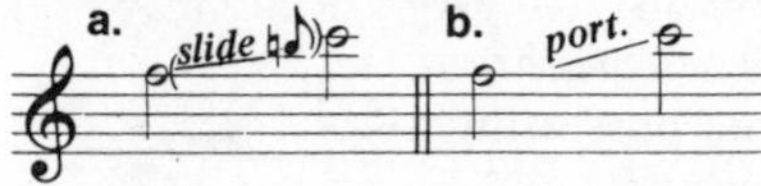

EXAMPLE 46 Portamento: a. The first finger slides from F to the grace note B; the second finger then stops C. b. The usual notation for portamento.

Portamento is a normal aspect of string technique and the slide may be done silently or made audible. Since this choice is usually made by the performer, portamentos may be added to passages even when they are not specifically notated.

Fingered Tremolos

The fingered tremolos involve the rapid change of pitch, with or without bowed tremolos. The alternation called for may be measured or unmeasured. The effect may be achieved by stopping and unstopping a single string or by alternating between pitches on two different strings. Unless instructions specifying the particular string(s) are included, the choice is left to the performer.

EXAMPLE 47 a. Unmeasured fingered tremolo. b. Measured fingered tremolo.

Bariolage

This string effect may be used to facilitate the performance of a passage or purely for a color effect. It involves the alternation between two or more strings, on the same instrument (often with one of the strings being open) using the lower-tuned strings to produce the higher pitches and vice versa.

EXAMPLE 48 An example of bariolage. Note the use of the "o" to indicate "open string."

Vibrato

Contemporary string playing techniques assume vibrato to be inherent to the sound of the instrument. In rapidly moving passages, little or no vibrato may be added to the shorter note values, but all longer notes receive an inflection produced by moving the stopping finger back and forth on the fingerboard. Vibrato is, therefore, a pitch undulation, the speed and width of which is controlled by the performer, a greater or lesser amount being used as the performer feels is appropriate. Composers may sometimes wish to call for more or less vibrato. To increase the amount of vibrato, the term *more vibrato* or *molto vibrato* is used. If one wishes the performer to obtain the stark, white tone associated with vibrato-less playing, the appropriate instruction is *no vibrato* or *senza vibrato.*

Pizzicato pitches decay rapidly, with the smaller instruments possessing a more rapid decay than the contrabass. The decay time may be increased by indicating *molto vibrato* on the pizzicato pitches.

When playing an open string, a performer may add vibrato by fingering a unison pitch on the next lower string or an octave above on the next higher string and adding vibrato to the fingered pitch.

If an orchestrator or composer wishes, after specifying a certain kind of vibrato, to return the decision regarding vibrato to the performer, the appropriate instruction is *normal vibrato.*

Since the terminology generally allows only the extremes to be easily indicated, composers often use the symbol ∿∿∿ to call for vibrato. The symbol, which will have to be explained to the performer in the instructions, can then be used as an analog to the desired effect. It shows changes in both the speed and the width of the vibrato.

EXAMPLE 49 Symbol showing vibrato changing from slow and narrow to fast and narrow to fast and wide to slow and wide to no vibrato.

Scordatura

Tuning the instrument to other than its normal pitches is called *scordatura* (German: *Skordatur*). This is usually specified so that the range of the instrument may be extended downward by a semitone or tone in order for a passage otherwise too low for the instrument to be performed. Other reasons for scordatura include the facilitation of special multiple stops and timbral effects. Among the latter are the solo violin part in the Mahler Fourth Symphony where all four strings of a violin are tuned a whole step higher to produce the sound of a toy fiddle, and in *Dance Macabre* of Saint-Saëns where the highest string of the violin is tuned down a semitone so that the unique open string sound of the interval of a tritone may be used to represent Death's fiddle.

Generally, most performers do not like to change the tuning of a string instrument by more than a whole step.[4] Another problem associated with the use of scordatura is the matter of retuning during a performance. This is often solved by using a second instrument.

The instruction for scordatura is simply a statement such as "tune D to D♭." One may also choose to draw a staff showing the tuning of all of the strings, with the instruction to tune in this manner.

[4]There may be some debate about the actual harm caused by scordatura. In general, tuning a string lower is considered less damaging than tuning a string higher with its concomitant increase in tension. The use of scordatura is, however, a very common technique on folk instruments (such as guitar, banjo, etc.).

Dampening Strings

After the strings have been set into vibration, they may be allowed to decay naturally or be damped. The indication to dampen the string(s) is shown in Example 50 and is the same symbol used for harps, guitars, piano strings, etc. The French name is *étouffer* (German: *dämpfen; Italian: velare.*) The same sign, placed where the note begins, is used to indicate a muffled string.

EXAMPLE 50 a. Dampen the string. b. Muffle the string.

Note that the sign is placed over the *attack* of the note for the muffled string effect (achieved by lightly touching a string with the left hand, avoiding unwanted harmonics) but is placed over the *release* point of the note to indicate dampening. To dampen the string, the left hand touches the string, causing the vibration to cease.

SPECIAL EFFECTS

There are a wide variety of special effects that can be produced on the orchestral strings. Although one could find creative ways to use many of these effects in special arrangements of common practice music, they are more usually associated with, and have often been generated by, the demands of contemporary composers. Thus, one should carefully examine the esthetic requirements of his project to determine the appropriateness of these or other effects. (N.B. All of the effects and devices discussed below will require an explanation of the technique and notation in the part or the score (or both) because one may not yet assume these to be common practice techniques.)

Special Bowing Effects

Bowing on the Bridge

Not to be confused with ponticello, which means playing *near* the bridge, bowing on the bridge means that the bow is placed *on* the bridge, where the string crosses, and is drawn.

Bowing the Tailpiece

With a well-rosined bow it is possible to produce a very resonant, rattly sound by bowing the tailpiece. Since the tailpiece is suspended between the four strings and the end pin, it is free to vibrate and produce a tone.

Scratch Tone

By placing the bow hairs flat against the string, pressing down into the string, and drawing with a continuing downward pressure, a very raspy, coarse tone called a scratch tone is produced. It may be called for by writing in the words *scratch tone.*

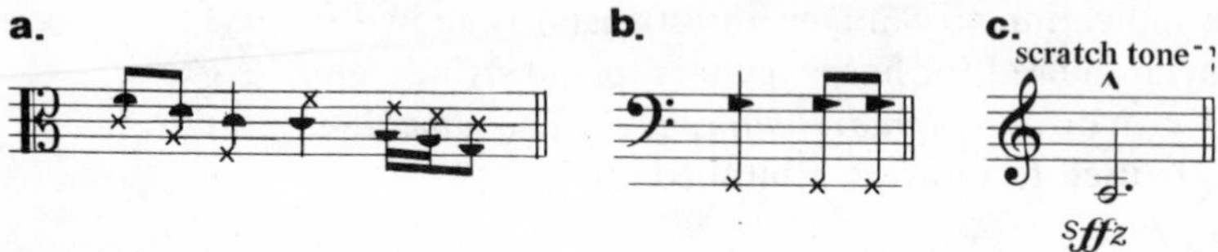

EXAMPLE 51 a. Notation for bowing on the bridge. b. Notation for bowing the tailpiece. c. Scratch tone notation.

Playing Behind the Bridge

Playing behind the bridge means playing the strings between the bridge and the tailpiece. Here the strings are very short and the pitches produced are very high and not predictable. The notation does not try to specify the pitches to be produced, but rather indicates the string to be played.

The tone may be produced either by bowing, including spiccato, legato, or ricochet bowings, or by pizzicato.

EXAMPLE 52 Notations for playing behind the bridge. a. Notation on a regular five-line staff. b. Notation using a four-line staff representing the four strings of the instrument. c. Pizzicato notation using a four-line staff.

Tapping Effects

"Silent" Fingering

A subtle effect is to call upon the performer to finger various pitches with the left hand without bowing or plucking the strings. Rather than simply stopping the strings as in normal playing, the left-hand fingers come down hard on the strings against the fingerboard, much like small hammers. The technique is reminiscent of the clavichord. Since this is a very delicate effect, it could benefit from electronic amplification.

Tapping the Instrument

Due to the natural resonance of the string instrument, a variety of interesting sounds can be produced by tapping at various places on the body of the instrument. The fingers may be used as well as other devices.

Striking the Strings

The strings may be struck with the palm of the performer's right (bow) hand producing a ringing sound. The left hand may finger various pitches. It is not always necessary for the performer to strike all of the strings, but selective striking is really only practical on the contrabass.

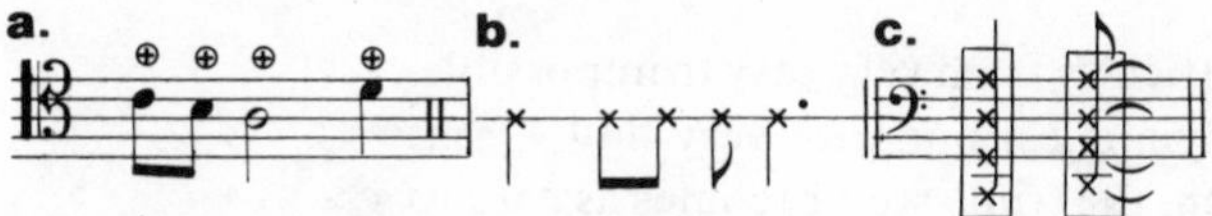

EXAMPLE 53 a. Notation for silent fingering. b. Notation for tapping on the instrument. c. Notation for striking the strings.

MULTIPLE STOPS

Bowed Multiple Stops

The curvature of the bridge enables the string performer to play any two adjacent strings with a single stroke of the bow and produce two pitches simultaneously, at any dynamic level, without increasing the normal pressure of the bow against the strings. (See Figure 2.) This two-note combination is called a *double stop*. If the performer applies more pressure from the wrist, thus causing the playing surface of the bow (i.e., the horsehair) to become slightly curved, it is then possible to play three adjacent strings with a single stroke of the bow producing a three-note combination, called a *triple stop*. (See Figure 3.) The increase in pressure will of course cause an increase in the dynamic level, but only a moderate amount of pressure is needed if the bow is only moderately stiff.

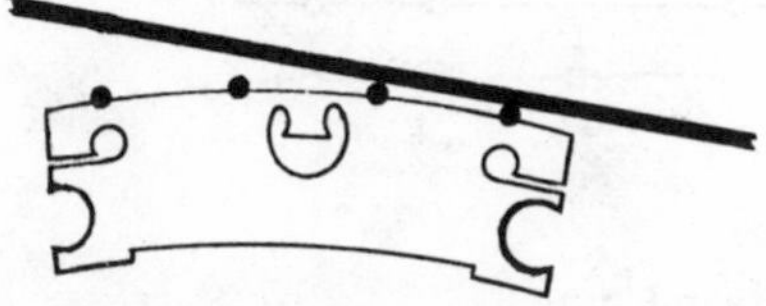

FIGURE 2 Bow under normal pressure engaging two strings.

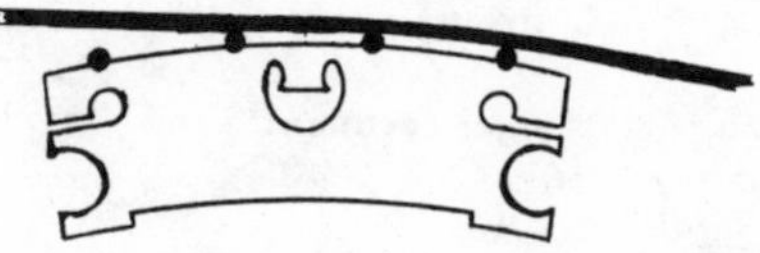

FIGURE 3 Bow under increased pressure engaging three strings.

If the bow is subjected to more pressure, enough curvature may be created to bow all four strings in one stroke, producing a *quadruple stop,* but only for a short period of time and at a loud dynamic level. Triple stops require louder dynamics than double stops, and quadruple stops are the loudest of all. Note that the bow must be only moderately stiff, for a very stiff bow will make it difficult to obtain three pitches and impossible to obtain four. Triple and quadruple stops are only playable given the correct combination of an elastic bow and sufficient wrist pressure.

Double Stops

The simplest multiple stop to produce is the double stop. Two notes being produced on one instrument are not the same as, and indeed have quite a different sound than, two notes being produced on separate instruments. Double stops may be played at any dynamic level and may be sustained almost as easily as a single tone. The double stops that use one or more open strings are very easy to perform and may be asked of even very inexperienced players. Those that require two fingered notes are playable so long as both notes are within the span of the performer's left hand. (See Appendix III)

Triple Stops

These three-note combinations vary in difficulty from very easy to impossible. Triple stops cannot be produced at soft dynamics, nor with very bulky, stiff bows. If two of the strings involved are open, the triple stop becomes as easy as the easiest double stop. If only one string is open, then one needs to be concerned that the stopped pitches can be achieved within the span of the performer's left hand. If all three strings must be stopped, then the technical difficulty is almost as great as with quadruple stops.

Quadruple Stops

Four-note combinations must of necessity be performed only on the smaller instruments (i.e., violin or viola), using very flexible bows, and at loud (fortissimo or more) dynamics. The more open strings involved, the easier the combination becomes.

To facilitate quadruple stops in which several stopped pitches are present, it is convenient to voice the chords so that each successive pitch, from bottom to top of the chord, is closer to the bridge than the previous pitch. (This applies to triple stops as well.) This is illustrated in Figure 4.

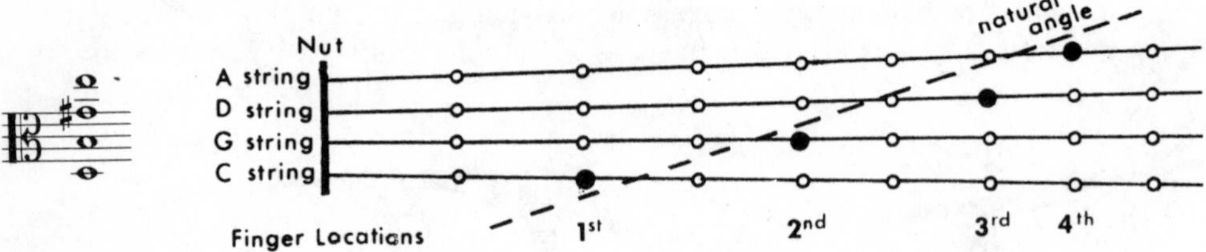

FIGURE 4 A naturally angled hand position—an easier hand position than Figure 5.

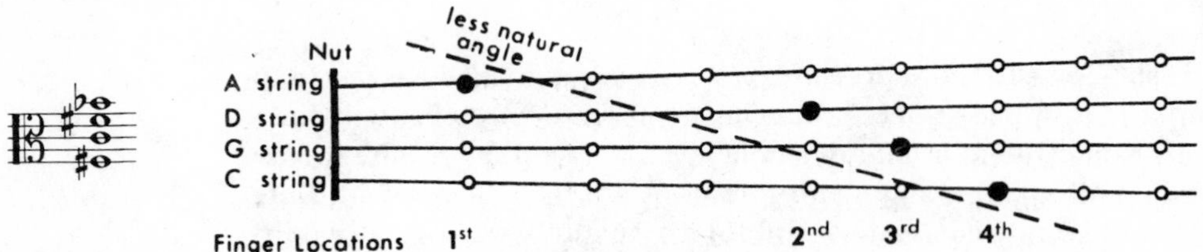

FIGURE 5 A less naturally angled hand position—not as easy as Figure 4.

The quadruple stop shown in Figure 5 is not necessarily unplayable. But, it is more difficult and more tiring. Unless one can verify the playability of a quadruple stop by asking an experienced string performer, it is wise to follow the prototype given in Figure 4, avoiding chords voiced like Figure 5. One needs to know, too, when planning multiple stops, that in the lower positions the performer's hand can span a fourth on the violin and viola, a major third on the cello, but only a major second between the first and fourth fingers on the contrabass.

Broken Chords

Since the possibilities of playing quadruple stops is limited to only certain instruments at certain dynamic levels, most quadruple stops are played as broken chords (arpeggiations). If one does *not* want a performer to arpeggiate a quadruple stop, it is necessary to mark the chord(s) *no arpeggio* or *without arpeggio* (French: *sans arpège.*) Often the notation will reflect the direction in which the chord is to be broken, but without instructions to the contrary, most performers will break the chord from bottom to top. If one wishes the arpeggiation to be from the highest pitch to the lowest, this symbol is used: ↓ .

EXAMPLE 54 Typical breaking of quadruple stops. The left one of each pair represents the usual notation; the right one, the approximate performance.

By utilizing the same hand positions and the same fingering precautions as for triple and quadruple stops, various stylistically typical string figures are possible. The most common is an arpeggiated chordal figure.

EXAMPLE 55 A frequently encountered string figure identical to broken quadruple stop.

Pizzicato Multiple Stops

When a double, triple, or quadruple stop is written to be played pizzicato, it will always be arpeggiated from the lowest pitch to the highest pitch unless specific indications to the contrary are given. If one wishes that two or more of the pitches be sounded simultaneously, a brace may be used.

Normally no symbol is required for the upward arpeggiation, but should one become necessary, to indicate alternation with downward arpeggiation, this is used: ↑ . This alternation between the upward and downward arpeggios is called *quasi-guitari,* and when this term is written above the music, one need not draw in the arrows.

EXAMPLE 56 a. Two pitches to be sounded together. b. Chords to be arpeggiated as shown. c. Two ways to write a quasi-guitar passage.

In passages calling for *quasi-guitara,* picks may be specified. Although most orchestral string players are not accustomed to picks, the use of them will save wear and tear on the fingers as well as enhancing the guitar imitation. The use of the pick in place of the fingers for other pizzicato passages is also possible.

FIGURE 6 The orchestral strings *(counterclockwise from lower left):* Contrabass, French-style bow, German-style bow; violoncello with bow; violin bow and violin; viola bow and viola. Note the relative sizes of the various instruments, the sloping shoulders of the contrabass, and the low C extension on the contrabass. Both the violoncello and the contrabass rest upon end pins, which extend vertically down from the bottom of the body, when played. (Photo by David Hruby.)

THE VIOLIN

	English	*French*	*German*	*Italian*
singular	violin (vln.)	violon (von.)	Violine *or* Geige (Vl. *or* Gg.)	violino (viol.)
plural	violins (vln.)	violons (vons.)	Violinen *or* Geigen (Vln. *or* Ggn.)	violini (viol.)

The Properties of the Violin

The violin is the highest pitched member of the string choir. It provides both the soprano and the alto parts in string ensemble writing. The violin is played by means of a bow held in the right hand of the performer or by plucking the strings with the right or left hand. The instrument is placed between the jaw and the shoulder of the player where it is held by the pincer action between these two points, allowing the left hand reasonable freedom to be placed anywhere between the nut and the bridge. Due to its small size, the violin is both the most responsive and agile of all the strings. Its compactness of design facilitates virtuoso performance skills.

EXAMPLE 57 The four strings of the violin are tuned as shown.

To specify the limits of the violin range it is necessary to give a highest and lowest pitch for each string. These limits, not including harmonics are:

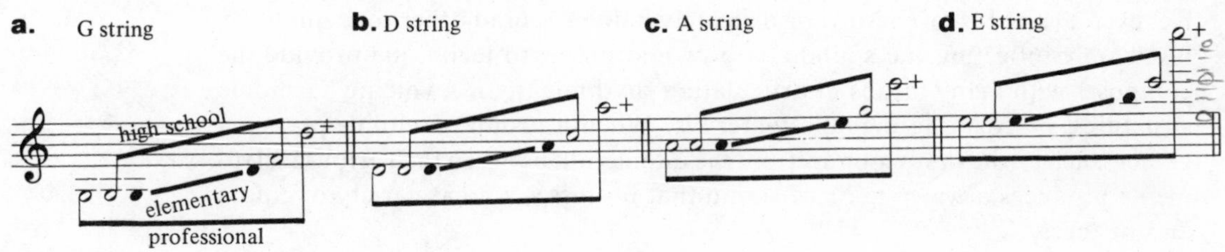

EXAMPLE 58 a. G string. b. D string. c. A string. d. E string.

The lowest string, G, is rich and dark in tone quality, becoming less well focused but with an increased intensity in the higher range. The D string is very calm and even "fuzzy" in quality, possessing the most introspective tone quality of any of the strings. The A string has a unique expressive quality that is more mellow than the E string in the same range. The E string is the most brilliant and has the best carrying power of the four strings. Played softly it can take on an almost unworldly shimmer.

The bow used to play the violin is longer than the instrument itself and is very responsive to both the pressure applied by the performer and the elasticity of the strings. Its length provides the player with flexibility in selecting bowings. The choices are more varied than with any other string instrument.

Pizzicatos are common in both solo and accompanimental writing for the instrument. The only technical problem in playing pizzicato on the violin is in the performance of repeated strummed chords arpeggiated from high to low. These can be made workable by moving the violin out of its usual performing position and holding it either in the player's lap or vertically in front of the performer. Simultaneous performance of two pizzicato pitches may be accomplished using one finger per string or, if the notes are on adjacent strings, by one finger catching both strings.

For professional performers there are very few performance limitations. For student performers, notes up to a perfect fifth above each open string are easy; for high school performers, a seventh above the open string is normal (a ninth for the concertmaster).

When composers or orchestrators who are not string performers first attempt to write for strings, they usually underestimate the ability of the string performers. Almost any one-line figure that remains within the range of the instrument is playable.

The flexible bow and small size work together to make quadruple stops possible at dynamics of *forte* and above. A wide assortment of idiomatic double, triple, and quadruple stops are easily produced, provided the cautions given earlier are heeded. (See pages 41-43). In solo and chamber music situations, virtuosity in the violin parts is expected and is normally found.

All natural harmonics up through the eighth partial are playable, with the lower partials being less susceptible to variations due to string, bow, and climatic variables. Artificial harmonics are excellent too, and, due to the small size of the instrument, even the artificial harmonics requiring the player to touch a note a perfect fifth above the stopped note are easy for almost all advanced players.

The violin is an expressive instrument capable of performing the most complex lines. It has excellent solo and ensemble qualities, for it can be both assertive, even over a full orchestra, or delicately hidden behind other tone qualities, just barely inflecting the sound. Its bow and pizzicato technique provide the composer with many means of articulating rhythmic figures, voicing harmonic structures, or covering melodic materials. When a group of violins plays together, such as the first violin section, the interaction between the various instruments produces a warm mass of sound that possesses a great variety of colors and nuances.

Typical Violin Scorings

As an example of traditional violin writing, the first excerpt is taken from Haydn's Symphony No. 103 in E♭ (the "Drum Roll"). This passage is played by the first violin section and is a good illustration of middle range section scoring for violins. The excerpt begins in measure 5 of the last movement.

EXAMPLE 59 First violin part from the fourth movement of Haydn's Symphony No. 103.

The melodic capabilities of the violin are shown in the following excerpt from Wagner's *Siegfried Idyll.* The first violins open the piece with a very relaxed and unhurried theme. Note that the theme does not require the use of the E string, thus contributing to its placid quality. The phrase mark does not indicate specific bowing but does imply that a general legato quality is appropriate.

EXAMPLE 60 Melodic writing for the violins: the opening of Wagner's *Siegfried Idyll.*

At the beginning of "On the Trail" from the *Grand Canyon Suite* by Ferde Grofé, a cadenza is written for solo violin which begins as follows:

EXAMPLE 61 The beginning of the violin cadenza from "On the Trail" by Grofé.[5]

In this passage from Richard Strauss's *Don Juan,* measures 1 - 5, almost the entire compass of the violin is explored, together with its dexterity. The orchestrator should notice that the second violin part is as difficult as the first and is not subordinate.

EXAMPLE 62 The opening of *Don Juan* by Richard Strauss.

Several of the string effects discussed earlier are displayed in this example of violin writing from the fourth movement of Arnold Schönberg's *Pierrot Lunaire,* Op. 21. Between measures 9 and 14 the composer calls for pizzicato, arco, ponti-

Strav. "L'histoire"

cello with bowed tremolo (unmeasured), trills, col legno tratto, and, in the last measure, natural harmonics. This represents a typical chamber music violin part from this century.

EXAMPLE 63 From *Pierrot Lunaire* by Schönberg.[6]

From Mahler's Third Symphony, first movement, beginning 3 measures after rehearsal number 50, comes this melodic line shared by the two violin sections. The alternation of equally important and challenging lines between first and second violins is typically good scoring practice in symphonic or chamber writing.

EXAMPLE 64 Good scoring practice: division of an important line between first and second Violins.

The following excerpt from Yehuda Yannay's *Two Fragments* for solo violin and piano shows a contemporary violin passage. Note the instructions for the different harmonics, the notation for glissandos, snap pizzicatos, and the instructions for which string to use. The little "o" over the last A of the first system and the A grace note in the last triplet mean that the performer is to use the open string. The composer uses "s.p." to mean *sul ponticello* and "s.t." to mean *sul tasto.* The horizontal wiggly lines following the pitches under the fermata represent a wide vibrato. (Two lines are used to represent both the stopping finger and the finger that touches the node; both must move together.)

[6]Used by permission of Belmont Music Publishers, Los Angeles, California 90049. Copyright © 1914 by U.E. © renewed 1941 by Arnold Schoenberg.

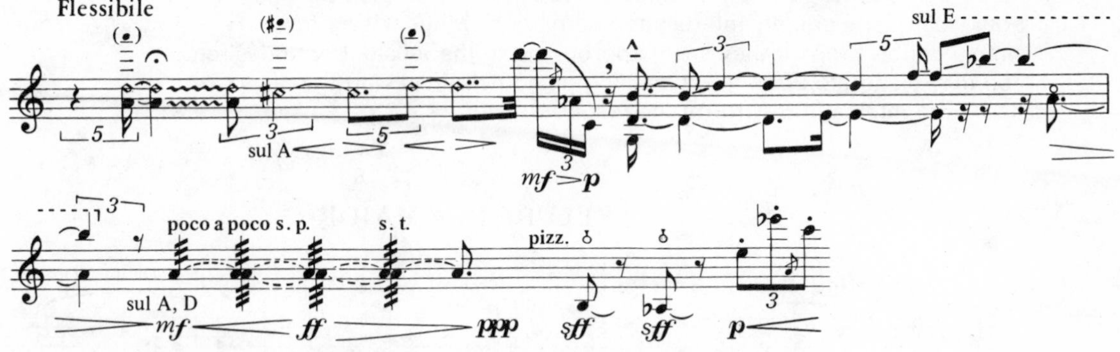

EXAMPLE 65 Excerpt from Yannay's *Two Fragments*,[7] beginning with the end of the second system, page 2.

Problem Set No. 6. Preparation of Scores and Parts.

1. Score the highest two lines of Bartók's "In Four Parts"[8] for two violins. Make at least the circled notes pizzicato, and do the same for all other similar passages. Perform the result, with a piano providing the lower two lines.

IN FOUR PARTS

[7]© Copyright 1970 by Media Press, Inc., Box 195, Media, PA 19063. All Rights Reserved. Used by permission.

[8]Copyright 1940 by Hawkes & Son (London) Ltd. Renewed 1967. Reprinted by permission of Boosey & Hawkes. Inc.

2. Score the following Chopin prelude for two violins and piano. Make both violin parts equally interesting and mark bowings. Use a few simple double stops if they seem appropriate to the music. If you desire, you may elaborate upon the remaining piano notes, making the piano part more interesting. Perform the results.

PRELUDE IN A MAJOR

3. Score the following movement from a Beethoven Sonatina for solo violin and piano accompaniment. Enrich the solo line with some easy-to-play double stops. Mark all bowings and have the finished product performed. (To make the result interesting, do some "enriching" of the piano part.)

SONATINA

4. Create an original passage for violin solo which uses several of the special effects discussed earlier on pages 39-41. Regardless of the compositional "merit" you may feel your efforts possess, be sure to have your example performed.

THE VIOLA

	English	*French*	*German*	*Italian*
singular	viola (vla.)	alto (alto)	Bratsche (Br.)	viola (vla.)
plural	violas (vla.)	altos (altos)	Bratschen (Br.)	viole (vle.)

The Properties of the Viola

The viola is the alto or tenor member of the string choir. It is pitched a perfect fifth below the violin. The body of the viola is both longer and deeper than that of the violin, but the proportions are not exactly adjusted for the difference in pitch. The bow is heavier than the violin bow, but the difference in size is not as great as the difference would be if the viola were simply a lower-pitched violin. The viola, due to its lower tone, sounds slightly more ponderous than the violin; but in the hands of a good professional performer, the virtuosity and agility of the viola is very nearly that of the violin. For purposes of performance, the instrument is held between the left shoulder and jaw of the player, the same as the violin.

EXAMPLE 66 The four strings of the viola are tuned as shown.

The alto clef is the normal clef for the viola. Very high passages on the D or A strings may at times be placed in the treble clef. A change of clef should usually be made only when an extended passage in the new clef will follow. Clef changes for isolated notes are generally avoided.

The ranges of the various strings, not including harmonics are:

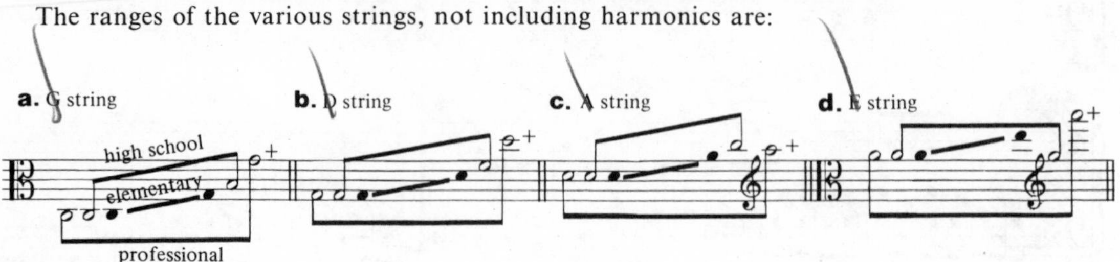

EXAMPLE 67 a. C string. b. G string. c. D string. d. A string.

The lowest string, C, has a dark, thick sound. Played loudly, it possesses a great deal of vitality; played softly, it is delicate but rich. The G string has a moderate amount of richness to its quality and the D string has a quiet warmth. The G and D strings together provide excellent tone qualities for accompaniment figures and subtle reinforcement of other instruments. The A string is quite unlike the other three strings in that it is capable of more penetration, more brilliance, and more reediness.

The viola is used both as an associate of the violins, doubling melodic lines at the octave or in unison with the violins, and as a small cello, reinforcing and doubling the cello lines. It can also serve well as the only bass instrument, providing a solid, but not heavy, foundation to the ensemble. Along with the second violin, it is usually given major responsibility for the inner voices, accompaniments, rhythmic figurations, and the harmonic underpinnings of a score. This keeps the viola busy and, unfortunately, often lessens the melodic opportunities for the instrument. However, as a mellow and somewhat melancholy solo voice, it is excellent.

The heavier bow used with the viola enables it to articulate the accented and rhythmic accompaniments so often assigned to the instrument. The characteristics of the viola bow and the violin bow are close enough to one another that the two instruments can match bowings with no problem. Pizzicato is excellent on the viola, having a little more ring than on the violin and significantly more body.

Harmonics are no problem and natural harmonics up to the 10th partial may be played. (The larger strings seem to favor the clear production of these tones.) Artificial harmonics are excellent, too. A few performers with small hands could have difficulty in lower positions with the harmonics produced by touching a note a perfect fifth above the stopped note. In higher positions, the problem should not exist.

Although the viola can play double, triple, and quadruple stops, quadruple stops are not idiomatic. When two or three pitches are written to be played simultaneously by the viola section, the usual practice is to play the part *divisi.* As with the violin, most double, triple, and quadruple stops that fit the hand well are playable *provided the dynamic is loud enough:* it should be *forte* and above for quadruple stops; *mezzo-forte* for triple stops. At softer dynamics all triple and quadruple stops will have to be broken.

Typical Viola Scorings

Since the viola is pitched a perfect fifth lower than the violin, many of the examples written for the violin would be equally possible on the viola if transposed. However, the practice has been generally not to treat the viola this way. Instead, viola writing has been in many ways less imaginative than violin writing.

It is true that the additional bulk of the viola does result in an instrument that is a little less responsive, but the difference is so slight that only at the outer limits of virtuoso technique would one encounter any significant differences.

The following excerpt from Wagner's "Good Friday Spell" in *Parsifal* is very typical of ensemble viola writing.

EXAMPLE 68 An accompaniment passage for viola section from Wagner's *Parsifal:* "The Good Friday Spell," (measures 139-150).

Although the next example, from César Franck's Symphony in D minor, may appear somewhat difficult, careful examination will reveal that all of the notes are playable from the same basic hand position. It is composed of an easily produced series of multiple stops that are broken in a rhythmic pattern.

EXAMPLE 69 Broken-chord passage from Franck's Symphony in D minor (second movement, measures 48-54).

The following example, from Nicolai Rimsky-Korsakov's *Scheherazade,* demonstrates the rhythmic vitality that the violas can generate:

EXAMPLE 70 Violas providing a rhythmic foundation in Rimsky-Korsakov's *Scheherazade* (fourth movement, measures 30-37).

The viola is not an overused solo voice. Except for chamber literature, examples of its use in solo and melodic roles are somewhat rare.[9] However, it is a beautiful melodic instrument. The following is a well-known passage from Tchaikovsky's *Romeo and Juliet* Fantasy Overture. Here it is in unison with the English horn. The combination is a rich romantic voicing.

EXAMPLE 71 Muted violas (doubled with english horn) from Tchaikovsky's *Romeo and Juliet* (measures 185-193).

At rehearsal number 49 in Aaron Copland's *Billy the Kid* the violas have this prominent line. Note the use of treble clef and the composer's avoidance of needless clef changes.

EXAMPLE 72 Viola line from Copland's *Billy the Kid.*[10]

In his composition *Elegy* for solo viola and tape, Roger Hannay takes advantage of many of the instrument's expressive qualities. This excerpt (from the middle of the third system on page two to the middle of the fifth system) illustrates two-voice writing, the use of glissandos, and a special instruction for the removal of the mute. Study it carefully.

[9]For an example of the viola in a solo role, the student should listen to *Harold in Italy* by Hector Berlioz.

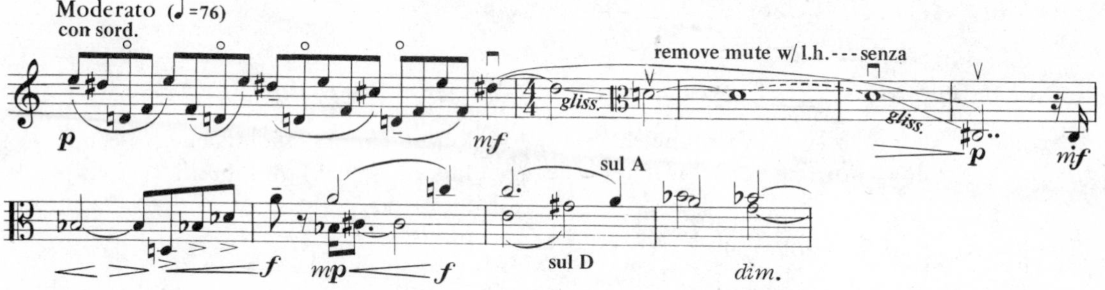

EXAMPLE 73 Solo viola part from *Elegy* for tape and viola by Hannay.[11]

Problem Set No. 7

1. Transpose the score and parts that were prepared for the violin and piano in exercise 3 of Problem Set No. 6 (page 50) down a perfect fifth, placing the violin part into the alto clef. Have the new version performed by a violist and pianist. Is it as easy for the violist to perform this part as it was for the violinist to perform the original?
2. Copy the tenor voice line of this Bach chorale harmonization into the alto clef for viola.

ACH WIE NICHTIG, ACH WIE FLÜCHTIG

J. S. Bach

3. Write a viola part separate from the two violin parts that you created for an arrangement of the Chopin Prelude in A Major in exercise 2 of Problem Set No. 6 (page 50). Use double stops if desired. If at all possible, play this viola part together with the two violin parts, filling in the missing notes on the piano.
4. Since contemporary special effects are usually closely allied with the creative (compositional) process, invent a passage in which several of the special effects discussed in this chapter are used. Have your piece performed.

[11]

THE VIOLONCELLO

	English	*French*	*German*	*Italian*
singular	violoncello (vc.)	violoncelle (vlle.)	Violoncell (Vcl.)	violoncello [(v)cello]
plural	violoncellos (vcs.)	violoncelles (vlles.)	Violoncelle (Vcle.)	violoncelli [(v)celli]

The Properties of the Violoncello

The violoncello, usually called simply *cello,* is the bass of the string choir. It is pitched an octave below the viola and possesses a rich, warm, clear tone. It is an excellent bass, harmonic, and melodic instrument. Like the other modern string instruments, it has four strings and is played both with a bow and by plucking.

EXAMPLE 74 The four strings of the cello are tuned as shown.

The limits for the range of the cello, given in terms of each string, are:

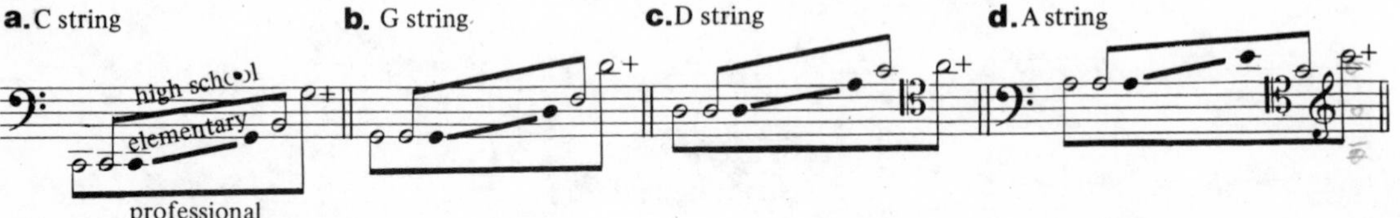

EXAMPLE 75 a. C String. b. G String. c. D String. d. A String.

The low C string has a heavy, rich tone quality; the G string, though of a similar sound, is a little lighter. At louder dynamics these strings offer a great deal of power, but at softer dynamics are amazingly easy to cover up. The D string has very little bite and is quite tranquil in quality. The A string is very expressive, powerful, rich and melodious, perhaps the most powerfully expressive string on any string instrument.

Higher notes for the cello are written in the tenor clef, although one should avoid changing clefs for only one or two isolated pitches. Passages that go too high for the tenor clef should be written in the treble clef. (One sometimes finds older cello parts written in the treble clef an octave above the intended pitch. This practice is to be avoided.)

The cello is supported on a peg that holds the body of the instrument off the floor. The performer steadies the cello with his knees while its neck rests against his left shoulder. This gives the performer's left hand great freedom of motion.

Because the strings are significantly longer than those on the violin or viola, pitches are farther apart than on the smaller instruments. Therefore, the composer or orchestrator should avoid very wide tremolos and remember that melodic leaps may require a little more time to execute. (See Appendix III:

String Fingerings.) The extra thickness of the body of the cello also makes it necessary for pitches that are a 10th or more above an open string to be played in a different manner than the lower pitches. To produce these high pitches the cellist must place his thumb on the fingerboard (toward the nut and away from the bridge) and stop the strings with his first, second, and third fingers. In these higher positions, the closer spacing of the pitches on the strings and the addition of the thumb, for stability and reference, make wide leaps and artificial harmonics easier to perform. It requires only a very short moment to place the thumb for the higher notes or to return to the lower positions.

The role of the cello in most ensembles is that of a bass as well as that of an alto, tenor, and even soprano voice. For its size and pitch range, the cello is a very agile instrument. Its standard repertoire consists of a variety of expressive melodic lines, arpeggios, and complex and intricate figures.

As a bass, it is clear, well-focused, and capable of the most subtle nuances or the most aggressive or exaggerated gestures. As a solo voice, it is very commanding in the upper register, but equally at home in the middle and lower ranges. The bow used on the cello is light and responsive and the cello can easily match bowings with the violin or viola. It is common to find the cello scored above the viola, for in that area of its range it is very assertive.

The cello pizzicato is quite successful, having excellent ringing properties and wide dynamic range. The pizzicato technique is light and rapid and the cello's speed in pizzicato is equal to the higher strings. The pitch is well-focused and centered. Pizzicatos on the natural harmonics are good and sustain well.

At a dynamic level of *forte,* triple stops are playable. At *mezzo-forte* and lesser dynamic levels, all triple stops are broken. Otherwise, multiple stops are as easy as on other string instruments, and the performance of broken chords may be more idiomatic to the cello than to any of the other orchestral strings.

All natural harmonics up through the 12th partial are good. Artificial harmonics are difficult in the lower positions, due to the string length, and had better be restricted to the harmonic produced by touching a minor third above the stopped string. Once the thumb positions are in use, then all artificial harmonics become playable.

Such effects as *ponticello* and *sul tasto* are more effective on the cello than on the other strings.

It doubles other instruments well, and, in larger ensembles, the cello section is regularly divided to provide two or more independent lines to the texture.

Typical Violoncello Scorings

This example from Felix Mendelssohn's *The Hebrides* Overture, Opus 26, shows the cello in both a melodic and an accompaniment role:

EXAMPLE 76 Violoncello writing in the opening of Mendelssohn's *The Hebrides.*

An often encountered accompaniment function of the cello is the performance of arpeggiated figures. The following excerpt is from Nicolai Rimsky-Korsakov's *Scheherazade* (beginning at letter H of the first movement). The figure is almost a cello cliché, very easy to play and very effective. The broken chord uses two open strings plus an E on the D string at the beginning and then gradually changes the composition of the figure.

EXAMPLE 77 A typical cello arpeggio figure.

As an example of the wide range over which the cello is written, the following example from *Also Sprach Zarathustra* by Richard Strauss is given.

EXAMPLE 78 An excerpt from Strauss's *Also Sprach Zarathustra* showing a wide cello tessitura.

Melodies played on the A string can often balance the full orchestra. The following melodic line begins the second movement of Brahms's Second Symphony, and the rest of the orchestra, scored moderately fully, is pitted against it. The cellos come through clearly.

EXAMPLE 79 Theme from the second movement of Brahms's Second Symphony, primarily using the cello's A string.

This cello passage is from "Nacht," the eighth section of Schönberg's *Pierrot Lunaire* (measures 16 - 19). It illustrates the use of *ponticello,* in measure 16 with unmeasured bowed tremolo, *tasto* in measures 17-18, and natural harmonics in measure 19. (See Example 42 on page 33.)

EXAMPLE 80 An example of twentieth-century cello writing, an excerpt from Schönberg's *Pierrot Lunaire.*[12]

This excerpt from Yehuda Yannay's *preFIX-FIX-sufFIX* illustrates the very high range of the cello. It is an example of technically demanding but playable cello writing. The composer is well aware of the properties of the cello, and has provided guides for the performer.

This symbol ⊓ is used to indicate "scratch tone." [symbol] means that the performer should make an accelerando; the reverse indicates a rallentando. This sign ‡ means ¼ tone sharp.

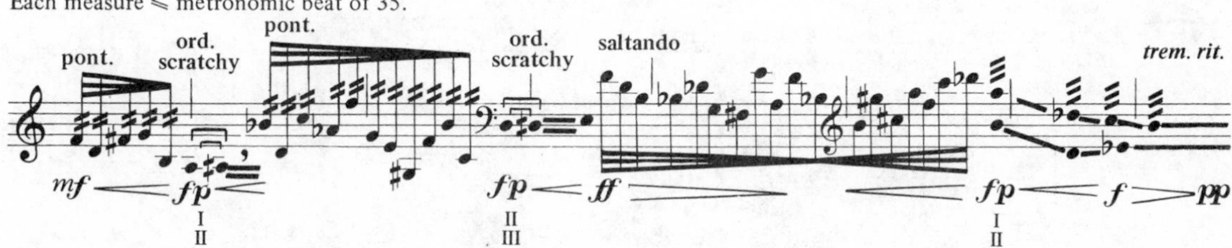

EXAMPLE 81 A contemporary cello passage: measures 40-47 from Yannay's *preFIX-FIX-sufFix.*[13]

Problem Set No. 8

1. Refer to the Bartók piece used for exercise 1, Problem Set No. 6 (page 49). In addition to the two violin parts, prepare a viola and a violoncello part. The final result should be a score and set of parts for a string quartet version of the original. (Maintain the use of pizzicato suggested in the original exercise.)

2. Write out a solo cello part, based in total on the lowest line in the following Chopin Prelude in B Minor. (Use tenor clef for some of the part.) What will need to be done with the one low B? Scordatura? Raise it an octave? Leave it out? Discuss this in class before you attempt the assignment. Have the result performed, with piano supplying the missing upper parts.

[12]Used by permission of Belmont Music Publishers, Los Angeles, California 90049. Copyright © 1914 by U.E. © renewed 1941 Arnold Schoenberg.

[13]© Copyright 1972 by Media Press, Inc. Box 195, Media, PA 19063. All Rights Reserved. Used by permission.

PRELUDE IN B MINOR

3. Copy the bass line of the Bach chorale harmonization given for exercise 2 of Problem Set No. 7 (page 55) for cello.

4. Make up a passage for violin, viola, and cello using several of the string special effects discussed in this chapter. Have your piece performed.

THE CONTRABASS

	English	*French*	*German*	*Italian*
singular	contrabass (cb.)	contre basse (c.b.)	Kontrabass (Kb.)	contrabbasso (c=bas.)
plural	contrabasses (cb.)	contre basses (c.b.)	Kontrabässe (Kb.)	contrabbassi (c=bassi)

The Properties of the Contrabass

The lowest voice in the string choir is the contrabass. It is also known as a double bass, bass viol, bass, or string bass. In contrast to the other orchestral strings the contrabass is a descendent of the viols, not the violins. (The characteristics that separate viols from violins are the shape of the body and the tuning system. The contrabass has sloping shoulders and is tuned in fourths. The violin, viola, and violoncello have shoulders with no slope and are tuned in fifths. See Figure 6, page 44.)

It is a large instrument, more than six feet in height, played by a performer who either sits on a tall stool or stands. Because of its size, the distance that a performer's hand must encompass simply to play two pitches a semitone apart is much greater on the contrabass than on the other strings. In fact, such large distances are involved on the contrabass that a performer can only span the interval of a major second between the first and fourth fingers in the lower positions. Tuning the strings a fourth rather than a fifth apart somewhat compensates for these limitations caused by the physical size of the instrument. (See also Appendix III: String Fingerings.)

The contrabass is the only transposing orchestral string instrument, sounding an octave lower than notated. The four strings are tuned to these pitches:

EXAMPLE 82 The four strings of the contrabass are tuned as shown.

The available pitches on each string (not including harmonics) are (as written):

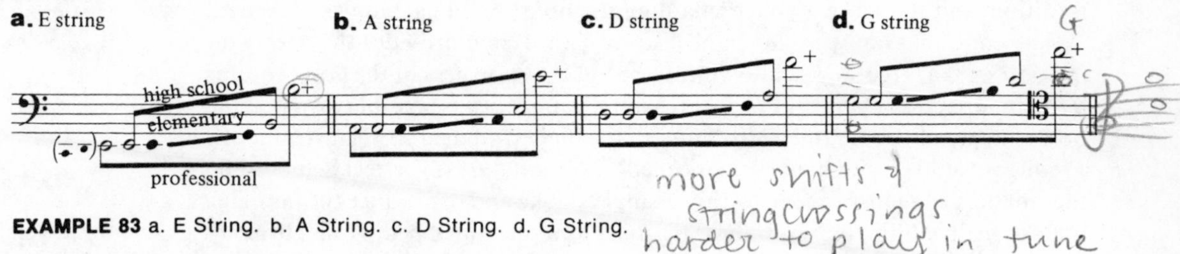

EXAMPLE 83 a. E String. b. A String. c. D String. d. G String.

The E string is very dark and somber. The tone is a little dull and foreboding. The A string has more buzz to it but is still quite ponderous and a trifle bland. The D string is much more mellow, reedy and rich. The highest string, the G, has a very rich quality and a larger range of expressive characteristics. It is capable of producing melodious or aggressive effects with equal ease. This string can rival any string in the orchestra for expressive playing, and yet it need not be of any particular disposition. It will adapt itself to the musical requirements.

In many scores, one finds pitches written for the contrabass that are below the E string. These very low notes are not available on most instruments and are therefore often omitted or replaced by a pitch an octave higher than written. There are three ways in which these low notes may be performed: One way, though seldom practical, is the use of scordatura. The contrabass has tuning pegs that are geared, rather than pressure-fit, and thereby somewhat easier to tune and retune. Another way, found almost exclusively in Europe, is the use of a five-string instrument, where the fifth string is tuned to the low C. The most common means of obtaining these pitches in the United States is by use of a low C extension (see Figure 6, page 44). This device consists of a string long enough to produce the low C, used in place of the normal E string, and a mechanism with four levers. Each lever controls a metal finger which in turn stops the string. These four keys are for E♮, E♭, D, and D♭, each stopping the string at the appropriate point. Most of the time the mechanism is locked so that the E key is stopping the string and effectively making the instrument's tuning the normal E, A, D, G combination. When the apparatus is used the keys are all released, increasing the effective length of the string down to C. As each key is depressed, its metal finger stops the string at the appropriate point to produce the required pitch. The keys are spring-loaded and unstop the string when not held down. Disadvantages to the low C extension are: It takes a second or two to lock or to release the mechanism; and when one of the keys is depressed it is impossible to stop another string in any usual manner, thus limiting fingering possibilities, especially the use of multiple stop fingerings.

Major orchestras often have half of the contrabasses equipped with low C extensions. Other organizations may have none so equipped, or at most one or two. It is always wise to provide an alternative (*ossia*) part for the basses without low C extensions whenever using these low notes.

Passages that become too high on the contrabass to be written in bass clef are usually written in tenor clef (like the cello) and very high passages may be written in the treble clef. A curious feature of contrabass notation is that all passages written in any clef are written an octave higher than the sounding pitch with the exception of harmonics in the treble clef. These are notated at sounding pitch to avoid ledger lines. Contemporary composers sometimes have not followed the tradition, and therefore a note explaining the notation of harmonics is needed.

The contrabass bow is short and heavy. This design provides the necessary mass to set the large strings into vibration; but the shortness of the bow requires frequent direction changes. For this reason it is not always possible to match the bow changes of the contrabass to those of the higher-pitched string instruments. Frequent, subtle bow changes are needed to obtain the same effect achieved by the smaller string instruments within a single stroke and to produce the familiar, but not really idiomatic, contrabass figure, a long sustained pedal tone. In a section of several contrabasses, staggered bow changes may be used. If only one performer is playing, then some considerable skill is needed to change bows with no audible break in the line.

The contrabass's pizzicato is one of its best assets. Due to the length and thickness of the strings and the resonance of the large body, the pizzicatos are warm, full, and well-sustained. In a variety of situations, loud or soft, its pizzicato can provide the only necessary underpinnings to an otherwise complex tonal structure. Jazz bass players have expanded the pizzicato resources to include double stops, tremolos, harmonics, and so on, not as special devices usable by only a few virtuosi, but as standard techniques within the capabilities of all professional players.

The size of the instrument makes the performance of artificial harmonics, in which a node a perfect fifth, perfect fourth, or major third above the stopped note is touched, impossible for most players. (Players with large hands can obtain these in the higher hand positions.) For most players, only the artificial harmonic produced by touching the node a minor third above the stopped note can be used, and this only in the higher positions. On the other hand, the natural harmonics on the string bass are more effective and more easily obtained than on any other orchestral string. The ranges of these harmonics place them in the middle of the string choir tessitura, making these harmonics especially good as alternatives to other string tones.

An effect developed by modern bassists is the *pulled* or *bent harmonic*. This is a natural harmonic produced while the performer stretches the string at a node. As the string is distended, the pitch of the harmonic is raised.

For all practical purposes, double stops are the only usable multiple-stops on the string-bass. These work best if one of the notes involved is an open string.

Like the violoncello (q.v.), the contrabass fingering technique requires the performer to shift to a thumb position when notes higher than a tenth above the open string are played. In these thumb positions, other multiple stops, including some triple stops, become playable. Use of these rather special multiple stops requires the composer to work closely with an experienced bassist.

Special effects, including bowing behind the bridge and on the tail piece, are all possible. In addition, such standard colorations as *sul ponticello* and *sul tasto* are even more effective on the string bass than on other instruments.

Typical Contrabass Scorings

The most obvious function for the contrabass is to play the bass line. A typical line is this one in the fourth movement of Beethoven's Ninth Symphony. While the cellos and violas play the theme, the bass adds this line:

EXAMPLE 84 Bass line from the fourth movement of the Beethoven's Ninth Symphony (measures 116-124).

In Richard Strauss's *Don Juan,* this bass line uses pitches lower than the low E. Strauss assumes that the extended range basses will be available. (The example begins 6 measures after rehearsal letter A.)

EXAMPLE 85 Contrabass Excerpt from Strauss's *Don Juan.*

The pizzicato bass line is a classic contrabass figure. This excerpt is from Dvořák's *New World Symphony* beginning 9 measures after rehearsal number 2 in the second movement).

EXAMPLE 86 From the second movement of Dvořák's *New World Symphony.*

The third movement of Gustav Mahler's First Symphony contains this solo for a single contrabass, muted:

EXAMPLE 87 Muted contrabass solo from Mahler's First Symphony (third movement, measures 3-10).

By keeping the tessitura lower, in the range of the middle strings, Saint-Saëns obtains a gravelly, tubby sound for "The Elephant" from *Carnival of the Animals.*

EXAMPLE 88 "Elephant" solo from *Carnival of the Animals* by Saint-Saëns.[14]

Color Studies by Jon Deak is a contrabass solo written by an accomplished bassist. In the movement "Fog White," Deak writes this passage. The indication TP means to bow tailpiece; BB means to bow below (on the tailpiece side) the bridge (no particular string is specified); note the instruction to pinch string IV and to scrape it with thumbnail; also, the reverse LH (left hand) pizzicatos are of interest. The diamond-shaped note heads represent the point at which the node is touched while the x represents the point at which the thumb touches and plucks the string. An arrow indicates a quarter-tone inflection.

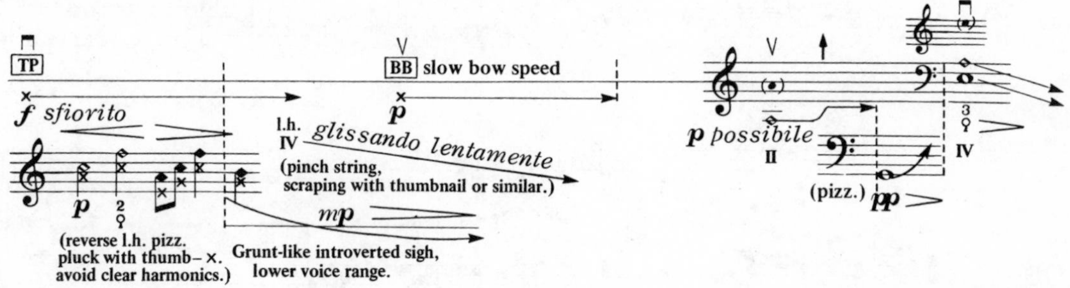

EXAMPLE 89 From Jon Deak's *Color Studies*.[15] All notation is an octave higher than it sounds; time is proportional.

Problem Set No. 9

1. Refer to the Bach chorale harmonization used in exercise 2 of Problem Set No. 7 (page 55.) In addition to the viola and violoncello parts that you have prepared, now prepare a contrabass part that is an octave lower than the violoncello part. If you would like, you could add two violin parts, covering the soprano and alto lines, thus producing a quintet version of the chorale.
2. Add to the violin and viola parts you have written for the Chopin Prelude in A Major, exercise 2, Problem Set No. 6 (page 50), a violoncello part and a contrabass part so that you totally replace the piano. Perform the resulting quintet.
3. Starting with the Bach Chorale Prelude, "Liebster Jesu, wir sind hier," below, copy the highest (soprano) line for violin; the second highest (alto) line also for violin; the middle (tenor) line for viola; the next to the lowest (baritone) line for violoncello; and the lowest (bass) line for contrabass. (Allow the contrabass to sound an octave lower than the notated pedal pitches.) If possible, have the quintet performed.

4. Using the Chopin Prelude in B Minor given in exercise 2, Problem Set No. 8 (page 60), write a solo contrabass part. Would you place the contrabass line at the original pitch or down an octave? What would you do about the notes out of the range in the latter case? Assume that you will only have a low E available unless you will actually have a performer available whose contrabass has a low C extension. Perform the final product with piano accompaniment.

5. Make a version of Chopin's Prelude in C Minor, given in Problem Set No. 1 (page 7), for an ensemble of two violins, viola, violoncello, and contrabass. Use your judgment as far as assignment of instruments to lines and use of higher or lower octaves than the original. Discuss in class problems of range, double stops, use of pizzicato (how can contrast be produced between the second and third phrases?) and other items. If at all possible, perform the results.

6. Compose a type of canon or round in which various contemporary string techniques and special effects are interchanged between the various instruments. Score it for violin, viola, cello, and contrabass. Have the result performed.

ORCHESTRAL STRINGS BIBLIOGRAPHY

Galamian, Ivan. *Principles of Violin Playing and Teaching.* Englewood Cliffs, N. J.: Prentice-Hall, Inc., 1962.

Green, Elizabeth A. H. *Orchestral Bowings and Routines.* Ann Arbor, Mich.: Ann Arbor Publishers, 1957.

Krolick, Edward. *Basic Principles of Double Bass Playing.* Washington, D.C.: Music Educators National Conference, 1957.

Leipp, Emile. *The Violin.* Translated by Hildegarde W. Parry. Toronto: University of Toronto Press, 1969.

Lorrin, Mark. *Dictionary of Bowing and Tonal Techniques for Strings.* Denver: Charles Hensen Educational Music and Books, 1968.

Menuhin, Yehudi, William Primrose, and Denis Stevens. *Violin and Viola.* New York: Schirmer Books, 1976.

Nelson, Sheila M. *The Violin and Viola.* London: Benn, 1972.

Potter, Louis. *The Art of Cello Playing.* Evanston, Ill.: Summy-Birchard Co., 1964.

Turetzky, Bertram. *The Contemporary Contrabass.* Berkeley: University of California Press, 1974.

Warfield, Gerald. "The Notation of Harmonics for Bowed String Instruments." *Perspectives of New Music,* (Fall-Winter, 1973 and Spring-Summer, 1974; double issue), p. 331ff.

Zukofsky, Paul. "On Violin Harmonics." *Perspectives of New Music* (Spring-Summer, 1968), p. 174ff.

3

INSTRUMENTATION: *The Woodwinds*

GENERAL WOODWIND INFORMATION

The Means of Producing Sounds

Woodwind instruments use one of these three methods of producing sounds:

1. A stream of air is directed over the edge of an embouchure hole, splitting the stream into two parts. One of these parts continues past the edge. The other, smaller part is directed into the hole, where it sets up a vibration. This is how sound is produced in flutes.
2. A pair of curved reeds, made from cane and separated slightly, are set into vibration against one another producing a rather nasal buzz. This is how sound is produced in oboes and bassoons.
3. A single flat reed made of cane is attached to a mouthpiece by means of a ligature, and vibrates against the mouthpiece with a "squawky" or "honky" quality. This is how sound is produced in clarinets and saxophones.

Terminology

Flutes are blown through an embouchure or blow hole which is located in the head joint. The head joint is closed at one end and possess a tapered (or conical) bore. The body of the flute has a cylindrical bore and has pads to cover various tone holes. On "closed-hole" flutes, the finger holes are covered by full, solid pads. On "open-hole" flutes these finger holes possess donut-shaped pads, the openings in which are covered by the performer's fingers as the pads are being depressed.

The double reeds—oboes and bassoons—are conical-bored and have an octave key operated by the performer's thumb. The reeds of the oboe attach to the body, while the reeds of all other double-reed instruments attach to a bocal which in turn attaches to the body. They both terminate in a bell.

The clarinets and saxophones are single-reed instruments. They have a mouthpiece to which the reed is attached by means of a ligature. The mouthpiece of the saxophone fits onto the conical metal body while the clarinet's mouthpiece attaches to a barrel joint and then to an upper and a lower joint ending with a bell. The clarinet bore is cylindrical. The performer's thumb operates a thumb or register key. The saxophones have an octave key (like the oboes and bassoons) and also end with a bell.

English	*French*	*German*	*Italian*
embouchure *or* blow hole	embouchure	Mundloch	imboccatura
head joint	corps supérieur	Kopfstück	testata
closed hole	trou fermé	geschlossenes Griffloch	foro chiuso
open hole	trou ouvert	offenes Griffloch	foro aperto
pad	tampon de clé	Klappenpolster	cuscinetto *or* tampone
tone hole	trou	Tonloch	foro
double reed	anche double	doppeltes Rohrblatt	ancia doppia
conical bore	perce conique	konische Bohrung	foro conico
octave key	clé d'octave	Oktavklappe	portavoce
bocal	bocal	das S	esse
bell	pavillon *or* bonnet	Schallbecher *or* Stürze	padiglione
reed	anche	Rohrblatt	ancia
mouthpiece	bec	Schnabel *or* Mundstück	imboccatura a becco *or* bocchino a becco
ligature	ligature	Ligaturklammer	legatura *or* fascietta
barrel	baril or barillet	Birne	barilotto
upper joint	corps de la main gauche	Oberstück	pezzo superiore
lower joint	corps de la main droite	Unterstück	pezzo inferiore
cylindrical bore	perce cylindrique	zylindrische Bohrung	foro cilindrico
register key	clef du pouce	Überblasklappe	portavoce
key	clef	Klappe	chiave
finger hole	trou	Griffloch	buco
key hole	trou de clef	Klappenloch	foro della chiave

Woodwind Articulations

The major components involved in wind articulations are the breath and the tongue. The interaction of these two elements provide all of the various types of articulations available to wind players. The working of the system can be broken down into three phases:

1. *Attack.*
   The tone begins when the tongue of the performer moves away from the back of the teeth, opening a passageway for the air through pursed lips.
2. *Steady-state.*
   The air from the player's lungs rushes into the instrument setting the

reed(s) and air column into vibration. The tone will continue as long as the flow of air continues.

3. *Release.*
   The tone stops when the flow of air ceases.

At every step the performer may introduce variations that modify the attack, steady-state, or release of the tone. Among these modifications are the use of various locations for the tongue and changes in the shape of the tongue; the speed, quantity, and direction of the air flow; the size and shape of the mouth and throat; and the method by which the air flow is stopped. The possible modifications and variations are certainly more vast than the number of articulation symbols that the composer has at his disposal. Therefore, the various articulations that are described in the following section are to be taken as *average* articulations. For example, there is not just one type of *staccato;* each instrument has its own characteristic staccato that it will produce naturally. In spite of the variety of staccatos produced by a mixed group of instruments, good ensemble is still possible because performers can overcome these differences and match each other's articulations.

There are three main classes or types of articulations to be found in woodwind music. These three are *legato, non-legato,* and *staccato*. Exact classification into these three categories, however, is often not so simple, for the extremes within each of the three classes, when heard in another context, may be judged to belong to another class of articulation.

EXAMPLE 90 Notation of the three main classes of woodwind articulation: a. Legato. b. Non-legato. c. Staccato.

Legato

Legato articulations are those in which, once the initial tone is started, the performer's tongue plays no audible role in the starting of subsequent tones. The tones of the passage sound smoothly connected and one perceives no break or separation between pitches. In addition, one does not hear any percussive attack or start to the notes. The notation for legato articulation for wind players is a slur.

Non-Legato

Non-legato articulations are characterized by each note being started by the tongue with very slight separations between the notes. The separations are usually only long enough for the player to re-position the tongue so that the next pitch may be started (a very rapid operation even for less experienced players). The main distinction between legato and non-legato articulations has to do with the use of air: Instead of using a constant, uninterrupted stream of air, as in legato playing, non-legato is a constant but interrupted stream of air which gives each note a separate attack and release.

Staccato

Staccato articulation is nearly the exact opposite of legato. In practice, it is an extreme example of non-legato. Staccato notation is somewhat ambiguous. The pitches are written full value, but the notation instructs the performer to insert spaces between the notes. Since the performer is not usually free to change the tempo, it is obvious that to achieve a staccato effect, the player must shorten the notes to provide the necessary spaces. Therefore, the staccato version of the passage in Example 90 may sound as follows:

EXAMPLE 91 One possible staccato performance.

In slow passages problems of interpretation arise. A famous example is the opening to Beethoven's *Egmont* Overture where the full orchestra has:

Sostenuto ma non troppo

EXAMPLE 92 The rhythm and articulation found in measures 2 and 3 of Beethoven's *Egmont* Overture.

Because of the slow tempo yet rather long note values, one may well wonder exactly what the staccato marking means. How long should those half notes last? To avoid such problems, it is a good idea to be more exact when indicating the length of notes and spaces in a staccato passage unless the speed of the notes is rapid enough to make such differences negligible.

Legato Shadings

Modification of the basic legato articulation is often desired. To achieve a variety of articulations, tenuto marks (-) and dots are used along with the slurs mentioned above. Although there is not universal agreement as to the "correct" interpretation of these notations, and interpretation without regard to historical and stylistic considerations is inappropriate, the following discussion represents typical current thinking and suggests usage that is practiced at this time.

The tenuto mark applied to a note in isolation is generally understood to add a stress to that note and often to extend the length of the note. When placed over a series of notes, all of which are under a slur, tenuto marks indicate that the phrase is to be played legato, that is, as connected articulation in which each note is slightly stressed but no discernable separation is heard between notes. Often the tongue is used to produce the stress, but due to the soft, quick stroke involved it may not be perceivable, and for this reason the articulation is sometimes called *legato tonguing.*

The dot, traditionally associated with staccato as discussed above, may be understood to represent an implication of separation in articulation. Another type of legato tonguing often used is indicated by notes with staccato-type dots, but placed under a slur. This is usually understood to mean a legato articulation in which each note is gently tongued with a short but perceptable space between the notes and no special stress associated with the tongue stroke. This articulation is more separated than normal legato, but not as separated as non-legato.

Between these last two types of legato tonguings is a third type which is notated with a line and a dot under a slur. This interpretive marking calls for both the delicate stress associated with the tenuto mark and the separation associated with the dot, but a little less of each.

EXAMPLE 93 a. Legato tonguing with some stress, but no separation. b. Legato tonguing, with some stress and some separation. c. Legato tonguing, with no stress but perceptable separation.

Non-Legato Shadings

The tenuto mark and the dot used together are also employed to obtain shadings of non-legato articulations. As mentioned above, the tenuto mark indicates that a note is to be stressed and at times lengthened. Therefore, when viewed as an articulation, the tenuto mark calls for a note to be more stressed and longer than a simple non-legato note. But it is also to be clearly tongued and separated in keeping with its non-legato character.

Adding the dot emphasizes the separateness of this stressed non-legato by increasing the space between the notes. This produces a note that is almost as short as staccato but more weighty.

Staccato Shadings

The only shading that is usually associated with staccato is staccatissimo. The indication is the use of a wedge (▼) over the note. This is interpretated to be a shorter note than the normal staccato, but neither more nor less accented or stressed.

EXAMPLE 94 a. Stressed non-legato. b. Stressed and separated non-legato. c. Staccatissimo.

So that the relationships between and among these various articulations may be more easily seen, the following chart is provided. Remember that not all performers and conductors will agree with all of the details of this chart, but it does generally reflect current practice.

EXAMPLE 95 A chart of various wind articulations.

In studying symbols used for wind articulations it must be remembered that many composers who were violinists or pianists have simply used string bowing symbols or piano articulation symbols for wind parts. Under these circumstances, other interpretations than the ones given in Example 95 will be appropriate. One especially troublesome symbol for the wind performer is illustrated in Example 96.

EXAMPLE 96 a. An often encountered notation. b. and c. Two different performance possibilities for that notation.

Since either (b) or (c) are equally plausible interpretations of (a), the orchestrator is advised to avoid (a) entirely and to use one of the other two instead, depending upon the effect desired. The ambiguity will thus be eliminated. It is always advisable to apply *only* wind articulation conventions to wind music, and to avoid string or keyboard symbols.

Other Tonguings

Double and Triple Tonguing

The discussion of articulations has up to this point dealt only with single tonguing techniques. Double and triple tonguing are also commonly available but may be assumed to be standard only on flutes and brass instruments (and not always among horn players.) Double and triple tonguing are possible on all winds and will undoubtedly become more widespread in the future.

Double and triple tonguing take advantage of the fact that, to create a fresh attack, one only needs to interrupt the air column. To accomplish this it is not always necessary to use the tongue position represented by the syllable "ta," i.e., putting the tongue against the back of the teeth; any means of interrupting the air column will do. Thus, the articulation of either "ta" or "ka" will create the effect of a note being tongued. Double tonguing consists of the syllable sequence of (approximately) ta-ka-ta-ka-etc. and triple tonguing consists of either ta-ka-ta, ta-ka-ta, etc., or ka-ta-ka, ka-ta-ka, or more commonly, ta-ta-ka, ta-ta-ka.

The choice of whether or not to double or triple tongue is usually left to the performer. Accomplished performers can execute either technique at almost any tempo and will choose to use one or the other (or neither) according to the musical requirements of the passage. If the composer-orchestrator wishes to specify that a passage be double or triple tongued, it is a simple matter of writing such an instruction into the part.

Flutter Tonguing

Flutter tonguing is possible on all wind instruments, although it is a more common technique for the brasses, flutes, and saxophones than it is for the clarinets and double reeds. In flutter tonguing, the performer allows his tongue to vibrate much as a rolled "r" is produced in some languages or as children sometimes imitate the sound of a machine gun.[1] It is difficult for less experienced players to do a flutter-tongued passage at softer dynamic levels or in the extremes of the ranges of the instruments (either high or low). But the use of this articulation at soft dynamics or range extremes should not be considered impossible. The difficulties encountered at these extremes are more noticeable at the start of a flutter-tongued passage, but become less so as the passage continues. Therefore, an attack at a *forte* level of a flutter-tongued note may be followed by a diminuendo to *pianissimo* and still be very playable even for younger musicians, while the opposite could be quite difficult. In fact, for less skilled players, an attack at a *pianissimo* dynamic may preclude flutter-tonguing from taking place.

Slap Tonguing

If the performer re-positions the tongue against the teeth or the reed to stop the air flow, a rather hard release is created. Common practice instruction suggests that, except for the double reeds, this is not an acceptable practice. However, the performer may be asked to produce this effect, even exaggerate it so that the release is especially hard and audible, to create an effect known as slap tonguing. The instruction to the performer would be simply *slap tongued.*

Special Attacks and Alterations to Sustained Tones

The wind instruments may produce modified attacks by the use of various phonemes on the attack other than the traditional "ta" or "tu." Among these are "da" or "du" which are commonly used to produce tongued legatos and non-accented attacks. Other consonants may be called for on the attack, such as

[1]Some performers produce the flutter tonguing roll in the throat. Other very good performers may not be able to flutter tongue at all.

"tsch" or "k" to produce altered attack envelopes. These special attacks are most effective on the flute, somewhat effective on the saxophones and brasses, and rather less effective on the other winds, where the effect becomes very subtle.

While a performer is sustaining a tone on a wind instrument, he usually attempts to keep the throat and mouth as unobstructed and as open as possible to insure a free tone quality that is rich and warm. However, alteration of the size and shape of the oral cavity and modification of the placement of the tongue during the steady tone can significantly change the quality, producing nasal, buzzy, or stuffy versions of the tone. To accomplish this, the performer adjusts the position of his mouth (i.e., jaw, cheeks, tongue) just as though to produce different vowels but without voicing the vowels. Similarly, the addition of consonant sounds to the end of a tone can produce varying, nonstandard releases.[2]

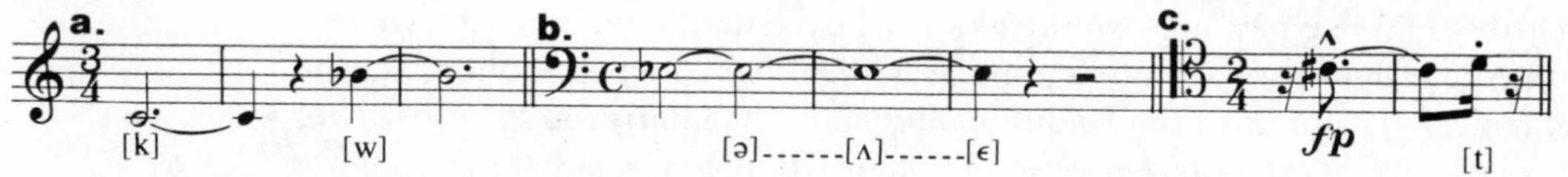

EXAMPLE 97 a. Consonants added to attack. b. Changing oral cavity during performance of a sustained pitch. c. Adding consonant to release.

SPECIAL WOODWIND EFFECTS AND DEVICES

Harmonics

All woodwind instruments can produce higher pitches that are partials found in the overtone series associated with pitches fingered within the lowest register of the instrument. The production of these partials is facilitated by the use of vent holes, register holes, or octave holes built into the instrument and the pitches thus produced are often incorporated into the keying system of the instrument.

When one of these partials is produced by controlling the air column and the embouchure and without the use of the venting, register, or octave holes, a washed-out, transparent note is produced. The result is called a *harmonic*. Harmonics are called for in flute and oboe parts quite frequently, less often in clarinet and bassoon parts. Saxophonists regularly use harmonics to extend the upward range of the instrument. The notation is a small circle (°) over the affected pitch(es).

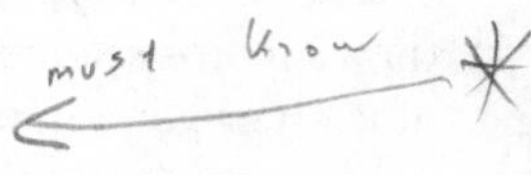

EXAMPLE 98 Harmonics are producible on and above the written pitches shown here.

[2]To avoid ambiguity, one should use symbols from the International Phonetic Alphabet (given in Appendix VII). Since most wind players will not know this alphabet, instructions explaining the symbols must be included.

Vibrato

Vibrato is possible on all of the woodwinds and to varying degrees is a standard aspect of woodwind tone quality. There are three types of vibrato commonly produced:

1. *Diaphragmatic vibrato* is produced by a pulsation of the air column controlled by the player's diaphragm.
2. *Jaw vibrato* is produced by tightening and loosening the embouchure around the reed as controlled by the jaw.
3. *Mechanical* (or instrument) *vibrato* produced by repeatedly moving the instrument as it is played, producing a constant disturbance of the air column.

Of these three types, one is more likely to hear a diaphragmatic vibrato used on the flute while a jaw vibrato is popular with jazz and rock saxophonists. The mechanical vibrato has been traditionally held to be inferior to the other two, but it does provide an alternative sound quality that can be either subtle or extremely rough and erratic as desired.

One may specify not only what type of vibrato is wanted, but also the speed and depth of the vibrato. (See pages 37-38.) If not specified, the type of vibrato used will be left up to the performer. The composer is also warned that not all performers can execute the diaphragmatic vibrato—not even all flutists.

The instruction to cancel vibrato is "no vibrato" or *non vibrato.*

Glissandos

There are two common, and often co-existant, means of producing woodwind glissandos. These are:

1. Inflecting the pitch by altering the embouchure and air column while changing the fingerings chromatically. The speed at which the fingers change depends upon the speed of the glissando.
2. Moving the reed into or out of the mouth, with or without altering the air column or embouchure. (On the flute, a rotation of the embouchure hole toward or away from the player's lips will produce a similar pitch change.)

Of these two types, the former is usable over a wide range, even the entire compass of the instrument, and may be performed rapidly or slowly, ascending or descending. (Ascending is usually considered to be easier.)

The second type of glissando is more limited in range, usually covering less than a major second. It may, however, be employed at the beginning and the end of a wider glissando to smooth out the execution. This second type may also be used to produce microtonal inflections (see page 82).

For additional discussion of glissandos and notation, see pages 35-36 and 127-29.

Flute Effects

Breath tones are produced by broadening the stream of air, thereby losing the normal focus of the tone. The effect is a subtle timbre modification which increases the white noise component of the tone. The result is a masked, whispy tone quality that seems to have no clear physical location in the environment.

Whistle tones are extremely delicate, pure, and quite soft notes produced by the performer barely directing a small stream of air into the flute. The sound is somewhat like a person whistling *sotto voce* between his teeth. Not all flutists have developed the ability to achieve these sounds. The dynamic level is limited to *piano* and softer.

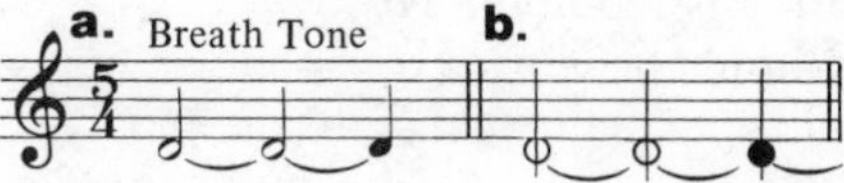

EXAMPLE 99 a. Traditional notation for a breath tone. b. An alternative notation, which would require an explanation in the part.

The head joint on all flutes and almost all piccolos is removable, and if the performer plays on the head joint alone, a rather uncontrolled tone is produced. If a dowel rod or similar device (drum stick, performer's finger, etc.) is placed into the open end of the head joint, the pitch of the tone can be controlled. As the device is moved into the head joint, toward the embouchure hole, the pitch is raised; as the device is removed, the pitch is lowered. This effect is very much like a slide whistle.

Double-Reed Effects

One of the woodwind effects that is unique to the double reeds is the *smack tone* which can be produced by sucking on the reed in a very noisy manner. The effect may be achieved on various pitches throughout the range of the instrument.

EXAMPLE 100 Recommended smack tone notation. An explanation in the part will be required.

The player of a double-reed instrument may remove the reed and play upon it alone (the bocal to which it is attached may be removed with it). A variety of squawks can be produced this way and, by cupping the performer's hands around the reed or bocal, and changing the amount of opening and the size of the cup formed by the hands, modification in the tone of the reed may be produced. The pitch range and dynamic range of the reeds are rather limited; the larger reeds produce lower but not necessarily louder sounds. On occasion, the double reeds have been attached to other instruments such as horns or trombones, often with special apparatus in order to assure a good joint between the reed and the instrument. The buzzing reeds will of course produce the characteristic double-reed squawk tone, but the amplification and filtering produced by the attached instrument will create an entirely new timbre.

Single-Reed Effects

Sub-tones are playable on both the clarinet and the saxophone. These are very easily produced in the lower register and are often used as a means of achieving required *pianissimos*. However, these represent such an extremely soft sound range that subtones are more often treated in modern music as special timbral effects. They can be easily covered, so careful scoring is required. To obtain these soft tones, subtone, *mezzo-voce,* or *sotto voce* should be written in the part.

In much the same manner as the detachable reed (or reed and bocal) of the double reeds, the mouthpiece and reed can be removed from the clarinet or saxophone and played by itself. Again, the hands may be cupped around the open end of the mouthpiece to modify the tone and pitch. The mouthpiece may also be attached to another instrument to produce special effects. (One such is the attachment of a clarinet or saxophone mouthpiece to a trombone and buzzing the reed while moving the slide. The effect is somewhat like an airplane roar.)

The opposite effect, in some respects, is the buzzing of the lips on the barrel of the clarinet after the mouthpiece has been removed. The buzzing, just like the lip buzzing of brass players, transforms the clarinet into a strange "keyed-bugle" device which can play overtones like a brass instrument (see page 125) and have its length altered like a woodwind. The same technique could be applied to the saxophone or flutes, but a slight modification of the opening of the tubing would be required to keep the performer's lips from being cut. The use of a regular or modified brass instrument mouthpiece suggests itself and leads to other ideas (such as the attachment of a brass mouthpiece to an oboe or bassoon, etc.). There is probably no end to the possible special effects one could develop.

The reassembly of standard woodwind instruments into different configurations may or may not be a special effect. Almost every young clarinetist must have at some time assembled and played the instrument without the upper (left-hand) section. This produces a piccolo clarinet with a strange tuning. The device has been used at least in improvisations, and could find other uses.

Contemporary Effects and Devices

Mutes

Mutes are not as common on woodwind instruments as they are on brasses, but they do exist. Handkerchiefs inserted partway into the bell of an oboe, saxophone, or bassoon have long been used to help control the assertiveness associated with the lowest notes of these instruments. More sophisticated versions of these mutes have been made of cotton or other absorbent material and equipped with "fingers" or other devices for securing the mute into the instrument. Other types of devices, usually soft and slightly smaller than the bell opening, have been used on clarinets and saxophones. Flute mutes seem to be generally uncalled for, but a piccolo mute, made from a round tube into which the instrument is inserted, with the head joint on the outside and with cloth-covered holes cut to allow the performer's hands to hold the piccolo in a normal playing position, has been used to reduce the loudness of extremely high notes. This same approach could be applied to other woodwinds.

Up to now, most mute usage for woodwinds has been devoted to the reduction of loudness rather than, as in the brasses, to the alteration of timbre. Experiments in the latter area might prove both interesting and rewarding.

Key Slaps

Key slaps also include "finger" slaps, produced by slamming the fingers down upon the open holes of the instrument. The actual key slaps are more often pad slaps, produced by rapidly popping the pads shut upon the holes they cover. When all of the holes closer to the mouthpiece, reed, or embouchure than the one being popped are already closed, the key slap will be pitched. When at least one hole—but better yet several holes—between the popped hole and the player's mouth is open, the result is a slap without definite pitch. Due to the acoustical characteristics of the performance environment, it is often necessary to close several pads at the same time to produce an audible sound.

Key slaps may be produced by themselves or with the attack of normally produced pitches. The type of slap produced on the flute and saxophones is easy to hear and quite effective. The slaps produced on the other woodwinds are not as resonant and thus less easily utilized. Electronic amplification greatly improves the versatility of these latter effects.

On the flute, a common technique is to cover the embouchure hole with the player's tongue or lip and then slap the keys. This produces a pitch that is a major seventh below the pitch of the last pad being closed, and is very resonant. (This effect could be achieved on the clarinet or saxophone if the mouthpiece were first removed.

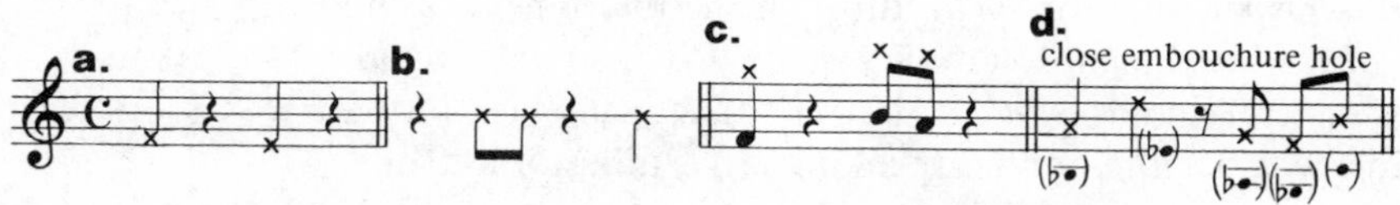

EXAMPLE 101 Recommended notations for: a. Pitched key slap. b. Key slap of unspecified pitch. c. Key slap added to normal pitch. d. Key slaps with embouchure hole closed.

Timbral Trills

Timbral or key trills are producible on all woodwinds and only require that the note to be affected be high enough in pitch within a given register so that there are keys or holes left uncovered when the pitch is performed. To obtain a key trill, the performer merely trills a key or hole which modifies the timbre of the sound without significantly affecting the pitch. The closer to the lowest depressed finger the hole or key to be trilled is located, the more obvious the pitch alterations will become; the further away, the less noticeable the pitch change, but the timbre variation will also be more subtle.

Double Trills

Double trills are producible only when an instrument has at least two separate vent keys, one playable by each hand, that will activate the same pitch. Thus, if a trill key from G to A♭ exists for the right hand and another, different, key for this trill exists for the left hand, a double trill may be playable. The process is straightforward. The player fingers the main note G and trills to A♭ in the normal way, and at the same time also trills from the G to the A♭ by moving the appropriate key with the other hand. But the second hand is ninety degrees out of phase with the first hand, thereby doubling the speed at which the trill is produced.

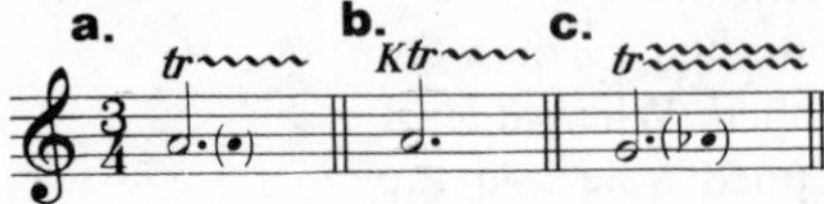

EXAMPLE 102 a. A possible notation for a key trill. b. Another notation for a key trill. c. A suggested notation for a double trill. (All will require an explanation in the part.)

Air Tones

Air tones are sounds produced by blowing air through the instrument with or without producing a more conventional tone. It may be done with the mouthpiece (or reed) removed or in place. If the normal tone production system is used with air tones, the composite effect is one of adding a windiness (white noise) to the main tone. Some performers are capable of going gradually from pure air sounds to normal tone and back. The technique is especially easy on the flutes, saxophones, and clarinets. On the double reeds there is more likely to be an audible attack as the reed begins to vibrate, but the transition from normal to air tones often works very well. Flute breath tones are an example of air sounds (see pages 76-77).

It is also possible to whisper, sing, or speak through the instrument, using the resonant qualities of the instrument to amplify or modify the vocal sound. Screams and other primative sounds work well, but for real intelligibility a dynamic range between a whisper and normal speaking levels is best. Electronic amplification can make this even more effective.

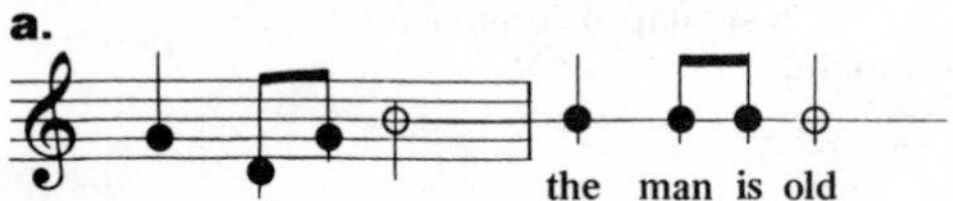

EXAMPLE 103 a. Air sounds added to normal tone. b. Whispering through instrument—no normal sounds. (Notation will require explanation.)

The alternation between sung and played pitches may be made to sound much like a variant of the instrument's timbre resembling a sort of timbral counterpoint.

Multiphonics

All woodwinds can produce multiphonics. There are at least two different approaches to the production of these sounds:

1. By playing one pitch and simultaneously humming another, producing two pitches with or without sum and difference tones (resultants).[3]
2. By blowing and controlling the air column or the venting of the column in such a way as to produce two or more simultaneous pitches.

The possible combinations of pitches producible as multiphonics vary greatly from specific instrument to instrument and from player to player. Although research is beginning to discover some consistently producible multiphones for each woodwind, a complete, reliable catalog is not available at this time. For this reason, a great many composers prefer to indicate simply that the performer is to play a multiphonic, show the approximate pitch area of the multiphonic, and indicate loudness, length, etc., leaving the rest to the discretion of the performer.

Another approach taken is to indicate a pitch or pitches that are to be heard within the multiphonic and allow the performer to select a playable multiphonic that contains the pitch(es).

The composer who wishes to have specific pitch content in the multiphonics needs to work closely with the woodwind player who is to perform the piece. When writing such a piece, it is important to realize that another performer may obtain totally different results, even with the same fingerings.

EXAMPLE 104 a. Notation of multiphonics where performer plays larger notes and hums smaller notes. b. Notation of indeterminate multiphonics. c. Notation of multiphonics in which some pitch content is specified.

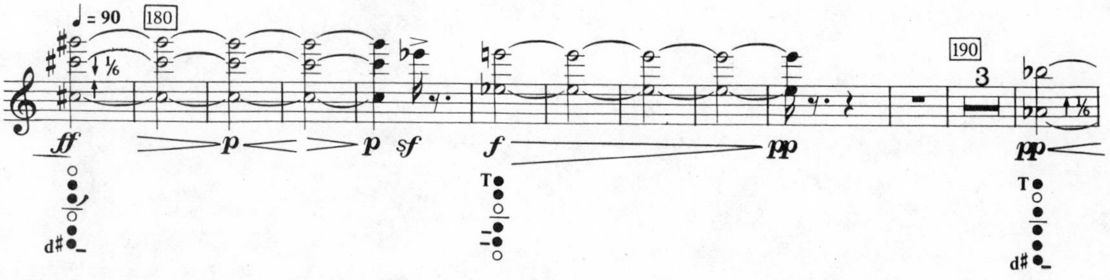

EXAMPLE 105 Notation of multiphonics which the composer worked out with a performer. Notation makes clear the specific pitches desired, including microtonal inflections and fingerings. Excerpt from Dennis Eberhard's *Paraphrases*[4] for woodwind quintet (flute part, measures 179-193).

[3]When two tones of different frequency interact with one another, *sum* (or *summation*) and *difference tones* result. Given a tone of 600 vibrations per second (Hertz) and another of 650 Hertz, the sum tone will be 1250 Hz (600 + 650 = 1250) and the difference tone, or resultant, will be 650 − 600 = 50 Hz.

Microtones

The use of microtones to inflect and ornament melodic lines has been practiced in the music of many cultures and styles. Although not usually discussed or taught as a part of the performance traditions of Western European art music, it is often encountered, especially in vocal performance and in some instrumental solos. All instruments of the woodwind choir have the ability to be pitch-inflected by the performer, and can therefore produce microtones. In jazz performance, the use of microtonal inflections has long been a standard part of the performance style. Microtones can be created by altering and controlling the air column through adjustments in the oral cavity and the tongue position as well as the throat opening, and by adjustments in the position of the reed or mouthpiece in the mouth and the amount of "bite" put on the reed by the jaws and lips of the performer. In the case of the flute, the rolling of the embouchure hole toward or away from the player's mouth will create pitch modifications of almost a semitone between the extreme positions.

In addition, special fingering may be utilized. By the use of *forked fingerings* (see Appendix IV) chromatic tones may be produced on woodwinds. If additional holes are covered below the fork, the pitch of the chromatic alteration may be lowered; by venting or half venting other, normally covered holes, the pitch may be raised.

One *can* obtain microtonal fingering charts for the various woodwinds. However, because the actual use of microtones in music varies greatly (some composers want microtonal inflections of unspecified size; others want even-tempered quarter or third tones; and still others want pitches that form specific intervallic ratios with other pitches), it should be clear that no one set of microtonal fingerings will produce all of these possible results and that truly accurate microtones in a given context are dependent upon the performer's ears and not a specific fingering. All of the instruments of the woodwind choir possess microtonal possibilities. The players may require special preparation.

WOODWIND BIBLIOGRAPHY

Baines, Anthony. *Woodwind Instruments and Their History.* 3rd edition. London: Faber, 1967.

Bartolozzi, Bruno. *New Sounds for Woodwinds.* Transl. and ed. Reginald Smith Brindle. London: Oxford University Press, 1967.

Weisberg, Arthur. *The Art of Wind Playing.* New York: Schirmer Books, 1975.

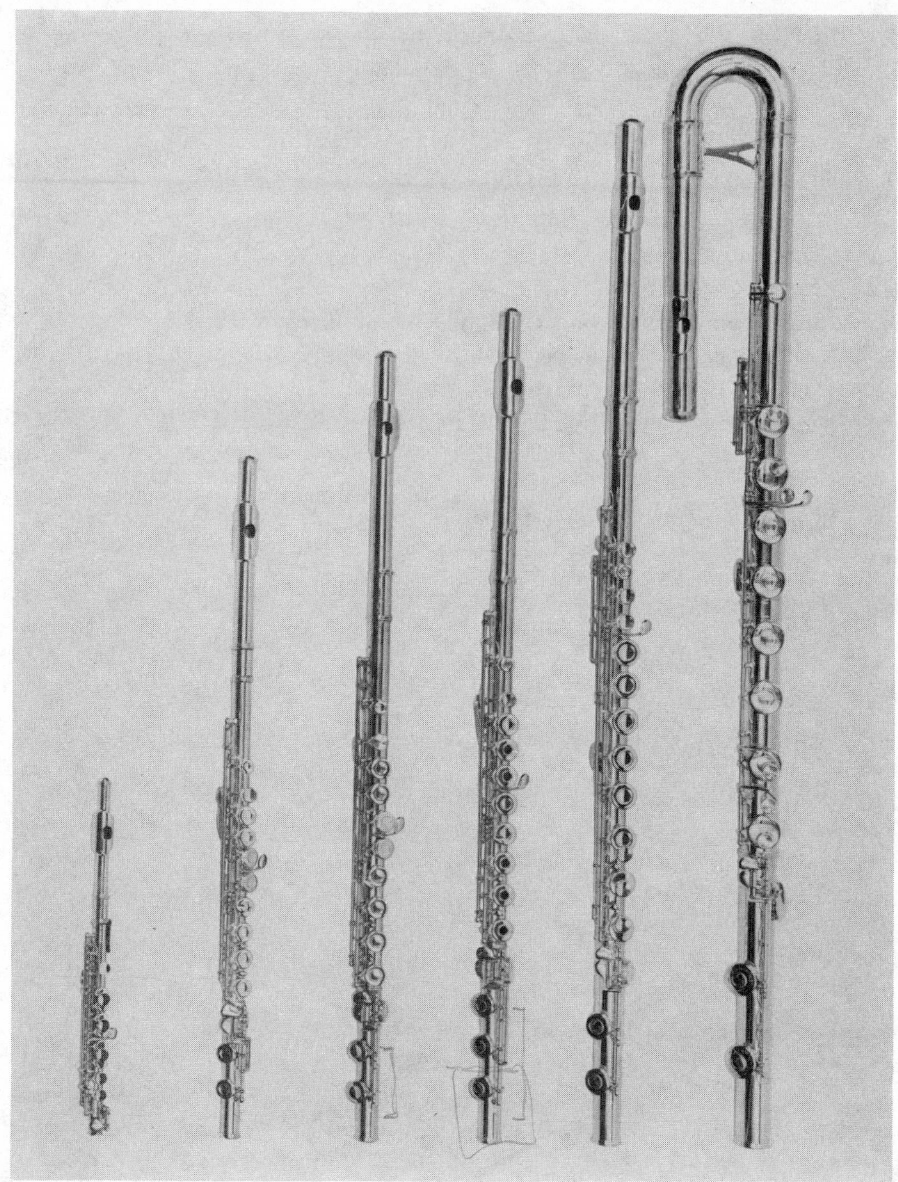

FIGURE 7. The flutes (*from left to right:* piccolo in C; E♭ flute; C flute with closed holes; C flute with open holes and B foot; alto flute in G; and bass flute in C. (Photo courtesy W. T. Armstrong Company, Inc., Elkhart, Indiana.)

THE FLUTES

	English	*French*	*German*	*Italian*
singular	flute [fl.]	(grande) flûte [fl.]	(grosse) Flöte [gr. Fl.]	flauto [fl.]
plural	flutes [fl.]	(grandes) flûtes [fl.]	(grosse) Flöten [gr. Fl.]	flauti [fl.]

The Properties of the Flutes

The flutes represent the highest-pitched (soprano) family of the woodwind choir. They are basically cylindrical-bore instruments. Older flutes were made of wood while modern instruments are generally made of metal. Wooden piccolos are still to be found, and are preferred by many players. The flute family consists of the following instruments:

1. Flute (or concert flute) in C.
2. Piccolo in C
   (French: flûte piccolo *or* petite flûte; German: Pikkoloflöte *or* kleine Flöte; Italian: ottavino *or* flauto piccolo)
3. Alto flute[5] in G
   (French: flûte alto en sol; German: Altflöte; Italian: flauto contralto).
4. E♭ flute
   (French: flûte tierce; German: Terzflöte; Italian: flauto terzino in mi♭).
5. Bass flute in C (rare)
   (French: flûte basse; German: Bassflöte; Italian: flauto basso).

With two exceptions, the flutes have the following written range:

EXAMPLE 106 Range of flute family.

The exceptions are the piccolos which have for the lowest note: and the concert flute which sometimes has a "low B key": This "B" key cannot yet be considered to be a standard feature and the composer should always provide an *ossia* passage for performers whose instruments do not possess the low B.

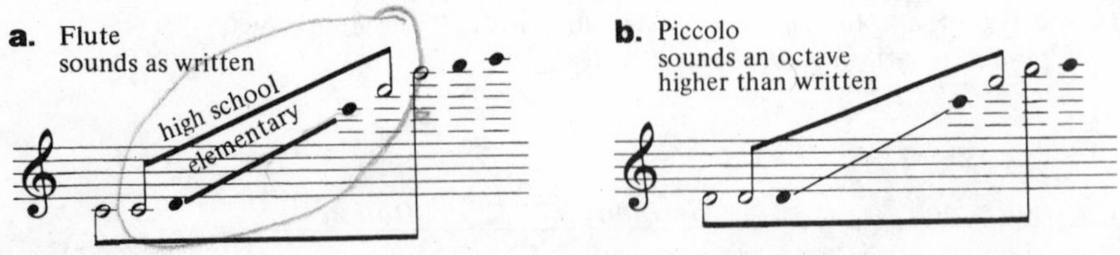

[5] In British scores and books one will find the alto flute often called a bass flute. The student is advised to avoid this practice.

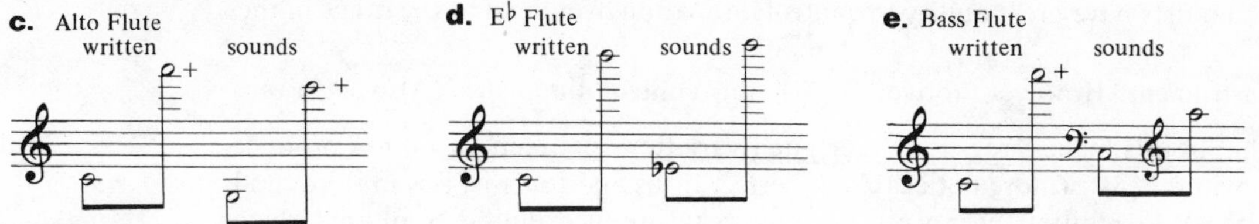

EXAMPLE 107 The written ranges, sounding ranges, and transpositions for the flutes. a. Flute (concert flute in C); sounds as written. b. Piccolo (in C); sounds an octave higher than written. c. Alto flute (in G); sounds a fourth lower than written. d. E♭ flute; sounds a minor third higher than written. e. Bass flute (in C); sounds an octave lower than written.

The flutes have the following natural dynamic curve:

EXAMPLE 108 Dynamic curve of flutes.

The lower range has a warm, dark quality, but with little ability to penetrate. The middle range is brighter and carries well. The highest register is brilliant, penetrating, and, when needed, shrill. The ability of the flute player to overcome these natural characteristics is dependent upon the performer's skill, but always qualified by the innate properties of the instrument.

The flutes are very agile instruments, capable of the fastest possible articulations and runs. Double, triple and flutter tonguing are standard techniques for all advanced players, and rapid scales or wide leaps present no problems, although downward leaps respond a bit slower than upward leaps. All flutes require a great amount of air, and opportunities to breathe must be provided in the music. The larger the flute, the more this breath problem (and the problem of playing loudly in the low register) is in evidence. The alto and bass flutes present the most serious problems in terms of breathing, and for this reason, alto flute solos must have extremely transparent accompaniments. For the same reason, bass flutes are often heard with electronic amplification, playing primarily short phrases. Extended passages, without gaps, can only be performed by two or more flutes, alternating and dovetailing with one another. All trills and tremolos[6] are possible with the following exceptions (as written):

EXAMPLE 109 Trills and tremolos not playable on the flute.

[6] Trills involve only major and minor seconds; tremolos are all wider intervals.

Flutists have great ability to control intonation over most of the range of the instrument. However, above  this control diminishes. Also, be aware that in this highest register slight pitch variations between two flutes produce obvious beats[7] (more noticeable in perfect fifths and fourths, less in thirds and sixths). In addition, even well-tuned intervals produce audible resultants which are clearly perceived in a lightly scored texture. In orchestra or band *tutti,* the resultants are usually not apparent.

In writing for flute, remember that the instrument tends to be easily covered below  and, although in this range it sounds full when played unaccompanied, it is nearly inaudible when instruments pitched below it are producing sounds rich in overtones. One should never expect the flute to balance with other instruments when it is scored in its lowest register. If such a voicing is necessary, the flute must be marked at a dynamic level louder than the other instruments.

To increase the sense of warmth and to produce a more velvety tone, two or more flutes playing in unison may be used in the lower register. The additional flutes, however, will not materially increase the ability of the listener to perceive the line unless the background is as transparently scored as is required when only one flute is used. In contrast, the use of more than one flute on a line in the middle and higher registers will increase mass, penetration, and carrying power.

The Piccolo

The piccolo has many of the same qualities of the flute and is, if anything, more agile and capable of faster articulations. All effects are possible and it is less easily covered in the lower octave of its range than the flute is in its comparable register.[8] The dynamic curve of the piccolo is like that of the flutes, but with more exaggeration of the contrasts. For sheer brilliance in the ensemble, the top octave of the piccolo cannot be surpassed by any natural acoustical instrument. In addition, solo piccolo in the middle and lower registers is an interesting and valuable voice, sounding a little colder and more breathy than the flute.

The Alto Flute

The alto flute, due to its larger dimensions, is a little less agile than the flute, but in the hands of a good player, this distinction is hardly a problem. The lowest register, below written  is dark and rich and a little more able to balance other instruments than is the flute in its comparable register; but it is still a voice that needs to be accompanied with care. Played softly in the lower register, the alto flute takes on almost a muted horn-clarinet quality. In its middle and upper registers, it becomes less distinguishable from the flute, although it never really achieves the brightness associated with the flute. All effects and articulations on the flute are also possible on the alto flute, but on the lower-pitched instruments

[7]Beats are low frequency vibrations (less than 6 vibrations per second) caused by the reinforcement and cancellation of two or more audio pitches.

[8]This is probably a result of the keenness of the human ear in the frequency range encompassed by the piccolo's lowest register, which is an octave higher than the comparable flute range.

they seem more sluggish. Much more air is required than with the flute, so it is necessary to write alto flute lines with more gaps for breathing.

The E♭ Flute

The E♭ flute, pitched a minor third above the concert flute, has properties of both the flute and the piccolo. Its lower register is not dynamically competitive with other instruments in the same range, but its middle and upper registers are bright and clear. It is as agile as the flute and would be a valuable alternative voice in a flute ensemble. However, its role as a substitute for the E♭ clarinet (see page 103) in the band is nearly the only function to which it is regularly assigned.

The Bass Flute

The bass flute is an exaggeration of the alto flute with all assets and liabilities magnified. Breathing is the chief problem, followed closely by lack of power. Amplification can be used to overcome the latter, and for this reason more examples of bass flute currently appear on recordings than one hears in live performance. Another problem which may seem to the arranger to be superficial, but most assuredly is not to the performer, is the problem of weight. The bass flute (and to a lesser degree the alto flute) is much heavier and longer than the flute or the piccolo. In addition to the obvious embouchure and finger adjustments, the matter of holding up a more bulky awkward instrument creates a fatigue factor that must be considered. In parts for the larger flutes longer rests are appreciated, to allow the performer to set down the instrument between periods of playing.

Other Flutes

In older band scores one often encounters parts for D♭ piccolo and D♭ flute. These instruments, which are almost obsolete now, are pitched a minor second above the piccolo and above the concert flute respectively. In all other ways they are similar.

Typical Flute Scorings

The flutes are equally at home in the performance of slow, legato passages or rapid, highly florid figures. As a family, they are second to none in their abilities to cover wide skips, slurred or staccato. But they function just as well in performing sustained pitches. The literature abounds with flute solos, duets, and trios which illustrate the many properties of the flute family.

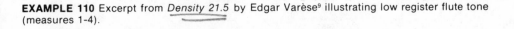

EXAMPLE 110 Excerpt from *Density 21.5* by Edgar Varèse[9] illustrating low register flute tone (measures 1-4).

[9]©1946 by Colfranc Music Publishing Corp., New York; by permission.

The following excerpt from Tchaikovsky's *Nutcracker Suite, "Danse Chinoise,"* (mm. 2-4) illustrates both the highest register and some of the flute's agility:

EXAMPLE 111 High-register flute passage from "Danse Chinoise" (measures 2–4) in Tchaikovsky's *Nutcracker.*

From the same work comes this famous example of a flute trio. Notice that the balance between the three flutes is good, even though the third part is quite low. This is because among themselves, flutes balance each other well no matter what ranges are employed. The orchestral accompaniment is light and without great mass or strong colors and thereby does not interfere with the flutes.

EXAMPLE 112 Writing for three flutes from Tchaikovsky's *Nutcracker:* "Danse des Mirlitons" (measures 3–6).

Also from the *Nutcracker* is this example of double tonguing. Notice that two flutes are assigned to the upper line and only one to the lower. Since the voicing is in octaves, the lower flute is not lost—the upper flutes provide not only a top line but also serve to reinforce the overtones of the lower flute, thus artificially creating a stronger lower octave tone.

EXAMPLE 113 Flute double tonguing in the "Marche" (measures 41-43) from the *Nutcracker.*

An interesting use of the flute and piccolo together is to be found in Borodin's *Polovtsian Dances* from the opera *Prince Igor*. Here, starting 8 measures before C, the piccolo and flute alternate the figure. The contrast between the two tone qualities is subtle but audible. Notice the use of dovetailing to help create the effect of a continuous line. Beginning in the fifth measure of the example given below, both instruments are to play, creating an octave doubling with the piccolo an octave above the flute.

EXAMPLE 114 Flute and piccolo dovetailing in excerpt from Borodin's *Polovtsian Dances.*

In "Well Pursed" for flute and piano, Paul Zonn has written this passage, which is typical of the whole piece. This excerpt begins with the last system on page two and ends with the second system on page three. The first figure indicates an accelerando; during the sustained C flutter tonguing is added, the small circle over the B♭ indicates a harmonic; the low F♯ in the first multiphonic is a resultant pitch; and the passage ends with a multiphonic tremolo. Time is proportional.

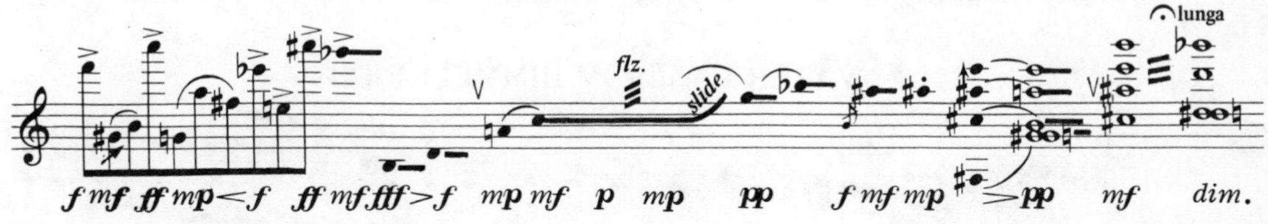

EXAMPLE 115 Excerpt from the flute part of Zonn's "Well Pursed."[10]

Problem Set No. 10

1. Score the first 21 measures of the Domenico Scarlatti sonata below for flute duet (two concert flutes). Raise the pitch level of the lower notes in measures 2–8 one octave to accommodate the flute's range. When more than two pitches are present in the original, select the pitches to be used in the duet for musical reasons. Prepare a score and, if at all possible, have the result performed.

SONATA

2. Score the Bach chorale below for flute quartet composed of piccolo, E♭ flute, concert flute, and alto flute. (Or, if available, E♭ flute or piccolo, concert flute, alto flute, and bass flute.) Transpose the whole chorale up an octave and assign the soprano line to the piccolo, the alto line to the E♭ flute, the tenor line to the concert flute, and the bass line to the alto flute (move the low F in measure 10 up an octave.) Prepare a score and parts and have the result performed. If these combinations are not available, discuss substitutions and then do the project using these alternative instruments.)

VATER UNSER IM HIMMELREICH

3. Write a short passage for solo flute that uses multiphonics, flutter tonguing, air tones, and other special effects. Have it performed for you.

FLUTE BIBLIOGRAPHY

Bate, Philip. *The Flute.* New York: W.W. Norton, 1969.

Dick, Robert. *The Other Flute.* London: Oxford University Press, 1975.

Heiss, John C. "For the Flute: A List of Double-stops, Triple-stops, Quadruple-stops, and Shakes." *Perspectives of New Music,* (Fall-Winter 1966), p. 139ff.

Howell, Thomas S. *The Avant-garde Flute.* Berkeley: University of California Press, 1974.

Putnik, Edwin. *The Art of Flute Playing.* Evanston, Ill.: Summy-Birchard Co., 1970.

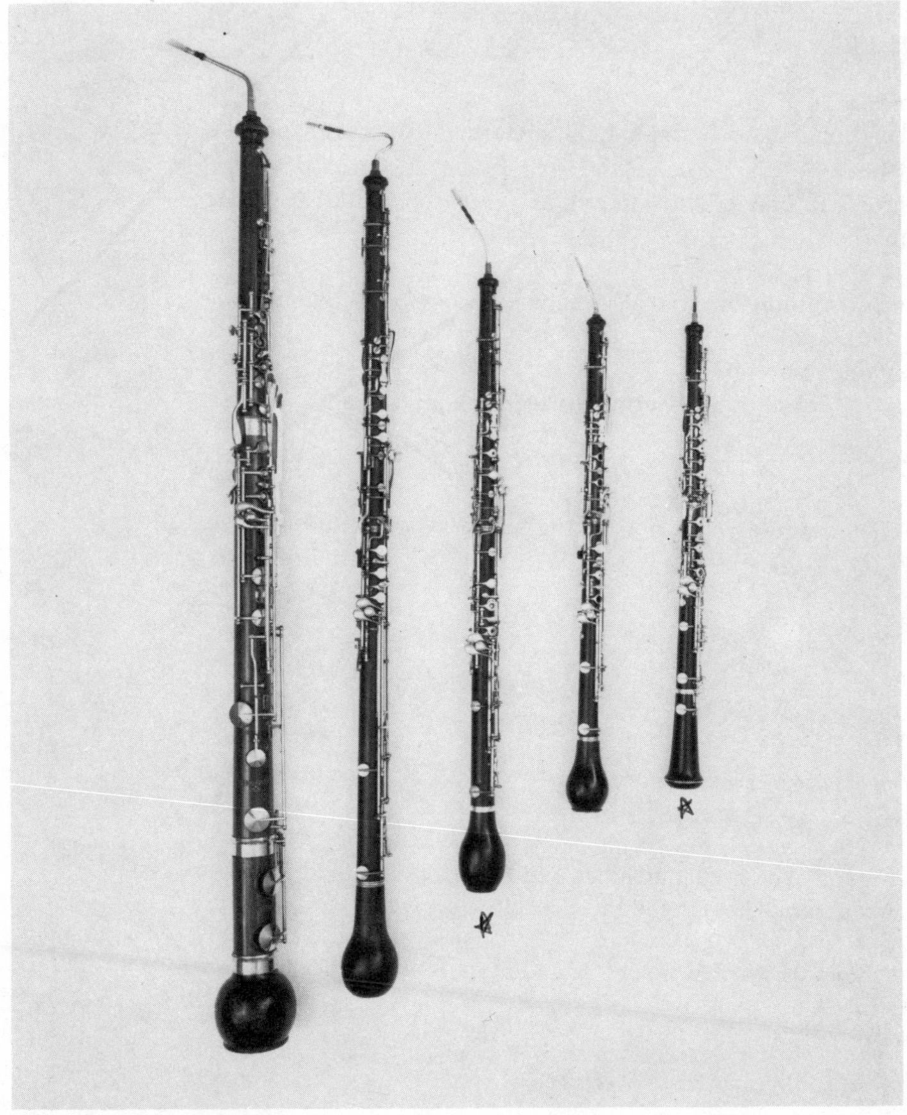

FIGURE 8. The oboes (*from left to right*) Heckelphone, baritone oboe, English horn, oboe d'amore, and oboe. (Photo by David Hruby.)

THE OBOES

	English	*French*	*German*	*Italian*
singular	oboe (ob.)	hautbois (hautb.)	Oboe (Ob.)	oboe (ob.)
plural	oboes (obs.)	hautbois (hautb.)	Oboen (Ob.)	oboi (ob.)

The Properties of the Oboes

If one considers the flutes to be the soprano family of the woodwind choir, then the oboes represent the alto family. Oboes are conical-bore, double-reed instruments made of wood. The oboe family consists of the following instruments:

1. Oboe in C.
2. English horn in F
   (French: cor anglais; German: Englischhorn; Italian: corno inglese).
3. Oboe d'amore in A
   (French: hautbois d'amour; German: Liebesoboe; Italian: oboe d'amore).
4. Baritone oboe in C (rare)
   (French: hautbois baryton; German: Bariton-Oboe; Italian: oboe baritono).
5. Heckelphone in C (rare)
   (French: heckelphone; German: Heckelphon; Italian: "Heckelphon").

With two exceptions, the oboes possess the following written range:

EXAMPLE 116 Range of oboe family.

The exceptions are the oboe itself which has a low B♭ (this low B♭ is found on all oboes and is not a special key),[11] and the Heckelphone, which has both a low B♭ and a low A.

Example 117 shows the written ranges, sounding ranges, and transpositions for the oboes:

[11]Some student models do not possess the low B♭ key, but these are not the usual orchestra or band oboes.

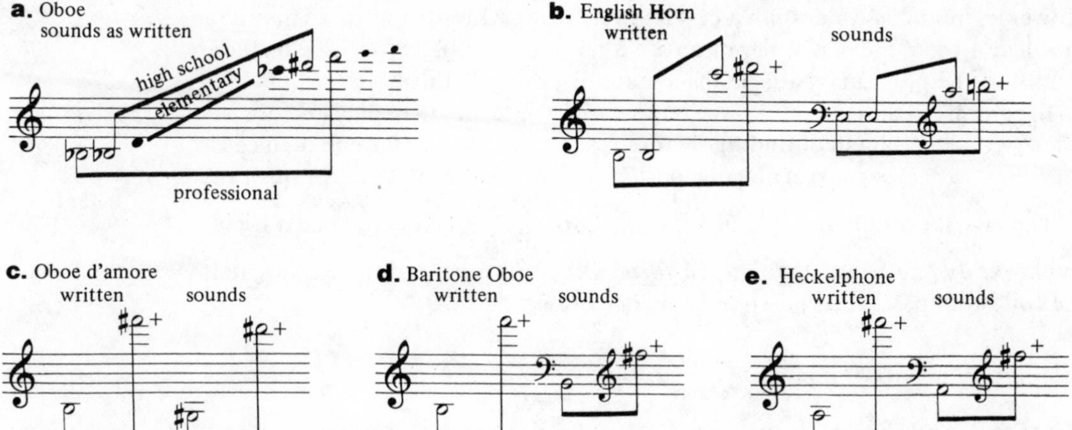

EXAMPLE 117 The written ranges, sounding ranges, and transpositions for the oboes. a. Oboe (in C); sounds as written. b. English horn (in F); sounds a fifth lower than written. c. Oboe d'amore (in A); sounds a minor third lower than written. d. Baritone oboe (in C); sounds an octave lower than written. e. Heckelphone (in C); sounds an octave lower than written.

The oboes have the following natural dynamic curve:

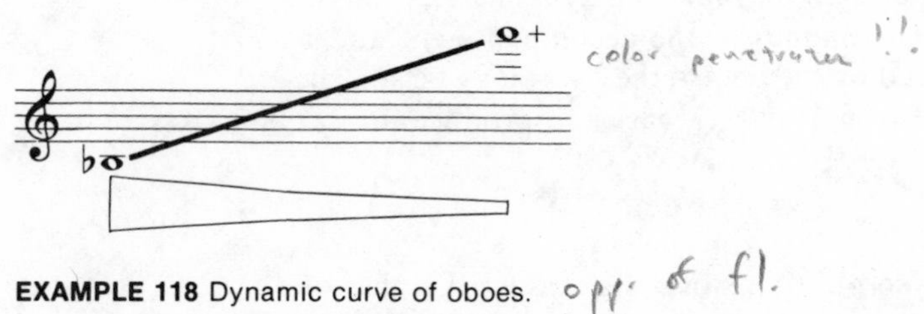

EXAMPLE 118 Dynamic curve of oboes.

Oboe tone is dependent to a great extent upon the style of the reeds used. It is, therefore, difficult to predict exact tonal characteristics. However, in general, the lower range has a rich, reedy quality that is difficult to subdue. The middle portion of the range is clear and possesses good ability to penetrate through most textures. The highest fifth or sixth of the range becomes thinner and much less rich in overtones. In this range the oboe's tone is not as characteristic as in the lower ranges but penetration is still extremely good.

Because many well-known passages for the oboe are slow and expressive, one often forgets that the oboe is very agile as an instrument. While they are perhaps not the dazzling performers the flutes are, the oboes are by no means sluggish or slow. Double, triple and flutter tonguing are not considered standard oboe techniques, but can be achieved by some performers. The oboes are capable of very smooth legatos, even when wide leaps are involved, as well as precise, clear staccatos. Rapid scales, a variety of trills, and ornaments sound clear on the oboe. Vibrato is a standard element of oboe tone and is used both as a means of modifying the tone quality and also as a method of intensifying the tone and shaping nuances.

All trills and tremolos are possible on the modern oboe. (See Appendix IV.) However, tremolos wider than a perfect fourth are awkward and speed may be a problem. Even if the performer discovers alternate fingerings to be used on these tremolos, the pitch may still be inaccurate or poorly defined.

In contrast to the flutes, the oboe requires very little breath to play and oboists often have the problem of finding themselves too full of air at the end of the passage. Rests are needed to enable the performer to exchange stale air for fresh air.

The lowest portion of the oboe's range, up to is very full and difficult to play at dynamics less than *mezzo-forte.* Orchestrators need to be aware that the following passage is possible in theory only:

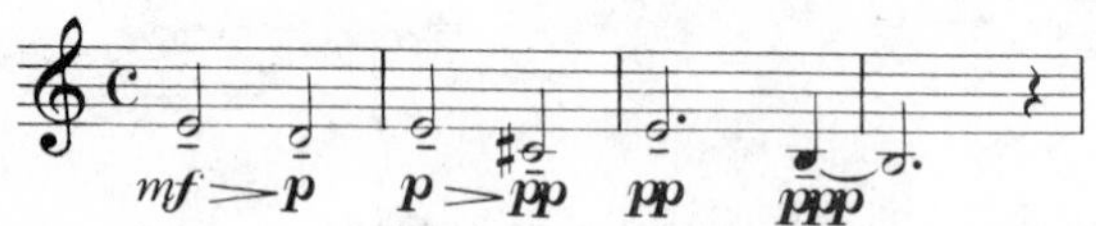

EXAMPLE 119 A virtually impossible oboe passage.

The actual performance will be louder than the indicated dynamics. By making the appropriate adjustments in the dynamics of the accompaniment and by controlling the amount of vibrato used by the oboist, the effect may be still successful. (Slurring the whole passage would make it easier to produce, too.)

The English Horn

The English horn has been used so often in slow, pastoral writing that one forgets that it is capable of many styles of performance. Even though it is larger than the oboe, the additional size does not decrease the responsiveness of the instrument. Any technical passage playable on the oboe is playable on the English horn.

The English horn has a more delicate and rounded sound than the oboe, but the precise attack, pointed staccato, and tone rich in upper partials are still present. These combine to give the English horn a veiled, poignant quality. The general lightness of the English horn tone allows it to blend with all instruments, especially at the unison. Added to an ensemble of clarinets, flutes, horns or strings, the English horn adds an incisiveness without being unduly assertive.

The Oboe d'Amore

The oboe d'amore is not encountered as often as the oboe or the English horn, but it is called for in works by Bach, R. Strauss, Debussy, and Ravel. The oboe d'amore is a little larger than the oboe and looks like a small English horn. In tone quality it is different enough from either to justify more frequent usage. It is darker and more mellow than the oboe, but brighter and more spritely than the

English horn. It is both an expressive solo voice in passages of a tranquil nature and responsive and flexible in florid or rapidly tongued passages.

The dynamic curves of the English horn and oboe d'amore resemble the curve of the oboe, but the lowest portion of the range is more easily controlled.

The Baritone Oboe

The baritone oboe would seem to be a potentially valuable addition to the oboe family, but its tone is very thin and stuffy, especially in the lowest register. Though an historically old instrument, little use has been made of it in either solo or ensemble scoring. In the hands of a skilled performer it can provide an interesting solo voice and a colorful tenor to the double reed section.

The Heckelphone

The Heckelphone has a full, reedy, and rich tone quality that provides both an excellent bass to the oboes and a pungent treble to the bassoons. It is an agile instrument with good clear tonguing capabilities. In most cases, it has been used either as a solo instrument, to exploit its rather unfamiliar voice, or as an extra double reed to fill out the double-reed family. Its expressive and technical properties are similar to the English horn's. In its lowest register it has a dark, foreboding quality that is haunting. In the upper register, its tone becomes more hoarse and nasal. The Heckelphone has seen some use in orchestral works by Richard Strauss, a trio by Hindemith, and in motion picture and recording studio writing.

Other Oboes

In older works, especially those by Bach, one sometimes encounters the obsolete *oboe da caccia* which is usually assumed to be equivalent to the English horn and is replaced with the latter in modern practice. In addition, there is an E♭ military oboe used in Europe but not found in this country. It is pitched a minor third above the normal oboe.

Typical Oboe Scorings

A good opportunity to hear the oboe in its middle-upper register is in the fourth movement of Beethoven's Third Symphony.

EXAMPLE 120 Oboe solo from Beethoven's Third Symphony (fourth movement, measures 373–377).

The oboe's middle-lower range is featured in the famous solo from the beginning of the third movement of Brahms's Second Symphony, Opus 73, a melody that exploits the pastoral quality of the oboe.

EXAMPLE 121 Oboe solo from Brahms's Second Symphony.

The oboe has good agility, as shown in this passage from Dennis Eberhard's woodwind quintet *Paraphrases.*

EXAMPLE 122 Some of the Oboe's agility Is Illustrated in this passage from Eberhard's woodwind quintet (measures 240-242).[12]

This example, a duet from Bartók's *Concerto for Orchestra,* illustrates the reedy quality of two oboes in thirds:

EXAMPLE 123 Writing for two oboes from Bartók's *Concerto for Orchestra* (second movement, measures 25–30).[13]

The most famous English horn solos tend to be slow and expressive. This excerpt from *The Pines of Rome* by Ottorino Respighi (beginning 4 measures before number 19) demonstrates both the English horn's expressive qualities and its flexibility:

EXAMPLE 124 English horn solo from *The Pines of Rome* by Respighi.[14]

Probably the most famous of all English horn solos is the one from Anton Dvořák's Symphony No. 9, "From the New World." Here are the first five measures of that solo:

EXAMPLE 125 English horn solo from Dvořák's "New World" Symphony (second movement, measures 7-11).

Problem Set No. 11

1. Score the Scarlatti movement given in exercise 1 of Problem Set No. 10 (page 90) for flute and oboe. Follow the suggestions given in that exercise with regard to problems of range. In addition, starting in measure 9, alternate pairs of measures between the two instruments to make the imitative character of the work more pronounced. If possible, have the result performed.
2. Score Bartók's "In Three Parts" for two oboes and English horn. Shift all of the pitches up an octave so that it remains within the range of the English horn. Have the result performed. (As an alternative, score the work for oboe, oboe d'amore, and English horn.)

[14]© Copyright 1925 by G. Ricordi, cspa, Milan. Used by permission of Associated Music Publishers, Inc.

IN THREE PARTS[15]

3. Using the Bach chorale harmonization given in exercise 2 of Problem Set No. 10 (page 90), score it for two oboes, oboe d'amore, and English horn (or you may substitute a second English horn for the oboe d'amore.) If possible, have the result performed.
4. Make up a six- or eight-measure duet for oboe and English horn which uses nothing but special effects including smack tones, timbral trills, and multiphonics. If possible, have it played.

OBOE BIBLIOGRAPHY

Bate, Philip. *The Oboe.* 3rd edition. New York: W.W. Norton, 1975.

Gossens, Leon and Edwin Roxburgh. *The Oboe.* New York: Schirmer Books, 1977.

Sprenkle, Robert and David Ledet. *The Art of Oboe Playing.* Evanston, Ill.: Summy-Birchard Co., 1961.

Zonn, Wilma. "Observations for Today's Oboists," *The Double Reed,* Vol. 1, no. 1 (March 1978), p. 6ff.

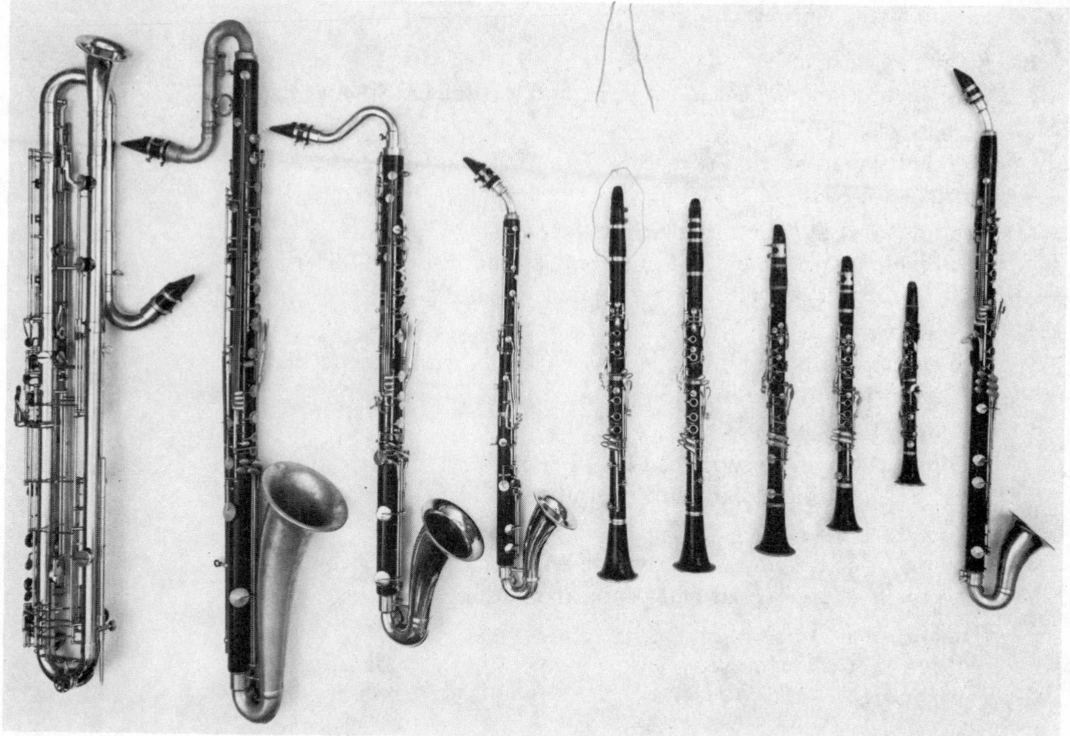

FIGURE 9. The clarinets (From left to right): B♭ contrabass clarinet, E♭ contra alto clarinet (sometimes called E♭ contrabass), B♭ bass clarinet, E♭ alto clarinet, A clarinet, B♭ clarinet, C clarinet, E♭ (soprano) clarinet, A♭ sopranino clarinet, and basset horn in F. (Photo by David Hruby.)

THE CLARINETS

	English	*French*	*German*	*Italian*
singular	clarinet (cl.)	clarinette (cl.)	Klarinette (Klar.)	clarinetto (cl.)
plural	clarinets (cls.)	clarinettes (cl.)	Klarinetten (Klar.)	clarinetti (cl.)

The Properties of the Clarinets

The clarinet is normally considered to be the alto or tenor member of the woodwind choir, but because of the many sizes of clarinets available and the wide ranges of each, a clarinet may be utilized in any role from soprano to bass. Clarinets are cylindrical-bore, single-reed instruments made of wood. Due to the acoustical properties of the cylindrical bore-single reed combination, clarinets behave like stopped pipes, overblowing at the twelfth rather than the octave.

The members of the clarinet family are:

1. B♭ and A clarinets
   (French: Si♭ and La; German: B[16] and A; **Italian: Si♭ and La**).
2. B♭ bass clarinet
   (French: clarinette basse en Si♭; German: B Bassklarinette; Italian: clarinetto basso in Si♭).
3. E♭ and (rare) D (soprano) clarinets
   (French: clarinette en Mi♭ and Re; German: Es and D Klarinette; Italian: clarinetto piccolo in Mi♭ and Re).
4. E♭ alto clarinet
   (French: clarinette alto en Mi♭; German: Es Altklarinette; Italian: clarinetto contralto in Mi♭).
5. B♭ contrabass clarinet
   (French: clarinette contrebasse en Si♭; German: B Kontrabass-klarinette; Italian: clarinetto contrabbasso in Si♭).
6. E♭ contra alto clarinet
   (French: clarinette contrebasse en Mi♭; German: Es Kontrabass-klarinette; Italian: clarinetto contrabbasso in Mi♭).
7. Basset horn in F (rare)
   (French: cor de basset; German: Bassetthorn; Italian: corno di bassetto).

The written range of the clarinets, with three exceptions, is:

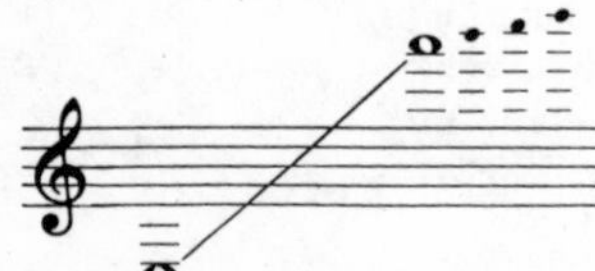

EXAMPLE 126 Range of clarinet family.

The exceptions are the bass clarinet, which possesses a low E♭ (and, for most symphonic players who own special instruments, even further down—to low C): and the B♭ contrabass clarinet and the basset horn, which possess written low E♭, D, D♭ and C: Example 127 shows the written ranges, sounding ranges, and transpositions for the clarinets. Note that all clarinets are written in treble clef, no matter what the sounding range.

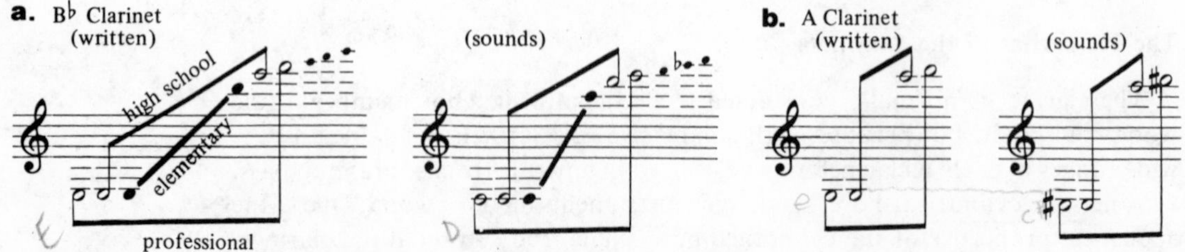

[16]In German, the pitch B♭ is called B while B♮ is called H; thus, Klarinette in B means clarinet in B♭ and not clarinet in B♮.

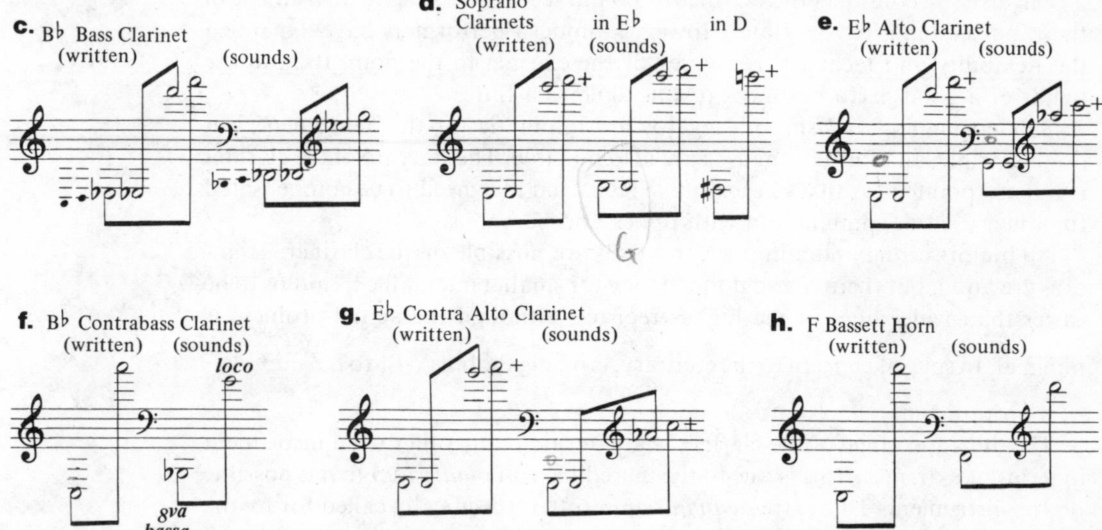

EXAMPLE 127 The written ranges, sounding ranges, and transpositions for the clarinets. a. B♭ clarinet; sounds a major second lower than written. b. A clarinet; sounds a minor third lower than written. c. B♭ bass clarinet; sounds a major ninth lower than written. d. Soprano clarinets (in E♭ and in D); sound a minor third and a major second higher than written. e. E♭ alto clarinet; sounds a major sixth lower than written. f. B♭ contrabass clarinet; sounds two octaves plus a major second lower than written. g. E♭ contra alto clarinet; sounds an octave plus a major sixth lower than written. h. F basset horn; sounds a fifth lower than written.

The dynamic curve for all of the clarinets is:

EXAMPLE 128 Dynamic curve of clarinets.

The lower part of the range, from written E to F♯, is called the chalumeau register and is very dark and rich in quality. The notes G, G♯, A, and B♭ are the throat tones and are quite pale and almost "fuzzy" in quality. Professional performers learn to overcome this natural limitation so that the listener is not aware of a change in tone quality in this register. From C upwards to about high C, the clarinet tone becomes bright and lively; this range is called the clarino register: . Above high C, the tone becomes increasingly flutelike in quality and may be shrill at a dynamic level of *forte* and a substitute for the flute when played softly.

One usually considers the clarinet to be the second most agile instrument in the wind section after the flute. However, modern performers have expanded the flexibility and technical resources of the clarinet to the point that, in the hands of a good performer, it is just as agile as a flute.

Single tonguing and smooth legatos are idiomatic for the instrument, but double, triple, and flutter tonguing are also possible. The staccato of the clarinet is not as "pointed" as that of the double reeds and may need to be compensated for when used in combination with oboes and bassoons.

All major second and minor second trills are possible on the clarinet. Tremolos are good, but there is a slight tendency for smaller intervallic tremolos to be easier than wider ones in the higher register, although the actual problem is minimal. In spite of concern to the contrary, crossing the break-B♭ to B —is no problem.

The dynamic range of the clarinet is greater than any other wind instrument in terms of extremes. This is due to the incredible soft *pianissimo* that is possible on the instrument. This extreme *pianissimo* (often specifically called for by the instruction *echo, subtone, sotto voce* or *mezzo voce*) can be produced by all moderately advanced performers and is available in all registers. A note may be attacked so softly as to be inaudible and may then be followed by a crescendo to a very penetrating *fortissimo*. The process may be reversed with equally good effect.

A very characteristic articulation found in rapid passages is the combination of two slurred notes and two tongued notes:

EXAMPLE 129 Typical clarinet articulation.

This is a clarinet cliché. Although its use may not be creative, it will provide an immediately recognized effect that in many conventional contexts sounds "right."

While writing solo passages for the clarinet, one should consider the significant difference between the clarinet registers. No other woodwind or brass instrument offers such a variety of tone color possibilities. In two-or-more-part writing, one may exploit these differences by placing a leading line in one register and an accompaniment figure in another. The register chosen for each function is simply a matter of taste, since the dynamic range available allows an appropriate balance to be maintained no matter what voicing is selected. With the wide pitch range available, three and even four separate clarinets may be used together, each within its own territory and, therefore, each with its own clearly perceived line.

Clarinets, in spite of their distinctive tone color, blend with other instruments more readily than any other woodwind. For this reason, one often finds the clarinet(s) doubling at the octave or in unison with other instruments or combinations of instruments. The effect, when the lower range of the clarinet is utilized, is generally one of added warmth or body. When the upper range is used, the effect is one of added brilliance or focus. Often the presence of the clarinet(s) in the ensemble is not readily apparent; but if the clarinets were to be removed, the contrast would be striking.

The B♭ and A Clarinets

These are the most common clarinets. The B♭ clarinet is the main woodwind of the concert band, and both are co-equally important in the orchestra or wind ensemble. The B♭ clarinet is preferred to the A clarinet, when both are available, in performing works in flat keys. The A clarinet, on the other hand, serves better in sharp keys. Many composers, orchestrators, or performers express a preference for one over the other for reasons of tone quality. This is not a minute point. The A clarinet is in general slightly darker in quality than the B♭ clarinet in the hands of the same performer. However, there is generally as much contrast between two different players as there is between the A and B♭ qualities. The A clarinet does provide a low C♯  not usually available on the B♭ clarinet. Selection of one over the other often results from an analysis of technical demands; for instance, a player will choose the instrument that provides the simplest fingering requirements in an important passage. The B♭ clarinet sounds a major second lower than written; the A clarinet sounds a minor third lower than written.

The B♭ Bass Clarinet

The bass clarinet has a rich, dark, and mellow chalumeau register that is very useful in many musical situations. Like all the other clarinets, its quality changes from register to register. The throat tones are transparent and the clarino register is diffused and windy. The bass clarinet's agility is almost equal to that of the B♭ clarinet, and in the hands of a good player it provides one of the most useful ensemble voices and one of the most distinguished solo voices (in any range) available among the woodwinds. It sounds a major ninth lower than written.[17]

The E♭ and D Soprano Clarinets

These high clarinets have all the characteristics of the B♭ and A clarinets; but the brighter more penetrating qualities of the higher range are amplified and fewer of the characteristic chalumeau qualities are available.

The E♭ and D soprano clarinets are often called for in scores, but the D clarinet is usually only found in professional ensembles, and sometimes not even there. These two represent a matched pair. The E♭ clarinet is more at home in keys employing flats while the D is more suited for keys employing sharps. In spite of this logical arrangement, the lack of availability of the D clarinet means that many famous passages written for it, such as in R. Strauss's *Till Eulenspiegel,* are routinely played on the E♭ clarinet, thus losing all the "key" advantage. The lower range of the E♭ clarinet sounds like a very pale version of the

[17]Older scores often show bass clarinet parts written in the bass clef. This notation, called German notation, indicates that the bass clarinet is to sound a major second lower than written. The treble clef notation, which is standard in this country, is called French notation and is the notation used here.

chalumeau register of the B♭ clarinet, and the highest notes, when played at louder dynamics, can be very shrill with a clearly reedy quality. The E♭ clarinet is useful in the band, where it expands the range of the clarinet family upwards. The instrument is agile and has an incisive staccato. The E♭ clarinet sounds a minor third higher than written; the D clarinet sounds a major second higher than written.

The E♭ Alto Clarinet

This instrument is primarily found in bands or clarinet choirs, where it provides a valuable tenor voice. It has a rich, reedy tone quality, not as dark as the bass clarinet, but more veiled and somber than the B♭ or A clarinets. The instrument has good agility and response. The alto clarinet at times has been pressed into service as a substitute for the basset horn, which it only slightly approximates. The alto clarinet is a little used solo voice that offers interesting possibilities to the imaginative orchestrator. It sounds a major sixth lower than written.

The B♭ Contrabass Clarinet

This clarinet is not usually made of wood, but of metal. Because it is turned back on itself four times and the tone holes are spaced much further apart than on the smaller instruments. A rather complex and delicate system of levers is employed to facilitate control.

The tone quality of the contrabass clarinet is, in the lowest register, very, very dark and capable of great power and clear *pianissimo*s. The higher range, while lacking the chalumeau qualities that first recommend the instrument, has a unique, colorless quality that exists in no other instrument. Agility is of course not as great as on the smaller clarinets, but the instrument can easily match the string basses and tuba in its ability to play rapid passages. It has a clear, focused pitch center that provides low notes with an easily perceived fundamental. The range downward extends to the lowest B♭ on the piano. It sounds two octaves and a major second below the written pitch.

The E♭ Contra Alto Clarinet

Pitched one octave below the E♭ Alto Clarinet, the E♭ contra alto (sometimes called E♭ contrabass) clarinet possesses a tone that is darker and more covered than the bass clarinet. This instrument is often used in bands to provide a woodwind bass that has the expressive capabilities and dynamic range of the clarinet.[18] The E♭ contra alto has more inertia than the bass clarinet, due to its size, but in the hands of a good player provides an additional dimension to the woodwind bass. It sounds an octave and a major sixth lower than written.

The Basset Horn in F

The basset horn is approximately the size of an alto clarinet, but has a smaller bore and produces a more subtle chalumeau quality than the clarinets. In the middle and upper ranges it is very similar to the B♭ or A clarinet in tone, but less dark and rather "whiney." Basset horns are called for in several Mozart works

[18]The performer can read bass clef tuba parts by simply changing the clef to the treble clef and adding three sharps to the key signature. This makes it possible to add E♭ contra alto clarinets to an ensemble even when separate parts are not provided.

and in the operas *Die Frau ohne Schatten* and *Elektra* by Richard Strauss. It is a transposing instrument in F, sounding a perfect fifth lower than notated. (In Strauss's scores, basset horn parts are sometimes notated in bass clef rather than the normal treble clef, in which case the sounding pitch is a perfect fourth *above* the written pitch.)

Other Clarinets

In eighteenth- and nineteenth-century scores, one finds parts for the C clarinet. There is in addition an A♭ sopranino clarinet (see figure 9 on page 99). The C clarinet, which is now rare, is a non-transposing instrument pitched a whole step higher than the B♭ clarinet. The A♭ sopranino clarinet sounds a minor sixth higher than written.

In many scores one finds parts for A bass clarinets. The rarity of these instruments accounts for the E♭ key on B♭ bass clarinets so that the latter can play all of the notes written for the A bass clarinet (which has an E for its lowest pitch). The relationship of the A bass clarinet to the B♭ bass is parallel to that of the A clarinet to the B♭ clarinet.

Typical Clarinet Scorings

Sibelius begins his First Symphony, in E minor, Opus 39, with a clarinet solo accompanied only by a timpani roll. It is a good example of the throat tone range of the instrument.

EXAMPLE 130 Middle-range clarinet solo from Sibelius's First Symphony (first movement, measures 1–16).

The clarinets are known for their ability to play many fast notes. This famous passage from the third movement of Rimsky-Korsakov's *Scheherazade* displays this agility. (The excerpt begins five measures before rehearsal letter A.)

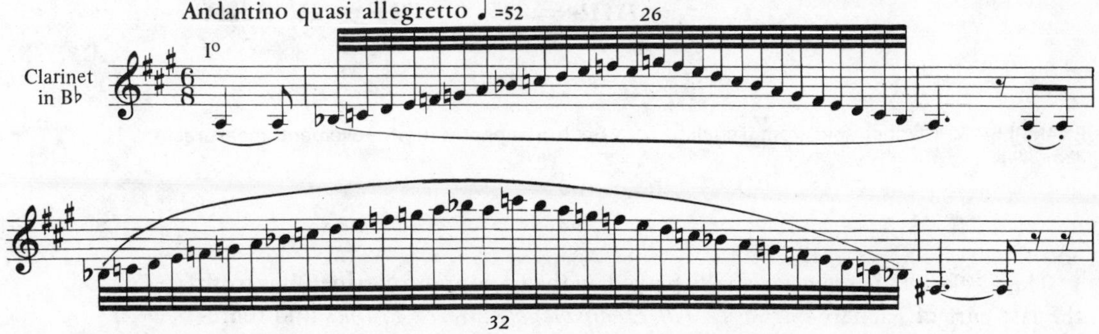

EXAMPLE 131 An example of typical clarinet agility, from Rimsky-Korsakov's *Scheherazade*.

This duet between two clarinets is found at the beginning of the Trio of the Minuet movement of Mozart's Symphony No. 39 in E♭. When listening to the passage, one is struck with the clear difference in timbre between the upper and lower lines; yet, since both are played by clarinets, the balance is excellent.

EXAMPLE 132 A model example of writing for two clarinets which takes advantage of the contrasting quality of different registers, from Mozart's Symphony No. 39.

In the first movement of Tchaikovsky's Sixth Symphony (*Pathétique*) in B minor, the clarinet has this familiar, expressive solo. The composer exploits the instrument's ability to play softly yet maintain a liquid and warm tone quality.

EXAMPLE 133 Clarinet solo from Tchaikovsky's Sixth Symphony (first movement, measures 325–334).

This D clarinet passage is usually played on the E♭ soprano clarinet. It is from the last part of Richard Strauss's *Till Eulenspiegel's Merry Pranks* and represents Till's last gasp.

EXAMPLE 134 D Clarinet solo from *Till Eulenspiegel* by R. Strauss.

That bass clarinet passages are not necessarily slow and stodgy is shown in this excerpt from Grofé's *Grand Canyon Suite.* (This passage is from the section called "On the Trail" and begins eight measures before letter C.)

EXAMPLE 135 Bass clarinet solo from *Grand Canyon Suite* by Grofé.[19]

In Igor Stravinsky's *The Rite of Spring* there is this bass clarinet duet which displays some of the bass clarinet's fluidity. (The passage begins two measures before rehearsal number 141.)

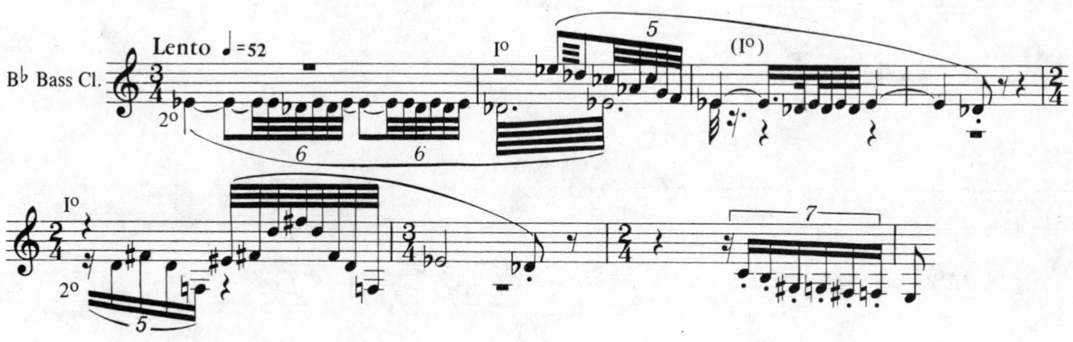

EXAMPLE 136 Rare bass clarinet duet, from Stravinsky's *Rite of Spring.*[20]

Problem Set No. 12

1. Score Schumann's "A Little Hunting Song" for an E♭ clarinet, two B♭ clarinets, and a bass clarinet. Prepare a score and a set of parts. Have the clarinet ensemble version performed. When there are fewer than four notes present, have two or more of the clarinets perform the same passage in unison, or give some rests. If you wish to change the octave in which some of the notes appear, do so.

2. Score Bartók's "In Three Parts" given in exercise 2, Problem Set No. 11 (page 98), for two A clarinets and an E♭ alto clarinet. Leave the pitches in the given octave. Have the result performed. (If the instruments are not available, substitute B♭ clarinets for the A's and bass clarinet or basset horn for the alto clarinet.)

3. Score the Bach chorale harmonization of "Vater unser im Himmelreich" given in exercise 2 of Problem Set No. 10 (page 90) for E♭ clarinet, two B♭ clarinets, alto clarinet, bass clarinet, and either B♭ contrabass or E♭ contra alto clarinet. Assign the soprano line to one B♭ clarinet, the alto line to another, the tenor line to the alto clarinet, and the bass line to the bass clarinet. Have the E♭ clarinet play the soprano line an octave above the original and the contrabass (or contra alto) play the bass line an octave below the original. (If the contra alto is used, the low F in measure 10 will have to remain at the original pitch.)

4. Compose a short piece for clarinet and flute (or clarinet and oboe) that uses special effects and extended techniques. Have the performers perform on portions of their instrument as well as the entire instrument correctly assembled. Have the piece performed.

CLARINET BIBLIOGRAPHY

Brymer, Jack. *The Clarinet.* New York: Schirmer Books, 1976.

Kroll, Oskar. *The Clarinet.* Transl. Hilda Morris, ed. Anthony Baines. New York: Toplinger, 1968.

Rehfeldt, Philip. *New Directions for Clarinet.* Berkeley: University of California Press, 1978.

Rendall, Geoffrey. *The Clarinet.* 3rd ed. New York: W.W. Norton, 1971.

Stein, Keith. *The Art of Clarinet Playing.* Evanston, Ill.: Summy-Birchard Co., 1958.

Tose, Gabriel. *Artistic Clarinet Technique and Study.* Hollywood: Highland Music, 1962.

Zonn, Paul. "Some Sound Ideas," *The Clarinet,* Vol. 2, no. 2 (February 1975), p. 17ff.

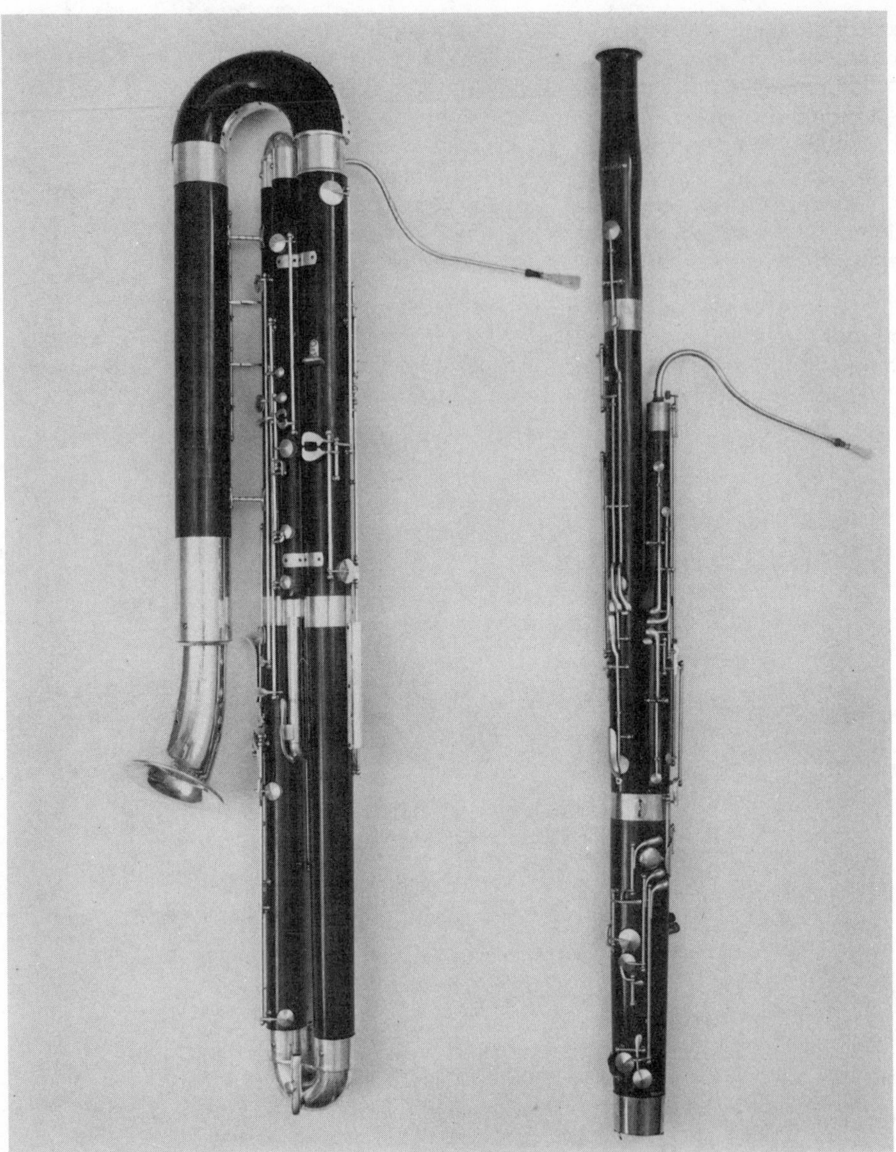

FIGURE 10. The Bassoons: (*left*) the contrabassoon and (*right*) the bassoon. The contrabassoon pictured is the so-called opera model, which is very compact so that it will not protrude from the orchestra pit. (Photo by David Hruby.)

THE BASSOONS

	English	*French*	*German*	*Italian*
singular	bassoon (bn.)	basson (bon.)	Fagott (Fag.)	fagotto (fag.)
plural	bassoons (bns.)	bassons (bons.)	Fagotte (Fag.)	fagotti (fag.)

The Properties of the Bassoons

The bassoon is the natural bass of the woodwind choir. It is a conical-bore, double-reed instrument usually made of maple.

The standard members of the bassoon family are:

1. bassoon
2. contrabassoon
   (French: contrebasson; German: Kontrafagott; Italian: contra-fagotto)

The written range of the German-style bassoon usually found in this country is:

EXAMPLE 137 Range of bassoon family.

There are two exceptions: The contrabassoon, in order to save weight and space, is sometimes provided with an optional, shorter bell section which limits the range of the instrument to written C: . However, the use of this bell is a choice made by the performer, and the shorter bell will not be employed when the lower notes are required. The second exception is the low A:  The low A is called for both in bassoon and contrabassoon parts in some scores. There is an extension made for the contrabassoon that enables it to reach low A, but there is no such extension for the bassoon. Therefore, bassoon passages which include the low A require the performer to insert a tube of the correct length into the bell. Since this makeshift extension affects the tuning and tone quality of the other low notes, it is usually inserted during the performance and kept in just for the passage where it is needed. With no opportunity to check and adjust the tuning, the effect is usually one of poor intonation. If pitch accuracy is not a particular concern, or if an opportunity exists to insert and tune the extension, its use becomes an additional resource. Note that with the extension in place, no low B♭ is available on the instrument.

The contrabassoon is a transposing instrument in C which sounds an octave lower than written.

EXAMPLE 138 Ranges of: a. Bassoon. b. Contrabassoon.

The notes in the higher range of the bassoon and contrabassoon are written in the tenor clef. Parts for less experienced bassoonists should be written in the bass clef. Professional performers read both clefs with equal ease, so parts with a high tessitura should be written in tenor clef for them. Avoid frequent clef changes.

The dynamic curve for the bassoons is:

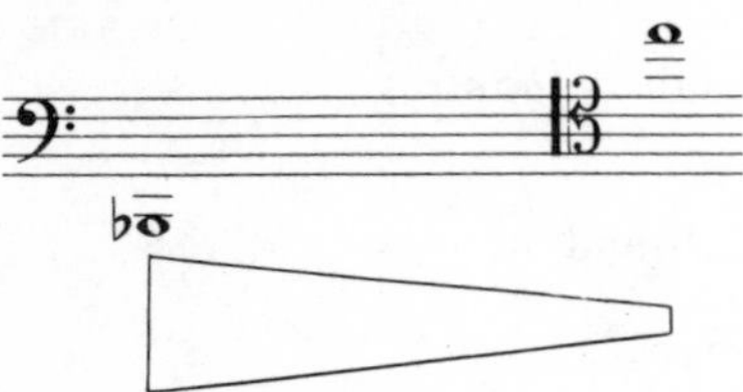

EXAMPLE 139 Dynamic curve for bassoons.

The lowest register is brittle and dry in tone quality, with a very rich overtone structure. Soft attacks and true *pianissimos* are almost impossible in this range. The middle range, from to , is more "hornlike" and transparent. Passages in this range blend well with almost any instrument or combination of instruments. From upward the tone is very focused and has a bright nasal quality that is unique. It is a quality totally unlike any other instrument's and is an excellent solo voice. It does not penetrate well and benefits from delicate accompaniment.

The bassoon is a very agile instrument, with the exception of rapid notes in the lowest fifth of its range to and above high G , where fingerings are awkward and the response is not always reliable. Wide leaps and rapid tonguing are especially idiomatic to the bassoon; so is its doubling of string melodies either in unison or an octave below. Between (approximately) F and A , the bassoon can be as expressive or as florid as any wind. In thin textures, it will hold its own against all but loud brasses.

Single tonguing is the usual technique employed by bassoonists in all but the fastest passages, but double, triple, and flutter tonguings are possible on the instrument and can be played quite easily by some performers. Very loud or very low passages may require frequent breaths, and these should be allowed for in the score.

Trills and tremolos involving notes from low G♭ downward are impossible, as are trills on all D♭'s, E♭'s, or G♭'s, or on high A:

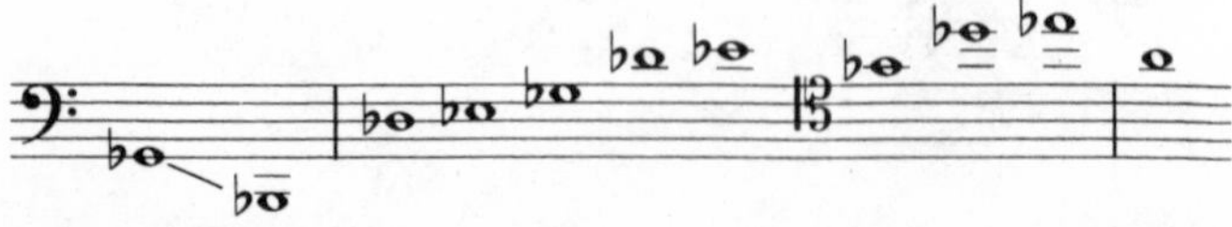

EXAMPLE 140 Trills (major or minor second) on these pitches are impossible.

One should also avoid rapid technical passages below low F. When such passages are necessary they are most effectively written by dividing the passage between two or more performers:

EXAMPLE 141 Bassoon part below low F divided between two players.

Adjustments in the embouchure can provide small amounts of control of the intonation, but it is necessary for bassoonists to change bocals if the tuning level of an ensemble alters by much. For this reason, most bassoonists carry several bocals with them at all times, and may even change bocals in the middle of a concert if the pitch level drifts too high or too low.

The Contrabassoon

Pitched an octave lower than the bassoon, the contrabassoon is the usual contrabass woodwind found in the symphony orchestra. The contrabassoon is slightly less agile than the bassoon, but when well played is expressive, facile, and possesses a well-focused, if reedy, tone. The tone quality of the contrabassoon is more growlly than the bassoon's, and its highest register is even more likely to be covered. Nevertheless, it adds an unobtrusive pitch center to extremely low string bass passages and is an excellent bass to any soft to moderately loud brass or woodwind ensemble.

Other Bassoons

Among older forms of bassoons sometimes mentioned, one finds the tenoroon, quartfagott, and the quintfagott. The tenoroon was a bassoon pitched a fifth above the modern bassoon. The quartfagott and quintfagott were older instruments pitched a fourth and a fifth, respectively, below the modern instrument. Later these same names were applied to small instruments pitched a fourth and fifth, respectively, above the bassoon. All are now obsolete.

Typical Bassoon Scorings

An example of the bassoon's solo voice is provided in this excerpt from Rimsky-Korsakov's *Scheherazade:*

EXAMPLE 142 Bassoon solo from *Scheherazade* (second movement, measures 5–11).

The dark, forboding quality of low-register bassoon played softly is heard at the beginning of Tchaikovsky's Sixth Symphony. The passage is scored as low as possible without forcing the performer into that portion of the range that is hard to control dynamically.

EXAMPLE 143 Opening of Tchaikovsky's Sixth Symphony (measures 1–11).

In his *Academic Festival Overture,* Brahms introduces the following theme with two bassoons. The ability of the instruments to perform staccatos gives this passage a spritely quality that is typical of much bassoon writing. (The excerpt begins with the pickup to the 21st measure after rehearsal letter F.)

EXAMPLE 144 Bassoon duet from Brahms's *Academic Festival Overture.*

The expressive quality of the bassoon as a solo voice is illustrated in the bassoon solo near the end of Igor Stravinsky's ballet, *The Firebird.* Beginning at rehearsal number 186, the solo bassoon has this plaintive melody:

EXAMPLE 145 Legato bassoon solo from *The Firebird* by Stravinsky.[21]

In Schönberg's *Theme and Variations* for Band, Opus 43a, this passage for two bassoons shows off the qualities of the instrument's lower-middle range:

[21] 1910 version.

EXAMPLE 146 Middle-low register writing for two unison bassoons, from Schönberg's Opus 43a (measures 227–233).[22]

On page 3 of *preFIX-FIX-sufFIX* for bassoon, horn, and violoncello, Yehuda Yannay writes this passage which shows the virtuosity and agility of the bassoon.[23]

EXAMPLE 147 Contemporary bassoon passage. (Tempo is proportional with 35 or more measures per minute.)

In the third movement of Brahms's Symphony No. 4 in E Minor, the contrabassoon has this exposed bass line:

EXAMPLE 148 A rare soloistic contrabassoon line, from Brahms's Fourth Symphony (third movement, last eleven measures).

Problem Set No. 13

1. Score the "In Three Parts" of Bartók given in exercise 2 of Problem Set No. 11 (page 98), for either an oboe (or B♭ clarinet) and two bassoons. Perform the result. (If three bassoons—or two bassoons and a contrabassoon—are available, score it for that combination instead.)
2. Score the Bach chorale harmonization given in exercise 2 of Problem Set No. 10 (page 90), for one oboe, one English horn, and two bassoons. Assign the soprano line to the oboe, the alto line to the English horn, the tenor line to the first bassoon, and the bass line to the second bassoon. Perform the chorale in this double reed version.

[22] Used by permission of Belmont Music Publishers, Los Angeles, California 90049. Copyright © 1944 by G. Schirmer.

[23] © Copyright 1972 by Media Press, Inc. Box 195, Media, PA 19063. All Rights Reserved. Used by permission.

3. Score the following excerpt from a Mozart sonatina for two B♭ clarinets and two bassoons. In general, assign the clarinets to the upper two lines and the bassoons to the lower two. However, it is not necessary to have all of the instruments play all of the time. It is also possible to have two (or more) instruments play the same line in the same or different octaves. Perform your work, if at all possible.

4. Compose a short piece for flute, oboe, clarinet, and bassoon. Use only unpitched sounds or effects for which the pitches are not specified (such as "any multiphonic"). Have your piece performed.

BASSOON BIBLIOGRAPHY

Biggers, Cornelia Anderson. *The Contra Bassoon: A Guide to Performance.*

Bryn Mawr, Penn.: Elkan-Vogel, 1977.

Cooper, Lewis Hugh and Howard Toplansky. *Essentials of Bassoon Technique (German System).* Union, N. J.: Toplansky, 1968

Langwill, Lyndesay Graham. *The Bassoon and Contrabassoon.* New York: W. W. Norton, 1965.

Spencer, William G. *The Art of Bassoon Playing.* Evanston, Ill.: Summy-Birchard Co., 1958.

FIGURE 11. The saxophones (*counterclockwise from lower left*): E♭ Contrabass; B♭ Bass; E♭ Baritone with a low A key; B♭ Tenor; E♭ Alto; B♭ Soprano; and E♭ Sopranino. (The bass saxophone in this photo was the property of John Phillip Sousa and was used in the Sousa Band.) (Photo by David Hruby.)

THE SAXOPHONES

	English	*French*	*German*	*Italian*
singular	saxophone (sax.)	saxophone (sax.)	Saxophon (Sax.)	sassofono (sas.)
plural	saxophones (saxes)	saxophones (sax.)	Saxophone (Sax.)	sassofoni (sas.)

The Properties of the Saxophone

The saxophones are conical-bore, single-reed wind instruments made of brass. Invented by Adolph Sax in the nineteenth century, the saxophone family is a complete set of instruments covering a wide pitch range. The family ranges from the high sopranino in E♭ to the equally rare contrabass in E♭. Included are the following members:

1. E♭ alto saxophone
   (French: saxophone alto en Mi♭; German: Es Altsaxophon; Italian: sassophono contralto in Mi♭).
2. B♭ tenor saxophone
   (French: * ténor en Si♭; German: B Tenorsaxophon; Italian: * tenore in Si♭).
3. E♭ baritone saxophone
   (French: * baryton en Mi♭; German: Es Baritonsaxophon; Italian: * baritono in Mi♭).
4. B♭ soprano saxophone
   (French: * soprano en Si♭; German: B Sopransaxophon; Italian: * soprano in Si♭).
5. B♭ bass saxophone
   (French: * basse en Si♭; German: B Baßsaxophon; Italian: * basso in Si♭).
6. E♭ sopranino saxophone (rare)
   (French: * sopranino en Mi♭; German: Es Sopraninosaxophon; Italian: * sopranino in Mi♭).
7. E♭ contrabass saxophone (rare)
   (French: * contrebasse en Mi♭; German: Es Kontrabaßsaxophon; Italian: * contrabbasso in Mi♭).

All of the saxophones, with one exception, have the following written range:

EXAMPLE 149 Range of saxophone family.

The exception is the baritone saxophone[24] which sometimes has a low A:

All of the modern saxophones are transposing instruments. The written and sounding ranges are as follows:

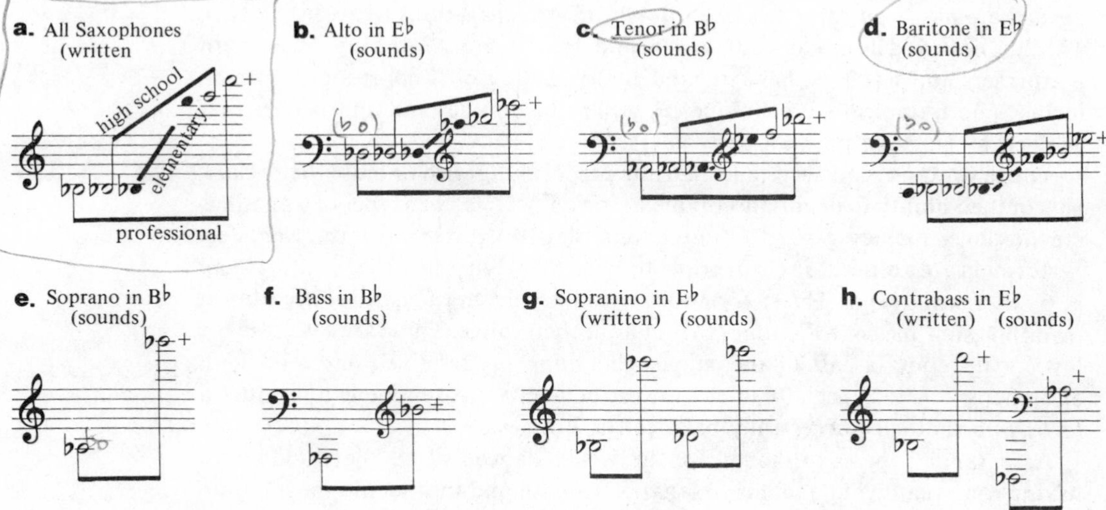

EXAMPLE 150 The written ranges, sounding ranges, and transpositions of the saxophones. a. All saxophones' written range is the same. b. Alto (in E♭); sounds a major sixth lower than written. c. Tenor (in B♭); sounds a major ninth lower than written. d. Baritone (in E♭); sounds an octave and a sixth lower than written. e. Soprano (in B♭); sounds a major second lower than written. f. Bass (in B♭); sounds two octaves and a major second lower than written. g. Sopranino (in E♭); sounds a minor third higher than written. h. Contrabass (in E♭); sounds two octaves and a sixth lower than written.

The natural dynamic curve for the saxophones is:

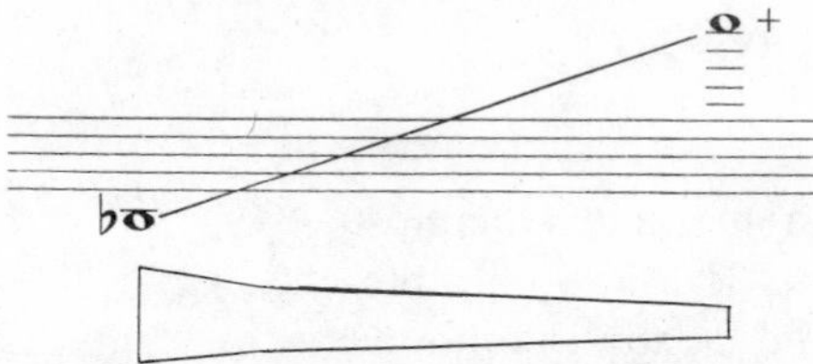

EXAMPLE 151 Dynamic curve for saxophones.

The lower portion of the saxophone range is very rich, reedy, and full. Played legato, it is quite velvety. In the middle of the range, from about G in the staff to high C, the tone becomes progressively more delicate, smooth and "flutey." Above high C, the tone in general resembles a very rich string-flute tone. Except in the lowest fifth of its range, the saxophone possesses excellent dynamic and tonal control. The lowest notes on the instrument are difficult to play at dynamics less than *mezzo-forte* and are almost impossible to attack softly unless

[24]Note, however, the sopranino and the contrabass, neither of which can play notes written as high as are playable by the other saxophones.

the performer is an exceptional player. This low register difficulty is more pronounced on the higher-pitched saxophones. (One often observes that baritone and bass saxophones seem to be capable of more delicate, controlled attacks in the lowest fifth of their ranges than the tenor or alto saxophones.)

There have been at least two schools of saxophone playing existing in this country: the jazz-popular school and the "classical" school. Within the recent past, there has been some breaking down of the separations between the two. This has occurred as modern composers and orchestrators, working closely with performers and teachers, have expanded the catalog of tonal resources which includes both traditional techniques as well as techniques and approaches first evolved by jazz and popular performers.

The saxophones are very agile instruments, ranking with or close to the clarinets in their ability to negotiate complex, florid lines. Various types of tonguings are possible, including single, flutter, and slap tonguing; however, very few performers are able to double or triple tongue. The dynamic range is wider than any other woodwind. The saxophones can, like the clarinets, produce almost inaudible subtones or echo tones throughout their range. These are easiest in the lower octave-and-a-half of the range, becoming progressively more difficult at higher pitches. Especially in the lowest octave, a saxophone can produce a *fortissimo* that can successfully balance the brasses.

As a family, the saxophones are the best balanced of all the woodwinds, having tone qualities and intensities that blend with one another in a most homogeneous manner. In fact, the string choir is the only instrumental combination that can cover a similar pitch range with as little timbral contrast.

The only techncal limitation that must be taken into account is the extreme difficulty of playing major and minor trills above high A:  . These are awkward, due to the rather complex fingerings required, and cannot be executed with the speed associated with trills in the lower registers. In general, all passages above this high A are a trifle more difficult than similar passages in other ranges, and in this register the saxophone loses a little of its agility.

Alto Saxophone

The alto has more literature than all the other saxophones and is the most frequently encountered member of the family. Its tone is rich and hornlike, sounding like a blend of the horn, bassoon, and cello. The E♭ alto saxophone sounds a major sixth lower than written.

Tenor Saxophone

This instrument has a long and distinguished association with jazz and popular music. The tone is more aggressive than that of the alto. If one describes the alto as being hornlike, then the tenor may well be considered organ-like. The B♭ tenor sounds a major ninth lower than written.

Baritone Saxophone

The baritone saxophone in E♭ is perhaps the most mellow of all the saxophones. It is pitched an octave below the alto and is the most commonly utilized bass member of the family. Due to the general shortage of low-pitched woodwinds, the writing for the baritone saxophone is traditionally bass-line writing.

Nonetheless, the baritone has an excellent solo voice that is much like a reedy euphonium in quality. All saxophones are capable of very clear articulations, but this is most in evidence in the baritone, which is unexcelled in the delineation of marcato or staccato figures. It sounds an octave and a sixth lower than written.

Soprano Saxophone

The B♭ soprano is the highest-pitched saxophone in common use. It is an excellent solo woodwind voice, possessing all necessary expressive properties needed for any situation. Its tone is reedy and slightly pungent in the lower register and it becomes sweeter and clearer in the higher range. It is a transposing instrument in B♭ and thus sounds a whole step lower than written.

Bass Saxophone

The B♭ bass saxophone is not heard as often as the other members of the family discussed above. Still, when well played, it can almost match the baritone quality for quality and add the additional advantage of four or five more semitones downward in range. The tone of the bass saxophone is more gravelly than that of the baritone and the articulation is a little less rapid. It is a very effective bass instrument that can rival the pizzicato of an electronic bass in clarity, incisiveness, and—to an extent—power.

Other Saxophones

Two saxophones pitched in C are sometimes found. These are the C soprano and the C melody (a sort of C tenor). The C soprano is a non-transposing instrument sounding as written. The C melody is pitched a whole step above the tenor saxophone. These are remnants of a whole family of saxophones built in F and B♭ rather than E♭ and B♭. Included in the family were F mezzo-soprano (alto) saxophone and an F baritone. These are all very rare.

Typical Saxophone Scorings

Although the saxophones have had a place in the concert band for years, there are few examples of the saxophone as a solo instrument in the symphonic literature.

The "Old Castle" from Ravel's transcription of Modest Moussorgsky's *Pictures at an Exhibition* features this alto saxophone solo (beginning at rehearsal number 20):

EXAMPLE 152 Alto saxophone solo from Moussorgsky's *Pictures at an Exhibition,* as orchestrated by Ravel.[25]

This tenor saxophone solo is from the second movement, "Kije's Romance," from Prokofieff's *Lt. Kije Suite.* (It begins at rehearsal number 18.)

[25]Copyright 1929 by Edition Russe de Musique; Renewed 1956. Copyright and Renewal assigned to Boosey & Hawkes, Inc. Reprinted by permission.

EXAMPLE 153 Tenor saxophone solo from *Lt. Kije.*[26]

In his Symphony in B♭ for Band, Paul Hindemith has scored this alto saxophone line:

EXAMPLE 154 Alto saxophone line from Hindemith's *Symphony for Band* (second movement, measures 2-5).[27]

In the concert band, the traditional saxophone quartet is composed of two altos, one tenor, and one baritone. Some earlier editions, around the beginning of the twentieth century, were scored for a quartet of one soprano, one alto, one tenor, and one baritone. This latter grouping is still the most commonly found saxophone quartet, an ensemble that has become quite popular over the last sixty years.

In the first movement of Hindemith's Symphony for Band, this passage for four saxophones is heard prominently. Notice the use of unison and octave scorings—typical saxophone voicings.

EXAMPLE 155 Saxophone quartet from Hindemith's *Symphony for Band* (first movement, measures 33-40).[27]

[26]Copyright by Edition A. Gutheil. Copyright assigned 1946 to Boosey & Hawkes, Inc. Reprinted by permission.

[27]Used by permission of European American Music, Clifton, N.J. Copyright 1951 by Schott & Co. Ltd. London.

Many interesting examples of saxophone writing are found in jazz and jazz-rock arrangements that are unpublished and generally unavailable. Much of the incisive and exciting ensemble writing heard in jazz scoring comes from the use of the saxophones in unison or in octaves. When octaves are used, a common distribution is two altos and one tenor on the upper line and one tenor and a baritone on the lower line. Chords are usually saved for backgrounds and punctuations of the line. When chords do appear, the typical voicing is (from top to bottom) alto, tenor, alto, tenor, and baritone. This is the traditional voicing.

An interesting effect available on the saxophone is the process of "stopping" the instrument. This is done by totally covering the bell with a book, or cushion, or performer's leg, etc. When stopped, the saxophone can produce a pitch a semitone lower than its normal lowest pitch. The stopping only works when the lowest pitch is fingered and played.

Problem Set No. 14

1. Score the Bach chorale-prelude below, "Vater unser im Himmelreich," for a saxophone quartet. Assign the top line to the soprano saxophone, the second line to the alto, the third line to the tenor, and the bass line, at the written pitch, to the baritone. Have the quartet performed.

2. Using the Mozart Sonatina given in exercise 3 of Problem Set No. 13 (page 116) score it for a saxophone quartet consisting of two alto saxophones, one tenor, and one baritone. (If the baritone does not possess the low A key, repeat the third-to-the-last chord for the last two chords.) If possible, have the quartet performed.

3. For an ensemble of one soprano, two altos, one tenor, one baritone, and one bass saxophone, score the Schumann "A Little Hunting Song" given in exercise 1 of Problem Set No. 12 (page 108). Do not have all of the instruments—especially the bass, soprano, and second alto—playing all of the time. Rather, alternate among several combinations, saving the full group for the *forte* passages or climaxes.

4. Using one flute, one oboe, two clarinets, and one bassoon, score the Bach chorale harmonization given in exercise 2 of Problem Set No. 10 (page 90). Assign the soprano line to the oboe, the alto to one clarinet and the tenor to another, and the bass to the bassoon. Assign the soprano, transposed up an octave, to the flute. (As an alternative, use one clarinet and one tenor—or alto—saxophone. Assign the clarinet to the alto line and the tenor saxophone to the tenor line.) Have the result performed.

5. Compose a short piece, 8-10 measures long, for a saxophone quartet of one soprano, alto, tenor, and baritone each. Use some of the special effects and tonguings discussed in this chapter. Use slap tonguing, multiphonics, and air tones among others. Have your piece performed, if possible.

SAXOPHONE BIBLIOGRAPHY

Dorn, Ken. *Saxophone Technique Vol. 1: Multiphonics.* Islington, Mass.: Dorn Productions, 1975.

Hemke, Frederick L. "New Directions in Saxophone Technique, Part One," *Selmer Bandwagon* 63, p. 14ff.

Rascher, Sigurd M. *Top-tones for the Saxophone.* Boston: C. Fischer Inc., 1941.

Schwab, William. "Quarter Tones for the Saxophone," *The Saxophone Symposium* (Winter 1976), p. 7ff.

Teal, Larry. *The Art of Saxophone Playing.* Evanston, Ill.: Summy-Birchard Co., 1963.

4 INSTRUMENTATION: *The Brasses*

GENERAL BRASS INFORMATION

The Means of Producing Sound

All brass instruments produce sounds by means of the performer's lips vibrating together, producing a "buzz" somewhat like a double reed. The mouthpiece is placed against the performer's lips, or embouchure, and collects the buzz and the air, which are directed into the instrument via the leadpipe. The instrument acts as a resonator for this buzz, amplifying and modifying it.

The tubing of the instrument is made of brass. The horns, flugelhorns, tubas, and related instruments, have conical bores (except through the valve section, where the tubing is cylindrical). The trumpets and trombones have cylindrical tubing most of their lengths. All modern brasses have tubing that flares at the end, terminating in a bell which helps to radiate the sound.

By changing lip tension the performer can produce different pitches. The pitches obtained by this method are the fundamental and the natural overtones of the instrument's tubing. (See Appendix VI.) Depending upon the skill of the performer and the characteristics of instrument, pitches up to the sixteenth partial and higher may be obtained. In addition to this bugle-like series of pitches, other pitches may be played by lengthening the tubing. Trombones are equipped with slides for this purpose; the other brasses use valves. All brass instruments are supplied with one or more tuning slides to make fine tuning adjustments.

Terminology

English	*French*	*German*	*Italian*
mouthpiece	embouchure	Mundstück	bocchino *or* imboccatura
leadpipe	bocal	Mundrohr	pezzo d'imboccatura

valves	pistons *or* cylindres	Ventile	pistoni
slide	coulisse	Zug	pompa mobile a coulisse
tuning slide	corps de recharge	Stimmbogen *or* Knie	pompa d'accordo
bell	pavillon	Schallstück *or* Stürze	campana

Brass Articulations

For the most part, all that was said about woodwind articulations is equally applicable to brasses (see pages 69-75). There are, however, two minor qualifications:

1. Double, triple and flutter tonguings are, if not easier than on most woodwinds, at least more commonly developed and exploited. Most high school brass players can execute flutter tonguing, and many can do double and triple tonguing as well. Among professional performers only hornists, as a group, tend not to have developed double and triple tonguing as standard techniques. Certainly, many hornists *can* double and triple tongue just as efficiently as the other brass players, all of whom are expected to have these skills, but little of the horn literature requires it.
2. Trombonists use the various legato tonguings to a greater extent than other instrumentalists, due to the nature of the slide and its operation. If the air flow were not interrupted during some slide changes—specifically those that lengthen the slide to obtain a lower pitch or shorten the slide to obtain a higher pitch—a glissando would result. If the glissando is not desired, the performer must of necessity stop the air during the slide change and re-attack the next note. If the effect is to be perceived as legato, the re-attacking must be a form of legato tonguing. It is not usually the composer's or orchestrator's problem to indicate these specific legato tonguings. Marking a trombone passage *legato* is sufficient. The performer will do the rest.

Special Attacks and Alterations to Sustained Tones

The brass instruments are capable of responding to a variety of attacks just as are the woodwinds. The steady-state of the tone and the release can be inflected, too. The discussion at page 75 is equally applicable to the brasses.

SPECIAL BRASS EFFECTS AND DEVICES

Vibrato

Except for popular and jazz styles, vibrato is not considered to be a normal aspect of brass performance. However, brass players can produce three types of vibrato: diaphragmatic, jaw, and mechanical. (See page 76.) Few brass players have a really well-developed breath or diaphragmatic vibrato to use. The jaw vibrato is usable and can produce a variety of effects, from a microtonal undulation of the pitch, through a shake or lip trill, to a raucous alteration in pitch covering a perfect fifth or more. The mechanical vibrato can be produced by moving the instrument while playing—most successful on the trombone, where a rapid movement of the slide can create a subtle vibrato not unlike that employed on orchestral strings (see page 37).

Lip Trills

A refined version of the jaw or lip vibrato is the *lip trill.* This is traditionally associated with the horns, but may be executed by all brasses. It is accomplished by changing lip tension, which allows the pitch produced by the instrument to alternate between two adjacent partials. (See Appendix VI.) When done rapidly on partials that are a whole step or half step apart, the effect is that of a trill. When executed on partials with wide spacings, the effect is comical (as in Mozart's *Musical Joke*). Not all brass players—not even all hornists—can perform effective lip trills.

Shakes

A less controlled version of the lip trill, one that is easier to perform than the lip trill but more difficult than the lip or jaw vibrato, is the *shake.* The performer achieves the effect by alternating between two adjacent partials. Since the effect is not intended to be subtle, the shake is obtained by moving the lips, jaw, tongue, or instrument as necessary. The shake is commonly heard in jazz contexts. If used in other situations, the notation could be confused with an upper mordant. Thus, an explanation of the effect desired would be necessary.

EXAMPLE 156 Notation for a shake.

Glissandos

There are three main types of glissandos that brass players may use. These include the following:

1. Valve glissandos.
2. Overtone or lip glissandos.
3. Slide glissandos.

The Valve Glissando

This glissando is possible on all valved brasses. It consists basically of the performer slurring from the starting note to the ending note in a very sloppy manner while moving the valves rapidly and at random. A common variation on the valve glissando is the half-valve glissando, in which the valves are depressed part way (some or all of the valves may be used) while the tone is bent by the player's lips from the starting note to the ending note. Both of these glissandos are playable in an ascending or descending direction.

It is possible to call for a valve or half-valve glissando that follows a specific contour by using analog notation.

EXAMPLE 157 a. Notation for a valve glissando. b. Notation for a half-valve glissando. c. Analog notation for a valve glissando that follows a contour.

The Overtone or Lip Glissando

Traditionally a horn technique, overtone glissandos may be produced on any of the brass instruments. These glissandos are obtained by slurring rapidly up or down the overtone series of the instrument. Traditional notation for these reflect the method of production by showing the series of pitches to be produced. The pitches may be those produced with or without valves depressed (or slide extended.) The partials of the overtone series are much closer together within the normal playing range of the horn and therefore the effect, when produced on the horn, is one of a strange, semi-diatonic scale. On the other brasses, except in the highest registers, the effect is more likely to be a rapid dominant seventh or ninth chord being arpeggiated.

The jazz "rip" glissando is a combination valve and overtone glissando, the amount of each depending upon the range being played, the instrument, the performer, and the style of the music. The possible confusion between the notation for the rip and the analog notation for valve glissando is obvious. For this reason, in situations where there could be doubt as to which is desired, an explanation to the performers is advisable.

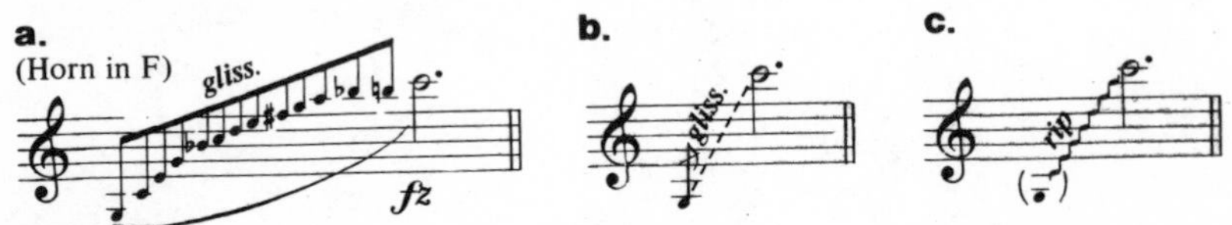

EXAMPLE 158 a. Traditional notation for an overtone glissando. b. Notation for an overtone glissando recommended by the Ghent Conference. c. Jazz glissando notation.

Even if one uses the traditional notation for an overtone glissando, or otherwise specifies in the part that an overtone glissando is desired, it is not a guarantee that an overtone glissando will be employed. The performer may be playing a different-sized instrument than the one for which the part is written and may therefore be unable to produce the specified glissando. However, most professional players are adept at substituting and intermixing valve, half-valve, and overtone glissandos while obtaining the sonic qualities required.

The Slide Glissando

This characteristic technique of the trombone is possible only because of the continuum of pitches available from one position to the next on the instrument.

It is not possible to produce an ascending slide glissando unless the slide is being shortened; nor is it possible to produce a descending slide glissando unless the slide is being lengthened. The composer-orchestrator needs to be sure that the trombonist can obtain the desired direction of glissando on the required pitches by using the same direction of slide motion. (See Appendix V.)

It is not necessary for a slide glissando to cover a wide interval to be effective. Glissandos of only a minor second work very well.

To a very limited extent, trumpets, tubas, and euphoniums with movable valve or tuning slides can obtain slightly effective slide glissandos. It is a little used device.

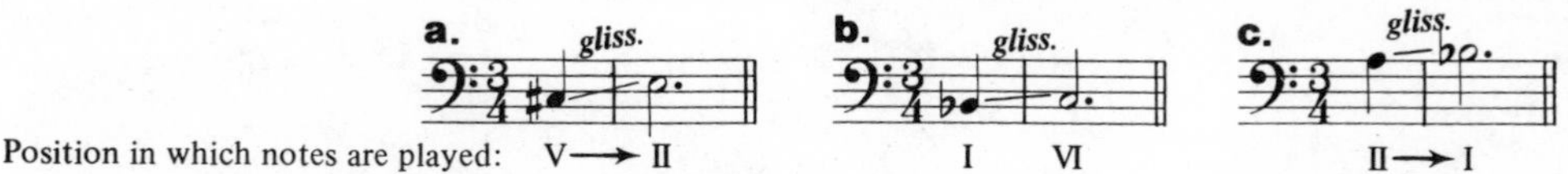

EXAMPLE 159 a. A playable slide glissando. The slide is being shortened from fifth position to second position. b. An unplayable slide glissando. The direction of pitch motion is upward, but it is impossible to shorten the slide from first position and the written B♭ is only playable in first position. c. An effective, short slide glissando.

For further discussion of glissandos and glissando notation, see pages 35-36 and 76.

Brassed Tone

At times, for added excitement, a composer will call for an effect which in English is *brassed* or *brassy* (French: cuiver (les sons); German: schmettern; Italian: metallizzare i suoni *or* produrre suoni metallici). This is a strident, forced sound with a very metallic quality. One can almost hear the brass vibrate. Since this is a forced effect, the dynamic must be *forte* or louder, or the instrument must be muted. (It is commonly associated with "stopped horn.")

Bells Up

This effect, which may or may not appear with brassed tone, is an additional means of providing excitement. In many circumstances the performers merely lift the bell of the instrument so that it points more directly toward the audience. This may mean to lift it over the stand or, in the case of the horn, to lift the bell off of the performer's knee (or away from his body, depending upon how it is held.) The effect alters the tone quality, by directing the axis of the instrument at the listener. The visual impact is also worth considering. Horn players do not remove their hands from the bell in the process. To do so would cause certain of the higher pitches to become so unstable as to be unplayable and all pitches to become sharp.

The instruction for this effect is, in English: bells up; French: pavillon en l'air; German: Stürze hoch *or* Schalltrichter auf; Italian: padiglioni in alto *or* campana in aria.

Contemporary Brass Effects

Air Sounds

Among the contemporary effects, one can call upon the brass players to blow air through the instrument, to whistle, hum, or sing into it, or to reverse the mouthpiece and blow through the back end. All of these produce sounds characterized by a high component of white noise or a hollow, empty resonance (or both). These are classified as air sounds. (See page 80.)

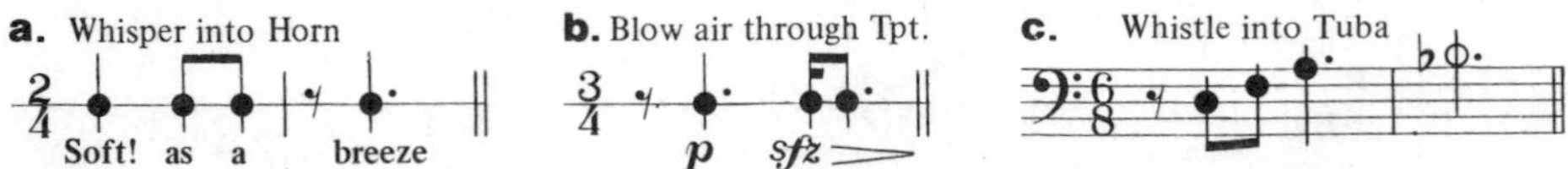

EXAMPLE 160 a. Whispering through instrument. b. Blowing air through instrument without producing normal tone. c. Whistling into instrument and obtaining specific pitches.

Smacking Sounds

These are produced by smacking the lips against (kissing) the mouthpiece. These were also discussed under special double-reed effects (page 77). Some brass performers have extended this technique to include the production of a sustained tone by the vibration of the lips while *in*haling through the instrument. The sound is not as full as the normal tone, but it is possible to play lines and figures this way.

Timbral Trills

These are the brass equivalents of woodwind key trills (page 79). The timbral trills are produced differently on the brasses. These are possible on any pitch for which there are two different fingerings. The performer alternates between two (or more) fingerings. On the trombone, timbral trills are possible when two different positions are available to produce the same pitch. The performer then changes between these positions while legato tonguing at the trill speed. A little thought and examination of the information in Appendix V will reveal that timbral trills are more likely to be possible in the upper registers of brass instruments.

Clicks

Various types of clicks can be produced on the brasses. One common click is the *valve click,* which is the sound of the valves being rapidly depressed and released, creating a sort of rattle or clatter.

Another type of click is produced by striking the instrument at various points with a fingernail, ring, mouthpiece, or other similar device. It is a quiet, metallic, percussive sound that may prove effective.

On the trombone it is possible to obtain a clicking sound by jerking the slide into first (completely closed) position.

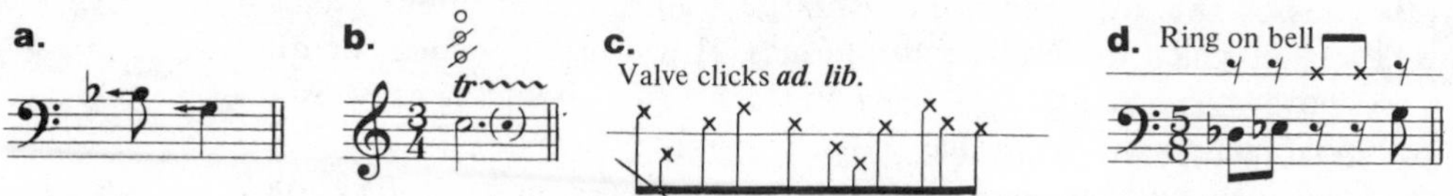

EXAMPLE 161 a. Smack tone. b. Timbral trill showing fingering to be used. c. Random valve clicks. d. Clicking the bell with a ring.

Mouthpiece Pop

By slapping the top of the mouthpiece with the palm of the performer's hand, a popping sound, known as a *mouthpiece pop,* can be produced. Different pitches can be obtained, but these depend upon so many variables outside the control of the composer or orchestrator that the notation of relative pitches is probably exact enough. However, in theory, at least, the pops may be changed by changing the valve combination depressed, and the total number of unique valve combinations available will be the total number of different mouthpiece pop pitches available.

Another kind of pop is available on the trombone: the *slide pop.* By separating the bell portion from the slide portion, the performer can seal both ends of the tubing leading to and from the latter section. After this is done, the slide may be rapidly disengaged from the internal tubing, producing a resonant pop. The same effect, but much softer, can be achieved by rapidly removing valve slides on other brasses without depressing the valves. However, these slides are not nearly as easily moved as the trombone's slide, and thus the effect is more difficult to place precisely in time.

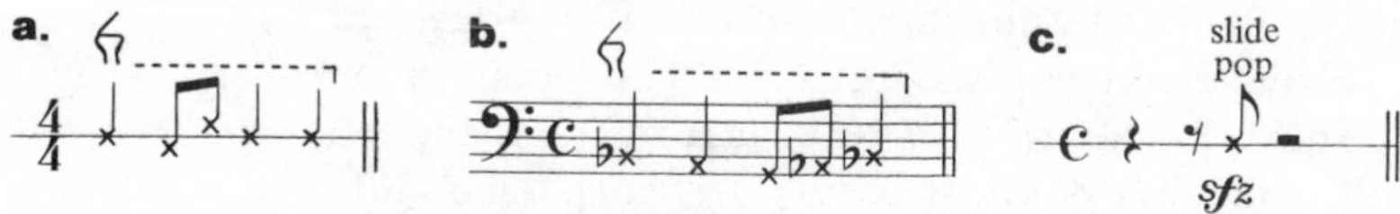

EXAMPLE 162 a. Notation for mouthpiece pop of unspecified pitch. b. Mouthpiece pop of specified pitches. c. Possible notation for a slide pop.

An obvious problem with all slide pops is the time required to disassemble and reassemble the instrument.

Multiphonics

The brasses can only produce one type of multiphonic: the performer plays one pitch and hums another. The technique is quite old, having been asked for in the cadenza from Carl Maria von Weber's Concertino for horn. When intervals such as perfect fifths or minor sevenths are produced between the sung and played pitches, and the performer attempts to match timbres as much as possible, recognizable chords and triads are produced. Various inversions of major and minor chords can be played. When other intervals are produced, rather curious sonorities appear. All of these are the result of summation and difference tones.

Of all the brasses, the tuba, because of its large mouthpiece and bore, seems to be the easiest on which to obtain multiphonics. However, performers on all of the brasses have shown an ability to learn the technique, giving the composer another valuable compositional device.

The recommended notation is to use small, cue-sized notes for the sung pitches and normal sized notes for those to be played. It is assumed that the octave in which the pitches are to be sung is optional unless specifically stated. (See also pages 80-81.)

EXAMPLE 163 Notation of playing and singing together from the author's *Cameos* for tuba alone.[1] Small notes are hummed, large notes are played.

Alternating singing with playing is a very usable technique on the brasses. If it is done rapidly, the effect can be one of interesting counterpoint. Any vocal effect can be alternated with the normal method of brass tone production (see Chapter 7).

Microtones

Of all the brasses, the trombone is the most ideally suited to the performance of microtones. The infinite variability of the trombone's slide allows the trombonist not only to play very well in tune but also to produce any pitch that lies along the length of its slide.

However, the horn, too, can produce microtones. Through a combination of lip adjustment and a change of the hand's position in the bell, the hornist can obtain any pitch within the chromatic range of the instrument. In the case of the horn, though, a price must be paid. The insertion of the hand further into the bell to lower the pitch also modifies the tone color. In passages where pitch is more important than timbre, the method works well. If timbre is important, then the amount of microtonal inflection available is limited.

Generally, members of the trumpet and tuba families are more limited in their abilities to play microtones than are the horns and trombones. But, instruments constructed with valve or tuning slides that may be moved during performance —this would include most of the professional models—can obtain inflections. If the main tuning slide is adjustable by means of some type of trigger, then any note played could be changed. If, on the other hand, only some valve slides are so equipped, then only pitches in which those valves are used can be altered.

The amount of pitch change that can be created varies among performers, specific models of instruments, and in different ranges. In general, brass players can bend or "lip" a tone downward further than they can lip it up. (Probably the difference is three or four times as far down as up for the majority of players.) In the lower register, the amount of inflection increases over that available in the upper register. (On the second partial, for example, most horn players can lip the pitch down a perfect fourth or more. On the 12th partial, few can lip downward even a minor second.) The use of variable slides or the hand of the performer becomes a valuable and necessary factor in the production of an infinite assortment of microtones.

In his piece written for Stuart Dempster, Ben Johnston exploits the trombone's ability to produce microtones. The composer calls for the performance of intervallic relationships involving "just chromatic semi-tones," "diatonic commas," and the different tuning ratios found between various pitches of the overtone series. Although extremely demanding to perform, it can be accomplished, due to the trombone's ability to achieve an infinite number of pitches within the limits of its range.

EXAMPLE 164 The opening of Ben Johnston's *One Man* for solo trombonist.[2] Key to notation: the Roman numerals indicate trombone slide positions; encircled numeral indicates F attachment; ♭‾ represents lowering the pitch by 44 cents; ♭- represents lowering the pitch by 93 cents; ♭-- represents lowering the pitch by 115 cents; and ♭̶-- represents lowering the pitch by 184 cents. These are logical and musically generated pitch relationships, but a more detailed account is beyond the scope of this book.)

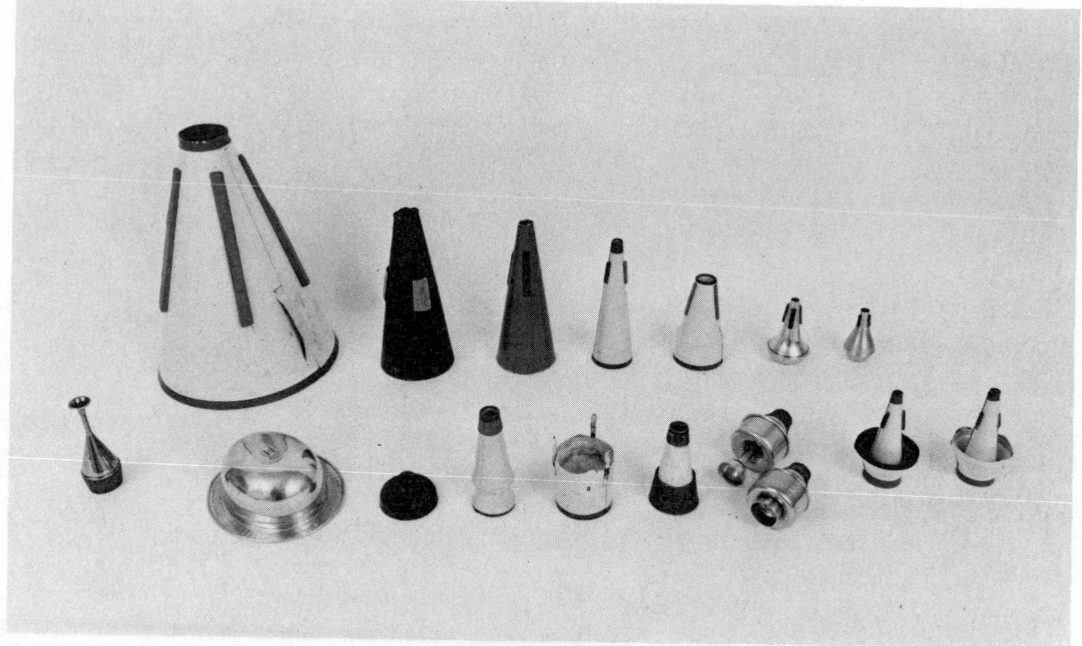

FIGURE 12. Brass mutes: (*back row from left*) straight mutes for tuba, euphonium, bass trombone, tenor trombone, horn, B♭ or C trumpet, piccolo trumpet; (*front row from left*) horn transposing mute; mutes for the trumpet: hat, plunger, solotone, bucket, whispa, two harmon mutes—one with stem in and one with stem part way out, mica, and cup. (Photo by David Hruby.)

Brass Mutes

Mutes are commonly called for in brass music. With the exception of the transposing mute for the horn, all of the mutes listed below are made for all of the brasses. However, only the straight mutes can be considered to be commonly available. The other mutes are rare for all brasses except trumpets and trombones.

mutes	*muting-type devices*
straight mute	plunger
cup mute	hat
mica mute	hand
harmon mute	handkerchief or cloth
whispa mute	music stand
bucket or velvetone mute	stopped horn and transposing mute
solotone or cleartone mute	horn devices

There are a number of appropriate instructions that can be used to indicate that the player is to insert or remove a mute. (If no specific mute is named, the performer will assume the straight mute to be called for.) These instructions, in four languages, are:

English	*French*	*German*	*Italian*
with mute *or* muted	avec sourdine	mit Dämpfer *or* gedämpft	con sordina
mute (verb)	mettre la sourdine	dämpfen	mettere la sordina
open *or* remove mute	enlever la sourdine *or* ôter la sourdine	Dämpfer weg *or* Dämpfer absetzen	togliere la sordina *or* via sordina
without mute	sans sourdine	keine Dämpfer *or* ohne Dämpfer	senza sordina

Straight Mute

The most commonly used mute is the *straight mute*. This mute is made of either metal or cardboard in the shape of a cone, closed at the large end and with a small opening at the other end. Three pieces of cork hold the mute in place and prevent the mute from totally blocking the egress of sound. Even though the two types of straight mutes are considered equivalent, the tone of the metal mute is definitely brighter and more pungent. To specify straight mute, write *st. mute* (See Figure 12, page 133).

Cup Mute

Use of the cup mute produces a rather colorless, nasal sound without any significant bite or edge. Heard in a solo voice, the sound produced is an almost ghostly distortion or a muffled echo, in contrast to the straight mute's brighter echo. An ensemble of cup-muted brasses sounds as though one is listening to a far-off brass section in which all of the instruments have colds in their noses. When needed, cup-muted brass may be used to fill out woodwind or string chords while making very little change in the tone quality of the chord. The cup mute is usually made of cardboard and is held in place in the bell of the instrument by three strips of cork thus allowing sound to escape around the mute. The instruction to use cup mute is *cup mute.*

Mica Mute

The *mica mute* is built like the cup mute but with one difference: there is a rubber edge around the cup which more completely covers the sound. The tone is similar to the cup mute—that is, nasal but colorless—but has even more of an echo quality. The mica mute also has more of a metallic edge to it, but with a far-off dynamic effect.

Harmon Mute

The *harmon mute* (sometimes incorrectly called a *waa-waa mute*) is made of metal. Since the part of the mute that fits into the bell is *completely* wrapped with cork, all of the sound is forced into and through the harmon mute. The small bell, or stem, may be removed or moved in or out of the mute to atune the mute to particular resonances within the instrument, the performance environment, or to a particular range of the instrument. With the stem completely removed, the harmon mute produces a sound that is less focused and almost devoid of a fundamental. With the stem in place, the tone is clearer, but the harmon mute always has an edgy quality much like breaking glass. It is a brass equivalent to ponticello. The directions to the performer to use a harmon mute are: *harmon mute, stem one-half out,* etc.

Whispa Mute

The *whispa mute* is the softest mute generally found. As with the harmon mute, all of the sound is forced through the whispa mute, which is filled with a sound-absorbent material like fiber glass. Small holes allow some sound to escape. The result is virtually inaudible except in a very quiet passage. It sounds like an instrument being played indoors two or three blocks away. (This mute is often used with amplification.) The directions to the performer are: *whispa mute.*

Bucket Mute

The *bucket mute,* which may be called a *velvetone mute,* is designed to allow some sound, but not a lot, to escape around the edge. The interior of the bucket is filled with cotton and cheesecloth-type material, not unlike old-fashioned bandages. The tone is mellow, not too loud, and with no edge at all, as if playing into a very heavy cloth coat.

Solotone Mute

The *solotone mute* (also called a *cleartone mute* or, because of the design, a *double mute*) is the rarest of all the listed mutes. The tone quality is very, very nasal with a little bite to it. The tone is resonant and may be fairly loud. The effect is something like listening through a telephone receiver over which indistinct sounds but not intelligible words can be heard, quite loud, but far away.

Mute Limitations

With all brass instruments, the use of a mute significantly changes the blowing characteristics. The mutes that force all sound through the mute create more change than the others. Because of these changes, passages that would be difficult normally may become almost unplayable with a mute in place. Although professional performers use mutes frequently enough to be familiar with the necessary adjustments between the two modes of performance, nonetheless, one should generally be a little more conservative when writing passages to be played muted. Time must be allowed in the part to insert or remove a mute. The time required to remove one mute and insert another is not simply twice the time required to insert a mute. Since a player has only one free hand with which to make all of the changes, it is necessary to remove and silently place down one mute (they tend to stick in the bell), then locate and insert the second mute. Mutes that do not significantly affect the pitch may be inserted or removed while playing.

Mutes are generally not available for alto horns, mellophoniums, flugelhorns, Wagner tubas, alto or contrabass trombones, or bell front tubas or euphoniums. The only mute available for the piccolo trumpet is the straight mute.

Muting-type Devices

Plunger

The use of a plunger (which is exactly like the plumber's plunger, only without a handle) originated in jazz, but the sound quality and effect is found more and more in modern music. When the bell of a brass instrument is covered with the plunger, the tone is quite muffled and stuffy. The traditional "dirty" sound is produced by flutter tonguing a covered note which changes to a non-fluttered uncovered note, usually of a different pitch (often higher, sometimes lower) approached by a glissando. A plunger held tightly into the bell of the instrument produces a "popping" sort of attack, especially if the notes are short and slightly accented.

Hat

The use of a hat is an effective way of reducing the intensity of an instrument while minimizing the distortion of the true tone. Specially made hats are available which attach to the music stand. If a passage is to be played into a hat, the instruction at the beginning would be *into hat,* and at the end *open* or *normal.* The use of the hat in musical contexts other than jazz should not be overlooked. Covering the bell with the hat is an effective muting device that avoids the tonal extremes of any of the standard inserted mutes. Hats are not very effective with tubas, but one might use a timpani head on a frame in place of the hat; it has been done effectively.

Hand Over the Bell

The player can, of course, place his hand over the bell of the instrument while playing. (Note: this has no effect on a tuba and very little on a euphonium.) The hand can be removed and replaced rapidly without the player having to move the instrument and without disturbing the embouchure. The effect of the hand is generally subtle, unless the performer places the hand too far into the bell. The device mainly softens the tone.

Hand in the Bell

If the performer places his hand into the bell far enough on one of the smaller brasses, the pitch will be lowered and the tone muffled or covered. This effect is often called for by use of the symbol ⊕. On the horn, where the normal playing position has the hand in the bell, this covered effect requires inserting the hand further into the bell. Usually, unless specified to the contrary, the performer of any brass will compensate for the pitch change caused by the inserted hand by lipping the pitch upward.

Rapid Covering and Uncovering

When using one of the mutes through which all of the tone is forced, such as the harmon mute or the solotone mute, or when playing an unmuted instrument, the performer's hand, a plunger, or a hat may be used to cover and uncover the bell of the instrument, producing what is often called a *waa-waa effect.*

Because writing the word *covered* or *uncovered* over each pitch would be awkward, two symbols have evolved: o for uncovered and + for covered. Therefore, any rapid alternation will require a series of + o + o symbols.

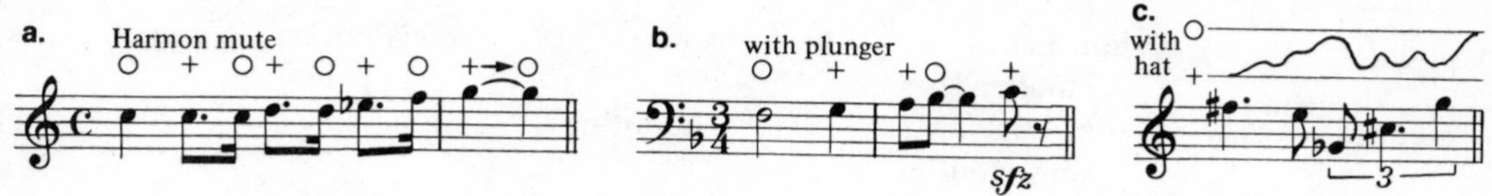

EXAMPLE 165 a. Notation for harmon mute and waa-waa effect. b. Notation for plunger and waa-waa effect. c. Analog notation for varying amounts of covering of the bell with a hat.

Handkerchief or Cloth Effects

Placing a cloth or handkerchief over the bell of the instrument reduces the strength of the higher partials, much as a hat will, but the effect is a little less pronounced. By the use of the cloth, the intensity of the tone can be reduced with little loss in the ability of the performer to control the tone or attack high notes. This effect is used on the trumpet in Charles Ives's *The Unanswered Question.*

Stuffing a handkerchief into the bell of the instrument produces a similar sound, only more pronounced. On the larger brasses, a large cloth would be required. If enough mass of cloth is in the bell the result becomes more like a hand-in-the-bell effect.

Into the Stand

This is an easy-to-achieve effect that reduces the loudness of the instrument without creating significant performance difficulties. By pointing the bell directly into the stand or folio from a distance of less than two inches, the tone of the instrument is made quite soft with only a slight loss of brilliance. The into-the-stand device allows the performer to play at a comfortable, moderately loud dynamic level while sounding much softer. It also greatly reduces the volume of the normal *pianissimo*. The appropriate written instruction is *Into Stand* and it is removed by the word *open*.

Stopped Horn

The normal playing position for the horn requires the performer to place his right hand part way into the bell of the horn. When the hand is placed as far into the bell as possible, a different sound is achieved. This technique is known as *stopped horn*. To obtain this effect, the performer must totally seal the bell, raising the pitch a semitone. Because of this pitch change, the performer must compensate by transposing the part down a semitone.[3] The tone quality of stopped horn is a combination of sounding very distant and possessing a metallic edge. At softer dynamics it is a delicate, buzzy coloration in the ensemble. At louder dynamics it has an ominous-sounding bite. The symbol to indicate stopped horn is a plus sign + over the note(s) to be stopped. The sign to remove the stopping effect is an o over the note. The change to and from stopped horn can be almost instantaneous.

English	*French*	*German*	*Italian*
stopped	étouffé *or* bouché	gestopft	chiuso
stop *(verb)*	boucher *or* étouffer les sons	stopfen	chiudere *or* tappare
stopped notes	sons bouchés *or* sons étouffés	Stopftöne	suoni chiusi

Transposing Mute (Stopping Mute)

As an alternative to hand stopping, a *transposing mute,* sometimes called a *stopping mute,* is made for the horn (see figure 12, page 133). It is fairly rare, usually owned only by professional performers. It cannot produce a perfect imitation of hand stopping, and it is primarily employed to obtain a stopped sound on lower pitches, for which the hand technique is normally not effective. It is also used to improve accuracy on especially problematic pitches. Since it is not a perfect imitation of stopped horn, the sound that is produced—noticeably more nasal and resonant than stopped horn—could be utilized as an alternative effect for the horn.

By covering and uncovering the end of the stem of the transposing mute, one can also produce a waa-waa effect on the horn that is very similar to a harmon-muted waa-waa on other brasses.

Other Hand Techniques

When the hand is not quite far enough into the bell to produce the stopped horn effect, a very covered sound is produced which is variously called *hand muting, half (or three-fourths) stopped,* or *echo*. It is a very soft, delicate, and distant horn sound. The horn straight mute approximates this effect.

As the performer moves his hand from the normal position into the bell toward the stopped position, the pitch will actually fall almost a semitone. This *hand glissando* can be called for by using the following notation:

[3]The composer or orchestrator must never do this transposition for the performer, but must simply notate the pitch to be played, and then adds the symbol + over the note(s) or the word *stopped.*

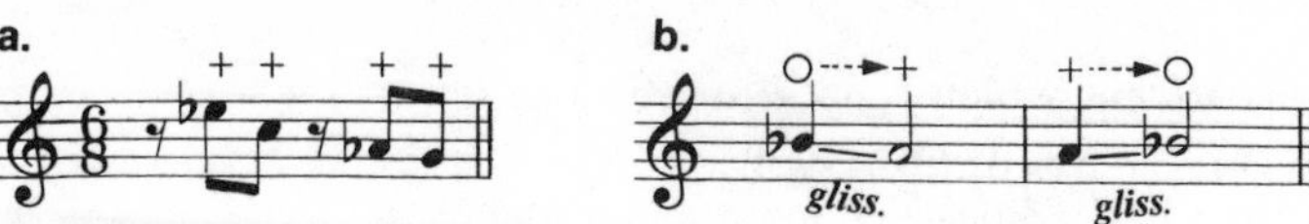

EXAMPLE 166 a. Notation for stopped horn. b. Notation for hand glissandos.

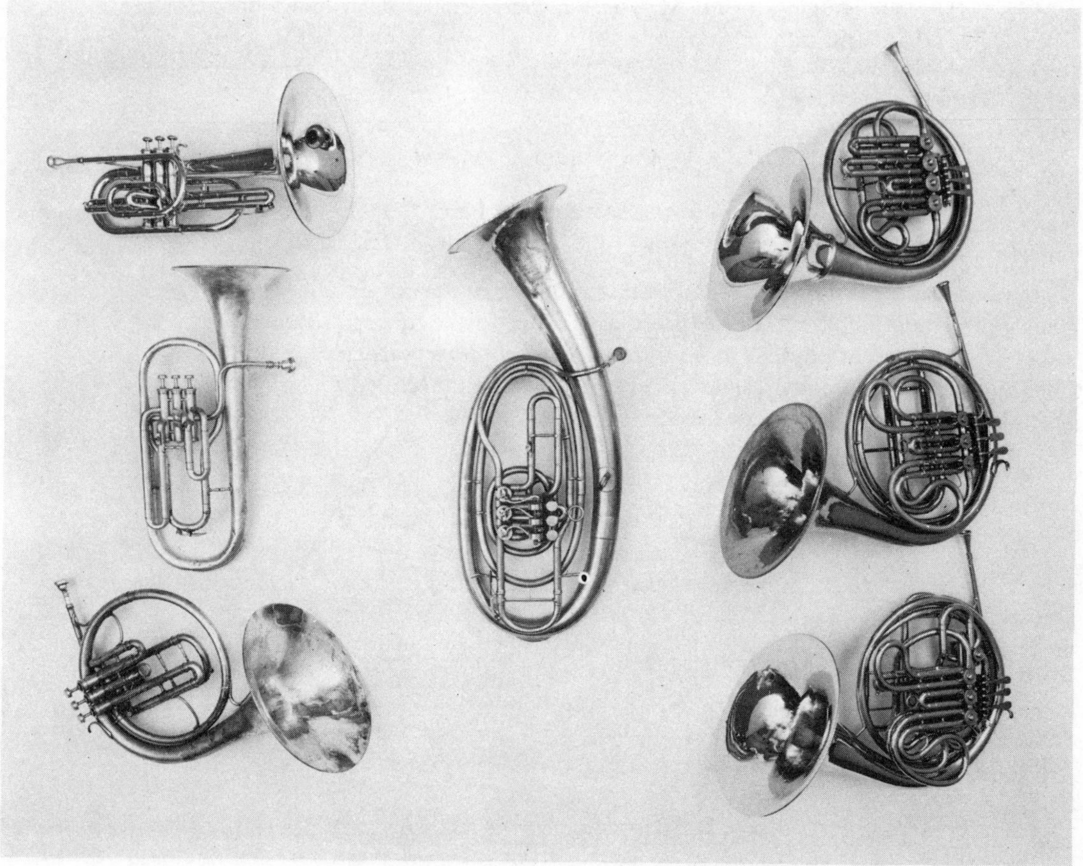

FIGURE 13. The horns: (*left column, top to bottom*) mellophonium, alto horn, and mellophone; (*Center*) Wagner tuba in F; (*right column, top to bottom*) single B♭ horn, single F horn, and double horn in F and B♭. (Photo by David Hruby.)

THE HORNS

	English	*French*	*German*	*Italian*
singular	horn (hn.)	cor (cor)	Horn (Hr.)	corno (cor.)
plural	horns (hns.)	cors (cors)	Hörner (Hr.)	corni (cor.)

The Properties of the Horns

The horn is a transposing brass instrument which represents the alto-tenor portion of the brass choir. Modern horns are usually pitched in F and have three or more valves to lengthen or shorten the basic pipe. The members of the horn family include:

1. Horn in F
   (French: fa; German: F; Italian: fa).
2. Alto horn in E♭ or F
   (French: bugle alto en Mi♭ or Fa; German: Althorn in Es or F; Italian: flicorno contralto in Mi♭ or Fa; the British call it tenor horn).
3. Mellophone in E♭ or F (rare).
4. Mellophonium in F, E♭.
5. Wagner tuba in F and B♭ (rare)
   (French: tuba Wagner, or tuba ténor, en Fa or Si♭; German: Wagner-Tuba in F or B; Italian: tuba wagneriana in Fa or Si♭).

There are single horns in B♭ or F; double horns in B♭ and F; and descant horns in B♭ and "high" F. These distinctions are of little concern to the composer. They represent choices of equipment made by the performer and with which the performer alone must deal. The horn is sometimes called *French horn.*

The ranges of the various horns are:

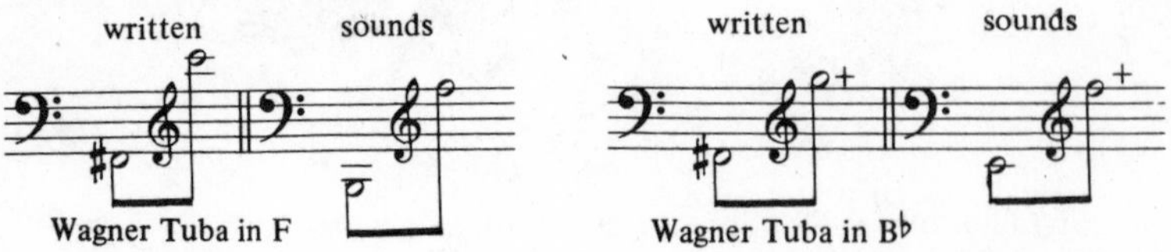

EXAMPLE 167 The written ranges, sounding ranges, and transpositions for the horn family. a. Horn in F; sounds a fifth lower than written. b. Alto horn, mellophone, and mellophonium; in E♭, sounds a major sixth lower than written; in F, sounds a fifth lower than written. c. Wagner tuba in F (bass); sounds a fifth lower than written. d. Wagner tuba in B♭ (tenor); sounds a whole step lower than written.

Because the relationship between the horn and the Wagner tubas is very slight—and between the horn and the alto horn, mellophone, and mellophonium nonexistant (except that they sometimes are substituted for one another)—the dynamic curves differ.

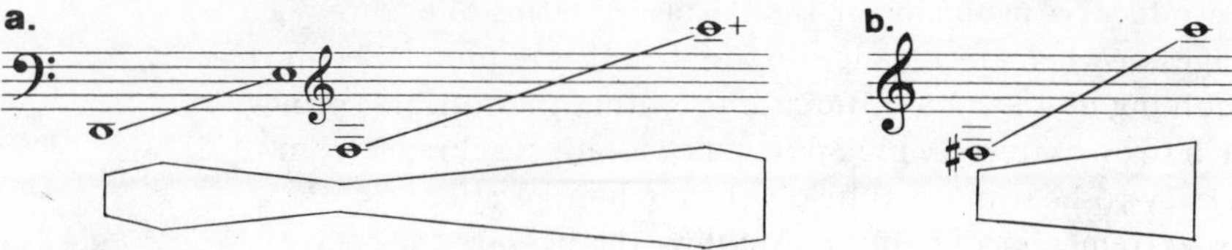

EXAMPLE 168 Dynamic curves for: a. Horn. b. Wagner tuba, alto horn, mellophone, and mellophonium.

Horn

In the lower register the horn does not have much ability to project and is easily covered, although its presence may be "felt" even when not heard. The horn is a warm, expressive solo instrument with, at softer dynamics, a haunting and dark quality that becomes more heroic and brilliant as the dynamic level or register increases. The most characteristic solo range is (at written pitch):

. While the higher range is sure to provide excitement, the lowest part of the horn's range lacks brilliance and power, yet can provide an unobtrusive but secure bass to all but the loudest passages.

The horn is not particularly agile, and leaps of more than an octave should be used sparingly. Its tonguing is not as incisive as other brasses; however some hornists can perform double and triple tongued passages, and flutter tonguing is no problem except at the extremes of the range.

Trills on the horn are of two types: lip and valve. The most characteristic horn trill is the lip trill and will be employed by most hornists unless it is impossible due to the physics of the instrument or unless a valve trill is specified. In general above written most whole-step lip trills are possible. Valve trills of minor seconds throughout the whole range work best, although wider trills are possible. Good lip trills are generally smoother than good valve trills.

One of the characteristic horn effects is stopped tones. These cannot be produced below written . If asked to perform stopped notes below this pitch, the performer will half-cover the bell or use a mute to approximate the effect. If a transposing mute is available, it will be used. Composers have too often been careless in calling for muted or stopped horn. Some passages marked *muted* allow no time to insert or remove the mute. Other passages marked *muted* show stopped horn indications (+) over the notes. Other stopped horn passages are written too low to be playable. In all of these cases, hornists have had to substitute some other effect for the one called for. This has led to a rather cavalier attitude among hornists toward the orchestrator's wishes regarding stopped and muted effects. The only means a composer or orchestrator has to offset this attitude is to be certain that all stopped or muted passages are playable as such. If the requirements appear well thought-out, the performer will play as directed.

The horn, in contrast to the other brasses, plays regularly in the range of its higher partials. This produces a problem for the hornist in terms of accuracy, especially in soft passages or when an entrance on a high note is required. Security is improved by: doubling in unison a difficult line (within the section); providing an easy approach to an extremely high note (such as approaching it from the octave or another easy-to-hear interval below the pitch in question: P4, P5, M3, or m3); avoiding extremes in dynamics; doubling the passage an octave lower within the horn section; or any combination of the above.

Due to the wide range of the horn and historically traditional scoring practices, hornists are usually either "high" or "low" performers, a distinction that exists in almost no other instrumental section. The high horn performers are traditionally assigned to the odd-numbered parts in an ensemble while the low horn performers are given the even-numbered parts to play. Thus the following ranges should serve as a guide:

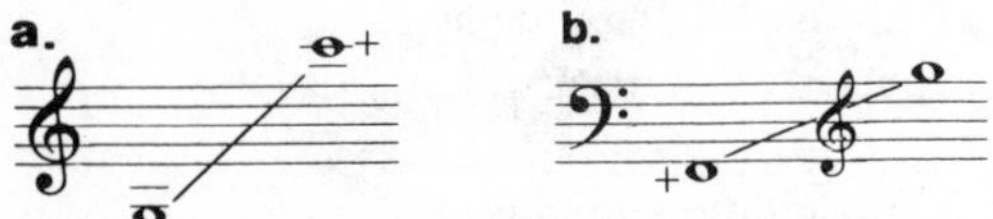

EXAMPLE 169 a. High horn range (first and third horn parts). b. Low horn range (second and fourth horn parts).

In important solos where the instrument is exposed, the given ranges should serve as guides, but the tessitura of the solo should determine whether it is assigned to a high or low hornist. Thus, a solo that goes "too low" for a high hornist would still be assigned to a high horn if the tessitura were more in his range. (The given ranges do not mean that the high hornists cannot play the low pitches or vice versa; indeed they can. But, the *specialization* of a high or low hornist is within one range or the other.) In non-solo situations, either part may be given notes outside of the usual range if these notes are also doubled in the other horn(s).

The normal voicing of a four-note horn chord is:

EXAMPLE 170 Traditional chord voicing for four horns.

This is sometimes called interlocking voicing. In professional situations it should be used at all times, except for a special musical need, such as completing a line within the same horn.

The first and second horn parts are treated as a matched pair in professional ensembles. Likewise the third and fourth horns form another pair. The high range solos are assigned to the first hornist about 60 to 75 percent of the time, with the remaining high horn solos assigned to the third hornist. The division of the low horn solos between second and fourth horns is more equal, with the very low solos almost always given to the fourth horn and the slightly higher and more agile solos given to the second horn. Seatings in most professional orchestras and bands, as well as good high school, college, and community organizations, are based on matching this distribution of assignments to the varying abilities of the horn players.

When writing horn parts in the bass clef one treats the bass clef in the same manner as is done in writing for the piano. (There is an old notation for bass clef notes often found in parts written for the historical natural horns; it is written an octave lower than the notation dictated by modern practice and should never be used by a contemporary writer for the horn.)

Horn players do not read high notes notated in the bass clef well. Therefore, one should never write notes above G 𝄢 in the bass clef.

Alto Horn, Mellophone, and Mellophonium

These are all basically the same instrument. The *alto horn* is the contralto member of the sax horn family[4] and the *mellophone* is simply a version of that instrument that is coiled to resemble a horn rather than a tuba. Both are fingered with the right hand and neither require the use of one hand in the bell. The sound is more blatant and aggressive than the horn's, and one is more likely to encounter these instruments in a marching band. These are the E♭ altos for which much early band music was scored (in place of horns).

The *mellophoniums* are variants of the above instruments. They are played in the same position as the trumpet, bell pointing forward. The bell is shaped more like a horn's bell than like either a mellophone's or alto horn's bell. These instruments were introduced by the late Stan Kenton, but are now being used in the marching band as a major inner melody instrument.

Wagner Tubas

In spite of the name, these are horns and not tubas as we know them. The instruments were first used in Wagner's *Ring* cycle of operas, and are traditionally played by hornists. Other examples of scoring for Wagner tubas exist in works by Anton Bruckner and R. Strauss. The Wagner tubas are built in two sizes, F and B♭. The tone, though somewhat hornlike, is also similar to that of the alto horn or euphonium. Except for professional situations, such as major orchestras or opera houses, few horn players have ever seen or played a Wagner tuba. (There is a model of euphoium made that looks like a Wagner tuba in shape but is not the same instrument.)

Typical Horn Scorings

In the first movement of Beethoven's Seventh Symphony, this duet appears for two horns. Due to the high register, it is considered to be a difficult, treacherous passage, even on modern valved instruments.

[4] Historically these are related to the old keyed bugles. The keyed bugle without keys but with valves became the flugelhorn, or soprano saxhorn, or soprano buglehorn. In Britain today, and in this country during the Civil War, the name for the E♭ version of the valved bugle was E♭ tenor, while on the continent and in current American usage, the name is E♭ alto.

EXAMPLE 171 Horn duet passage from Beethoven's Seventh Symphony (first movement, measures 88–96). This effective but high passage was scored for natural horns in A; here it is transposed to F.

The vertical sonorities created are typical of writing for natural horns. Many musicians refer to this type of passage as being written in "horn fifths" due to the unique but correct voice leading to and from the one perfect fifth that is produced. To capture this characteristic eighteenth- and early nineteenth-century horn sound, the following intervallic successions should be used, transposed into the key of the music:

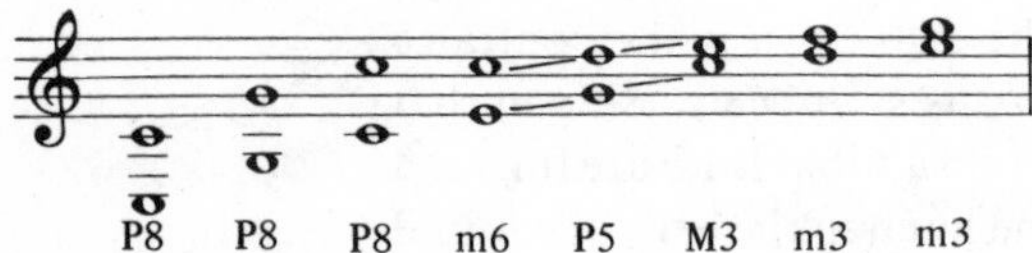

EXAMPLE 172 The usual intervals used with natural horns, notated as though in C major.

The second movement of Tchaikovsky's Fifth Symphony features one of the most famous of all horn solos:

EXAMPLE 173 Andante cantabile solo from Tchaikovsky's Fifth Symphony (second movement, measures 8–12).

In the third movement of Brahms's Third Symphony, the following horn passage is found. The horn is heard prominently, although it is doubled in the oboe at the octave above and in the flute two octaves above. (The excerpt is from the pickup to rehearsal letter B.)

EXAMPLE 174 Lyrical horn line from Brahms's Third Symphony.

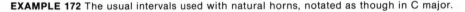

The Overture to *Semiramide* by Rossini opens with this horn quartet. Notice the interlocked voicing and division of responsibilities between high and low horns. It is typical of horn voicing.

EXAMPLE 175 Horn Quartet writing by Rossini, from *Semiramide* Overture.

This passage, which starts with a solo by the third horn and builds up until the full section is playing, is from Richard Strauss's *Till Eulenspiegel's Merry Pranks.* The high notes in this example are easy to obtain due to the unison and octave doublings. Since the composer expects this to be heard through the full orchestra, he has doubled the final gesture at the octave. This is a good scoring practice when one wishes the horns to be heard.

EXAMPLE 176 From R. Strauss's *Till Eulenspiegel* (beginning at rehearsal number 29).

This passage from Jan Bach's *Four 2-Bit Contraptions* for flute and horn shows the possible agility and flexibility one could require of the horn. It is a difficult passage, one that many good horn players would find challenging to execute up to tempo. The excerpt is from the beginning of the second movement, "Calliope."

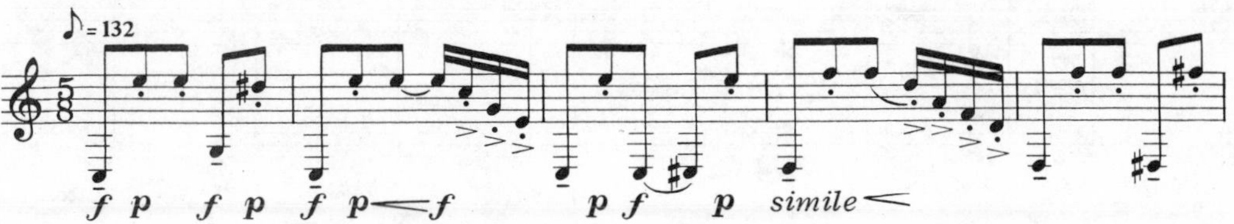

EXAMPLE 177 An example of horn agility from Jan Bach's *Four 2-Bit Contraptions.*[5]

One of the works that calls for Wagner tubas is Bruckner's Seventh Symphony. Here, near the beginning of the second movement, one can hear a quartet of two B♭ tenors and two F basses. The instruments are played by the fifth, sixth, seventh, and eighth hornists.

Adagio ♪ = 63
Tenors in B♭ I II
p cresc.
dim.
Basses in F I II
p cresc.
dim.

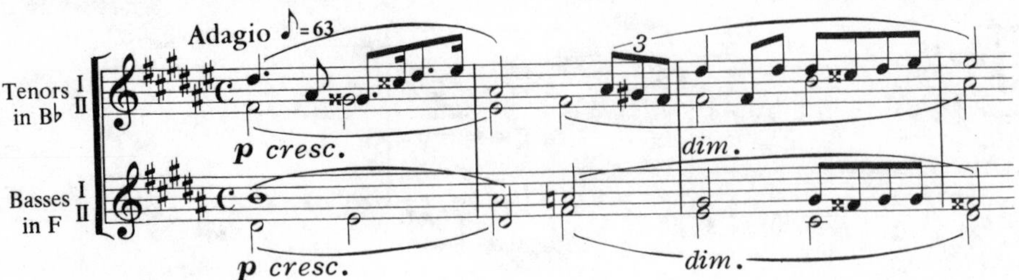

EXAMPLE 178 Beginning of the second movement of Bruckner's Seventh Symphony.

Problem Set No. 15

1. Score "Dolly's Funeral" by Tchaikovsky for horn quartet. In keeping with the mock tragedy of the piece, use muted and stopped horn devices. Be sure to voice the horns with first and third horns higher than second and fourth. Alternate the melodic interest at least between first and third. If possible, have the result performed.

DOLLY'S FUNERAL

P. Tchaikovsky. Op. 39

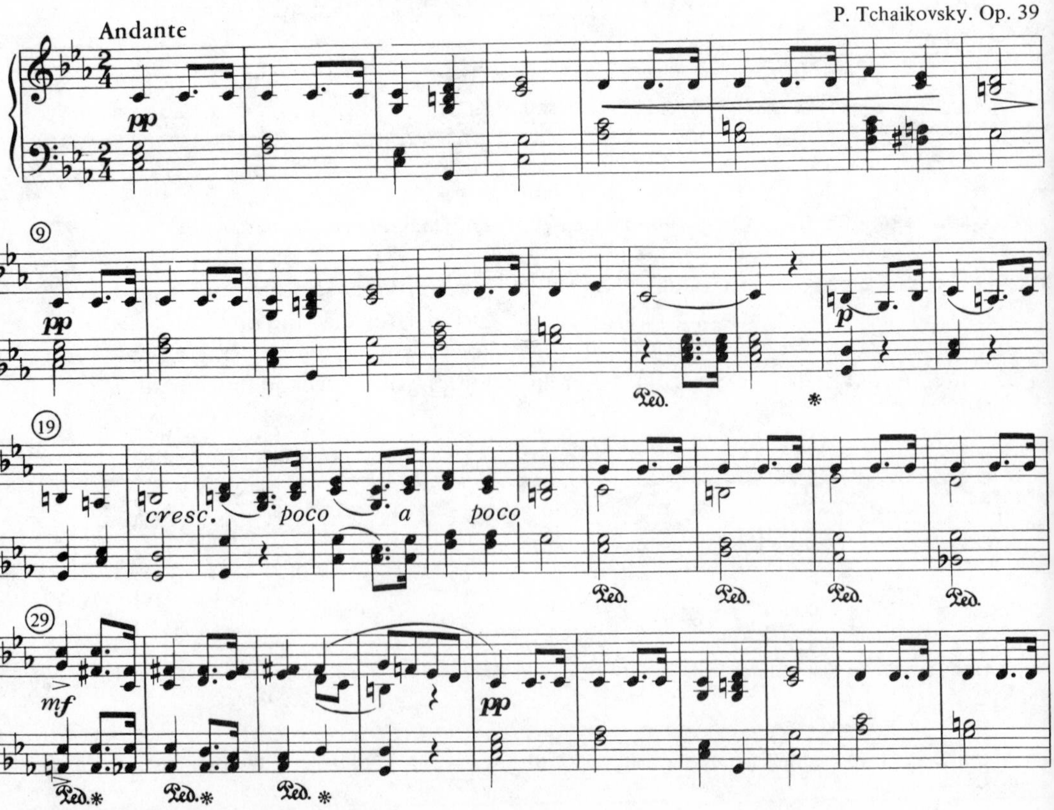

Andante
pp
9
pp
p
19
cresc.
poco
a
poco
29
mf
pp

2. Score this Beethoven sonata movement for solo horn. Transpose the top line down an octave, assign it to the horn, and give the remaining notes to the piano as an accompaniment. Have the piece performed.

L. Van Beethoven

Allegretto

p

7

mf

14

cresc.

dim.

21

p

28

p

34

3. Write a second horn part for this first horn part using "horn fifths" (see Example 172). Have two horns play the result. What harmonic progression is implied by these two lines?

4. Write a short passage of about 12 to 20 measures in length in which various horn devices such as muted and stopped horn, lip trills, glissandos, air sounds, etc. are used exclusively. Have your composition performed if at all possible.

HORN BIBLIOGRAPHY

Farkas, Philip. *The Art of French Horn Playing.* Evanston, Ill.: Summy-Birchard Co., 1956.

Franz, Oscar. *Complete Method for the Horn.* Transl. Gustav Saenger. New York: Carl Fischer, 1906.

Gregory, Rubin. *The Horn.* New York: Praeger, 1969.

Howe, Marvin C. *A Critical Survey of Literature, Materials, Opinions, and Practices Related to Teaching the French Horn.* Doctoral dissertation, University of Iowa. Ann Arbor, Mich.: University Microfilms, Inc., 1966.

Morley-Pegge, Reginald. *The French Horn.* London: E. Benn, 1960.

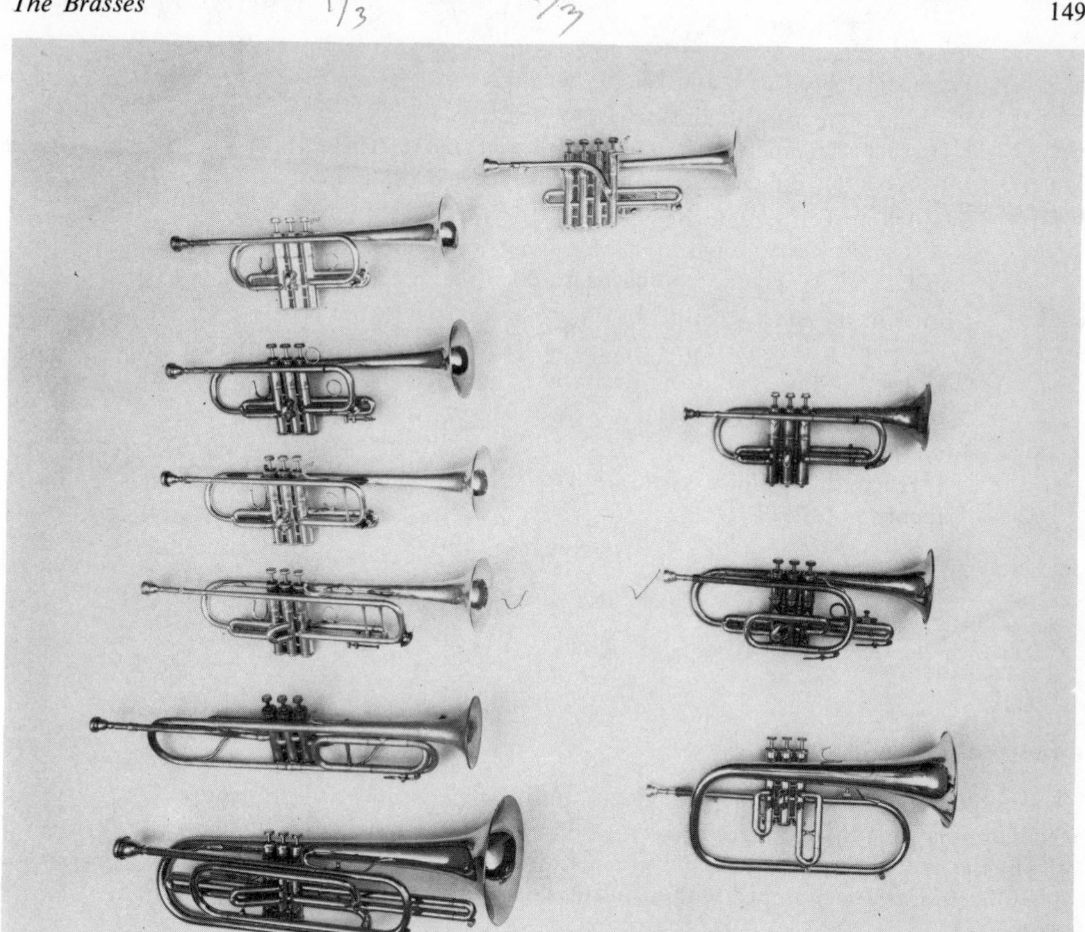

FIGURE 14. The trumpets, cornets, and flugelhorn: (*center top*) piccolo trumpet in B♭ or A; (*left, top to bottom*) E♭ trumpet, D trumpet, C trumpet, B♭ trumpet, E♭ bass trumpet, B♭ bass trumpet; (*Right, top to bottom*) E♭ cornet, B♭ cornet, B♭ flugelhorn. (Photo by David Hruby.)

THE TRUMPETS

	English	*French*	*German*	*Italian*
singular	trumpet (tpt.)	trompette (tromp.)	Trompete (Tr.)	tromba (tr.)
plural	trumpets (tpts.)	trompettes (tromp.)	Trompeten (Tr.)	trombe (tr.)

The Properties of the Trumpets

Trumpets, cornets, and flugelhorns are the soprano and alto members of the brass choir. These instruments are made in a variety of sizes including the following:

1. Trumpet in B♭, C, D, and E♭.
2. Piccolo trumpet in B♭ and A
   (French: trompette piccolo en Si♭ and La; German: Pikkolotrompete in B and A; Italian: tromba piccolo in Si♭ and La).
3. Bass trumpet in E♭ and B♭
   (French: trompette basse en Mi♭ and Si♭; German: Basstrompete in Es and B; Italian: tromba bassa in Mi♭ and Si♭).
4. Cornet in B♭ and E♭ (rare)
   (French: cornet or cornet à piston en Si♭ and en Mi♭; German: Kornett or Piston in B and Es; Italian: cornetta or cornetta a pistoni in Si♭ or Mi♭).
5. Flugelhorn in B♭
   (French: bugle a pistons en Si♭; German: Flügelhorn in B; Italian: flicorno in Si♭).

The most common written range of the trumpets is:

EXAMPLE 179 Range of the trumpet family.

The exceptions to this range include pitches up to an octave above those given, which are playable by many performers; availability of these pitches is limited only by the skill of the individual player. In addition, the piccolo trumpets and some flugelhorns are equipped with a fourth valve which allows the player to play these (written) lower notes: . Added to these exceptions is the possible performance of the low F by the use of movable tuning slides (available on professional-quality three-valve trumpets and cornets and the performance of pedal tones. These pedal tones, written are possible on all trumpets. (Some performers have developed the ability to produce subpedals, which are an octave below the pedals shown above.) Pedal tones are easier to perform on the high-pitched trumpets and the flugelhorns.

The ranges for these various trumpets, cornets, and flugelhorns are as follows:

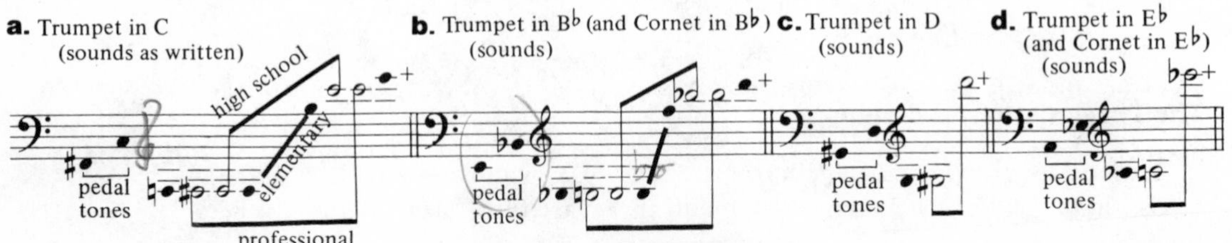

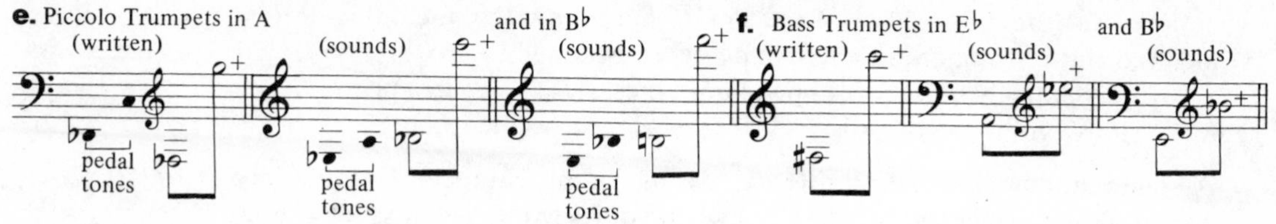

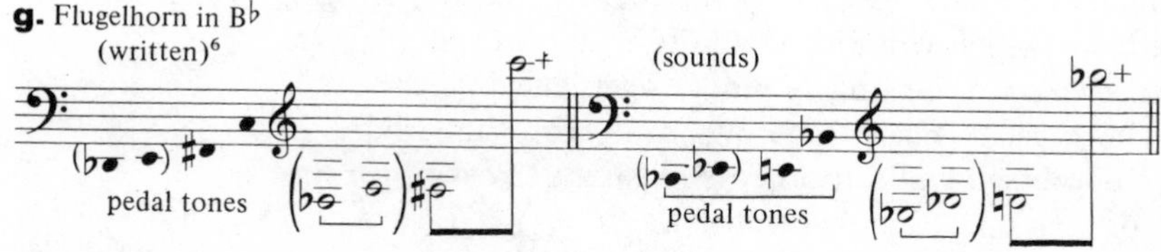

EXAMPLE 180 The written ranges, sounding ranges, and transpositions of the trumpets. a. Trumpet in C; sounds as written. b. Trumpet in B♭ (and cornet in B♭); sounds a whole step lower than written. c. Trumpet in D; sounds a whole step higher than written. d. Trumpet in E♭ (and cornet in E♭); sounds a minor third higher than written. e. Piccolo trumpets in A and in B♭; sound a major sixth and a minor seventh higher than written. f. Bass trumpets in E♭ and B♭; sound a major sixth and a major ninth lower than written. g. Flugelhorn in B♭; sounds a whole step lower than written.

The trumpets have a natural dynamic curve, relative to the written range that looks like this:

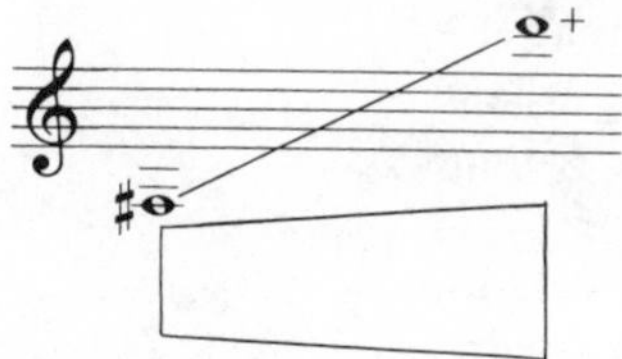

EXAMPLE 181 Dynamic curve for the trumpets.

The difference in power between the lower and higher notes is more a matter of the attention-getting quality inherent in the high notes on any brass instrument, when the physical effort required of the performer becomes evident to the listener. The trumpet has the ability to command attention in any range and can carry through any texture.

Traditionally, trumpets were cylindrical-bore brass instruments from the mouthpiece on for only two-thirds of the length, while the last third of the tubing leading to the bell was conical. Current designs produce an instrument with a conical bore for the first and last third of its length, while the middle third is cylindrical. The tone of the trumpets is bright, penetrating and clear.

Trumpet players have long considered the acquisition of dazzling technique to be an important aspect of their training and, consequently, the trumpets are as a class the most agile of the brasses. This agility is manifest in all aspects of performance, especially the fingering of rapid passages, the flexibility shown in

[6]Notes in parentheses available on four-valve models only.

wide leaps, ascending or descending, and in rapid tonguing, including double, triple, and flutter tonguings. This highly developed technical prowess is facilitated by the relatively shallow, cupped mouthpieces; the light, fast piston valves; and the short tubing.

All major and minor second trills are possible on the trumpets. Tremolos of a minor third and larger are not easy to execute quickly but are possible if both pitches can be played with the same fingering or with two closely related fingerings (i.e., fingerings in which only one finger moves between the two fingerings). Other, easy fingering patterns which will also facilitate trills and tremolos are those fingerings in which two or more fingers move together while the other finger(s) remain fixed. The most difficult fingerings are "cross fingerings" in which one finger must be depressed while another is released. Cross fingerings limit the speed of a trill or tremolo. (See Appendix V.)

All slurs are possible on the trumpets, with those greater than an octave ascending and those greater than a sixth descending being particularly challenging. Upward slurs are relatively difficult while downward slurs and leaps are more natural.

Solo writing for the trumpet is very straightforward. Almost any conceivable line that lies within the range of the instrument is playable by a good performer. Although difficult, even *pianissimo* entrances on higher pitches may be called for and executed. In general, lines that lie well and are easily performed will be those that move stepwise or which contain intervals found in the natural overtone series. (See Appendix VI.)

Writing for two or more trumpets presents no special problems. Lines that employ good voice leading, and which lie well for the trumpets individually, will work well together. Closely spaced dissonances between two trumpets are especially biting at dynamics of *mezzo-forte* and louder. However, three trumpets or more playing closely spaced dissonances actually provide less bite.

The trumpet is noted for its brilliant and commanding voice which can dominate an orchestra or band. But, it also possesses a delicate *pianissimo* which is very usable.

B♭, C, D, and E♭ Trumpets

The B♭ trumpet is the standard instrument in both the band and the orchestra. One will usually encounter the C trumpet only in professional situations. The differences between the two lie mainly in the slightly more brilliant sound of the C trumpet and considerations having to do with fingering problems, ease of transposition, or response of specific pitches. The choice between these two instruments is made by the performer.

The D and E♭ trumpets, although sometimes selected by the performer to facilitate a certain passage, are more often specified by the composer or orchestrator. These are both brighter, less mellow instruments than the B♭ or C trumpets. One would use either of these smaller instruments to obtain greater ease of performance and a little more edge to the sound in the upper registers. These trumpets have very clear, clean tones. The selection of the E♭ over the D (or vice versa) would be determined by technical concerns.

A or B♭ Piccolo Trumpets

These are really a single instrument equipped with an adjustable leadpipe which, when extended, tunes the trumpet to A, and when pushed in, tunes it to B♭. The piccolo trumpet has a smaller, more compact sound than the E♭ or D trumpets. When played at moderate or soft dynamics it becomes almost flute-like; at louder dynamics it can be strident and even shrill. Originally intended to facilitate performance of works such as Bach's Second Brandenburg Concerto, the piccolo trumpets also find use in making some extended high passages easier to endure for the performer, and as a unique instrument in its own right.

E♭ and B♭ Bass Trumpets

These rare instruments are only seldom called for in standard literature.[7] The E♭ bass trumpet (sometimes called an alto trumpet) is pitched a perfect fifth below the B♭ trumpet. It has a duller sound than the B♭ or C trumpet and a little less agility. Stravinsky calls for this instrument in *The Rite of Spring*. The B♭ bass trumpet, pitched an octave below the regular B♭ trumpet, is dark and possesses a full, sonorous quality.

B♭ and E♭ Cornets

The cornet is a compromise instrument, being constructed in such a manner as to be in between the trumpet and the soprano saxhorn (flugelhorn) in design and tone. In contrast to the traditional trumpet, the traditional cornet had the first third of its tubing cylindrical and the last two-thirds conical. Modern cornets have the same apportionment of cylindrical and conical tubing as the trumpet, but with a slightly smaller bore and a shallower and tubbier bell. The cornet is more mellow than the trumpet in tone and is well adapted to the performance of lyrical, though often technically brilliant, lines. Long a mainstay of the military, and now the concert band, the cornet has also found use in orchestral music.

Nineteenth-century composers, especially French composers, often called for a pair of cornets along with a pair of trumpets in their orchestral scores. Although this offered a timbre contrast that was exploited to a limited extent, the main value of these valved cornets was to provide pitches not available on the natural trumpets. Valves were applied to cornets for use in military bands long before valves were applied to the trumpet.

The small E♭ cornet is now rare, usually being found only in large Salvation Army bands. It is pitched a perfect fourth above the B♭ cornet with which most Americans are more familiar.

Flugelhorns

The flugelhorn (or soprano saxhorn) is a valved descendant from the old keyed bugle. This instrument is, except for the short portion of tubing that is found within the valve mechanism, a purely conical-bore brass. It is quite mellow and dark in tone, having more of the quality of a horn than of a trumpet.

Pitched in B♭ and therefore possessing the same range as the B♭ cornet or B♭ trumpet, the flugelhorn has been rediscovered by modern jazz musicians. Interest in these mellow, high brasses is also shown by composers and orchestrators who seem pleased to have an alternative to the trumpet tone for special effects. Some models of the flugelhorn are equipped with a fourth valve, greatly expanding their usuable range.

[7]These instruments, when called for, are usually played by trombone or euphonium players.

Other Members of the Family

In addition to the trumpets discussed above, there are F and G trumpets that sound a perfect fourth and perfect fifth, respectively, above notated pitch, and an A trumpet that sounds a minor second below the B♭ trumpet. Bass trumpets have been built in E, D, and low C, sounding a minor sixth, minor seventh, and octave lower than written. Cornets have been built in A and C sounding a minor third below written pitch and at written pitch. A soprano flugelhorn in E♭, sounding a minor third higher than written, was used as a soprano voice in American bands from around the time of the Civil War (even though the parts called for "cornets"). One can also find alto flugelhorns pitched in E♭ (which are bell-front, trumpet-shaped alto horns; see page 143). Some European sources indicate the existance at one time of a flugelhorn in C.

Trumpets, cornets, and flugelhorns have probably been built in every possible key. However, all but the most common of these must be considered very rare musical curiosities.

Typical Trumpet, Cornet, and Flugelhorn Scorings

A very typical trumpet solo is this excerpt from Ravel's orchestration of Moussorgsky's *Pictures at an Exhibition.* In the opening "Promenade," an unaccompanied C trumpet plays the first two measures and is joined in the third and fourth measures by a wind tutti. This is the solo trumpet line:

EXAMPLE 182 Opening trumpet solo from Ravel's scoring of *Pictures at an Exhibition.*[8]

An equally dramatic beginning is provided for Mahler's Fifth Symphony. Again, a solo trumpet starts the piece. The rest of the ensemble joins in measure 12 on the second half note. This is written for trumpet in B♭.

EXAMPLE 183 Opening of Mahler's Fifth Symphony.

[8]Copyright 1929 by Edition Russe de Musique; Renewed 1956. Copyright and Renewal assigned to Boosey & Hawkes, Inc. Reprinted by permission.

In an unusual scoring, Tchaikovsky wrote this passage for two trumpets in unison in his Sixth Symphony. At the climax of the martial third movement, the two trumpets in A become the dominant forces in the orchestra. (This example begins in measure 214.)

EXAMPLE 184 From Tchaikovsky's Sixth Symphony, third movement: two trumpets in unison.

From *Scheherazade* by Rimsky-Korsakov comes this illustration of rapid tonguing for a pair of A trumpets. The tempo is fast and the articulation is usually a combination of triple and double tonguing. (The excerpt is from measures 568-573 of the fourth movement.)

EXAMPLE 185 An illustration of rapid tonguing, characteristic of the trumpets, from Rimsky-Korsakov's *Scheherazade.*

In *Polyphony,* a work for solo trumpet, Charles Whittenberg writes the following passage which includes half-valve notes, wide leaps, extremes of range and dynamics, and flutter tonguing, all of which is very idiomatic for the instrument.

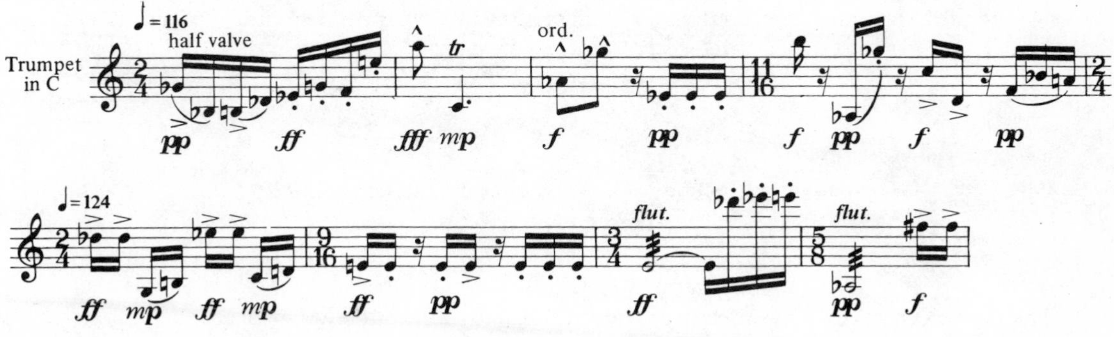

EXAMPLE 186 Excerpt from Whittenberg's *Polyphony* for solo trumpet[9] in C (measures 67–74).

[9]Copyright © 1970 by Josef Marx, McGinnis & Marx Music Publishers, 201 West 86th Street, New York City 10024. Used by permission.

This famous trumpet part from the Second Brandenburg Concerto by Bach is written for a high F trumpet, sounding a perfect fourth higher than written, but it is usually performed on the piccolo trumpet. Execution of the trumpet part from this piece, even on the high piccolo trumpet, is still very difficult, due to the high tessitura.

EXAMPLE 187 Trumpet passage from the first movement of Bach's Second Brandenburg Concerto (measures 26–34).

In *The Rite of Spring,* Stravinsky has written this passage for two C trumpets and an E♭ bass trumpet, all muted and scored entirely in octaves. The bass trumpet will need to be equipped with an extendable tuning slide or a fourth valve in order to play the low F natural. Other possibilities include the use of a bass trumpet pitched in D or lower. (The excerpt begins at rehearsal number 132.)

EXAMPLE 188 Trumpet ensemble in octave unison from Stravinsky's *Rite of Spring.*[10]

The next example displays the virtuosity traditionally associated with cornet playing. This is from Stravinsky's *Petrushka* (beginning the fourth measure after rehearsal number 69).

EXAMPLE 189 B♭ cornet solo from *Petrushka.*[11] (This passage is often performed on the trumpet.)

In Holst's First Suite in E♭ for Band, the cornet is featured in this lyrical solo from the second movement. It, too, is for B♭ cornet. (The excerpt begins in measure 3 of the Intermezzo.)

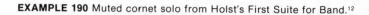

EXAMPLE 190 Muted cornet solo from Holst's First Suite for Band.[12]

In *Lincolnshire Posy,* Percy Grainger calls for a solo flugelhorn to play the main theme of "Rufford Park Poachers." (The solo begins in measure 18 of the third movement.)

EXAMPLE 191 Flugelhorn solo by Grainger.[13]

Problem Set No. 16

1. Score the Beethoven sonata movement in exercise 2 of Problem Set No. 15 (page 147) for solo cornet, flugelhorn, or trumpet. Leave the solo line in the original octave and assign all of the other notes to the piano. If possible, have the piece performed in turn by a B♭ or C trumpet, by a cornet, and by a flugelhorn.

2. Score this excerpt from Lasso's *Penitential Psalm No. 6* for two B♭ trumpets and an E♭ trumpet (or A or B♭ piccolo trumpet if available). Transpose all three parts up an octave for the setting.

3. Rescore Tchaikovsky's "Dolly's Funeral" from exercise 1 of Problem Set No. 15 (page 146) for four horns and two B♭ trumpets. Alternate the two trumpets with the leading horn lines to obtain more varied timbres and effects. Use some mutes on the trumpets as you see fit. (However, do not forget proper horn voicings.) Perform the completed work.

4. Compose a duet for one horn and one trumpet in which many of the contemporary special effects are utilized in both parts. Exploit contrasts as much as possible. Have the results performed, if possible.

TRUMPET BIBLIOGRAPHY

Bate, Philip. *The Trumpet and Trombone.* (2nd ed.) New York: W.W. Norton, 1978.

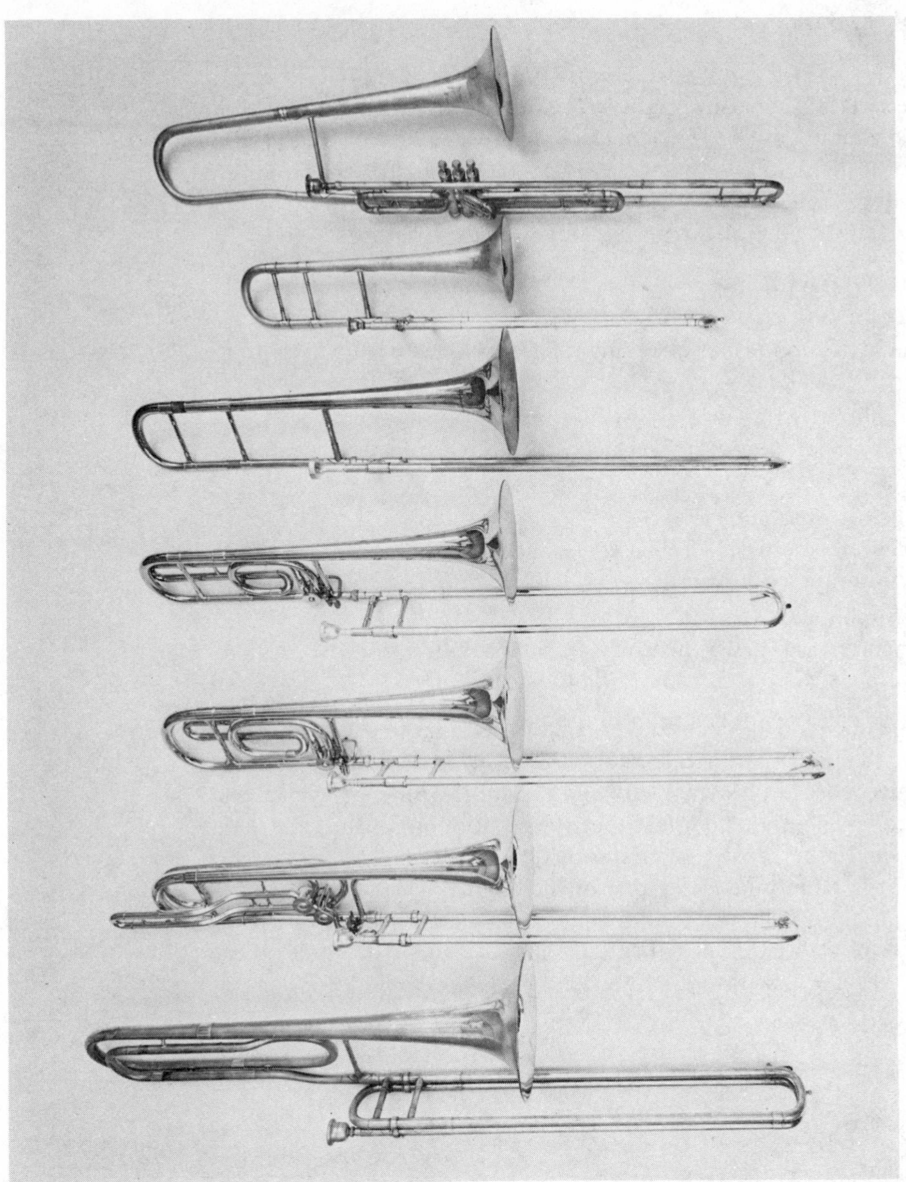

FIGURE 15 The trombones: (*top to bottom*) valve trombone, alto trombone, tenor trombone, tenor trombone with F attachment, bass trombone with F attachment (only), bass trombone with F and E attachments, and contrabass trombone. (Photo by David Hruby.)

THE TROMBONES

	English	*French*	*German*	*Italian*
singular	trombone (trb.)	trombone (tromb.)	Posaune (Pos.)	trombone (tr-ne)
plural	trombones (trbs.)	trombones (tromb.)	Posaunen (Pos.)	tromboni (tr-ni)

The Properties of the Trombones

The trombone is a primarily cylindrical-bore brass instrument played with a cupped mouthpiece. It is the natural tenor voice in the brass choir and the only modern brass instrument that utilizes the movement of a slide for obtaining pitches other than those available from the overtone series of its basic pipe.

The first two-thirds of its length are cylindrical while the last third is conical, ending in a flaring bell. The five different instruments in the trombone family are:

1. Tenor trombone.
2. Bass trombone
   (French: trombone basse; German: Bassposaune; Italian: trombone basso).
3. Alto trombone
   (French: trombone alto; German: Altposaune; Italian: trombone contralto).
4. Contrabass trombone (rare)
   (French: trombone contrebasse; German: Kontrabassposaune; Italian: trombone contrabbasso).
5. Valve trombone
   (French: trombone à pistons; German: Ventilposaune; Italian: trombone a pistoni *or* trombone a macchina).

The most visible distinguishing characteristic of the trombone is its slide. By means of the slide the performer can lengthen the basic pipe of the instrument and thereby produce more pitches than would be available from the pipe were no means of changing the length available. Since the positioning of the slide is infinitely variable between its closed, or first, position and its most extended, or seventh, position, the trombone is capable of the most flawless intonation of any wind.

The trombones are all written at concert pitch. Therefore, they possess the following ranges, all of which sound as written:

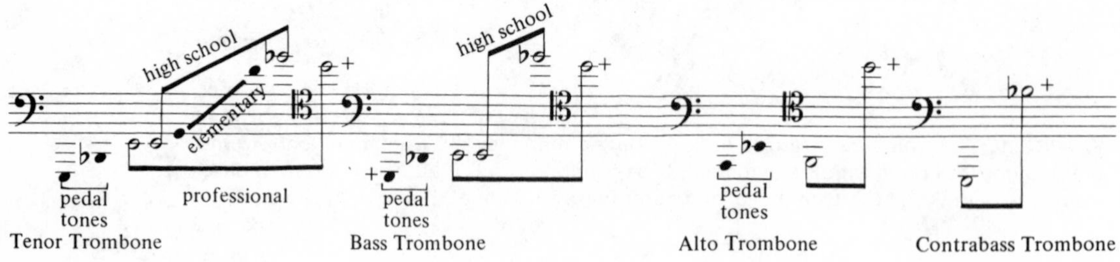

EXAMPLE 192 Trombone ranges.

The tenor trombone has the following dynamic curve:

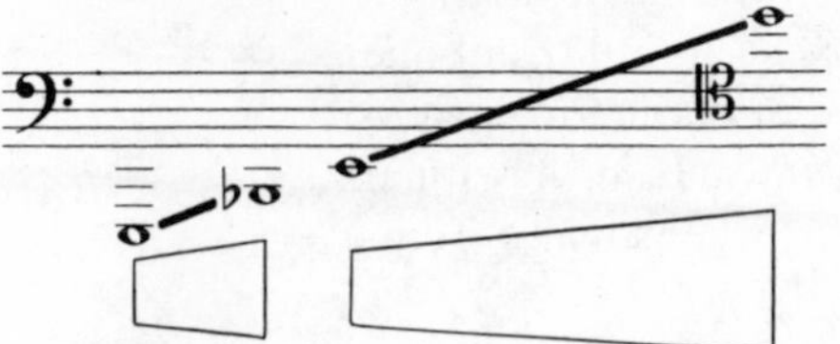

EXAMPLE 193 The dynamic curve of the tenor trombone.

Throughout its range, the dynamic curve of the trombone is very uniform. Thus, no matter how the trombones may be voiced, the balance is excellent. The pedal tones on the tenor are very strong on B♭ and A, becoming weaker at the lower pitches. The larger bore of the bass trombone makes the lower portion of the range stronger and the pedal tones retain good power, at least to F. The alto trombone is not as strong in its lowest register, but still remains usable throughout all registers.

The trombone possesses a very full, rich, and sonorous tone quality. In *pianissimo* passages, one or more trombones can provide a soft cushion of sound. At these softer dynamics, it is almost hornlike in its mellowness. In *fortissimo,* either in unison, octaves, or chords, the trombone is as assertive as the trumpet, but even more massive and powerful. Trombones played loudly are capable of being heard in any context.

The voicing of trombone passages does not present any significant problems to the composer or orchestrator, since trombones work well in any voicing. Chords in open or close voicing are good, as are unison or octave doubling of a line. The traditional usage of the trombones has been to perform sustained chords, which they do well. Trombones balance horns well, trumpets excellently, and also blend with all possible woodwind or woodwind and brass combinations. They provide a rich and secure tenor-bass voice that is often needed by an otherwise treble-dominated ensemble.

In the upper portion of the trombones' ranges dexterity is good, due to the existance of more alternative positions for various notes. In the lower portion of each range agility is somewhat limited, due to fewer alternative positions and greater slide movement between most notes.

The characteristic legato of the trombone is tongued legato (legato tonguing; pages 71 and 72), which is utilized to avoid glissandos when changing slide positions. A true (slurred) legato is also possible if the two notes to be connected are both played with the slide in the same position or if the slide movement from the first pitch to the second pitch is opposite to the direction of the pitch change (i.e. if the second pitch is lower than the first but played in a shorter slide position).

The trombone possesses an ability to respond to fast tonguing, including double and triple tonguing, and may be flutter tongued with ease. Within the limits of the slide speed, which is often faster than a non-trombonist might imagine, it is a responsive and flexible instrument.

In the nineteenth century orchestra, a familiar trombone section consisted of an alto, a tenor, and a bass trombone, scored in the alto, tenor, and bass clefs, respectively. In the modern orchestra and concert band, the trombone section is more likely to consist of two tenors and a bass trombone. In the band, the assignment of two or three performers to each part (i.e., six to nine trombonists) is common. The usual distribution of parts in a jazz band is three tenors and one bass trombone. Current practice is to use tenor and bass clef for all trombone parts, the only exceptions being that bass clef only is used in music for elementary or high school bands or orchestras and for jazz bands. In professional writing, the alto clef may be used for very high passages or when an alto trombone is specified.[14]

The Tenor Trombone

This is the mainstay of the trombone family. In non-professional situations it is not unusual to find tenor trombones assigned to all trombone parts. Typically, the small-bore tenor trombone has a fairly bright, rich tone quality that is admired for its clarity and focus. Many performers prefer a larger-bore tenor which possesses fullness of tone and good power. The large-bore instrument also is capable of a more mellow tone when needed.

In the upper portion of the range, from about B♭ upward, the tenor demonstrates good agility, due to the number of pitches in this range that have several alternative positions and because, from middle C upward, all notes can be played in the first three positions (I, II, or III.) (See Appendix V.) In the lower range, some passages may be impossible due to long slide travel between certain pitches. The following passage requires alternation between position I and VII —all the way in to all the way out—and thus cannot be performed rapidly:

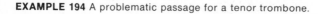

EXAMPLE 194 A problematic passage for a tenor trombone.

To improve agility and to add a few semitones to the lower portion of the trombone's range, many performers play a tenor trombone with an F attachment. This attachment provides, by means of a valve operated by the performers left thumb, an additional length of tubing that may be added to lower the fundamental from the first B♭ below the bass clef to the F below that. This provides more position alternatives throughout the range of the trombone. Thus Example 194, played on an instrument with an F attachment, could become an alternation between A♯ (III on the F) and B♮ (II on the F).

The extra tubing added to the tenor trombone when the F attachment is used increases the length of the basic pipe enough to require each semitone along the slide to be further out than the corresponding position when the F attachment is

[14]Two types of treble clef notation are sometimes found. One type merely uses treble clef for pitches too high for tenor clef; it is a non-transposing notation. Another type of notation, which is now obsolete, treats the tenor trombone as a transposing B♭ instrument, written a major ninth above sounding pitch in the treble clef. This notation was used by converted cornet or trumpet players playing valve trombones.

not used. Therefore, with the F attachment in operation, the performer has only six slide positions to use. This limits the downward range of the tenor with F attachment to the range given for the bass trombone. Notice that low B is not playable. To correct for this, an extra tuning slide is provided which the performer may draw before playing a low B to enable him to produce the pitch. This requires time and is not a very practical maneuver. As a general rule, one is better off avoiding low B naturals if possible.[15]

As a caution, since the use of the F trigger (valve) requires the left thumb, it is not possible to use a plunger, or hat mute, with the trigger unless some special device can be attached to allow the left hand to move to the bell and still operate the trigger.

The Bass Trombone

The normal American bass trombone is the same length as a tenor trombone with F attachment. Thus, it has the same range and limitations. But, it has a larger bore and possesses a darker, more sombre tone quality. The bell also is larger in diameter. The instrument is especially constructed to facilitate the performance of the pitches from [musical example] downward and to make the performance of the pedal tones more secure. Since it requires quite a bit of air, opportunities to breathe need to be planned into the part.

Because the performance of a low B natural is more likely to be asked of a bass trombone than a tenor, the inability to obtain this note readily is a real problem. Therefore, most professional bass trombonists have turned to a model with two valves controlled by the left thumb: a bass trombone with and F and an E (sometimes E♭) attachment. The second attachment provides the low B and also offers alternative positions in the lower register, where the bass trombone is most valued.

Unless one knows to the contrary, it is always wise to assume that the bass trombone will not have an E attachment (just as one must assume that the tenor will not have an F attachment) and to prepare parts accordingly (i.e., providing ossia passages).

The Alto Trombone

Once given up for lost, the alto trombone is making a modest comeback. This rise in popularity has been due to a renewed interest in older music written specifically for the alto trombone, to the interest shown by some contemporary composers in its lighter, sweeter sound, and to the relative ease it offers in the performance of some of the high nineteenth-century orchestral parts. It has a distinctive, delicate tone quality, and it blends well with all woodwinds, brasses, and voices. It lacks the imposing power and grandeur of the tenor and bass trombones, but within its register, it can easily hold its own. It possesses no special attachments, and therefore it does present technical problems in its lower register, below [musical example].

[15]It is possible to lip the pitch down to the B from the C, but this is not always an acceptable solution, due to the tone quality of the lipped pitch.

The Contrabass Trombone

The contrabass trombone has all the response and endurance problems of the bass trombone, magnified. It is often a single trombone, so that in its most effective range it has both the limitation of slide technique of the single tenor and the slow response associated with all long pipes. It is common to find tubas performing parts intended for the contrabass trombone. However, as a cylindrical brass, it is a unique bass sound, not replaceable by the tuba. Scored with care and an understanding of the performance problems, it is an effective and majestic voice not easily forgotten but not often available.

The Valve Trombone and the Trombonium

These are both tenor trombones in which the slide mechanism has been removed and a set of three piston valves added. The valves provide increased technical opportunities but bring with them a loss of intonation and remove the need for special legato articulations. This often causes the sound not to be perceived as trombone at all but more like a very brightly toned euphonium. The loss of the slide mechanism makes the characteristic glissando unavailable.[16]

Other Trombones

In addition to the instruments discussed above, there are slide trumpets, which are virtually soprano trombones, pitched an octave above the tenor, and the European-style bass trombone, which is an instrument without a trigger attachment and pitched in G or F. Because of the longer slide on these bass trombones, an extention or handle is attached to the slide and the performer moves the slide by means of this lever. Both of these instruments are rare in this country.

Typical Trombone Scorings

The solo tenor trombone in the upper register is a heroic and majestic voice. The trombone solo from the "Tuba Mirum" of Mozart's *Requiem* offers an excellent example of this use of the trombone. (The excerpt is from measures 8 to 12.)

EXAMPLE 195 Tenor trombone solo from Mozart's *Requiem.*

The following trio appears in the last movement of Brahms's First Symphony. It provides an example of the sort of ensemble scoring which is traditionally associated with the trombones. Listening to the passage will provide a good aural sense of trombone articulations. A study of the voicing will reveal that a variety of chord voicings are effective on trombones.

[16]A model of the valve trombone has been built that includes both a slide and the set of valves, but it is not commonly found.

EXAMPLE 196 A trombone chordal passage from Brahms's First Symphony.

The following trombone line, divided between two performers, is found in Mahler's Fifth Symphony (first movement, beginning at rehearsal number 17). Because of the overlapping of the two parts, one never hears a break in the line. (This *bell up* instruction is often understood to mean that the performer should stand up.)

EXAMPLE 197 One line divided between two trombones from Mahler's Fifth Symphony.

In *The Firebird,* Stravinsky makes use of the ability of the trombone to produce glissandos. In spite of the use of alto clefs, the composer assumes that both of the higher trombones are tenors and that the bass is equipped with an F attachment. (To see if you understand how the instruments function, try to figure out in which position each glissando begins and ends.) The excerpt is from the 1910 version.

EXAMPLE 198 The three trombones (beginning at rehearsal number 179) in *The Firebird.*

The trills in the seventh and eighth measures of the excerpt are lip trills. The trill in the second trombone will be played in position VI (F to G). The trill on the A may be in II or IV positions (A to B natural.) (See also page 127.)

An interesting example of contemporary writing for the trombone is the following passage from Morgan Powell's *Inacabado* for trombone unaccompanied. The X notes, circled or uncircled, are to be sung. If double stems are attached, they are to be both sung and played. The passage begins with a harmon mute in the bell, but with the stem removed. The small "dots" represent tapping the mute with the stem. (The excerpt is from the second and third systems of the piece.)

EXAMPLE 199 Excerpt from Powell's *Inacabado.*[17]

Problem Set No. 17

1. Score the Bach chorale harmonization of "Christ lag in Todesbanden" for four trombones: one alto, two tenors, and a bass. Transpose the chorale down a whole step. Write the alto in alto clef, one tenor in tenor clef, and the other tenor and the bass in bass clef. Have the chorale performed.

CHRIST LAG IN TODESBANDEN

J. S. Bach

2. Score "Dolly's Funeral" from exercise 1 of Problem Set No. 15 (page 146) for three tenor trombones and a bass trombone. Use at least a straight mute in one of the parts. Perform the result.

3. Score the Lasso excerpt from exercise 2 of Problem Set No. 16 (page 158) for three tenor trombones. Write all parts in the bass clef, sounding in the same octave as the original example.

4. Score the chorale given in exercise 1, above, for two B♭ trumpets and a tenor and a bass trombone. Leave it in the original key. Have the example performed.

5. Compose a short piece of about 16 to 20 measures for two trombones in which various special effects, mutes, and contemporary devices are used. Have your piece performed.

TROMBONE BIBLIOGRAPHY

Gregory, Robin. *The Trombone.* New York: Praeger, 1973.

Kleinhammer, Edward. *The Art of Trombone Playing.* Evanston, Ill.: Summy-Birchard, 1963.

(See also Trumpet Bibliography.)

FIGURE 16. The tubas: (*left to right*) BB♭ tuba, CC tuba, F tuba, tenor tuba. (*above right*) euphonium. (Photo by David Hruby.)

THE TUBAS

	English	*French*	*German*	*Italian*
singular	tuba (tu.)	tuba (tuba)	Basstuba (Btu. *or* Btb.)	tuba (tuba)
plural	tubas (tu.)	tubas (tubas)	Basstuben (Btu. *or* Btb.)	tube (tube)

The Properties of the Tubas

The name "tuba" is and has been applied to a variety of instruments. The modern tuba is a bass (or contrabass) saxhorn, possessing a conical bore. The instruments are made in various lengths and may differ greatly in terms of the actual bore used. Generally these instruments are used to provide the bass of the brass choir. Among the more commonly encountered tubas are these:

1. Tuba (contrabass) in B♭ and C
   (French: contrebasse à pistons, saxhorn contrebasse, *or* tuba; German: Kontrabasstuba *or* Tuba; Italian: tuba contrabbasso *or* tuba).

2. Tuba (bass) in F and (rare) E♭
   (French: tuba basse, contrebasse à pistons, *or* tuba; German: Basstuba *or* Tuba; Italian: tuba bassa *or* tuba).
3. Euphonium in B♭ and (rare) C
   (French: euphonium, euphonion, saxhorn tuba, tuba ténor, *or* basse à pistons; German: Euphonium, Baryton, *or* kleiner Bass; Italian: eufonio *or* flicorno basso).

The variety of names used in the various languages gives an insight into a problem that plagues scholars and musicians. There are similarities between names for dissimilar instruments, and often the same instrument will be called by many different names. Americans call a euphonium a *baritone,* while the English use the term *baritone* to refer to a tenor horn; the French call a Wagner tuba (see page 143) a *tuba ténor,* while also calling a euphonium a *tuba ténor,* and the Germans use *Tenor-Tuba* for the Wagner tuba only. Add to this the diversity of shapes, bores, and tunings found among various manufacturers, nationalities, and even regions and it is easy to see how much confusion there can be in discussing tubas. (In this book, current American terminology is used.)

Most tubas and euphoniums are equipped with four valves, either rotary or piston, and a few tubas have a fifth valve. Tubas are produced in three different shapes: upright, bell front, and helicon. Most professional models are upright. A few student models are bell front. The familiar Sousaphone seen in the marching band is the only modern version of the helicon design one is likely to encounter; it is a special variation of the helicon with a movable bell and very large proportions.[18]

Student model tubas, and this includes Sousaphones, are usually made with only three valves. The lack of the fourth valve reduces the range of the instrument and creates intonation problems in the lower register.

The written ranges for the tubas are as follows. (All tubas are concert pitched instruments that sound as written.)

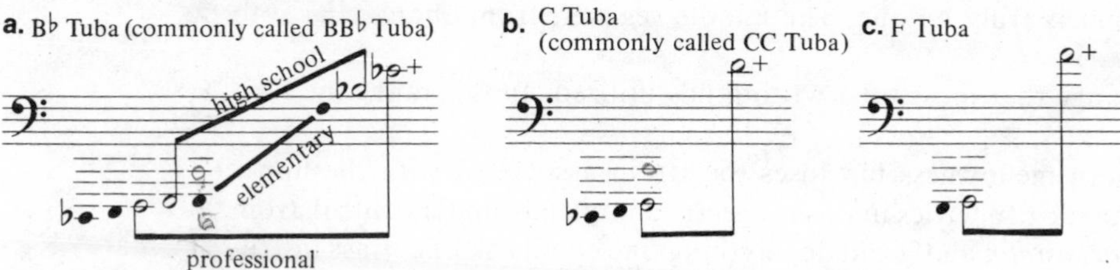

EXAMPLE 200 Tuba ranges.

[18]A helicon is a brass instrument that is shaped in a circle so that it may be carried over the shoulder and around the neck of the performer. Euphoniums and tenor horns have been made in the helicon shape, but these are usually only found in museums at this time.

In band scores and some orchestral scores one finds the B♭ euphonium part written in the treble clef. In these cases, the instrument is treated as a transposing instrument in B♭ and the parts are written a major ninth higher than sounding pitch. The more commonly accepted notation is to write the euphonium in the bass clef at sounding pitch. (Tenor clef may be used for very high pitches in professional situations.)

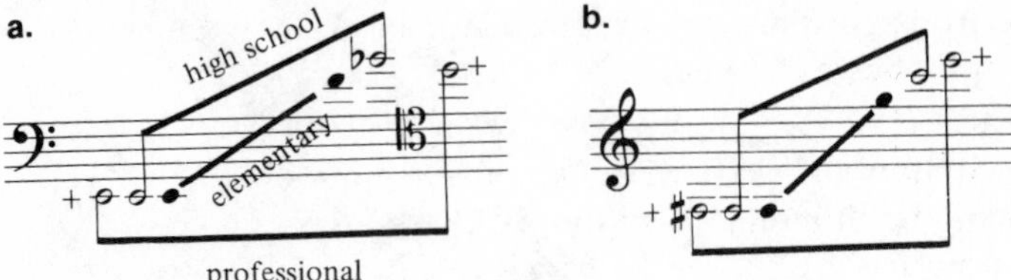

EXAMPLE 201 Range of B♭ euphonium. Two styles of notation: a. Bass clef; sounds as written. b. Treble clef; sounds a major ninth lower than written.

The tuba has a fairly uniform and balanced expressive quality throughout its range. As with all brasses the higher pitches are more difficult and possess a "strained" quality while the lower pitches are more flabby and lack some focus.

EXAMPLE 202 Dynamic curve for the tuba(s).

Nonetheless, the tuba is a very agile instrument that can single, double, triple and flutter tongue passages as rapidly as any of the brasses. The only limitation is the fact that it requires a lot of air, especially in the lower register and especially at louder dynamics: thus, the arranger needs to provide ample opportunities to breathe.[19]

In the upper register, above the tuba has, at medium and soft dynamics, a smooth hornlike quality, but with more ability to cut through the texture than the horn does. At *fortissimo* dynamics, the tuba has a power and richness in this range that is truly unique. The middle register, from about to is the range that most tuba writing has utilized. In this range the tuba retains its smooth mellowness but loses the strain associated with the upper register. Its dynamic properties in this range are completely under control, from *pianissimo* to *fortissimo,* and it can do anything one could ask of a brass instrument, from slipping into the texture unnoticed to totally dominating a full orchestra or band *tutti.*

[19]Some wind players, especially tubists, have developed the ability to circular-breathe. The technique calls for the inhaling of air through the nose while sustaining the tone by the use of air stored in the performer's cheeks. By this method a tone may be sustained for several minutes without an interruption. The number of performers who do this, however, is limited.

In its lowest register, below [music notation], the tuba loses some of its agility and cleanliness, due to the greater inertia associated with a long air column and slow vibrations. One should not expect great fluidity in this lowest range of the tuba, but it is still the most clear-pitched and dynamically varied bass voice of the band or orchestra.

In theory, these pitches are available on professional model tubas [music notation]. However, not all performers can produce them, or may not be able to produce them in a manner that they find satisfactory. If these tones are available at all, they are best approached stepwise, or, if approached by leap, should be within *tempo rubato ad libitum.*

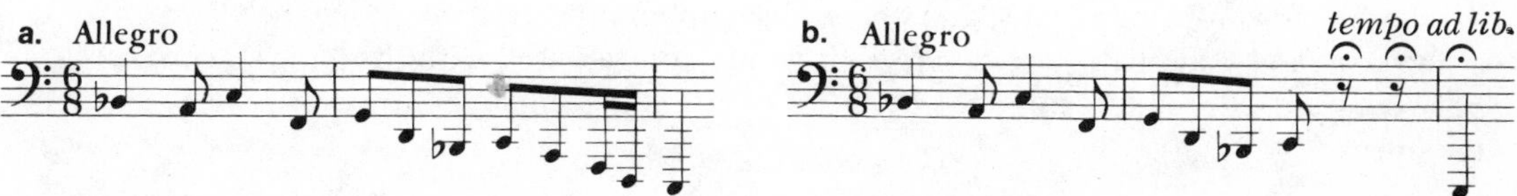

EXAMPLE 203 a. An almost impossible approach to contra C. b. A playable passage using contra C.

In writing for the tuba, one should always use ledger lines for the low notes. Do not write the part an octave higher than it is to sound and ask the performer to play it in the lower octave. The tubist is accustomed to reading the ledger lines and is not accustomed to changing octaves.

The composer need not specify the tuba on which a given part is to be performed. The choice of instrument is usually a decision made by the performer. The CC tuba and the F tuba can play the same pitches, so the choice will be made on the basis of tone quality differences relative to the hall, tessitura, ease of fingering certain passages, or blend with other instruments. All other criteria being equal, the F tuba is a bit brighter in quality than the CC, but seldom is this subtle difference of sufficient audibility to be of concern to the composer.

The tubas may be scored for in a variety of ways, although the traditional usage of the instrument—playing the bass line or doubling the bass line an octave lower than the general pitch level—is still dependable. The tuba is a mellow, smooth, and potentially powerful solo voice throughout the bass and tenor ranges. The use of more than one tuba is rare, but these instruments blend well with each other and the ensemble achieved by two or more tubas is excellent. However, when writing in the lowest octave for two tubas together, avoid intervals between the tubas of less than a fifth or sixth, except for special effects.

The Euphonium

In the United States, the names *baritone horn* and *euphonium* have been used interchangeably for the same instrument. At one time there was an instrument called a tenor horn, one variety of which was pitched in B♭ like the euphonium, but possessing a small bore. There was also a large-bore instrument of the same pitch called a *baritone* or *bass horn.* Since these are obviously related to the tuba family, the name *tenor tuba* has been used, although the latter term, in this country, is usually applied to an instrument of the same pitch with a *very* large bore and a much darker sound (see Figure 16 page 168). Over the years, elements of the old baritone and old tenor horns have gradually merged into an instrument now usually called a *euphonium*.

The euphonium is more agile and flexible than the tuba, requires less air, and can negotiate its lowest register with ease. It is a noble and sonorous instrument that has proven its value in the modern band even though its use in the orchestra is rare (an omission that, may in part be due to the confusion in names discussed earlier).

The combination of euphonium and tuba is commonly heard in bands, brass sextets, and brass choirs. Traditionally, the two instruments are used together as a bass line, with the tuba and the euphonium playing the same material in octaves. At other times, the euphonium may provide a tenor voice to the ensemble. A quartet of two or three tubas, and one or two euphoniums could certainly be a powerful and majestic brass section that would contrast well with the trombone choir and, depending upon the dynamic level, either blend or contrast with the horns.

Typical Tuba Scorings

Near the beginning of the third movement of Mahler's First Symphony, one of the presentations of the canon theme is assigned to the tuba. (The excerpt begins 7 measures after rehearsal number 2.) The general range of the passage indicates that it would work well for F tuba.

EXAMPLE 204 Melodic writing for the tuba from Mahler's First Symphony.

This passage for two tubas from Richard Strauss's tone poem *Also Sprach Zarathustra* demonstrates some of the tuba's agility. (It begins at rehearsal number 10.)

EXAMPLE 205 Writing for two tubas from *Also Sprach Zarathustra.*

A well-known example of solo tuba writing occurs in Wagner's Prelude to *Die Meistersinger.* Beginning 9 measures after rehearsal letter J, the tuba carries an important line of the counterpoint which culminates in the famous tuba trill.

EXAMPLE 206 Famous tuba line from *Die Meistersinger.*

This rather high solo from Stravinsky's *Petrushka* is intended to evoke the image of a bear dancing and therefore is most effective when played on one of the larger instruments. (The excerpt is from the third measure after rehearsal number 100 in the fourth tableau.)

EXAMPLE 207 Very high tuba passage from *Petrushka.*[20]

This solo from Ravel's scoring of Moussorgsky's *Pictures at an Exhibition* is from the "Ox Cart" movement. It is often performed on the euphonium instead of the CC or the F tuba.

EXAMPLE 208 Tuba solo from Ravel's scoring of *Pictures at an Exhibition.*[21]

In *Midnight Realities* for tuba unaccompanied by Morgan Powell, the performer is asked to sing and play simultaneously. The notation system uses X's or ◇'s for sung pitches, while a stem down from an X indicates to play and sing the note at the same time. (The excerpt consists of the last two systems of the piece.)

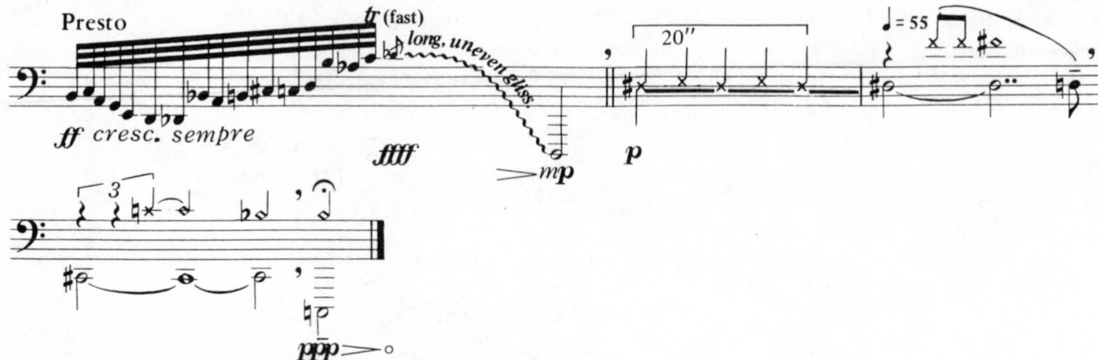

EXAMPLE 209 *Midnight Realities* by Morgan Powell.[22]

In Gordon Jacob's arrangement of the *Giles Farnaby Suite* for band, this euphonium solo is featured in the seventh section, "Tell Mee, Daphne," beginning at rehearsal letter B.

EXAMPLE 210 A euphonium solo by Gordon Jacob.[23]

Two euphoniums are called for in Schönberg's *Theme and Variations* for band, Opus 43a. This important duet begins in measure 62 of variation II.

EXAMPLE 211 Writing for two euphoniums by Schönberg.[24]

Problem Set No. 18

1. Score the Bach harmonization of "Christ lag in Todesbanden" given in exercise 1 of Problem Set No. 17 (page 166) for two euphoniums and two tubas. Transpose the original down a major third for your setting. Have the result played.
2. Score "Dolly's Funeral" from exercise 1 of Problem Set No. 15 (page 146) for two trumpets, two horns, two trombones, and a tuba. Use various mutes, special effects or other devices. Have the piece performed.
3. Score "A Little Hunting Song" from exercise 1 of Problem Set No. 12 (page 108) for two trumpets, one horn, one trombone, and a tuba. Double lines, change octaves, and use mutes as you desire. Have a brass quintet perform the completed work.
4. Write a duet for tuba and euphonium that uses multiphonics and other contemporary effect and devices. Have the duet performed.
5. Using as many mutes as are available and a wide variety of special effects, compose a short work for trumpet, horn, trombone, and tuba. Prepare a score and parts and have the piece performed.

TUBA BIBLIOGRAPHY

Bevan, Clifford. *The Tuba Family.* New York: Scribner, 1978.

BRASS BIBLIOGRAPHY

Benade, Arthur H. "The Physics of Brasses," *Scientific American,* Vol. 229, no. 1 (July 1973), pp. 24ff.

(See also Woodwind Bibliography, page 82.)

5

INSTRUMENTATION: *The Percussion*

GENERAL PERCUSSION INFORMATION

Percussion instruments are traditionally defined as those instruments that produce a sound when struck or shaken. However, composers have regularly assigned the production of additional special sound effects to percussionists and percussion performers have gradually added more types of sounds and production methods to their repertoire so that it is now difficult to define percussion exactly. Percussionists may be called upon to blow a whistle, crank a siren, bow a cymbal, turn on a tape player, or break glass, in addition to the traditional methods of producing sounds.

The Basic Percussion Strokes

The basic sound producing gesture in percussion music is the single stroke. This consists simply of striking a sound-producing object once with something capable of setting the object into vibration. By various combinations of these single strokes, a set of common "stickings" may be assembled:

English	*French*	*German*	*Italian*
single stroke	coup simple	einfacher Schlag	colpo singolo
flam	"flam"	einfacher Vorschlag	colpo preceduto da acciaccatura
drag	"drag"	Doppelter Vorschlag	gruppetto di due note
ruff	"ruff"	dreifacher Vorschlag	ruff or rullo
open roll	roulement ouvert	offener Wirbel	rullo rimbalzato
closed roll *or* buzz roll *or* crush roll	roulement fermé	dichter Wirbel	rullo stretto

The *flam* is a rapid combination of two single strokes, one played by each hand. The notation is:

The *drag* is a rapid combination of three strokes, notated like this:  and usually played either *right-right-left* or *left-left-right* (abbreviated R-R-L and L-L-R). Rapid double strokes as used in the drag may lack rhythmic clarity and precision at faster tempos. At slower speeds, and in certain contexts where effect is more important than accuracy, double strokes are no problem.

The *three-stroke ruff* is notated this way:  and is usually performed R-L-R or L-R-L.[1]

Some percussionists define a *ruff* as consisting of three or more strokes, while others define a ruff as consisting of four or more strokes. The typical notation for four or more strokes would be:  = a four-stroke ruff;  = a five-stroke ruff. Typical performance would be L-R-L-R and R-L-R-L-R, respectively, or the reverse. Ruffs are generally considered to be too rapid for double strokes, but there are some excellent performers who use R-L-L-R sticking with good effect.

The *roll* is a controlled alternation of sticks or hands, which produces the effect of a continuous sound. There are two types of rolls used by percussionists: the first type is called the *open roll.* It is produced by using the muscular control in the wrists of the percussionist to control and limit the rebound of the sticks to one per stroke. The second type of roll is the *closed, buzz,* or *crush roll,* which involves letting the sticks achieve a natural multiple bounce off the struck surface. The speed of the bounce and the concomitant return to the surface for another stroke is related both to the loudness and the grip of the hands on the sticks. As with other percussion strokes, the speed and amount of rebound is also affected by the resiliency of the struck surface and the natural springiness of the sticks used. During a closed roll, at least two bounces will be produced per stroke to achieve the effect of a continuous sound. Normally, composers have not specified the type of roll desired and the choice has been left to the performers. The notation for either type of roll is or or 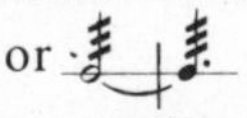 , etc., depending on the time value. (The number of slashes through the note stem or over the head should be enough to guarantee an unmeasured rhythmic figure. Usually three slashes is enough. At slower tempos when three slashes could be realized as perceivable thirty-second notes, four slashes would be better.)

Ending the Roll

If one wishes to hear a clear, accented stop on the end of a roll (a final, single stroke), then this notation should be used: $\frac{4}{4}$. If on the other hand, one wishes the roll simply to end, with no accented stop, then this notation is to be used: $\frac{4}{4}$ or  .[2] With no accent indicated, there will be

[1] Many composers and performers make no distinction between a drag and a three-stroke ruff; therefore, the double sticking of the drag may be used in the ruff.

[2] Rudimental drummers will end every roll, no matter what notation is used, with a clear, stop stroke, and the only kind of roll they will play is an open roll. This style of drumming, once the norm, is dying out.

very little space between the rolls and very little articulation at the beginning of each. Accents 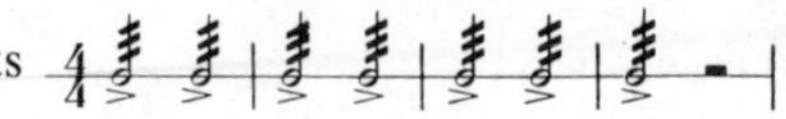 would call for more space and more articulation.

In older music a trill sign was used to indicate a roll. This symbol should *never* be used for this purpose, since it is possible to play trills on many percussion instruments, and therefore the trill sign should be reserved for such use.

Rolls on Two Instruments

A roll on two instruments employs the actions of a typical roll but, instead of alternating strokes on a single instrument, the player strikes one instrument with the left hand and another instrument with the right hand. If both instruments produce good bounce, the effect is very similar to that of two separate players, each rolling one of the instruments with a normal two-stick roll. The notation for this roll is exactly like that for a pitch tremolo: 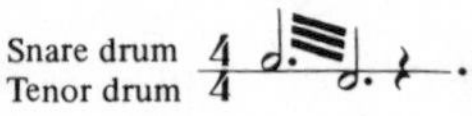 Snare drum Tenor drum . (When soft mallets are used, double stroke rolls on two different instruments are *not* possible.)

Other Strokes and Articulations

Deadsticking

A special variation on the single stroke is known as *deadsticking*. This involves the use of the muscle control in the wrists of the performer to stop a stroke from rebounding. The stick hits the instrument and remains in contact with the instrument's surface. The symbol for this special stroke is , , etc.

Rim Shots

Another special stroke is the *rim shot*. The symbol for this is 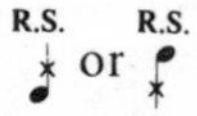 R.S. or R.S. . Two possible methods of producing rim shots exist. In one method, the player holds one snare drum stick on the rim of the drum with the tip pressed against the middle of the head and strikes this stick with the other stick. The point of impact is between the rim and the tip. The second type of rim shot is more difficult, but does not involve both hands. In this second method, the stick is almost thrown at the drum head. The angle of impact is such that the tip strikes the head at the same time as the handle of the stick strikes the rim. Both rim shots sound somewhat like a pistol shot.

Another stroke related to the rimshot is usually used by jazz or rock drummers. It is a modified rim shot played by pivoting the stick very slightly on the tip, which is held against the head, and tapping the handle against the rim. It is performed by one hand and produces a delicate tapping sound.

Scraping

The roll symbol is used to show how long a *scrape* is to last. If one wishes the performer to scrape a tam-tam with a triangle beater for the first three beats of a

4/4 measure, the notation would be: scrape. When an extended scraping motion, such as with a triangle beater or a brush, is to describe a circular pattern over the surface of the instrument, this symbol is used: scrape.

Bowing

The notation of bowing in percussion parts is the same as the notation used in strings. The basic bowings are usually limited to down bows, up bows, and bowed tremolos. (See pages 26-28, 30-31.)

On the Rim

In addition to all the above effects, the percussionist may be called upon to play *on the rim,* which means to perform the various rhythms written in the part by hitting the rim and not the drum head. This produces a clicking sound. Sometimes this *on the rim* effect may be produced by simply clicking the sticks together. These two strokes are more commonly found in parade drumming than in other styles of playing.

The Notation of Durations

The duration of a percussive sound is usually a result of the instrument's natural resonance or the result of artificially sustaining the vibration by the use of a roll, scrape, or bowing technique. Some percussion instruments have such a dry, non-resonant sound that almost no symbol available indicates the true shortness of the duration. Other percussion instruments like the tam-tam have such a long ring that two successive downbeats could cause the second attack to come before the full impact of the first has become fully audible. Notating such a sound with even a whole note is totally inadequate to convey the true resonance that is heard.

To solve the notation problems caused by the natural sustaining qualities of a percussive sound, observe the following rules:

1. Instruments with short decay times should be written in convenient, easy-to-read notation, with no effort made to indicate the true shortness of the sound.
2. Instruments with long decay times should be written showing either:

   a. the exact duration desired

   or

   b. that the sound should be allowed to decay naturally.

a. b. c.

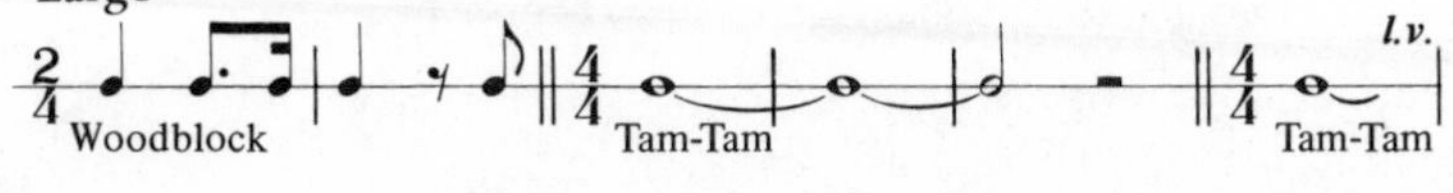

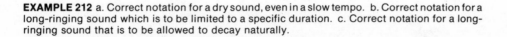

EXAMPLE 212 a. Correct notation for a dry sound, even in a slow tempo. b. Correct notation for a long-ringing sound which is to be limited to a specific duration. c. Correct notation for a long-ringing sound that is to be allowed to decay naturally.

Should one need to further clarify the notation, the following terms should be used:

English	*French*	*German*	*Italian*
choked *or* dry	sec	trocken	secco
let ring	laissez vibrer *or* laissez résonner	klingen lassen *or* ausklingen lassen	lasciar vibrare

Notation for artificially sustaining sounds by use of rolls, scrapes, and other devices has been discussed above. These notations are to be used no matter what the natural characteristics of the instrument.

Notation of Pitch

Certain percussion instruments produce specific pitches and are called *definite-pitched percussion* (see pages 187-98). For these instruments, pitches are notated on a five-line staff just as one would notate string or wind instrument pitches. Percussion instruments that produce no one specific pitch are called *indefinite-pitched percussion,* and do not require the five-line staff (see pages 199-213). For these instruments, a single-line staff is clearer and is preferred.

Even among the indefinite-pitched instruments, however, one can hear relative pitch differences, such as between several woodblocks, for example. It is not at all uncommon to find scores that call for high, medium, and low (or—less accurately—small, medium, and large) woodblocks or other indefinite-pitched instruments. Even these three pitch gradations can be notated clearly on a one-line staff, while four or five relative pithes are more clearly expressed on a two-line staff. One should never use more than a five-line staff for percussion notation.

English	*French*	*German*	*Italian*
high	aigu *or* haut, *or* clair	hoch	alto *or* acuto
medium	moyen	mittel	medio *or* mezzo
low	grave *or* bas	tief	basso *or* grave

EXAMPLE 213 a. One-line staff notation for a single snare drum. b. One-line staff notation for three (high, medium, low) woodblocks. c. Two-line staff notation for five (very high, high, medium, low, very low) tom-toms.

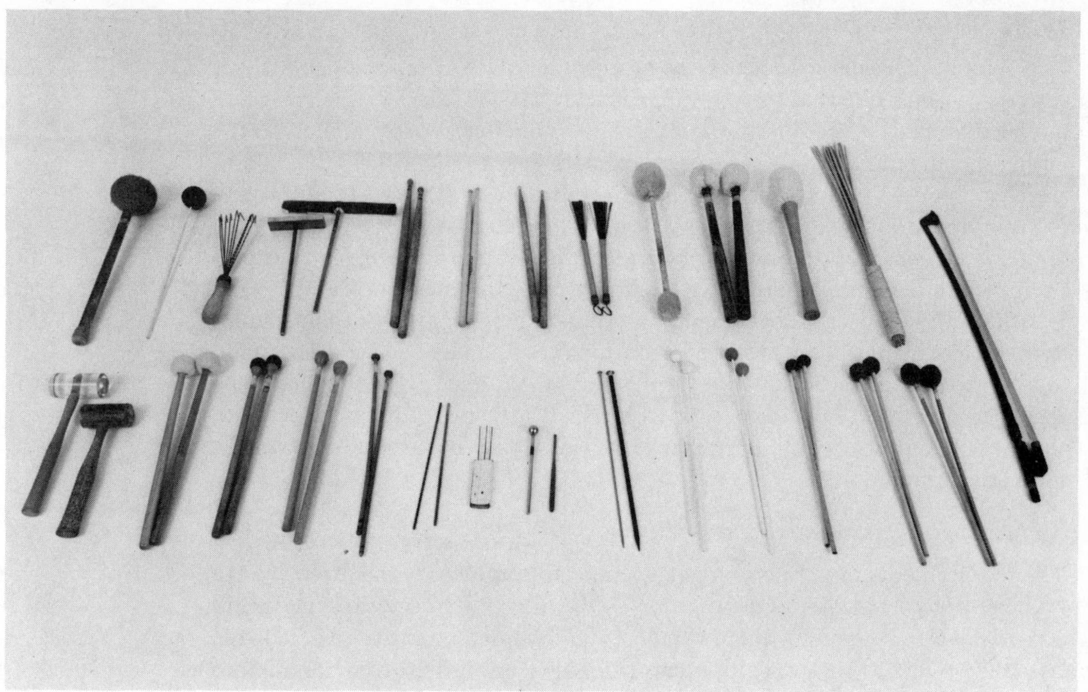

FIGURE 17. Percussion mallets, sticks, and beaters: (*upper row, left to right*) tam-tam beater, superball mallet, cymbal rake, metal and wood cluster bars, a pair of parade snare drum sticks, a pair of concert snare drum sticks, a pair of jazz snare drum sticks with plastic tips, a pair of wire brushes, two-headed bass drum beater, a pair of bass drum roll beaters, a concert bass drum beater, a switch; (*lower row, left to right*) plastic and rawhide chimes hammers, a pair of medium hard timpani mallets, a pair of hard timpani mallets, a pair of wooden timpani mallets, a pair of brass mallets, two different triangle beaters, a three-pronged guiro scraper, a steel mallet, a single-pronged guiro scraper, two knitting needles, a pair of plastic mallets, a pair of wooden mallets, a pair of rubber mallets, a pair of hard yarn mallets, and a pair of soft yarn mallets; (*far right*) a bow. (Photo by David Hruby.)

Percussion Mallets, Beaters, etc.

The object used to set an instrument to vibrating is very important. It is not simply a matter of hitting an instrument with the "correct" beater, but, more important, of obtaining the desired sound. If the student does not fully understand the effect of mallet selection, he should try the following experiment. Strike a suspended cymbal with a triangle beater, then with a fingertip, and then with a felt mallet. Try to make all strokes equal in terms of speed of the stroke, length of the stroke, force of the stroke, and point of impact. The very clear differences heard are a result of the mallets used.

Beaters, mallets, and sticks often exist in varying degrees of hardness, different sizes, and with different heads or ends. All of these variables enable the performer to select the striker that will best achieve the desired sound. It is also important for the composer and orchestrator to become familiar with the different beaters and their variations.

Degrees of Hardness and Softness

In general, the harder a mallet is, the more attack one will hear in each stroke; at softer dynamics this is perceived more as a dryness or staccato quality, while at louder dynamics it becomes more of a *sforzando* effect. A soft mallet, on the other hand, will tend to minimize the attack clarity, generally causing the sound to seem to "bloom," to have a slower developing attack envelope. At soft dynamics, this approximates a percussive legato or brush-stroke bowing, while at louder dynamics, it becomes a *rinforzando* attack. The medium-hard mallet is an approximate compromise between these two extremes.

Considering size, larger strikers produce more sluggish attacks than smaller ones of equal hardness. Therefore, a hard timpani mallet will give a drier attack than a hard bass drum beater. The hardest possible attack would probably be from a triangle beater, knitting needle, iron nail, fingernail, or brass mallet. The softest possible attack would probably be provided by the largest, softest bass drum beater obtainable.

Mallet Specifications and Changes

The requirements of percussion performance often include the rapid change of mallets or beaters. Special instructions to the player are necessary to explain which mallet is to be held in which hand (or that two mallets are to be held in the same hand). Since this information can get very complicated to write out and difficult to read and comprehend quickly during performance situations, symbols representing these mallets, beaters, and sticks have been developed and are often used in new music.

English	*Symbol*	*French*	*German*	*Italian*
*snare drum sticks		baguettes de tambour	Trommelstöcke	bacchette da tamburo
*snare drum sticks with plastic tips		baguettes de tambour en plastique	Kunststoff—Trommelstöcke	bacchette da tamburo di plastica
rubber mallets		baguettes en caoutchouc	Gummischlegel	bacchette con l'estremitá di gomma
*plastic mallets		baguettes en plastique	Kunststoff-Schlegel	bacchette di plastica
*yarn mallets		baguettes recouverte de fil	Garnschlegel	bacchette ricoperte di filo o di lana
*timpani mallets		baguettes de timbales	Paukenschlegel	bacchette per timpani
*wooden timpani mallets		baguettes de timbales de bois	hölzernen Paukenschlegel	bacchette per timpani di legno

*brass mallets		baguettes de laiton	Messingschlegel	bacchette d'ottone
wooden mallets		baguettes de bois	Holzschlegel	bacchette di legno
steel mallet		baguette en acier	Stahlschlegel	bacchetta d'acciaio
plastic hammer		marteau en plastique	Kunststoff-Hammer	battaglio di plastica
*rawhide (Chimes) hammer		marteau	Glockenhammer	battaglio, martello, *or* battente
*triangle beater		baguette de triangle	Triangelschlegel *or* Triangelstab	battente da triangolo
*bass drum beater		mailloche	Schlegel für Grosse Trommel	bacchetta da grancassa
*two-headed bass drum beater		mailloche à double tête	zweiköpfiger Schlegel	mazzuolo a doppia testa
*wire brushes		brosses	Besen *or* Stahlbesen	spazzola
switch		fouet *or* verge	Rute	spazzolino
*guiro scraper		râpe	Raspel	raspa
*knitting needle		aiguille à tricoter	Stricknadel	ferro da calza
bow		archet	Bogen	arco *or* archetto
*hand		main	Hand	mano
*fist		poing	Faust	pugno
finger		doigt	Finger	dito
*finger nail		ongle de la main	Fingernagel	unghia

*coin	©$	pièce de monnaie	Geldstück	moneta
*handles (of the mallet)		manche	Stiel *or* Handgriff	manico
*hard		dur	hart	duro
*medium		moyen	mittel	medio
*soft		doux *or* mou	weich	soffice *or* morbido

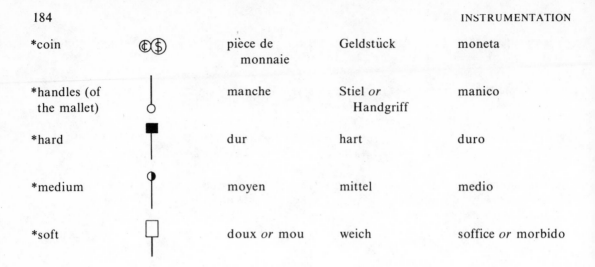

To call attention to the specified mallets and any changes in mallet requirements during the course of a piece, the symbols for the mallets are to be placed in boxes. Mallets indicated on the left side of the box are for the left hand and mallets on the right side of the box are for the right hand. The end of the mallet that points up (toward the top of the box) is the end to be used to strike the instrument. Here are some examples:

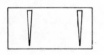

Symbol	*Meaning*
	Hard yarn in the left hand, wire brush in the right hand. Strike instrument with yarn and wire ends.
	Snare drum stick in each hand. Strike instrument with handles of sticks.
	Two soft rubber mallets in the left hand, one medium yarn mallet in the right hand. Strike instrument with rubber ends of rubber mallets and handle end of yarn mallet.
+	Pick up triangle beater.
−	Put down hard timpani mallet.

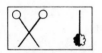

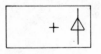

It is not uncommon to specify two mallets or beaters per hand. This is standard technique on the keyboard percussion instruments, like the marimba, in order to obtain (rolled) chords. However, it may be used in other situations to minimize mallet or stick changes. It only works well with smaller, lightweight mallets.

In addition to the various mallets and sticks listed above, percussionists may be asked to use cluster bars on keyboard percussion instruments. These cluster bars are made of metal or wood and may or may not have felt applied to the striking surface or edge. The bars have handles attached to them. The length of the cluster bar will be the size necessary to produce the required cluster (from a minor second to an octave or more) on the instrument for which it is intended. Most cluster bars are made for specific compositions and passages.

In any type of music where a mallet or stick change is called for, the indication of which stick(s) is (are) to be used should be placed over the music to which it applies and not over rests preceeding the passage. Percussionists read ahead.

In very uncomplicated percussion parts where many mallet changes are not required, the use of the symbols may not be necessary. However, the composer should always remember that specifying the mallet to be used is as important as specifying the instrument. The processes by which the percussionist picks up, uses, and puts down mallets cannot be left to chance but rather must be carefully planned.

The final selection of the specific mallet is left to the conductor or performer. This is as it should be since in the actual acoustical environment in which the piece is performed, the results achieved aurally from the specified mallets (and instruments) may not match the conception.

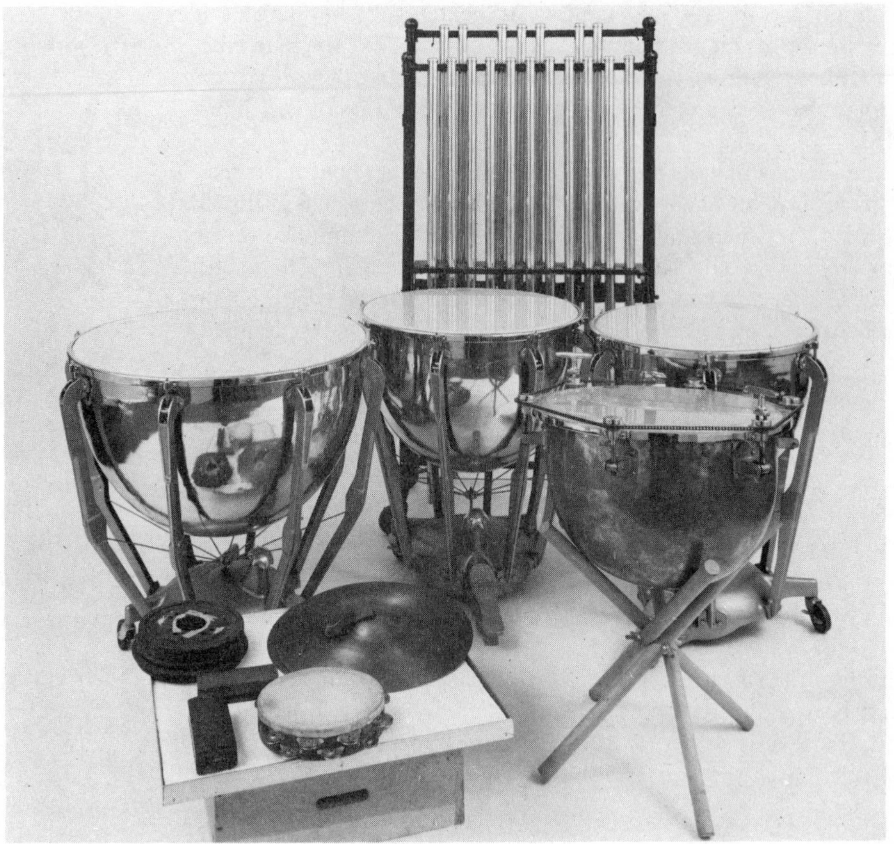

FIGURE 18. Percussion instruments: (*rear*) tubular chimes; (*middle, clockwise from left*) 32″ timpano, 28″ timpano, 23″ timpano, piccolo (20″) timpano; (*foreground, on tray, clockwise from upper left*) automobile brake drum, crash cymbals, tambourine, large and small woodblocks. The three large timpani are pedal-tuned; the piccolo timpano is tuned by means of a key and the chain mechanism. (Photo by David Hruby)

Striking Points

It is equally important to specify *where* on an instrument the mallet is to strike. The difference between hitting a drum in the center of the head (producing a "dead" sound) and hitting it nearer the edge (producing a fuller, more normal sound) is immense. One may also strike an instrument on its edge (rim), side(shell), frame, resonators—in fact, any part of the instrument. It is not uncommon to strike one instrument with another, such as a suspended cymbal with a finger cymbal, and so forth. All of these methods of producing sounds must be specified and explained in the part since they are out of the ordinary.

PERCUSSION INSTRUMENTS

The instruments of the percussion family may be placed into one of four categories:

1. Wooden instruments (called *woods*).
2. Metal instruments (called *metals*).
3. Skin-covered instruments (called *skins*).
4. Other sound sources.

The Woods

The wooden percussion instruments probably are the oldest percussion. The characteristic sound of a wooden instrument is a rapid decay and high-pitched partials. Smaller wooden instruments possessing more rapid decays are characterized by brittle, dry sounds much like *clicks* or *snaps*. Larger wooden instruments produce warmer sounds more like *thumps* and *thuds*.

The Metals

The metal percussion instruments are characterized by very long decay times and often slow attack times. The smaller metal instruments have bright, bell-like sounds with great quantities of dissonant partials present. The decay time of these small metal instruments is very slow. Larger metal instruments possess metallic crash-tone qualities—an initial crash followed by a crescendo brought about by the appearance and stabilization of more and higher partials. This is all followed by a very long decay.

The Skins

In these instruments, an animal skin (or a plastic substitute) is stretched over a frame. The small skins have rather hollow, well-focused sounds while the larger skins have a boomy, thuddish quality. Skins generally have longer decay times than woods, but the decay times are significantly shorter than the decay times of metals. With skin instruments, the resonating structure to which the skin is attached plays a major role in determining the tone quality, pitch range, and pitch definition of the instrument.

Other Sources

Sounds taken from nature and from the surrounding environment are included in this category. Among the more commonly heard are auto horns, police whistles, bird calls, etc. Humorous effects are often specified, like slide whistles, or unique sounds like sandpaper blocks.

It is often convenient to divide these four categories of percussion instruments into two subcategories:

1. Instruments with definite pitch.
2. Instruments with indefinite pitch.

The former produce pitches that are clearly defined within the tuning system in use. The latter produce sounds that may be heard as higher or lower than one another but which possess no clearly defined pitch (at least within the pitch system in use). Thus we have xylophones and orchestral bells in the first subcategory and woodblocks and cymbals in the second.

The Percussion Instruments with Definite Pitch

The following lists include some of the more commonly encountered definite-pitched percussion instruments. (The pictograms given, if marked with an asterisk, were endorsed by the Ghent conference.)

The Wooden Instruments with Definite Pitch

English	*Symbol*	*French*	*German*	*Italian*
*marimba	Mar	marimba	Marimbaphon	marimba
*xylophone	Xyle	xylophone	Xylophon	xilofono *or* silofono
xylorimba *or* xylomarimba		xylorimba	Xylomarimba	xilomarimba *or* silomarimba

The Metal Instruments with Definite Pitch

English	*Symbol*	*French*	*German*	*Italian*
*orchestral bells	Glsp	jeu de timbres *or* carillon	Glockenspiel	campanelli
*vibraphone	Vib	vibraphone	Vibraphon	vibrafono
*tubular chimes		tubes de cloches	Röhrenglocken *or* Rohrenglockenspiel	campana tubolare *or* campane tubolari
celesta	Cel	célesta	Celesta	celesta *or* celeste
*button gong		gong	Buckelgong	gong
*gong		gong	Gong	gong
*crotales		crotales *or* cymbales antiques	Zimbeln	crotali
steel drum		tambour d'acier	Stahltrommel	tamburo d'acciaio
*handbells	A E	clochettes à mains	Handglockenspiel	sonagli a mano
*almglocken		sonnailles de troupeau	Almglocken	campane da pastore

*anvil		enclume	Amboss	incudine
musical saw		scie musicale	Spielsäge	sega cantante
*flexatone		flexatone	Flexaton	flessatono
tubaphone		tubaphone	Tubaphon	tubofono

The Skin-Covered Instruments with Definite Pitch

*timpano and timpani	30″ 25″	timbale and timbales	Pauke and Pauken	timpano and timpani
roto-tom		roto-tom	Tom-Tom-Spiel	roto-tom-tom

The Other Sound Sources with Definite Pitch

*slide whistle		sifflet à coulisse	Lotosflöte	flauto a culisse
musical glasses		coupes de verre	Gläserspiel	bicchieri di vetro

Definite-Pitched Woods

The *marimba* has a range of:  . It is usually written on the grand staff like the piano. The tone is dark, mellow, and similar to a cello or lower-register saxophone. The marimba is not used as much in large ensembles as other keyboard percussion simply because it is very easily covered due to its very soft tone. The marimba is played with yarn or soft rubber mallets. Normal marimba playing calls for rolling every pitch that has a duration longer than a quarter note. To facilitate chords, much music for marimba requires the use of two mallets in each hand. (More than two mallets per hand is still a trick and not yet standard technique.) Parts in which four mallets are required are generally relaxed in tempo and much more chordal than countrapuntal. Fast-moving, intricate lines for more than one mallet per hand are for the virtuoso.

The *xylophone* may be considered to be the soprano marimba but is more often used for its own special qualities. The xylophone in its high register can be heard in any musical texture. The wood of the xylophone's bars is much harder than the wood used on the marimba and it often has resonators below the bars like the marimba. The lowest octave tone is darker and more like the marimba, but the rest of the range is brittle, hard, and incisive, not unlike hardwood being broken, with a definite "pop" to the attack. It is played with plastic or rubber mallets. The written range of the xylophone is: 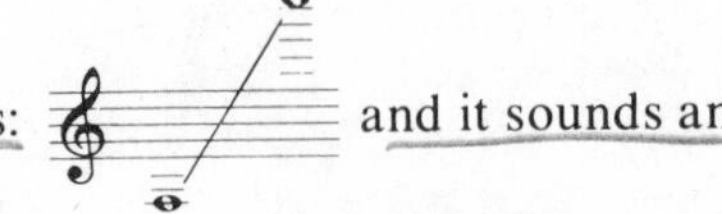 and it sounds an octave higher than written. The sound of the xylophone has no durational component as far as musical notation is concerned. It decays immediately. The only way to sustain the tone is with a roll, but this must be used carefully by the composer or orchestrator. In the wrong situation, rolled xylophone may even sound humorous. The decay is so rapid that one hears each stroke, even in the fastest roll.

The *xylorimba* is a cross between the xylophone and the marimba. Rare in this country it is sometimes found in European scores. The range is: and it sounds as written (although some scores expect it to sound an octave higher). Higher parts for this instrument may be performed on the xylophone instead while lower parts may be performed on the marimba.

Definite-Pitched Metals

The *orchestral bells,* sometimes called *glockenspiel,* have the following range: The instrument is usually played with brass mallets but rubber or plastic mallets may also be used. It is generally agreed that the instrument sounds two octaves higher than written. The tone quality is very clear and bell-like and in rapid passages tends to blur very quickly. Successful glockenspiel parts usually are limited to a few very important pitches. The technique usually involves single strokes, although rolls are sometimes called for. The latter often sounds like an alarm clock going off.

A version of the glockenspiel designed to be carried upright is sometimes found in bands. It is called the *bell-lyre,* due to the lyre shape of its frame. The range is less than the glockenspiel's. Some bell-lyres are built as transposing instruments in B♭ to enable the performer to read from solo clarinet or cornet parts.

The *vibraphone* has metal bars placed over resonators. In the resonators are small paddles connected to a shaft that is rotated by an electric motor. The instrument also has a damper pedal that removes a set of dampers from contact with the metal bars. The range of the vibraphone is: . It is usually played by striking the bars with yarn or soft rubber mallets. The tone of the vibraphone is mellow and velvety, becoming brighter in the upper register. With the damper pedal depressed[3] the tone rings for quite a while. With the damper in contact with the bars, the tone sounds slightly choked. When the paddles in the resonators are turned at slow speeds, with the damper depressed, the undulation produced is slow and gentle. At faster motor speeds, it is a wavy pitch vibrato. On better instruments the speed of the motor can be varied over a continuum, while on cheaper models only one or two speeds are available. All models can be played with the motor turned completely off as well; without the undulation, the vibraphone has a very cool, placid sound. As a special effect, there is a type of glissando that can be obtained by placing a hard mallet on one of the metal bars at the node (point at which it is suspended) and pressing down. The performer then strikes the bar at the center with another mallet and slides the first mallet out toward the edge of the bar. The effect is a very subtle and quiet glissando over the range of about a minor second. Other methods of producing sounds include bowing the edge of the bars.

The *tubular chimes* (or *tubular bells*) sound very much like church bells or grandfather clock chimes. The written range is: [musical staff]. The physics of vibrating tubes is complicated and because of this the exact pitch produced by tubular chimes is subject to some debate. The perceived pitch of each tube is not physically present, but is interpreted by the ear from the various complex modes of vibration present in the composite tone. Thus, some listeners are convinced that the chimes sound an octave lower than notated while others maintain that the pitch center is as the above notation.

These instruments are intended to be used at those points in a musical score where highly representational chiming is required. However, other uses are possible. The normal tone is produced by striking the upper corner of an individual chime with a chimes hammer. If the chime is struck with a brass mallet like the one used on the orchestral bells, and the point of articulation is the top of the chime instead of the normal striking area, a totally different set of partials is brought out. This other sound is hollow, clangorous, and "whining," but not as loud as the normal chimes tone. Chimes are equipped with dampers, operated by the performer's foot, that are usually removed (depressed) before striking. For special effects the dampers may be left on to provide a dry sound. Since all the chimes tubes together are affected by the damper when it is on, individual damping of some tubes by hand may be called for in special circumstances.

When only one or two pitches are required in a performance, it is common for the performer to remove the required tubes from the frame and to suspend them from a special, smaller frame. In this situation, there is no damper pedal.

The *celesta* is a keyboard instrument. The performer plays it much as a pianist plays a piano but the keys control hammers that strike metal bars connected to wooden resonators. A damper pedal is operated by foot, and when it is depressed the tones are allowed to decay naturally. When it is not depressed, the tones decay more rapidly, but not quickly enough to be considered staccato. The range

[3]The symbol of depressing the damper pedal is 𝆮 the same as is used on piano (see pages 223-225).

of the celesta is:  It sounds an octave higher than notated. It is usually written on two staves, like the grand staff on the piano. The celesta is used primarily as a coloring instrument, adding a silvery quality to the texture or providing a delicate, filigree decoration. Extended use of the celesta to provide harmonic materials is rare. Its tone is like a refined and mellow glockenspiel; it is never as brilliant as the latter instrument and indeed one often has difficulty hearing it in an orchestral texture. Like many softly voiced instruments it needs aural space in order to come across distinctly. There now exists an electronic instrument that is constructed to sound like the celesta, only it has the advantage of overcoming the problem of being too soft through amplification. In many performance situations this is very helpful.

Gongs are of many types. The most commonly encountered gongs are made of thick, heavy brass with deep sides and a circular surface. This surface may be smooth or, in the case of the *button gong,* it may have a raised dome in the middle. Gongs are usually struck with a timpani mallet, bass drum beater, or gong or tam-tam beater. Other means of articulating gongs include triangle beaters, wire brushes, and rubber or plastic mallets. The tone of the gong resembles the more familiar tam-tam, but has a definite pitch. When writing for gong, one may specify a pitch but usually not the octave. Most percussionists do not possess gongs or, at most, own only one or two. Thus, one's selection of pitches and octaves is usually limited.[4]

Crotales are also known as antique cymbals. These are heavy, thick brass plates that look like fat, flat cymbals of various small diameters. When struck, the crotales produce clear, bell-like sounds, not unlike a water glass struck with a spoon. The usual means of striking the crotales is with a brass mallet, although plastic mallets, triangle beaters, and any other hard mallets may be used. Usually the crotale is suspended from a string that passes through the thickened middle and is held by the performer. Recently percussionists have been mounting chromatically arranged sets on larger boards and playing these more like a vibraphone or glockenspiel. This arrangement allows additional techniques (including rolls) to be employed and makes possible the use of crotales as melodic instruments. The usual range available is: . With this notation, the crotales sound two octaves higher than written. Because scores exist in which they are written at sounding pitch, it is wise to specify the system of notation you are using.

[4]Puccini's *Turandot* requires an octave of gongs from to It is possible that an opera company may possess gongs for all of these pitches.

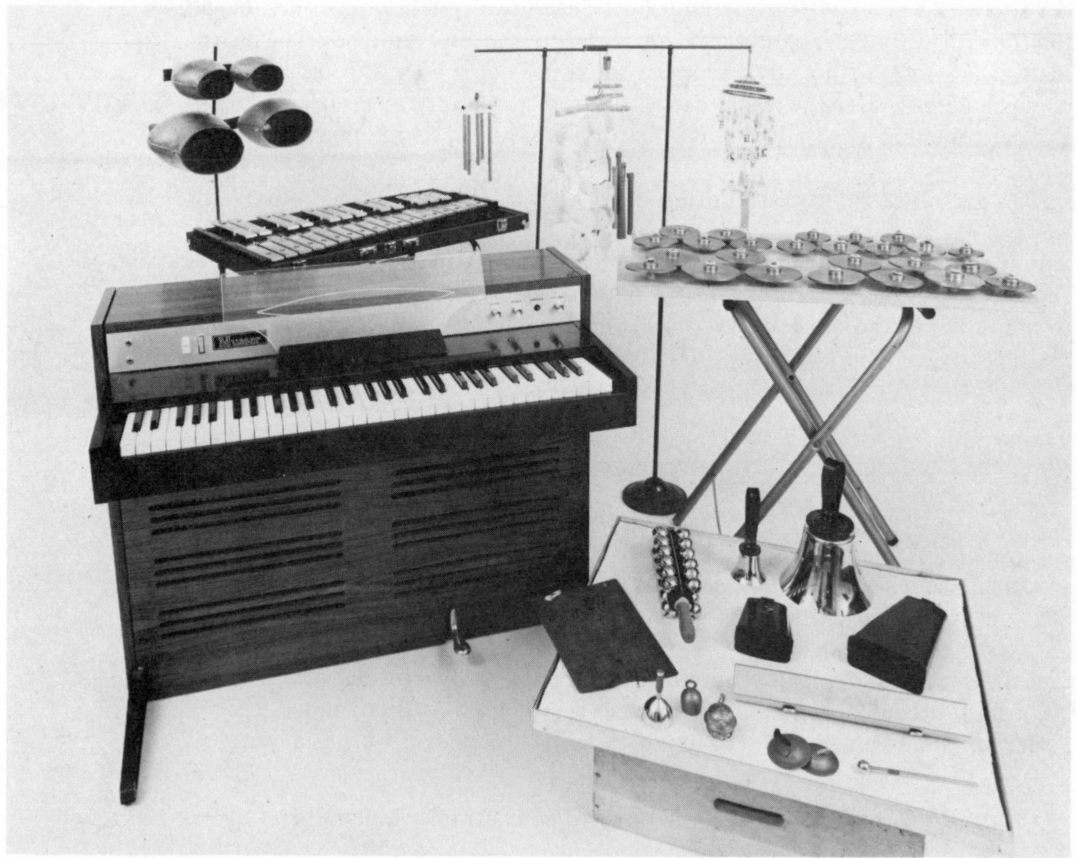

FIGURE 19. Percussion instruments: (*clockwise from center left*) celesta, orchestral bells, four almglocken, metal wind chimes, bamboo wind chimes, glass wind chimes, crotales; (*on tray, clockwise from left*) bell plate, sleighbells, small handbell, large handbell, large cowbell, anvil, steel mallet for anvil, finger cymbals, and three miscellaneous bells; (*in center of tray*) small cowbell. (Photo by David Hruby.)

Steel drums are instruments strongly associated with Trinidad. These instruments are made from 55-gallon steel oil drums. The lowest drums, or *pans* as they are called, are not cut down, but are used full-size. The slightly higher-pitched pans are cut down to 18 to 24 inches in depth. The highest-pitched pans are from 6 to 12 inches deep. The lowest-pitched, full-sized drums can only produce two or three pitches per drum. The medium-low cello pans and the slightly higher-pitched tenor pans can produce from five to ten pitches each. Both the guitar pans and the higher-pitched alto pans can produce about fourteen notes while the highest-pitched soprano or single tenor pans may have as many as twenty-nine notes.

Steel drums are tuned by hammering the heads of the oil drums, creating various-sized but carefully tuned sections that are in different planes. Each section is lettered with its pitch. Since the pitch of a section is directly related to the size of the section (larger sections produce lower pitches) it is only logical that the lowest-pitched pans would also produce the fewest pitches. The instruments are struck with a stick wrapped with strips of rubber, but other mallets could be used. Due to the resonance of the drums, rolls take on a sustained quality that resemble a cross between a marimba and a pipe organ celeste stop.

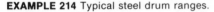

The overall range of a steel drum band is: . Individual pans vary in actual notes available; however, these approximate but typical ranges should be of value. Except for the soprano pans, it requires two or more drums to obtain all of the pitches given within each range.

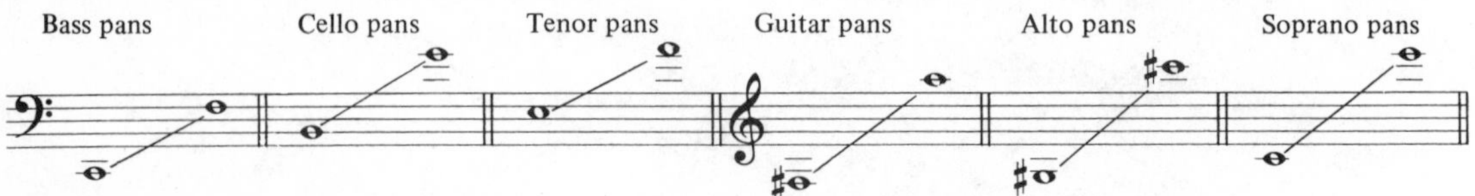

EXAMPLE 214 Typical steel drum ranges.

The drums are not typically chromatic but are normally diatonic, with selected, frequently needed chromatic pitches such as F♯, C♯ and B♭ included.

Handbells are made in sets of up to sixty-one bells covering a range of

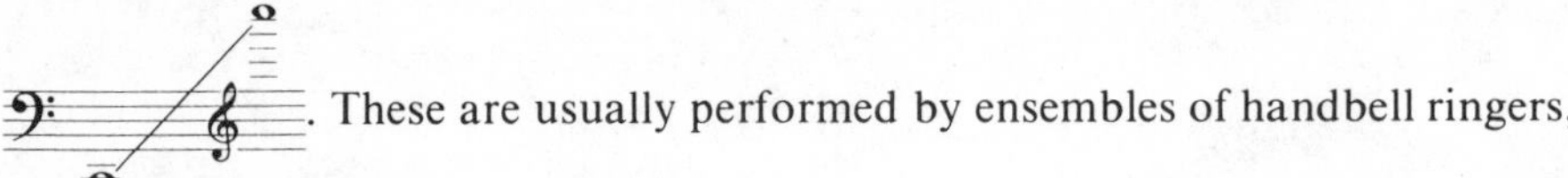

. These are usually performed by ensembles of handbell ringers, each of whom holds one or two bells in each hand and rings the required bell at the required time. Composers usually specify only one or two handbells, and then usually call for relative pitch (i.e. *high* or *low*) only; or specify the pitch but not the octave.

Almglocken are Swiss cowbells and possess definite pitches. The available written range is from to *8va*. The instruments are played with various mallets, such as rubber and yarn, and are often arranged in keyboard fashion to facilitate melodic performance. The tone is sorrowful and hollow with a clear "boink" on an accented attack. The instruments sound an octave higher than notated.

Anvils have been specified in operas by Wagner and Verdi, as well as in other works for band and orchestra. The instrument usually used is a metal bar with a definite pitch. In writing for the anvil, one calls for specific pitches but not specific octaves except by relationship: (two C-sharps an octave apart, etc.) Anvils are usually struck by a steel mallet or a metal hammer.

The *musical saw* may be a regular hand saw, of the rip or cross-cut variety, played with a bow (cello or double bass). By bending the saw, the performer can control the frequency of vibration, thus producing melodic lines and figures. These lines are characterized by glissandos and a tone quality which resembles buzzy humming. Another version is made from the same flexible steel and is about three inches wide and four to six feet long, with a handle on one end and the other end welded to a heavy base plate. The performer stands on the base plate and bows the saw. By gripping the handle with the other hand and bending the saw, different notes are produced. The range of the musical saw is about:

The *flexatone* consists of a triangular piece of spring steel held at two corners to a frame that is attached to a handle. Also attached to the handle are two springy wires with wooden knobs on the ends. The performer shakes the whole assembly, causing the two wooden knobs to alternately strike the triangular piece of spring steel. The third, unattached corner of the steel triangle is located so that the performer may apply more or less pressure to the triangle with his thumb. More pressure produces higher pitches. The tone quality is like the musical saw but, due to the striking, the sound is accompanied by a constant rattle. The usual range for this instrument is:

Brass or copper tubes from about four to twelve inches in length are suspended from fine ropes and arranged in xylophone (keyboard) fashion to produce the *tubaphone.* The instrument dates to the beginning of the twentieth century, and is not often seen in this country. Its tone has a unique, hollow, bell-like quality. Because the tubes are suspended, a very subtle vibrato is achieved. The range of the tubaphone, sounding two octaves higher than written, is: The tubaphone is usually played with rubber, plastic, or wooden mallets.

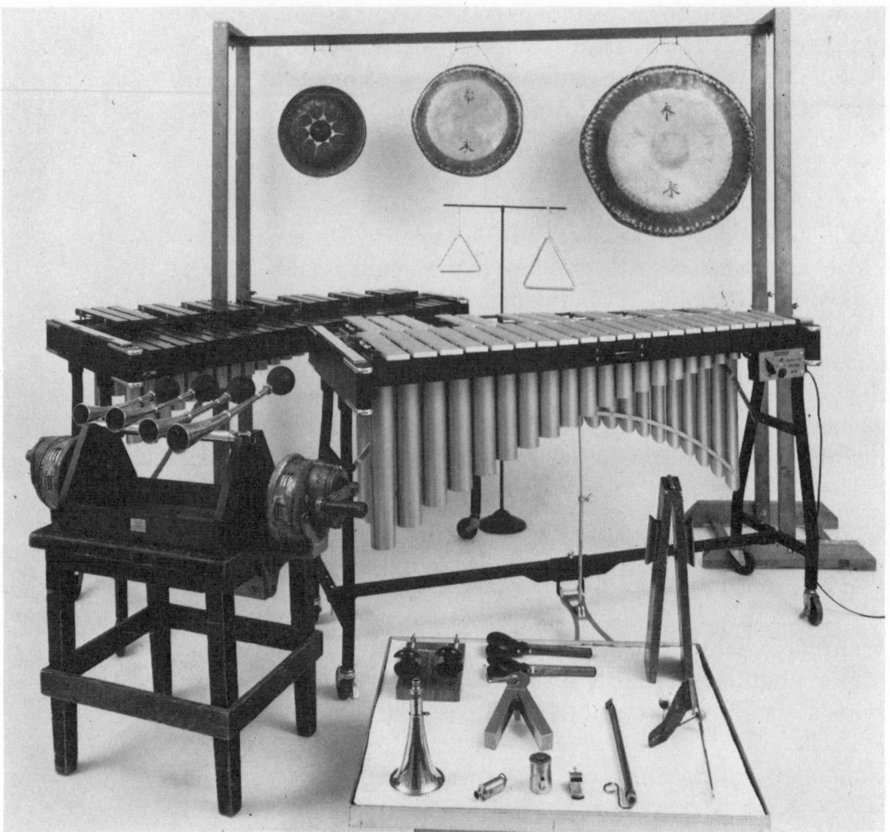

FIGURE 20. Percussion instruments: (*hanging in rear, above, left to right*) button gong, small tam-tam, large tam-tam; (*hanging below*) small and large triangles; (*middle, left*) xylophone; (*right*) vibraphone; (*left foreground*) four auto horns setting on bench with two (hand-cranked) sirens; (*on tray, back row, left to right*) mechanical castanets, hand castanets, whip or slap-stick; (*in center of tray*) ratchet; (*front row of tray, left to right*) large mouth siren, small mouth siren, bird whistle, police whistle, slide whistle, and flexatone. (Photo by David Hruby.)

Definite-Pitched Skins

The *timpani* are probably the best known definite-pitched percussion instruments. They are made in a variety of sizes and have different methods of tuning. Some timpani are equipped with a crank on the side of the drum that is mechanically connected to tension rods spaced around the drum. When the crank is turned, all of the rods are tightened or loosened together. Another system has the crank (or a place to attach a tuning key) on the top of the drum with all the tension rods connected through a chain and gear mechanism. When the key or crank on top is turned, all the tension rods turn, too.

The most common method for tuning timpani is through the use of a pedal, generally operated by the performer's right foot. It somewhat resembles an accelerator pedal and when one "steps on the gas" the pitch goes up, and when one moves the pedal in the other direction the skins loosen and the pitch goes down. It is possible that repeated, heavy impacts may stretch the head or cause a slight amount of slippage in the tuning mechanism. To minimize these concerns, allow an opportunity to check the tuning before any really important solo passage or passage of extreme dynamic level. Checking the tuning does not take nearly as long as the initial tuning. To check the tuning, allow at least six seconds per drum. For the initial tuning or retuning, allow at least fifteen seconds for each pitch to be tuned.

Originally the heads of timpani were made of skins, but most are now plastic. The tone quality of the timpani is affected by the amount of tension (the tuning) on the head. When the head is very loose (flat) the tone is long and rumbling and the attacks sound dull and very thumpy. When the head is very tight (sharp) the sound is hard and pingy. Traditional timpani performance usually avoids either extreme, and so whenever possible drums are selected that place most of the notes to be played in the middle of the timpani's range. In studying and using the following chart, keep in mind that even though the range of each timpano is fairly wide, the sound desired by the performer is close to the middle of the range. For special effects, extremes of range can be specified, although it is often necessary to attach an instruction assuring the performer that what is requested is not a mistake and that the composer really does desire that effect.

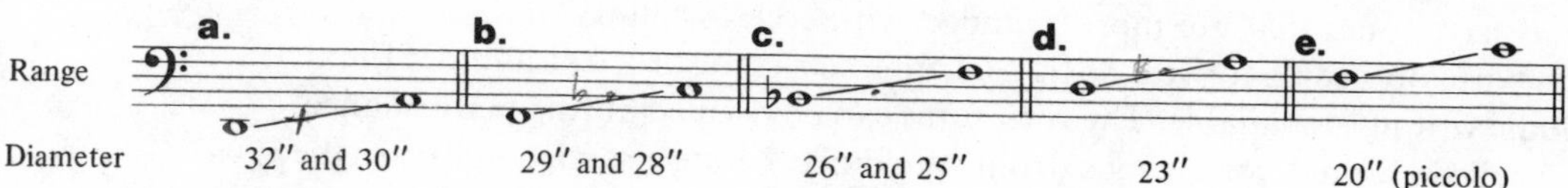

EXAMPLE 215 Timpani ranges, according to size.

The timpani may be struck by any of the mallets listed previously in the section on general percussion information (see pages 181-84). The usual choice is, of course, timpani sticks. The tone may be altered by muffling the drum, which involves placing a piece of cloth on the head of the drum to reduce the vibrations. Various different tone qualities can also be obtained by striking different areas on the head. Striking dead center on the drum, a darker, more ominous sound with less ring is obtained.

In addition to the normal way of playing the timpani, it is possible to obtain interesting sounds from the shell of the kettle, the frame, and the rim. The rolling or bouncing of coins on the heads is sometimes called for and it is not uncommon to place an object, such as a bowl gong or a cymbal, on the head and roll the object on the head while varying the tension with the pedal.

On timpani equipped with pedal tuning mechanisms, glissandos are very playable. Depending upon the effect desired, there are several ways of indicating these.

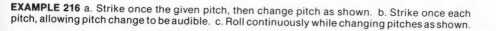

EXAMPLE 216 a. Strike once the given pitch, then change pitch as shown. b. Strike once each pitch, allowing pitch change to be audible. c. Roll continuously while changing pitches as shown.

The dynamic range of the timpani, depending upon the sticks used, is from an inaudible *pianissimo* to a *fortissimo* that can completely cover a band or orchestra.

The *roto-toms* were originally developed as practice pads for timpani performers. They are tunable drums made in a variety of sizes. The roto-toms have no resonators but are simply metal frames over which the heads, usually plastic, are stretched. By rotating the drum clockwise on its base, the head is tightened and the pitch raised. Rotating the drum counterclockwise lowers the pitch. The sizes and ranges of the various drums are:

EXAMPLE 217 Roto-tom ranges, according to size.

The two highest-pitched drums possess very brittle and dry tones. The larger drums have tones that are more rounded with a clear "plink."

One usually scores for sets of these drums so that a sufficient number for all melodic writing is available. The roto-toms can be retuned during performance, but a rolled glissando on a single drum would necessitate an assistant to turn the drum while the performer rolls. Roto-toms may be played with a wide variety of sticks and mallets.

Other Definite-Pitched Sound Sources

The *slide whistle* is most often treated as a sound effect and a comic one at that. One can expect a performer to produce the shape of a line, but exact pitches are more difficult, though not impossible. Its range is usually: . The most characteristic effects on the slide whistle are the long glissandos (up or down) and a (wide) vibrato added to a line or tone.

Thin-walled drinking glasses may be struck gently with a small beater to produce a delicate, high-pitched bell sound. These *musical glasses* can be tuned by adding varying amounts of water to each glass; the more water, the lower the pitch. Another means of performance uses the performer's fingers, wet with vinegar, to rub the rims of the glasses. Usually only one or two pitches are specified, but sets of glasses could be arranged to produce scales. The typical range is:

FIGURE 21. Percussion instruments: (*clockwise from upper left*) lion's roar, bass drum in a swivel stand, tenor drum, four roto-toms, (Korean) temple blocks, piccolo snare drum, field drum, snare drum; (*in center*) musical saw. (Photo by David Hruby.)

The Percussion Instruments with Indefinite Pitch

These are some of the more commonly encountered indefinite-pitched percussion instruments. Included in the list are some for which a definite pitch may be ascertained but which are seldom available by specific pitch. These latter types include automobile brake drums and slit drums, among others. (The pictograms endorsed at the Ghent conference are indicated with asterisks.)

The Wooden Instruments with Indefinite Pitch

English	*Symbol*	*French*	*German*	*Italian*
*woodblock	▭	bloc de bois	Holzblock	blocco di legno cinese
*temple block	⊖	temple-bloc	Tempelblock	blocco di legno coreano

*claves	claves	Claves *or* Holzstab	claves
castanets	castagnettes	Kastagnetten	castagnette *or* nacchere
*guiro	güiro	Guiro	guiro
*maracas	maracas	Maracas	maracas
*cabasa	cabaza *or* calebasse	Cabaza	cabasa
jaw bone of an ass *or* quijada	quijada	Schlagrassel	mascella d'asino
vibra slap	vibra slap	Vibraslap	vibra slap
*slit drum	tambour de bois *or* tambour à fente	Schlitztrommel	tamburo di legno a fessura

The Metal Instruments with Indefinite Pitch

*finger cymbals	cymbales digitales	Fingerzimbeln	cimbalini
*crash cymbals	cymbales	Becken-Paar	piatti *or* cinelli
*suspended cymbal	cymbale suspendue	Hängendes Becken	piatto sospeso
*sizzle cymbal	cymbale sur tiges	Nietenbecken	piatto chiodat
*hi-hat cymbal	cymbale à pédale *or* cymbales charleston	Hi-Hat Becken *or* Fussbecken	hi-hat *or* piatti a pedale
*Chinese cymbal	cymbale chinoise	chinesische Becken	piatto cinese
*triangle	triangle	Triangel	triangolo

*cowbells		cloche de vache	Kuhglocken	campanelli da mucca
*tam-tam		tam-tam	Tamtam	tamtam
graduated bells		cloches gammes	tonleiterartige Glocken	campane a scala
*bells		cloches	Glocken	campane
*sleighbells		grelots	Rollschellen	sonagliera *or* sonagli
*bell plate	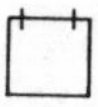	cloche en lame de métal	Plattenglocke	campana in lastra di metallo
bowl gongs *or* cup-bells		clochettes	Schalen-glöckchen	piccole campane
tubo		tubo	Tubo	tubo
cymbal tongs *or* metal castanets		castagnettes de fer	Gabelbecken	castagnette di ferro
*automobile brake drums	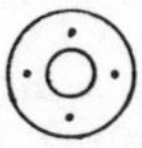	auto-brake-drums	Auto-brake-drums	auto-brake-drums
iron pipe		tuyau de fer	Eisenröhre	tubo di ferro
chains		chaîne	Kettenrassel	catena

The Skin Covered Instruments with Indefinite Pitch

*snare drum (with snares on)		caisse claire *or* tambour (avec timbres)	kleine Trommel (mit Schnarr-saite)	tamburo piccolo (colle corde)
*(with snares off)		(sans timbres)	(ohne Schnarr-saite)	(senza le corde)
piccolo snare drum		petit tambour	Pikkolotrommel	tamburo acuto

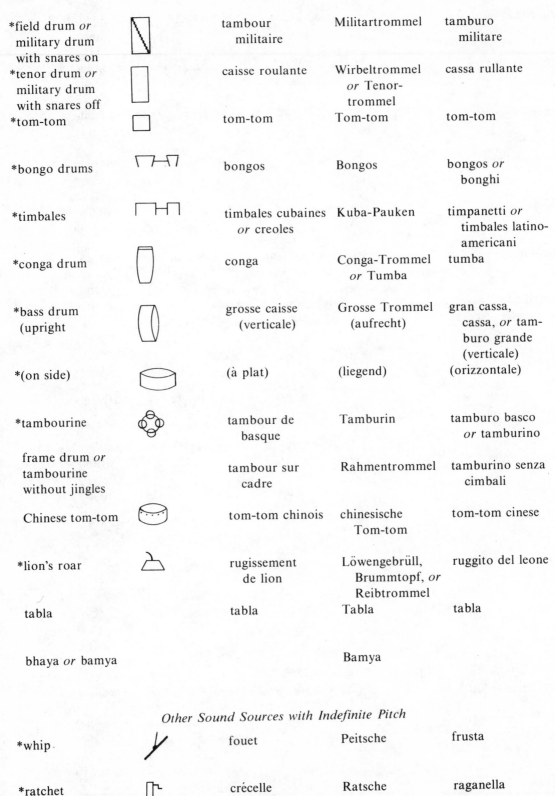

*field drum *or* military drum with snares on		tambour militaire	Militartrommel	tamburo militare
*tenor drum *or* military drum with snares off		caisse roulante	Wirbeltrommel *or* Tenor-trommel	cassa rullante
*tom-tom		tom-tom	Tom-tom	tom-tom
*bongo drums		bongos	Bongos	bongos *or* bonghi
*timbales	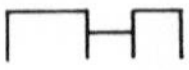	timbales cubaines *or* creoles	Kuba-Pauken	timpanetti *or* timbales latino-americani
*conga drum		conga	Conga-Trommel *or* Tumba	tumba
*bass drum (upright		grosse caisse (verticale)	Grosse Trommel (aufrecht)	gran cassa, cassa, *or* tamburo grande (verticale)
*(on side)	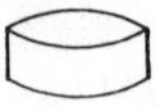	(à plat)	(liegend)	(orizzontale)
*tambourine	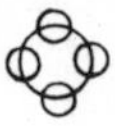	tambour de basque	Tamburin	tamburo basco *or* tamburino
frame drum *or* tambourine without jingles		tambour sur cadre	Rahmentrommel	tamburino senza cimbali
Chinese tom-tom		tom-tom chinois	chinesische Tom-tom	tom-tom cinese
*lion's roar		rugissement de lion	Löwengebrüll, Brummtopf, *or* Reibtrommel	ruggito del leone
tabla		tabla	Tabla	tabla
bhaya *or* bamya			Bamya	

Other Sound Sources with Indefinite Pitch

*whip		fouet	Peitsche	frusta
*ratchet	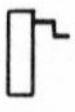	crécelle	Ratsche	raganella

*police whistle		sifflet à roulette	Trillerpfeife	fischietto a pallina
*bird whistle		appeau	Vogelpfeife	richiamo per uccelli
*duck call		conard	Entenquak	gracidio di anitra
*mouth siren		sirène a bouche	Sirenenpfeife	sirena a fiato
*siren		sirène	Sirene	sirena a mano
*auto horn		trompe d'auto	Autohupe	clacson
*thundersheet		tonnerre à poignée	Donnerblech	tuono a pugno
*sandpaper blocks		papier de verre	Sandpapier *or* Sandblöcke	carta vetrata
wooden wind chimes		baguettes de bois suspendues	Holz-Windglocken	bacchette di legno sospese
bamboo wind chimes		bambou suspendu	Bambusrohre	tubi di bambù
metal wind chimes		baguettes metalliques suspendues	Metall-Windglocken	bacchette di metallo sospese
*glass wind chimes		baguettes de verre suspendues	Glas-Windglocken	bacchette di vetro sospese
shell wind chimes		baguettes de coquille suspendues	Muschel-Windglocken	bacchette di conchiglia sospese
*wind machine		machine a vent	Windmaschine	macchina del vento
*klaxon horn		klaxon	Hupe (Claxon)	clacson
*pistol shot		coup de pistolet	Pistolenschuss	pistolettata
stones		phonolithes	Klingsteine	pietra sonora

Indefinite-Pitched Woods

The *woodblock* is a solid piece of wood that has been partially hollowed out. It is usually played by being struck with a hard rubber or plastic mallet, although other possibilities exist. The sound is hard, dry, and brittle, with just a little resonance. Pitch and tone can be varied by striking the woodblock at different points, by changes of mallet, and by distortion of its shape using hand pressure. It sounds something like an unpitched xylophone. Due to its lack of sustaining power, it is primarily an instrument for delineating attacks. To sustain a sound would require a roll that would have each stroke clearly discernible.

Temple blocks, sometimes called *Chinese temple blocks,* are actually of Korean origin. They are more hollow-sounding than woodblocks and tend to ring just a fraction longer. Temple blocks are often used in music of a pseudo-oriental character and for that reason usually come in sets of five different sizes. The five sizes seem to approximate the effect of a pentatonic scale, even though the temple blocks do not themselves give any clear, singable pitches. They are played with rubber or yarn mallets. Rolls are moderately effective, due to the slightly longer ring of these instruments.

Claves are two cylinders of wood about six inches long and one inch in diameter. One cylinder is held loosely in the player's hand and struck with the other. The sound is a very hollow, brittle click, bright and well-focused. (The claves make excellent sopranino woodblocks.)

Castanets are flat, partially hollow pieces of hard wood or plastic mounted in pairs to click together. The castanets used in bands and orchestras usually have handles attached to them or are mounted on a base or frame. The hand-held instruments are often slapped against the performer's knee. The frame-mounted (or mechanical) castanets are struck with the performer's hands. Besides the obvious Spanish flavor they provide, castanets may also add a bright snapping click to any texture.

Guiro is a Latin American instrument made from a hollow gourd. It has a slit lengthways and has been serrated crossways. It is scraped back and forth with a three-pronged metal fork or a wooden stick (guiro scraper) producing a *pianissimo* ratchet sound. In addition to atmospheric uses, the guiro can provide an edge of excitement to a glissando or rapid scale passage.

Maracas are hollow gourds that have been loaded with steel shot or seeds and to which handles are attached. The normal performance technique is to shake the maracas in a steady rhythm. Other less characteristic uses would be extended rolls or quick, staccato shakes to accent or highlight an effect.

Like the guiro and maracas, the *cabasa* is a Latin American instrument. It is a large, heavy gourd with a handle attached. The outer surface of the gourd is rough and the gourd is covered with a loose netting of ceramic beads. The performer holds the instrument in the palm of one hand, preventing the beads from moving, and rotates the gourd with the other hand. The sound is a rather loud, shuffling-like rattle.

Jaw bone of an ass is literally what the name says. It is not wood, but has the sound of a wooden instrument. The jaw bone is struck by the heel of the hand, and the teeth—which are loose in the jaw—rattle. The sound of the jaw bone, or *quijada* as it is often called, is a mixture of a rattlesnake rattle and a large rubber band having been plucked. The only source for the instrument is Mexico; it has become scarce in recent years. For this reason a substitute instrument, the *vibra slap,* has been produced from heavy steel rod, bent into the shape of a pistol grip. One end has a wooden ball attached while the other end has a small tapered wooden box, open on one end, fastened to it. In the box are rivets that are free to bounce up and down. The performer holds the vibra slap by the "pistol grip" and strikes his hand with the wooden ball, producing an acceptable imitation of the jaw bone sound.

Slit drums are wooden drums. Most are homemade and resemble apple boxes that are completely enclosed but with different sized slits cut into the sides. They are played with various mallets and sticks. The sound they produce has a hollow, thumpy quality that changes relative pitch and timbre as various parts of the drum are struck; this sound could be described as a tenor-bass woodblock quality. Slit drums can produce specific pitches, but one seldom has a *set* of pitches available. Nor is it especially easy to build a drum that will produce a specific pitch. Therefore, unless one's own situation offers other possibilities, it is usually best to write for slit drums as indefinite-pitched instruments.

Indefinite-Pitched Metals

Finger cymbals are very small cymbals, about an inch and a half in diameter, that have loops of string attached to them. They are usually used in pairs; one cymbal is held in each hand and the two are brought together rim to rim. The tone is high-pitched and somewhat bell-like, perhaps even a little "tinny." A finger cymbal may also be suspended from a frame and played with a stick or mallet; in this playing position, a triangle beater works well.

A pair of large cymbals (each with a strap or handle attached to the middle), held in the hands and played by striking together are called *crash cymbals.* Normally crash cymbals are between 14 and 30 inches in diameter. The most common effect called for is simply a note or series of notes which are realized by the performer bringing the cymbals together with a combination crashing and sliding motion. Two other effects are sometimes called for: roll and tremolo. The roll involves a repeated circular sliding of two contacting cymbals past each other at a distance varying continuously from 0 to 3 inches apart. The tremolo requires the performer to crash the cymbals together and then quickly move the vibrating cymbals toward and away from the audience, creating a Doppler effect.[5] To work effectively, the tremolo requires a very quiet texture after a fairly loud crash of the cymbals or the effect, which is subtle, will not be audible.

If a cymbal is allowed to hang from a frame or rack, it becomes a *suspended cymbal.* Suspended cymbals are played with snare drum sticks, yarn mallets, wire brushes, triangle beaters, and other mallets capable of producing a sound. The raised center of a cymbal, known as the *dome* or *crown,* is often struck instead of the main plate surface. The sound achieved by striking the crown is bright and bell-like. The edge may also be struck, giving a slightly darker effect, or it may be bowed or scraped with a triangle beater or other object. Another effect is to scrape the surface of the cymbal, from the crown to the edge or vice versa, with a triangle beater, coin, or other items.

A *sizzle cymbal* is a suspended cymbal that has been caused to "sizzle" or

[5]The Doppler effect, named for Christian Doppler, a mathematician and physicist (1803-1853), is the apparent raising of the pitch heard by a listener as a sounding object approaches, and the apparent lowering of the pitch as the sounding object recedes.

rattle. There are three ways the sizzle cymbal effect may be achieved. In one method, the cymbal is specially constructed with holes drilled through it and rivets loosely fastened into these holes. In a second method, an arm with hinged ends is loosely pivoted above the dome of the cymbal and each end of the arm is allowed to touch lightly the surface of the cymbal. When the cymbal is struck the hinged ends bounce, on the cymbal's surface creating a sizzle. The third method of producing a sizzle involves hanging a lightweight chain, such as a pull chain for an electric light, over the cymbal. The chain is secured to the center of the crown of the cymbal and lies across the cymbal's surface and over the edge. In sound, the sizzle cymbal is to the suspended cymbal as the snare drum is to the tom-tom. Performance techniques are the same as those for the suspended cymbals. However, the rattle effect causes the decay to remain audible for a longer period of time.

The *hi-hat cymbals* are a pair of cymbals of about 12 to 16 inches in diameter mounted on a special stand. One cymbal is mounted crown downward while the other cymbal is mounted above it, crown upward. A mechanism in the stand is connected to a foot pedal operated by the performer. Depressing the pedal brings the two cymbals tightly together; releasing the pedal allows the two cymbals to separate. Hi-hat cymbals are regularly found as a part of the jazz drum set. They are usually played with snare drum sticks or wire brushes. The written notation for these instruments includes signs indicating the opening and closing of the cymbals. When the cymbals are to be closed (pedal depressed) the symbol is +. When the cymbals are to be opened (pedal up) the symbol is a small o.

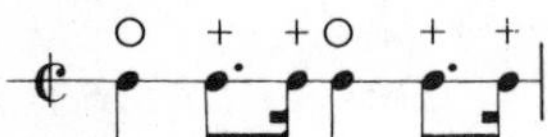

EXAMPLE 218 A typical hi-hat passage.

Made of metal with a different composition than our usual "Turkish" cymbals, the *Chinese cymbal* is equipped with a more plateau-shaped dome. The sound, although definitely cymbal in quality, has more rattle or splash to its attack. It is a cross between a tam-tam quality and a cymbal quality.

The *triangle* is a bright, perky, high-pitched bell sound that can add brightness to any ensemble. Made in the shape of a triangle, as the name implies, it may be suspended from a rack or frame, or held in the performer's hand. In the latter position, the damping of the sound is facilitated. It is usually struck with a metal rod called a triangle beater. One beater is normally assumed but two enable the performer to play intricate rhythmic figures. The triangle, like all metal instruments, has a long decay time.

Cowbells are made in a variety of sizes. The shape is more angular than that of the almglocken (see page 194) and the tone is decidedly less hollow and more metallic. The decay time of cowbells is fairly short when compared to other metals of the same size. Cowbells are made in a variety of special shapes which have special names like *samba bells,* etc., and are struck with snare sticks, yarn or rubber mallets, wire brushes, or other available beaters.

The *tam-tam*[6] is an oriental instrument with a very slow attack or rise time and an even longer decay. The tone quality is dark, ominous, mysterious, and filled with dissonant partials. Tam-tams come in a variety of sizes from small dinner bell sizes (about 6 inches in diameter) to large concert hall models that are over 36 inches in diameter. The tam-tam may be struck, scraped, or bowed. The traditional sound is obtained from a large beater with a metal core which is covered with soft sheepskin and padding. Tam-tams take so long to "bloom" that precise rhythmic figures are impossible (unless they are struck with a small, hard beater like a triangle beater). A single, hard stroke with the soft beater may require two to three seconds to crescendo up to full volume and may take 15 to 30 seconds to decay. On the other hand, a soft stroke appears a bit more rapidly, but is more felt than heard. A special tam-tam effect, called a *water gong,* calls for a tam-tam to be lowered into and raised out of a large tub of water while played. As the tam-tam is lowered, the apparent pitch is also lowered; as it is lifted out of the water, the pitch is raised. The sound produced is thus a tam-tam glissando.

Graduated bells and *bells* in general may be called for in a piece of music. Percussionists have shown great ingenuity in seeking out various types of bells to use in their performances. Among the bells more commonly used have been Indian elephant bells, dinner bells, and even large bells from carillons or ships. Unless the composer knows what bells are available to his performers, it may be impractical to do more than describe the quality of sound and relative pitches (*high* or *low,* etc.) desired. One may ask for a set of bells of like quality, arranged in some scalar order, but it is frequently more practical to allow the performer to have the final say in the selection and scaling of the bells. Thus, though these bells may produce specific pitches, treating them as indefinite pitches is often the most practical approach.

Sleighbells are just that, attached to a handle and shaken by the performer.

The *bell plate* is a heavy steel slab, from 3/16 of an inch to 3/4 of an inch in thickness and having a surface area of from 24 to 350 square inches. The bell plate is suspended by a rope or thong and may be struck by a variety of mallets, especially brass or steel mallets, or by steel hammers. The sound is a very metallic clank, which is more resonant when larger plates are used. Depending upon the composition of the metal, the bell plate may be definite- or indefinite-pitched, but the selection of pitches is usually limited.

The names *bowl gongs* or *cup bells* are applied to a variety of resonant, brightly toned metal dishes that one may strike with any of the rubber, plastic, yarn, or brass mallets. Again, these exist in many shapes and sizes, and though they may possess a specific pitch, the selection available is usually limited.

The *tubo* is a Latin American instrument. It is a tube, sealed on both ends with steel shot inside, that the performer shakes in a manner similar to maracas. Some versions of the instrument have been made of wood.

The *cymbal tongs* or metal castanets are a pair of very small cymbals attached to a curved handle that resembles a pair of sugar tongs. By squeezing the tongs together and then immediately releasing the pressure on the tongs, a very high pitched metallic clink is produced.

[6]For many years, percussionists and composers have used the term gong for both tam-tams and gongs. The recent practice, reflected in this book, is to reserve the term *gong* for definite-pitched instruments and *tam-tam* for indefinite-pitched instruments.

Brake drums are just that—automobile brake drums. They are whatever pitch they happen to be, but percussionists often go to the trouble of locating a variety of pitches. The tone quality is that of a dark bell. (They sound not unlike the bells used on locomotives, but slightly more refined.) Since the availability of pitches is subject to the whim of circumstances, it is usually practical to specify relative pitches, as in the case of bells and slit drums. Mallets used are plastic, rubber, timpani, yarn, brass, etc.

Various sizes of *iron pipe* produce various pitched clanks and clangs. These may be struck by any one of a number of hard mallets, hammers, or beaters; or one may choose to strike two pipes together. Again, it is usually practical to treat these as possessing only relative pitches.

Chains may be used either to obtain the literal sound of chains or as large, heavy metallic rattles. One may drop a chain onto a wooden or metal surface, or may alternately lift the chain with one hand and lower it with the other. Constantly moving and scraping a chain over a surface is effective and can produce the equivalent to a chain roll.

Indefinite-Pitched Skins

The *snare drum* and the methods of playing it are the bases for much modern percussion technique. The snare drum is two-headed, with snares on one side. It is usually held on a stand and played with two hard wooden sticks. The *piccolo snare* is a smaller version of the snare drum—not so much smaller in diameter, but less deep. Snare drums are made in a variety of depths from the piccolo, which is only about 3 to 4 inches deep, and the *orchestral snare,* which is about 6 to 7 inches deep, to the *field* or *military drum* which is from 18 to 36 inches deep. The snares used on all of these drums are either gut or wire wound (both types being found) and are from one or two to a dozen or more in number. The snares stretch across the bottom of the instrument and impart a buzzing rattle to every stroke. (One may specify gut or wire snares in a score if one wishes.) All modern drums with snares have mechanisms for loosening the snares and thereby eliminating their effect. The correct direction for removing the snares is *snares off.* The instructions for tightening and therefore using the snares is *snares on.* (one or the other of these instructions should be placed at every entrance in a snare drum part, since performers regularly take the snares off when the drum is not being played to avoid annoying buzzes caused by sympathetic vibrations.)

The *tenor drum* is a military or field drum with the snares off. It may be a separate, snareless instrument, or a snare drum with the snares switched off.

One may call for *muffled drum,* which involves having the performer place a cloth on the head of the drum to deaden the sound. (French: sourdiner, *not* avec sourdine; German: dämpfen, *not* mit Dämpfer; Italian: sordinare, *not* con sordina) Because in other languages the instructions *to muffle* is so similar to the instruction *to mute,* one may find percussion parts where the composer has unintentionally and incorrectly called for "muted" drums. The instruction is both ambiguous and incorrect. It means neither to remove snares nor to muffle, and must be avoided.

All of the above drums are regularly played with wire brushes and sometimes yarn mallets in addition to the various types of snare drum sticks. The tone of these drums, lower for the bigger drums, is tight and rattly. With snares off, they sound much like tom-toms and at times are used as tom-toms in some situations.

FIGURE 22. Percussion instruments: (*counterclockwise from lower right*) pair of bongos, three steel drums (bass pan, cello pan, and guitar pan), thunder sheet, conga drums, four tom-toms; (*on tray, clockwise from lower left*) sandpaper blocks, pair of claves, pair of maracas, vibra slap, jawbone of an ass, guiro, cabasa. (Photo by David Hruby.)

match inst w/ category)

2 types o' snares

Tom-toms are straight-sided drums which, in the past, have been made with two heads and exposed rims. Currently, many percussionists are showing a preference for single-headed tom-toms, which produce a slightly more resonant tone. Tom-toms are made in a variety of sizes and are played with snare drum sticks, yarn or rubber mallets, brushes, and similar strikers. The tone is hollow and sprightly, but a little duller than the tone of bongo drums.

The *bongo drums* are smaller, single-headed drums with sides that taper in at the bottom. Originally played only by the performer's hands, the bongos have the covered rims characteristic of hand drums. The tone is tight with a "pop" on the attack and a rapid decay. Bongos are still played by hand, but, even more often, are struck with small yarn mallets or lightweight sticks.

The pitch of the *timbales* is a little lower than the bongos and a little higher than the tom-toms. The shells are straight-sided with exposed rims. The bottom may be open, or may curve under, somewhat like timpani, but with a large hole cut out. The tone is more resonant than the bongos and a little more lively than that of the tom-toms. The original performance style for these single-headed drums involved the tapping of a steady rhythm on the metal shell (with the right hand) while the left hand performs accents on the head. Lightweight sticks, similar to snare sticks, are used on the timbales.

Conga drums are single-headed drums on a barrel-shaped body that is 18 to 30 inches tall. The sound is very resonant and hollow, with a great deal of "boinkiness" to the tone. The drums are played with the hands. Even though three sizes (*quinto, conga, tumba*—i.e., small, medium, large) exist, a performer usually only plays one drum, obtaining a variety of pitches by hitting the drum at various points on the head and with various portions of the hand. To facilitate usage as a hand drum, the conga drum, like the bongos, has covered rims. Complex, repetitive rhythmic figures with a lot of pitch and accent inflections are typical of Conga drum playing.

The *bass drum* is the lowest-pitched drum found in Western music. It is a two-headed drum with a very dark sound. At softer dynamics, the pitch seems to be even lower than at *fortissimo* passages. (Often the effect of the bass drum is felt rather than heard.) Like most percussion instruments, it possesses a tremendous dynamic range. The bass drum is usually played with a heavy, felt-covered beater. For rolls, a pair of lighter, felt-covered mallets, larger than timpani sticks, are commonly employed. Modern usage calls for the bass drum to be suspended from a circular frame so that the drum may be positioned vertically or, to facilitate rolls, horizontally.

The *tambourine* is an old instrument. It is a hoop of wood over which a skin head has been stretched. The sides of the hoop have slits cut into them and in each slit there are two metal jingles (or jangles) mounted so that they may shake against one another. There are three typical ways of performing the instrument: One method consists of beating out rhythms on the head with one's hand, sticks, or a combination of one's hand and knee. A second method is to shake the instrument. The third method is called a thumb roll and is produced by rubbing one's thumb along the edge of the head, against the "grain." The shake, or shake roll, is notated like any percussion roll but with the instruction *shake*. The thumb roll, which is a very delicate effect and always of short duration, is notated as a roll with the instruction *thumb roll*. One sometimes finds a headless tambourine which can produce two sounds: a rhythmic jingling or the shake roll. This form, although not a new instrument, is now most frequently seen in rock bands.

The *frame drum,* or tambourine without jingles, is a skin head mounted on a frame with no resonator. It is usually played with the hand or a soft-tipped stick. Stroked gently, it produces a delicate, snareless drum effect. Struck more vigorously, the head produces a brittle rattling, but of soft volume.

The *Chinese tom-tom* was the forerunner of the modern tom-toms. It is made in a variety of sizes. The body is about one half as thick as the diameter of the head, which is attached to the body by round-headed tacks. The instrument is played with a soft rubber or yarn mallet, usually in single strokes, and it is similar in tone to a bongo drum but with greater decay time.

The *lion's roar* is a friction drum. It is made like a single-headed drum on a straight-sided shell. To the middle of the head is attached a gut string that is about 4 to 6 feet long. The drum portion is firmly mounted and the performer, with rosined fingers or a rosined cloth, grips the string near the head (holding the string tightly yet letting it slip through his fingers) and slides his hand down the string. The low-pitched whine that is produced does resemble the roar of a lion. Various sizes of the instrument exist, often with names that reflect the highness or lowness of the growl produced.

A pair of Indian drums, the *tabla,* have recently become more frequently used in percussion writing and performance. The lower-pitched of the two, the *bhaya* (or *bamya*), looks much like a small timpano with a shell of metal. The higher-pitched drum, the *tabla* (for which the pair of drums is named), is cone-shaped with a shell of wood. The tension of the single heads of these drums is adjustable, due to various straps of leather and wooden rods. Subtle and complex pitch modifications are produced in performance by pressure on the head exerted by the heel of the performer's hand. A special feature of these instruments is a circular black spot located on the head of the drums. This spot of a hardened paste, the formulation and application of which dates to ancient rituals, is responsible for the unique timbre and tuning of these drums. Western percussionists are usually not equipped to produce the pitch intricacies characteristic of indigenous Indian music where the tabla are melodic instruments. Therefore, in Western music, one must usually treat the tabla as indefinite-pitched instruments. The tabla are hand drums.

Other Indefinite-Pitched Sound Sources

The *whip* or *slapstick* is two boards attached with a hinge. The performer opens the boards and brings them together rapidly, making a sound that is much like a buggy whip. Besides imitating a whip, it is often used to provide accents. Repeated notes need to be well spaced to allow for preparation (opening) of the boards.

The *ratchet* is four strips of hardwood, clamped at one end and with the other end pressed against a wooden or plastic gear. The gear has a crank that may be turned by the performer. When the crank is turned, a clattering rattle is produced. Dynamics may be controlled by the performer grasping the instrument in such a way that his left hand's finger can limit the travel of the wood strips, thus softening the otherwise loud sound.

The *police whistle* (sometimes called a referee's whistle), the *bird whistle,* and the *duck call* are all what the names describe.

FIGURE 23. Percussion instruments: (*rear, left to right*) sizzle cymbal, three suspended cymbals; (*middle*) marimba; (*front, left to right*) pair of timbales, two slit drums (on floor), hi-hat cymbal, two-headed tom-tom (attached to bass drum), stool for the set drummer, set bass drum with foot pedal, large two-headed tom-tom. (Photo by David Hruby.)

The *mouthsirens* are very high-pitched, breath-activated instruments, while the (hand-cranked) *siren* is like the acoustical sirens heard on fire engines in the 1930s through 1950s.

Auto horns are usually the rubber bulb-operated types associated with early automobiles.

The *thundersheet* is a large sheet, about 4 feet by 8 feet, of galvanized iron or aluminum, approximately 1/16 of an inch thick. It is best suspended from a frame so that one person may shake it. The sound is the stereotyped thunder effect of moderate loudness. The dynamics can be varied somewhat by the intensity of the shake it is given. Larger sheets, though more representational of thunder, are rare.

Sandpaper blocks are two blocks of wood covered with sandpaper on one side and with handles attached to the other. The performer holds one block in each hand and rubs the two together. The sound is that of a soft hiss and is usually of short duration. Rolls are possible, but tend to be little used.

Wind chimes are suspended from a rack or frame and are performed by being shaken or brushed in some way. The sound is a random clattering the specific quality of which depends upon the material from which the wind chimes are made. Typical materials used for wind chimes are wood, bamboo, plastic, shell, glass, steel, or brass. Once set into motion, wind chimes are difficult to stop; thus, one needs to allow a long time for the sound to cease.

The *wind machine* is a large amount of canvas laid loosely over a set of wooden rods that are arranged roughly in the form of a cylinder and attached to a crank enabling a performer to turn the rods. When the rods are turned past the cloth a whirring, windlike sound is produced. As the crank is turned faster, the pitch raises and the volume increases. It could easily be replaced by electronic imitators or recordings of wind.

The *klaxon horn* is named for the Klaxon Automobile Horn Company. It is a mechanical horn that was used on automobiles in the 1920s and 1930s. A metal plunger is rapidly depressed, causing the horn to produce its characteristic sound: "Ah-OO-ga." The term has also been used to mean any mechanical and (later) electrical horn. It is often necessary to study the musical context before one can determine what sort of horn is intended by the name klaxon.

The *pistol shot* is just that, produced with blank cartridges. To create more of a cannon effect, the pistol may be fired into a large metal (garbage) can.

Stones, musical stones, prayer stones, etc. are various names used for actual stones that produce very resonant clacks when struck together, or when struck with a hard mallet, beater, or stick. Although not common in this country, an interesting assortment of stone instruments have been produced. Included among these is a xylophone-type instrument, the *lithophone,* made of stone disks. The instrument is rare.

There are, in addition, special instruments invented or developed by percussionists and composers and called for in various pieces. A list that included these special instruments would be out-of-date as soon as it was compiled. Many of these special instruments are made out of items such as coffee cans, aluminum foil, blocks of wood, aluminum rods, and other sound-producing objects and materials.

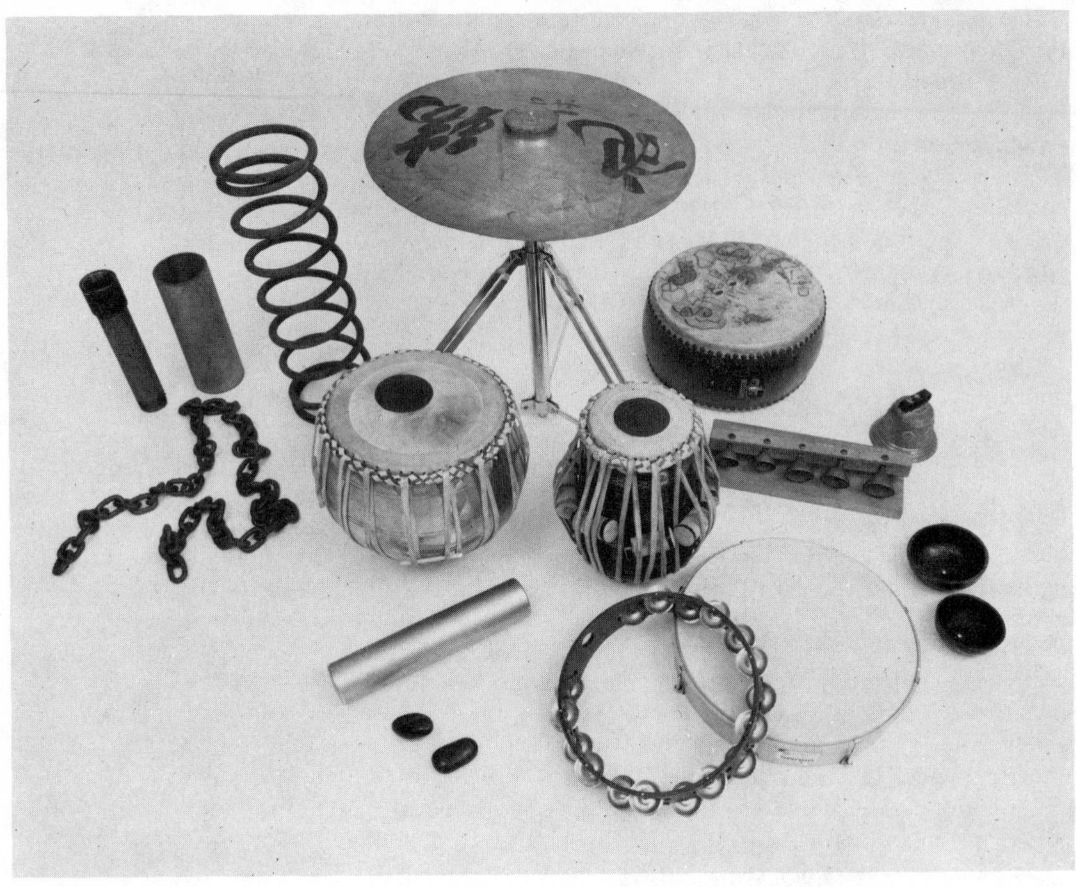

FIGURE 24. Percussion instruments: (*Back, Left to Right*) two iron pipes, automobile (**coiled**) spring, Chinese cymbal, Chinese tom-tom; (*middle, left to right*) chain, tabla (**bhaya** on left, tabla on right), five graduated bells, a Swiss bell; (*Foreground, Left to Right*) tubo, stones, headless tambourine, frame drum, and two bowl gongs. (Photo by David Hruby.)

The Drum Set

In jazz, show, and rock music, one encounters the *drum set* or *trap set*. The drum set is nothing but a variety of percussion instruments, arranged so that one performer, using both hands and both feet, can provide a wide assortment of percussive effects. The exact instruments to be found in a drum set will vary with the requirements of the musical style and the taste of the performer, but these are generally the basics:

1. A pedal-operated bass drum.
2. High-hat cymbals.
3. A snare drum.
4. High and low tom-toms.
5. Medium and large suspended cymbals.

The following are often added to the set: woodblock, šizzle cymbal, cowbell, third tom-tom, small suspended cymbal, second bass drum, triangle, various sound effects.

The cymbals used in a drum set have special names. The largest is usually called the *ride* or *bounce cymbal* and is used to carry the constant "beat" often heard in jazz or swing. These are usually between 18 and 25 inches in diameter. The next most common is a *crash cymbal* (not to be confused with the orchestral crash cymbal pair) which is a thin, 14- to 18-inch diameter cymbal used to accent the rhythmic figures. A very small (7- to 11-inch diameter) cymbal is also found which is called a *splash* or *choke cymbal.* One sometimes finds a cymbal between the ride and crash cymbals in size which is known as a *crash-ride* or *show cymbal.* The high-hat cymbals used in a drum set are sometimes called *sock cymbals.*

TYPICAL PERCUSSION SCORINGS

The following example shows typical percussion scoring as found in many nineteenth- and some twentieth-century works. Notice the use of a five-line staff for the timpani and one-line staves for the indefinite-pitched instruments.

EXAMPLE 219 First four measures of "Fandango Asturiano," the fifth movement of *Capriccio Espagnol* by Rimsky-Korsakov.

The dry, hard sound of the xylophone has often been used in connection with death dances. (Examples date from the seventeenth century.) Here is typical writing for the instrument from Saint-Saëns's *Danse Macabre.*

EXAMPLE 220 Xylophone passage from *Danse Macabre.* (This excerpt begins eight measures before rehearsal letter C.)

In the prologue to the first act of *Götterdämmerung,* Wagner wrote this part for the orchestral bells. The part is notated an octave higher than is the current practice.

EXAMPLE 221 Orchestral bells part from "Siegfried's Rhine Journey" by Wagner (measures 468-474).

Tchaikovsky wrote perhaps the most famous celesta part in the literature. The following is the beginning of the "Dance of the Sugar Plum Fairies" from the *Nutcracker Suite:*

EXAMPLE 222 Celesta solo from the *Nutcracker.*

In George Crumb's *Ancient Voices of Children* the composer has written a musical saw part. Here is a typical line for the saw, which is to be played with a violoncello or contrabass bow.

EXAMPLE 223 Musical saw passage from *Ancient Voices of Children* (second movement).[7]

Stravinsky calls for five timpani—including a piccolo timpano—and two players in *The Rite of Spring*. This passage, which uses all of the timpani plus the tam-tam and bass drum, is from two measures before rehearsal number 176.

EXAMPLE 224 Five timpani, tam-tam, and bass drum passage from *The Rite of Spring*.[8]

Snare drum scoring often appears like the following excerpt from the first movement of Prokofieff's *Lieutenant Kije Suite:*

EXAMPLE 225 Snare drum writing from the "Birth of Kije" movement of *Lieutenant Kije*.[9]

In the third movement of Crumb's *Ancient Voices of Children,* three percussionists establish this ostinato. The ostinato figure is two measures long, but is repeated until the end of the movement. The meter signature 6/♪ is another way of writing 6/8. The X-shaped note heads indicate whispered words.

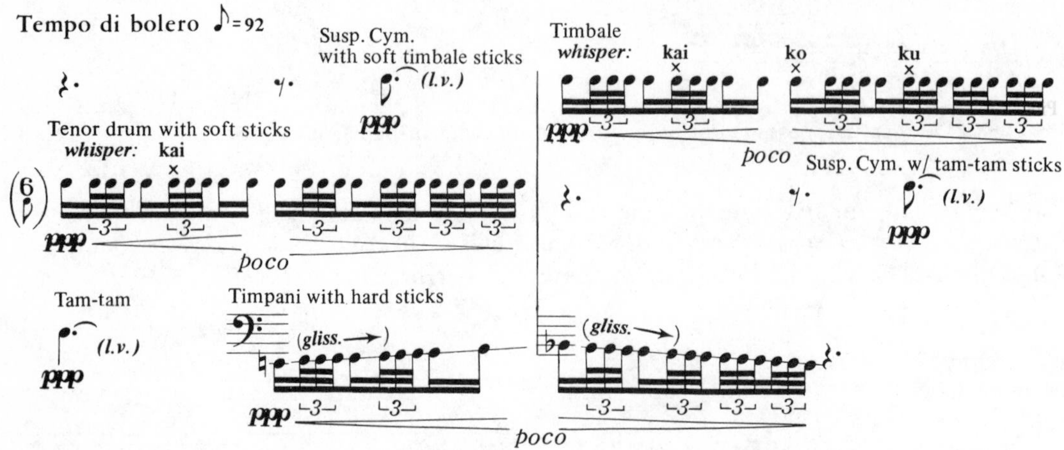

EXAMPLE 226 Percussion ostinato by George Crumb.[10]

In *Outline* for flute, percussion, and string bass, Pauline Oliveros wrote this passage for the percussion. (Excerpt is from page 3.)

EXAMPLE 227 Percussion part from a section of Oliveros's *Outline.*[11]

One of the first percussion ensemble works was *Ionisation* by Edgard Varese. The following example is the first score page from this work. The Arabic numerals to the far left (1 through 13) are used to identify the performers. Studying this score and the way in which the instruments are assigned to the performers should be valuable. This particular approach to score and part layout uses one line for each indefinite-pitched instrument.

EXAMPLE 228 First score page from Varèse's *Ionisation.*

Problem Set No. 19

1. Use the rhythmic pattern below and divide it up into various rhythmic figures. Assign these figures to the following instruments: suspended cymbal, woodblock, high and low tom-toms, claves and triangle. Have some of the completed scores performed *by class members.*

2. Score the Bach chorale harmonization below for vibraphone, marimba, and timpani. Assume that the vibraphonist and the marimbist can only use two mallets and that there are four timpani tuned to . For the purposes of sustaining the sound, write rolls on all notes that are a quarter note or more in duration. If possible, have the finished works performed.

JESU, MEINE ZUVERSICHT

J. S. Bach

3. Using the Beethoven Sonatina given in exercise 3 of Problem Set No. 6 (page 50), score it for a quartet of percussionists. The first percussionist has a snare drum and triangle; the second percussionist has a high and a low tom-tom; the third percussionist has a suspended cymbal and woodblock; and, the fourth percussionist has five temple blocks. You will have to ignore pitches, but you may wish to observe melodic contours. Use rolls, flams, etc. to color and inflect the parts. Have these "transcriptions" performed in class.

4. Using the following ostinato figure (either rhythmically or melodically or both) write a percussion piece for three performers using any available percussion instruments. For example, the steady eighths may be realized as the given pitches on a xylophone or marimba; as a steady series of eighth

notes on a woodblock or triangle; or as a series of eighth notes, but with added flams, rolls, etc., on the snare drum or tom-tom. The isolated clusters and pitches may be also treated as merely isolated percussive sounds or as pitched sounds. Do four or five differing repetitions and have the results performed in class.

5. Do exercise 4, above, with an ostinato written by a member of the class.
6. Repeat exercise 3, above, using another piece of music given in this book.
7. Using another Bach chorale harmonization or another grouping of instruments (or both), repeat exercise 2, above.
8. Write your own rhythmic pattern and treat it according to the instructions given in exercise 1, above.

PERCUSSION BIBLIOGRAPHY

Avgerinos, Gerassimos. *Handbuch der Schlag-und Effektinstrumente.* Frankfurt: Verlag Das Musikinstrument, 1967.

Blades, James. *Orchestral Percussion Technique.* 2nd edition. New York: Oxford University Press, 1973.

Blades, James. *Percussion Instruments and Their History.* London: Faber, 1975.

Kotoński, Wlodzimierz. *Schlaginstrumente im Modernen Orchester.* Mainz: B. Schott's Söhne, 1968. (German edition of a Polish original.)

Peinkofer, Karl and Fritz Tannigel. *Handbook of Percussion Instruments.* Transl. from the original German by Kurt and Else Stone. Mainz: B. Schott's Söhne, 1976.

Reed, H. Owen and Joel T. Leach. *Scoring for Percussion.* Englewood Cliffs, N. J.: Prentice-Hall, 1969.

Smith-Brindle, Reginald. *Contemporary Percussion.* New York: Oxford University Press, 1970.

INSTRUMENTATION: *Other Instruments*

THE KEYBOARD STRINGS

The Pianoforte

English	*French*	*German*	*Italian*
pianoforte *or* piano	pianoforte *or* piano	Pianoforte *or* Piano *or* Klavier	pianoforte *or* piano

EXAMPLE 229 The range of the piano.

The tone quality varies from the lowest notes,[1] which sound gonglike, through the middle range, the most characteristically piano portion of its compass, to the top, flutey, bell-like register.

Pianos come in various models and designs, from the 12-foot concert grand to the various upright and spinet pianos. The larger pianos possess a more resonant tone quality and are characterized by full, rich bass pitches. The smaller pianos lose their lowest octaves' resonances.

Each key, when depressed, throws a hammer toward the strings. Before the hammer strikes the strings of a particular note, a damper is lifted that allows the strings to ring. The hammer then strikes the strings and returns to its normal

[1]Certain manufacturers add this lowest octave to the range of the piano to improve the resonance and richness of sound in the upper registers. The sound of these extra bass notes is "thuddy," with a rather wooden, percussive quality, and they are therefore not often actually played.

position. As long as the performer's finger depresses the key, the damper remains off the strings, allowing them to continue to ring until their tones have died away.

From about tenor C upward, all hammers strike three strings when activated. From on downward, each hammer strikes two strings. Below , each hammer strikes but one string.

Above there are no dampers on the strings, since the decay of these high-pitched strings is so rapid that in order to be heard at all, maximum ring must be obtained.[2] These high-pitched strings also vibrate sympathetically with the sounding of lower-pitched strings.

By depressing the far right-hand pedal, called the *damper pedal,* the performer can remove all dampers from all strings, allowing maximum sympathetic vibrations throughout the piano's range.

The middle pedal, called the *sostenuto pedal,* catches only the dampers that have been lifted by the performer's fingers and keeps them up, even after the fingers have been removed from the keys. It is important to realize that the sostenuto will only hold dampers off *after* they have been lifted by the depression of the key(s) and before the key(s) is (are) released, so the pedal must be depressed after striking the key(s) but before the key(s) is (are) released.

The far left-hand pedal, called the *una corda* pedal, physically shifts the whole key-hammer mechanism to the right so that the hammers will strike only one string instead of three (or two). When the effect is no longer desired and the left-hand pedal is to be released, the instruction is *tre corda.* In Beethoven and in modern works, one can find indications such as *due corde* which indicates that the *una corda* is only to be depressed far enough to reduce the number of strings sounding to two. It is possible to call for *poco a poco due corde,* or—starting from *una corda*—to call for *poco a poco tre corde.* (The former is found in Beethoven's Opus 101 piano sonata.) Neither of these is actually performable since the hammers must always strike one, two, or three strings but, the sound ideal can be accomplished.

Abbreviations commonly used for the three piano pedals are: Ped. (for the *damper* pedal); *Sos* (for the *sostenuto* pedal); and *U.C.* (for the *una corda*). The use of T.C. for the release of the *una corda* is also found. More precise pedallings, including the gradual depression or release of a pedal, can be indicated as follows:

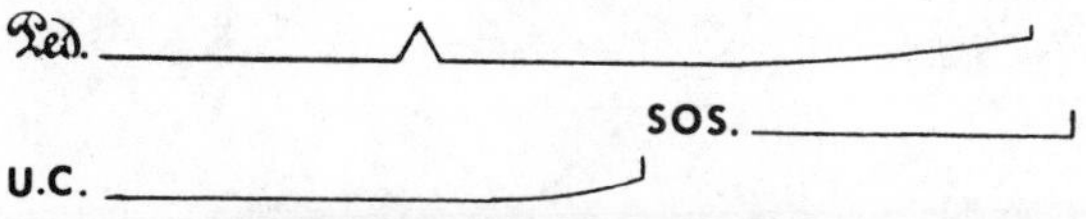

FIGURE 25. Precise pedaling notation. (Note the order from top to bottom; this is standard practice.)

[2] These exact points vary with manufacturer and model.

English	*French*	*German*	*Italian*
key	touche	Taste	tasto
damper	étouffoir	Dämpfer	smorzo *or* smorzatoio *or* smorzatore
hammer	marteau	Hammer	martello *or* martelletto
damper pedal	pédale forte *or* pédale de résonance	Fortepedal	pedale di risonanza *or* pedale del forte
sostenuto pedal	pedale de prolongation	Tonhaltepedal	pedale tonale *or* pedale solleva-smorzatori
una corda	una corda *or* avec pédale sourdine, *or* avec céleste	una corda *or* mit Verschiebung	una corda
tre corde	toutes les cordes	alle Saiten	tre corde

Characteristics of the Piano

The piano has no sustaining power to speak of. Once a note is struck, it immediately begins to die away. Therefore, a *crescendo* during a single pitch is impossible as is a *crescendo* during a chord, unless the chord is *rolled* (tremolo). For this reason too, slowly moving chordal music, such as one associates with the pipe organ, is not at all idiomatic for the piano. On the other hand, chimelike effects in which the decay is a desired coloristic effect, are very good and well provided by the piano.

The piano's ability to play staccato is almost on a par with the string pizzicato and the xylophone. It is an excellent instrument for dry, clean playing and for clarifying an attack with which it is associated. It is especially useful for minimizing the muddiness often found in low-pitched passages performed on other instruments.

Some Limitations

The large space between the thumb and index finger is, on the right hand, located at a lower pitch level than are the short spaces between the other fingers; on the left hand, the situation is reversed. This means that when large stretches are needed, the spacing of the pitches needs to be like this: left hand] larger interval

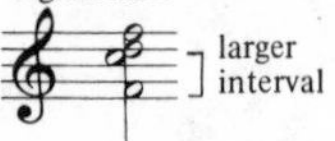

It is possible for the thumb of either hand, or any of the fingers, to play two notes at the same time. For the thumb, the two pitches may be either two adjacent white keys or two adjacent black keys (such as F♯ and G♯)] thumb.

For the fingers, the only possibilities are adjacent white keys.

The normal limit for the distance between the thumb and little finger is an octave. A ninth is possible for some players and, in rare cases, one can find a performer than can span a tenth. However, *the closer together the thumb and index finger are required to play* in a given chord, *the more restricted the span between the thumb and little finger must be.*

Special Effects

Among the special effects available on the piano is the obtaining of resonances by silently depressing a key or several keys or by depressing the damper pedal and then playing another instrument (such as a flute) into the piano, allowing the strings to vibrate sympathetically. Without involving another instrument, the piano can accomplish much the same effect by having the performer depress some keys silently and, while these are being held down, strike other keys. The reverse, depressing a key silently and then striking a chord, also works well.

The use of the interior of the piano provides for several interesting effects. Rubbing the strings with the finger tips (flesh) or fingernails with or without depressing the dampers or some of the keys, provides for a pseudo-harp effect. Plucking individual strings also works well, as does damping strings before, during, or after playing them in the normal manner. By moving the finger along a string, carefully touching the nodes, one can produce a series of natural harmonics just as one can on other string instruments. Scraping a fingernail along the wrapped bass strings provides the effect of very rapid attacks.

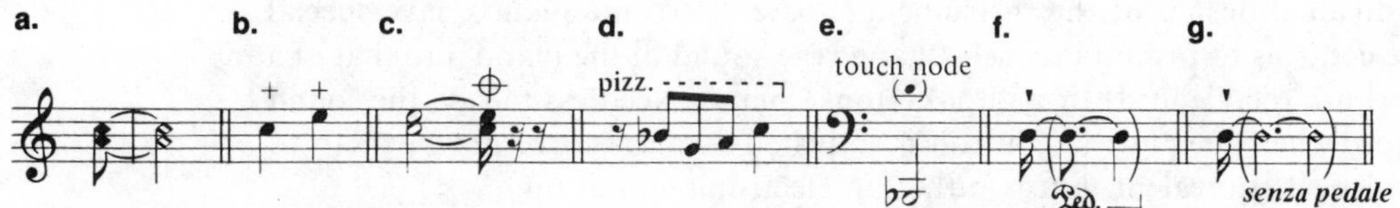

EXAMPLE 230 a. Depress keys silently. b. Stop or muffle string with finger. c. Dampen with hand. d. Pluck the strings. e. Harmonic produced by touching node to obtain small note pitch when key is struck. f. Catch and sustain with pedal. g. Catch and sustain with key.

Among effects requiring special equipment are many that utilize percussion mallets, sticks, or guitar picks. Most of these are similar to those discussed above, but modified due to the mallets or other devices used to start the sounds. Other possible sounds, not related to those discussed before, are the slipping of a sheet of paper or cardboard under the dampers to create a quasi-harpsichord (cembalo) effect. Waxed paper or aluminum foil could be used for other sounds.

When these devices get more complex, it often requires taking time to prepare the piano. In this process, one can attach nuts and bolts to the strings at particular nodal points, or insert erasers at certain spots, or place paper clips on the strings. All of these modify the sound of the piano and (especially) expand the percussive attributes of the instrument. Rosined strands of material, much like the bow hair used on orchestral strings' bows, can be threaded under individual strings of the piano and pulled back and forth, producing a bowed piano effect. As with all of the piano interior effects discussed, time is required for the performer to move from a normal, seated playing position to the interior performance position, which is usually a standing position. For some effects, it may be necessary for the performer to move around to one of the sides of the instrument.

The Electronic Piano

There are basically two types of electronic pianos manufactured. One type utilizes small metal bars that are struck when a key is depressed and then the sound of the bars ringing is amplified and broadcast through a speaker system. This type of electronic piano comes closer in sound than any other to imitating the acoustical piano.

The other type of electronic piano is purely electronic. The depressing of a key turns on an electronic oscillator, the attack characteristics of which are controlled by the speed at which the key is depressed. Once the tone begins to sound, it also begins to decay, unless it is sustained by the use of a pedal. Since the tone of this type of electronic piano is controlled by electronic means, it is possible to modify and alter any component of its sound. These pianos do not imitate the sound of acoustical pianos as well as the metal-bar pianos, but they offer more interesting sound possibilities.

Characteristics of Electronic Pianos

Most electronic pianos, no matter the manufacturer, are equipped with controls for regulating the loudness, attack characteristics, and decay time of the instrument. The amount of control for each of these aspects of sound varies with the individual design of the instrument. Some electronic pianos have special timbre controls to instantaneously change the sound of the piano into that of a harpsichord (clavichord) or a "honky-tonk" piano. Needless to say, the sound produced when one of these controls is activated does not correspond exactly to its acoustical equivalent, but is rather an electronic imitation.

A few electronic pianos have a full 88-note keyboard. Most, however, have shorter keyboards of 61 keys or so. The actual number varies from model to model. On some of the shorter-keyboard models, a separate control for changing octaves is provided. With this control it is possible to play a certain note by depressing a key and then, by switching the control, cause the same key to produce a pitch an octave higher.

Other possible characteristics of the electronic piano are inherent in the fact that it *is* electronic. Being such, its output can be processed by an electronic device capable of modifying audio signals.

Toy Pianos

In general, toy pianos are not at all like pianos, except for the most superficial characteristics. The internal mechanism tends to be a primitive collection of metal rods which produce a sound when struck by "hammers" activated by the keys. Most cheaper models usually offer no more than eight notes, approximating the diatonic scale from, nominally, C to C. (One cannot be sure without trying the instrument which octave may be involved nor how close to concert tuning the piano may be built.) On the other hand, more expensive models are chromatic and cover a range of a tenth, a twelfth, or more. The sound of the toy piano is tinny and decays rapidly. Examples of its use may be found in George

Crumb's *Ancient Voices of Children,* Terry Riley's *In C,* and Donald Jenni's *Cucumber Music.*

The Harpsichords

English	*French*	*German*	*Italian*
harpsichord	clavecin	Cembalo *or* Clavicembalo	cembalo *or* clavicembalo *or* arpicordo

The harpsichord produces its tone by the action of a quill plucking a string. The quill is attached to a jack which is raised when a key is depressed. The harpsichord is an old instrument that has been reborn in our time. Historical instruments were generally fairly simple and lacked many of the features found on modern versions, although most of the modern devices do have historical prototypes.

The instrument may have one or two keyboards (*manuals*). Some larger instruments may even have three keyboards or possess a pedal clavier. Each keyboard has one or more sets of strings that are activated by the jacks of that keyboard. On most modern instruments the upper manual has two sets of strings tuned to produce the unison pitch (8′) and the octave above (4′ pitch.)[3] The lower manual will often have three sets of strings tuned to the 8′ and 4′ pitches as well as an octave lower (16′ pitch.) One may occasionally find an instrument with a set of strings tuned two octaves above unison (2′ pitch.)[4]

The control of these sets of strings, called *stops* or *registers,* is by foot-pedals or hand-drawn levers or knobs. The latter are more historically accurate. The upper keyboard is often equipped with a device called a *damper* for changing the timbre of the strings to that of a lute or guitar. This mechanism mutes or damps the strings, allowing the pizzicato attack characteristic to be more clearly perceived. By the use of a *coupler,* it is possible to interconnect the two manuals so that by playing keys on the lower keyboard the same keys on the upper keyboard are simultaneously activated.

English	*French*	*German*	*Italian*
quill	bec *or* plectre	Kiel	plettro
jack	sautereau	Springer *or* Docke	salterello
register *or* stop	registre	Register	registro
damper *or* mute	étouffoir	Dämpfer	smorzatore
coupler	accouplement	Koppel	accoppiamento

a.

b.

EXAMPLE 231 a. Most modern harpsichords possess this range. b. Historically accurate harpsichords may have either of these ranges.

[3]For an explanation of these pitch symbols, see pages 240-241.

[4]On historical instruments the use of 16′ or 2′ tunings was rare.

The harpsichord has a very delicate sound with almost no means of controlling dynamics except for the use of registers, couplers, or the damper, and these effects are subtle compared to the typical dynamic ranges associated with modern instruments. Writing for the harpsichord requires careful control of the balance when other instruments are involved. (The judicious use of amplification is often valuable.) Examples of modern uses of the harpsichord are found in the music of Manuel de Falla, Frank Martin, and Elliott Carter.

HARPSICHORD BIBLIOGRAPHY

Albarda, Jan H. *Wood, Wire, and Quill.* Toronto: Coach House Press, 1968.

Hubbard, Frank. *Three Centuries of Harpsichord Making.* Cambridge, Mass.: Harvard University Press, 1965.

THE HARPS

The Double-Action Harp

English	*French*	*German*	*Italian*
harp	harpe	Harfe	arpa
double-action harp	harpe à double mouvement	Doppelpedalharfe	arpa a doppio movimento

The modern double-action harp is unique. No other instrument operates on the same principles. The harp has forty-seven strings covering the following range:

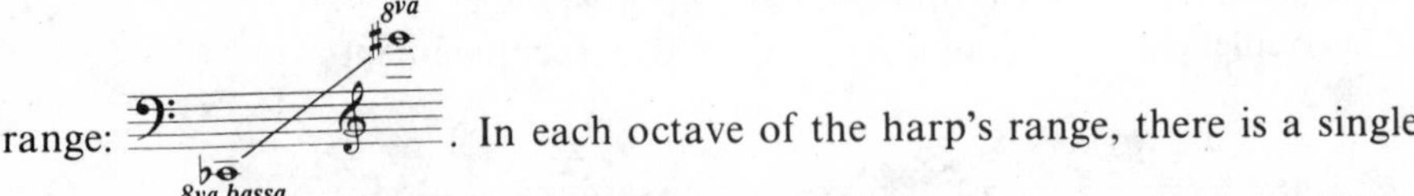

. In each octave of the harp's range, there is a single string for each pitch class—in other words, a C-class string for playing C♭, C, or C♯; a D-class string for playing D♭, D, or D♯; and so on through a B-class string for playing B♭, B, or B♯. Since at any one time a string can only be tuned to one pitch (for example F♯), it is impossible to play both a particular pitch and its sharped or flatted variant (say an F and an F♯) together.

The selection of the specific tuning of a string is controlled by a foot pedal. There are seven foot pedals, one for each pitch class, so that if one wishes to tune a C string to C♯, one places the C pedal in the C♯ position, but then all C strings

FIGURE 26. (*left*) troubadour harp; (*right*) double action harp. (Photo by David Hruby.)

become C-sharps. However, this problem is offset somewhat by the fact that all strings have three tuning positions: flat, natural, or sharp.[5] Thus, though F and F♯ cannot be played together, E♯ and F♯ *can* be played at the same time.

The pedals that control the tunings are located at the base of the harp—three on the player's left and four on the player's right. Looking down from where the performer sits, the pedals look like this:

[5]On most harps, the lowest two strings are not affected by the pedal mechanism. Therefore, these must be tuned to the pitches required in a piece prior to the performance. Changing the pitches of either of these strings during a performance is seldom practical.

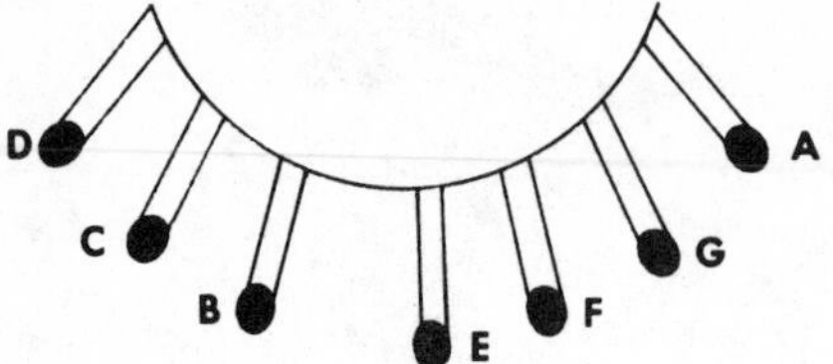

FIGURE 27. The pedals of the harp.

In order that the mechanism of the double-action harp function as intended, it is necessary for the unstopped strings of the harp to be tuned to the C♭ major scale. If this is done, one will end up with a scale of C♭, D♭, E♭, F♭, G♭, A♭, B♭ in each octave. If one were to effectively shorten any of these strings by the appropriate amount, the pitch of the shortened string would rise one half-step. This is what the pedal tuning mechanism of the harp does. When the pedal is moved from the "off" position to the first "on" position, it causes a mechanical stopping device to shorten the strings associated with that pedal's pitch class. The amount each string is shortened is just enough to raise the pitch a semitone. When the pedal is moved from the first "on" position to the second "on" position, another device shortens the string again, this time raising the pitch another semitone. Thus, when the pedal mechanism is off, the pitch will be, for example, C♭. When the pedal moves into the first "on" position, the string is shortened to C♮, and when the pedal is moved into the second "on" position, the pitch is raised to C♯.

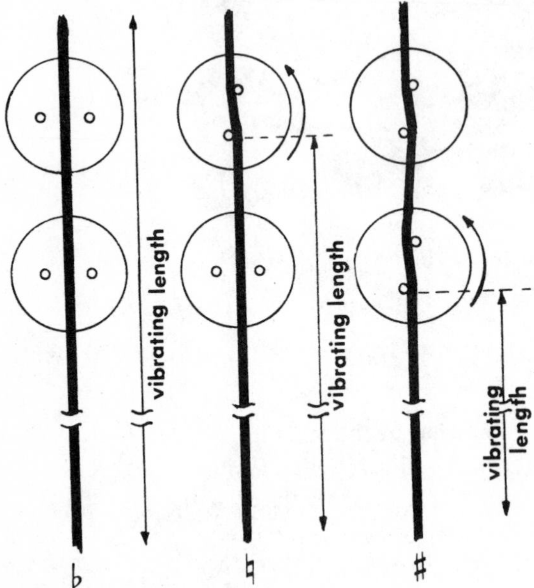

FIGURE 28. The effect of the harp's tuning mechanism on a string. (left) mechanism "off" producing flatted pitch; (center) mechanism in first "on" position producing natural pitch; (right) mechanism in second "on" position producing sharped pitch.

Because of the mechanical requirements of the instrument, the pedals must operate in this fashion: When the pedal is not depressed—that is, when it is all the way up, in the top notch—the stopping mechanism is off. When the pedal is moved down to the middle notch and latched in that position, the mechanism is moved into the first "on" position. When the pedal is moved all the way down into the bottom notch and latched in that position, the mechanism is moved into the second "on" position:

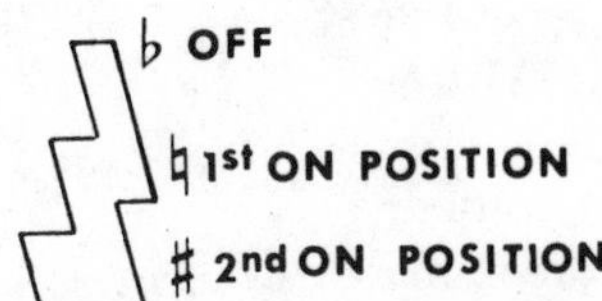

If one wished to have the harp play a G harmonic minor scale, the harpist would have to arrange the pedals in a particular way to obtain the needed pitches. Thus, the notes of the scale (G, A, B♭, C, D, E♭, F♯) would be translated into the following pedal positions: G = 1st "on" position (middle notch); A = 1st "on" position (middle notch); B♭ = "off" position (top notch); C = 1st "on" position (middle notch); D = 1st "on" position (middle notch); E♭ = "off" position (top notch); and F♯ = 2nd "on" position (bottom notch). Writing out all of this information for the harpist would be quite an annoyance, but not telling the harpist in advance how to arrange the pedals could leave the performer in a situation in which he or she might be totally unprepared for a particular passage and—because the pedals were not set correctly—unable to play the passage. What the orchestrator is expected to do is to indicate to the harpist how to set the pedals and when to change the pedals. One way would be to simply list the tunings of the strings (settings of the pedals). This is usually done in the order in which the pedals *appear* on the harp from left to right. Thus, for our scale above, we would list these settings: D♮ C♮ B♭ E♭ F♯ G♮ A♮. A symbolic system that a lot of harpists use (and which anyone writing much for the harp should learn) involves a pictogram of the harp pedals, showing the pedal settings required. For our scale, the pictogram would look like this: . Each heavy vertical line represents a pedal, while the light vertical line represents the centerline of the harp; pedals to the left of this line are on the left side of the harp and pedals to the right of this line are on the right side of the harp.

In the normal playing position, one foot is placed on either side of the instrument and the instrument is tipped back to rest on the right shoulder of the player. Changing two pedals, one on each side of the instrument, at the same time, is about as complicated a pedaling as one wishes to call for. It is possible to change two pedals on the same side simultaneously if the pedals are side by side and if the direction, the starting notch, and the amount of movement are all the same.

Changing two pedals on the same side at the same time, but involving pedals that are not adjacent or which move in different ways, would require having the harpist place both feet on the same side of the instrument. This is theoretically possible, but the loss of balance this would cause the harpist would make one wish to avoid such a maneuver, unless it was specifically tried and approved by a competent harpist.

Music for the harp is written on two staves, like piano music, with the upper stave usually representing the right hand and the lower the left hand. Treble and bass clefs are used and either clef may be placed in either staff. Because of the position in which the harp is held, the harpist's left hand can reach further down the harp than his right hand can. Both hands can be employed in the higher range of the instrument, but only the left can be expected to reach the lowest octave.

The hand technique used in modern harp playing involves the use of the thumb and three fingers on each hand. (The little finger is not used at all.) Therefore, chords involving four or fewer notes per hand are idiomatic, while chords involving more than four notes per hand are unplayable. In the playing position, both of the harpist's thumbs are closer to the performer (and therefore in the higher range) than are the fingers. For this reason, chords in either hand should avoid large intervals between lower pitches and instead favor large intervals between higher pitches: This: —not this: . This principle of voicing chords with the larger interval above the smaller intervals is true for both hands. Average hands can span an interval of a tenth from thumb to ring finger.

Pitch Problems

The harp presents some pitch problems for the composer. These stem from the fact that not all pitch configurations are possible. For example, this chord is not playable on the harp: while this chord is: . A skilled harpist would, upon encountering the first chord, rewrite it as the second chord *if the necessary pedal changes can be made in time.* A well-written harp part should not require the performer to rescore it before it is performable; this means that for certain passages a lot of effort and thought on the part of the composer may have to go into the harp part. The solution may be to use enharmonic equivalents, forgetting for the moment "correct" spellings, or perhaps the whole passage may need to be rewritten just to enable the harp to produce a particularly important sound.

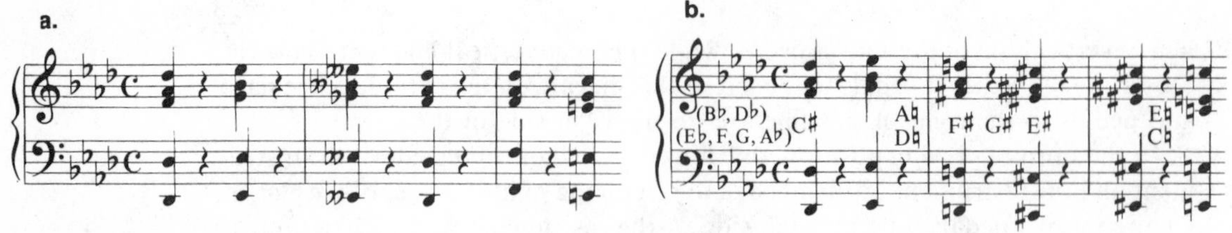

EXAMPLE 232 a. A Passage that is unplayable on the harp. b. The same passage now written to be playable on the harp.

Pitch Assets

The pitch characteristics of the harp are not all problems. Some of the characteristics are assets to the composer. The enharmonic possibilities lead to a common harp effect which is the playing of a tremolo using two different strings each tuned, enharmonically, to the same pitch. This allows the harpist to use a separate finger on each string, thereby increasing the loudness of the passage, the speed of the alternation, and improving the control available to the performer.

A similar effect, produced at soft dynamics and with less clearly defined articulation, is called *bisbigliando* or "whispering" (French: chuchotant; German: flüsternd; Italian: bisbigliando). It may be achieved with the enharmonic or with normal tremolos.

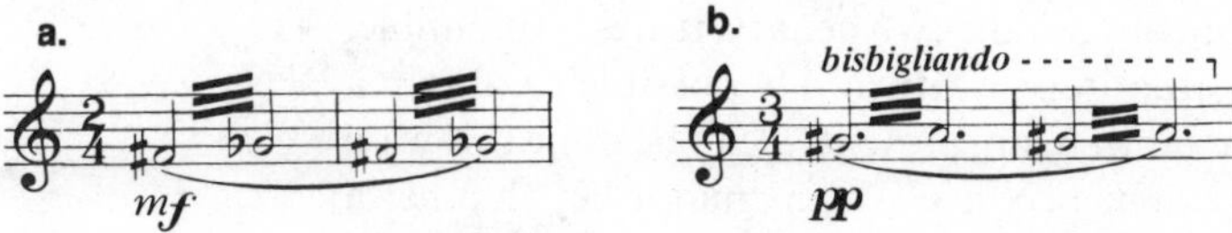

EXAMPLE 233 a. Enharmonic tremolo. b. Normal tremolo played *bisbigliando.*

The enharmonic tuning of strings is especially valuable to reinforce lower tones that are often weak, or to bring out important pitches. Whenever possible, harpists prefer to obtain rapidly repeated notes by the alternation of two strings tuned to the same enharmonic pitch. Because replacing a finger on a vibrating string can often cause an unwanted buzz, rapid repetitions sound better and cause fewer performance problems for the player if it is possible to alternate strings.

The Glissando

Among the most recognizable harp effects is the glissando. These are produced by having the performer strum the strings of the harp in a continuous motion up or down (or both). One-handed, two-handed, single-note and multiple-note glissandos are all possible.

EXAMPLE 234 a. Single-note or one-finger glissando. b. A three-note glissando. c. A one-note glissando in both hands.

In selecting the pitches for harp glissandos, the composer can have a great deal of freedom, since he can specify the tuning desired for each string. The changing of tunings in the middle of the glissando is possible, but requires special consideration. If one wishes to have a harp glissando that is harmonically a dominant seventh chord in B♭, one would like to have the following (and only the following) pitches in the glissando: F, A, C, E♭. But, as the harpist's hand moves over the strings, all seven strings in each octave are going to vibrate. It makes it necessary, therefore, to also select tunings for the B, D, and G strings. The B string can be tuned to B♯ (enharmonically C) and the D string can be tuned to D♯ (enharmonically E♭) but the G string is going to be G♭, G, or G♯. Probably, of the three choices, the G-natural tuning is the least objectionable, but then the chord actually heard in the glissando will be a dominant ninth chord and not a dominant seventh. Another possibility would be to tune the E string to E♯, reinforcing the root of the chord and leaving it for the D♯ to provide the seventh. As much of an improvement as the latter suggestion would seem to be, in almost all situations the difference between the two pedal settings is inaudible.

If one wishes to summarize the situations in which it is possible to obtain a dominant seventh chord without the ninth being present, it can be done this way: dominant seventh chord glissandos can be produced in any major key that has a key signature of three or more sharps or five or more flats or an enharmonic equivalent of one of these keys. In all keys involving two or less sharps or four or less flats in the signature, or their enharmonic equivalents, the closest approximation to a dominant seventh chord is a dominant ninth.[6]

Possible dominant-seventh glissandos	*Dominant ninth glissandos*
Key of C♭ (or B♮)	Key of F (or E♯)
C♯ (or D♭)	G
E (or F♭)	A♭ (or G♯)
F♯ (or G♭)	B♭ (or A♯)
A	C (or B♯)
	D
	E♭ (or D♯)

On the other hand, full diminished seventh chords present no problems for harp glissandos. It is possible to set the pedals of the harp in such a way as to produce only the pitches that make up any of the possible fully diminished seventh chords.

Harmonics

Harmonics are produced on the harp by touching the string at the middle node while plucking the string with the thumb. It is a one-hand execution requiring very careful positioning of the hand in order to both pluck the string and to touch the node. In the right hand, the knuckle of the first finger touches the node while in the left hand the heel of the hand touches the node. Usually, harmonics sound an octave higher than notated. Since there are examples of harmonics being written at sounding pitch, a note to the performer explaining the

[6]It is possible to silence the unwanted ninth, or other pitch, during a glissando by having the harpist deaden the unwanted strings successively with one hand while playing the glissando with the other. (A note to this effect would be required in the part.) This is not practical in very fast glissandos. Also, whether indicated or not, harpists often use two hands on a glissando to increase the loudness, making it impossible to stop any of the strings.

notation in use is necessary. Harmonics using the third and higher partials are possible, but there is no standard notation. One would have to explain to the performer what harmonic is desired, and how it is to be produced.

Pedal Glissando

The pedal glissando is especially useful in solo music or melodic playing of a popular or jazz quality to inflect the pitches. It is executed by preparing to move a pedal before playing a note or chord, but only moving the pedal after the string(s) has (have) been plucked. The effect will work either as an ascending or descending inflection, but the latter is less subject to the buzz caused by the pins (that stop the string) being struck by a vibrating string.

Sons Étouffes

When a very dry staccato is desired, the appropriate instruction is *sons étouffes* or *dampen* (French: sons étouffes; German: dämpfen; Italian: velare *or* coprire.) Normally, this involves the replacing of a finger on the string immediately after plucking the string. When the procedure is not possible, due to the need to move the finger to a new position, other fingers or the heel or palm of either hand may be used to damp the sound. A symbol that is used for the effect is: ⊕ and by the use of this symbol it is possible to indicate the damping of a single note, a part of a chord, or a whole chord. Normally, when *sons étouffes* is not specified, it is assumed that the tone of the harp is allowed to ring until it fades away naturally. Should there be some doubt as to whether the tone is to ring or be damped, the indication *laissez vibrer* or *let vibrate* is used (French: laissez vibrer; German: klingen lassen; Italian: lasciar vibrare.) The common abbreviation is L.V.

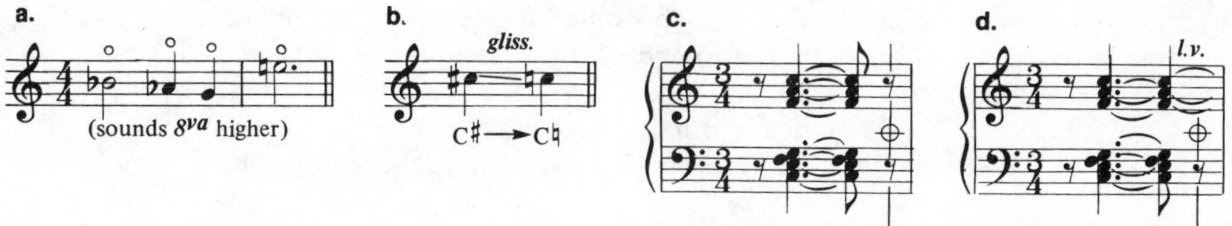

EXAMPLE 235 a. Harp harmonics. b. Pedal glissando. c. *Sons étouffes,* all notes to be silenced on the last eighth note. d. *Sons étouffes,* lower strings to be silenced on the last eighth while the upper strings are allowed to ring.

Quasi Guitara

A sound that resembles a guitar or lute is achieved by plucking the strings very low near the soundboard rather than near the middle as is usual. The instruction for this effect can be either *quasi guitara* or *près de la table.* (French: près de la table; German: Resonanztisch; Italian: presso sulla tavola.)

Special Effects

Special effects sometimes called for in harp writing include plucking the strings with the fingernails; playing glissandos with the nails; tapping on the sounding board or other parts of the instrument; using a metal rod that slides along a string to achieve a glissando, weaving paper, cloth, or other substances between the strings to change the timbre; scordatura; and the use of picks, combs, brushes, and various percussion mallets and beaters on the strings or other parts of the instrument.

Solo Writing

Solo writing for the harp is more effective when it involves full chords and a fairly busy texture. However, a great amount of intricate counterpoint is neither clear nor idiomatic. Often a single chord, note, or other coloration is more effective than too many notes would be.

When dealing with tonal music that modulates to keys with more sharps (toward the dominant) it is best to take advantage of the enharmonic capabilities of the harp and to start the harp part in a very flat key (for example F♭ rather than E.) If the direction of the modulation is toward the subdominant, then start in as sharp a key as is possible (E♯, not F). Even though it is not always possible to follow the foregoing suggestions, one should at least consider the possibilities before writing. It is also imperative to indicate the pedal setting in the harp part at the beginning and to keep track of all changes throughout the piece.

The Troubadour Harp

The *troubadour harp* is a smaller, simpler version of the large concert harp. It has no pedals and its principles of operation are, therefore, different. The troubadour harp has 33 strings, 7 per octave, and its range is: . The only chromatic alterations possible are achieved by raising the pitch of the strings. Each string has a lever mounted at the top on the left-hand side. When the lever is raised, the string is shortened enough to raise a pitch a semitone. Since each string has a separate and independent sharping mechanism, certain tonal possibilities exist on the troubadour harp that do not exist on the double-action harp. For example, the following chord is playable on the troubadour harp: .

Since the sharping levers are on the left side of the instrument, the performer must be allowed rests in the left-hand part in order to make any tuning changes. It is also necessary to make series of changes one after another, unless the strings to be raised are side by side. This takes time and requires the left hand to be utilized for pitch changes at these points and not for playing notes.

Fingering patterns and possibilities are the same as on the double-action harp. Harmonics can be played and, of course, glissandos. Tuning requires planning. In pieces in flat keys, the performer will need to tune the B-naturals to B-flats and E-naturals to E-flats, etc., as required. These can then be raised to naturals as the piece progresses, by the use of the levers. Instructions at the beginning are used to tell the performer of any levers that should be preset, such as "Fix F♯ III and IV" (meaning to sharp the F's in octaves III and IV). Octaves are numbered on both the double-action and troubadour harps like this:

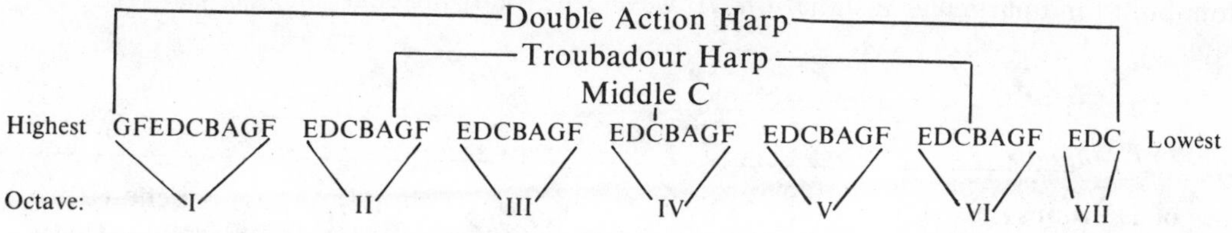

HARP BIBLIOGRAPHY

Rensch, Roslyn. *The Harp.* New York: Praeger Publishers, 1969.

Salzedo, Carlos. *Modern Study of the Harp.* New York: G. Schirmer, 1948.

THE ORGANS

The Pipe Organ

English	*French*	*German*	*Italian*
organ	orgue	Orgel	organo

The modern pipe organ consists of between one and several hundred sets (*ranks*) of pipes, controlled by one or more keyboards. Each rank of pipes has a unique tone quality. Since each pipe can only produce one pitch, it is necessary to have one pipe for each key.

The keyboards played by the performer's hands are called *manuals.* The written range of a manual is:

The keyboard played by the feet is called the *pedal clavier* and it usually has a written range of: 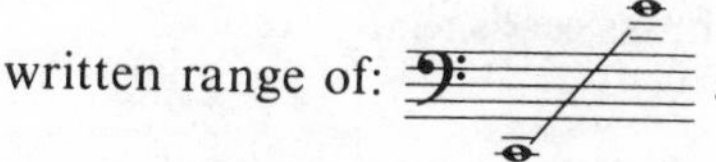 .

In a typical organ, each manual controls several musically related ranks of sixty-one pipes.[7] Such a group of ranks is known as a *division* or an *organ.* On a typical two-manual instrument, the upper manual controls the Swell Organ while the lower manual controls the Great Organ. Other divisions found on some instruments are the Choir Organ, the Positive Organ, the Solo Organ, the Echo Organ, the Antiphonal Organ, and the Bombarde Organ. The pedal clavier controls the Pedal Organ. A pedal rank typically contains thirty-two pipes.

It is not possible to say what characteristics an organ will have without examining the instrument in question. Each pipe organ is custom-designed and

[7]Typically for a variety of reasons, ranks with more and fewer pipes may be found.

custom-built for a particular installation. However, the following chart may be helpful:

Number of Manuals	*2*	*3*	*4*	*5*
Names of Divisions	Swell (U) Great (L)	Swell (U) Great (M) Choir (L)	Solo (U) Swell (UM) Great (LM) Choir (L)	Echo (U) Solo (UM) Swell (M) Great (LM) Choir (L)
	or	*or*		
	Great (U) Positive (L)	Swell (U) Great (M) Positive (L)		

(U=upper; L=lower; M=middle; UM=upper middle; LM=lower middle.)

Other variations are possible.

Within any one of these divisions, pipes possessing various tone qualities will be found. Some ranks will be made of loud, assertive pipes. Others will be composed of softer, more delicately toned pipes. So that the organist can control the tone quality of the instrument, mechanisms are connected to each rank to allow the pipes to speak when the appropriate keys are depressed or to *stop* the pipes from speaking. Each of these controls is called a *stop*. There is usually one rank of pipes associated with each stop. The physical device that the organist actually moves to activate a stop is called a *stop tab* or a *stop knob*.

The various tone qualities found on pipe organs can be divided into six classes:

1. Foundation stops.
2. Flute stops.
3. String stops.
4. Hybrid stops.
5. Chorus reed stops.
6. Solo reed stops.

Of these, the first four types are known as *flue* stops while the last two are *reed* stops. The distinction between flues and reeds is based upon the way the tone of the pipes is produced. Flue stops are made like whistles or recorders with the air column striking a fairly sharp lip. The reed pipes are made with brass reeds that work much like a New Year's Eve horn.

English	*French*	*German*	*Italian*
rank	registre *or* tirant	Zug	tirante
manual	manuel	Manual	manuale
pedal clavier	clavier de pédalier *or* pédalier	Pedalklaviatur	pedaliera
division *or* organ	orgue	Orgel *or* Werk	organo
Great Organ	grand orgue	Hauptwerk	grand' organo
Swell Organ	récit	Schwellwerk	corpo d'organo in cassa espressiva
Choir Organ	orgue de choeur	Chororgel	organo corale *or* organo del coro

Positive Organ	positif	Positiv	organo positivo
Echo Organ	clavier d'écho	Fernwerk *or* Echowerk	organo eco
stop tab	bouton du registre	Registertaste	tasto del registro
draw knob	pommette	Registerknöpfe	pomelli dei registri *or* bottoni dei registri
flue pipe *or* labial pipe	tuyau à bouche	Lippenpfeife	canna ad anima *or* canna labiale
reed pipe	tuyau à anche	Zungenpfeife	canna ad ancia
foundation stops	fonds	Grundstimme	registro di fondo
flute stops	jeu de flûte	Flötenstimme	registro di flauto
string stops	jeux de gambe	streichende Stimme	registri violeggianti *or* registri gambati
reed stops	jeux d'anches	Zungenstimmen	registri ad ancia *or* registri a lingua

Foundation Stops

These are the tone qualities that are uniquely those of the organ. They are metal pipes which are allowed to sound naturally. Among the names one finds associated with foundation stops are Principal, Diapason, Dulciana, Prestant, Dolcan, Octave, and Montre. According to most contemporary theories of organ design, foundation stops should be included in every division of the pipe organ.

Flute Stops

This is the largest family of pipes on the organ. Flutes are made from open pipes, stopped (covered) pipes, half-covered pipes, and harmonically blown pipes. (The latter are pipes that have air forced through them at sufficient pressure to cause them to sound an octave higher than one would expect.) The characteristic of flute tone is its strong fundamental and little overtone development. Among the names found for flute stops are Gedeckt, Bourdon, Quintaton, Stopped Diapason, Hohlflöte, Clarabella, Melodia, Flûte d'Amour, Nachthorn, Flûte Conique, Blockflöte, Rohrflöte, Koppelflöte, Chimney Flute, and Harmonic Flute.

Classical organs and classically designed organs consist primarily of foundation and flute stops.

String Stops

These stops are made from pipes that are narrower than the foundation or flute pipes. String tone is not imitative of orchestral string tone, but is applied to organ pipes that have a tone rich in upper partials. Among the string stops are Violone, Gamba, Viola Pomposa, Æoline, and Salicional.

Hybrid Stops

These stops have tone qualities that are between foundation and flute tone, or flute and string tone, and include the following: Gemshorn, Erzähler, Phonon Diapason, Tibia, and Geigenprinzipal.

Chorus Reed Stops

These reed stops have characteristically buzzy voices. In spite of the individual names by which these stops are known, they are not at all imitative of orchestral or historical instruments. The softer-toned stops add subtle color to other tonal combinations. The louder-toned stops, like trumpets, produce a brilliant and fiery mass of sound. These reeds may be used for solo or ensemble passages. Common names include Oboe, Trumpet, Bombarde, Fagotto, Clarion, Posaune, and Vox Humana.

Solo Reed Stops

These stops do often sound exactly like the historical or orchestral instrument for which they are named. These stops appeal to those who wish to recreate the orchestral voices on the organ, but these reed stops can function effectively in combinations, too. Some of the more common solo reeds are Orchestral Oboe, Trompette, Tuba Major, Schalmei, Krummhorn, Clarinet, Regal, and Cor Anglais.

Organ Pitches and Mutation Stops

If one examines a pipe organ or the specifications (listing of stops) for a pipe organ, one notices that most organ stops have a name and a number. For example, one will see *Diapason 8′* or *Oboe 4′*. The numbers are organ nomenclature for pitch. The system is based upon the fact that an open pipe, or air column, eight feet long will produce a pitch that is low C:  . If one doubles the length of the pipe to 16′, the pitch produced will be an octave lower. If on the other hand, one divides the 8′ pipe in half, making it 4′ long, it will sound an octave higher. Therefore, the 8′ designation is used to indicate that the pitch of the stop is exactly that of the notes played. A 4′ stop sounds an octave higher than the notes played and a 16′ stop sounds an octave lower than the notes played. A chart of these commonly found footages and the sound produced is given below.

Footage	*Sounds*	*Note heard if middle C key depressed*	*Footage*	*Sounds*	*Note heard if middle C key depressed*
32′	2 octaves lower		2-2/3′	Perfect 12th above	
16′	1 octave lower		2′	2 octaves above	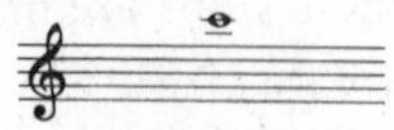
10-2/3′	Perfect 4th lower		1-3/5′	Major 17th above	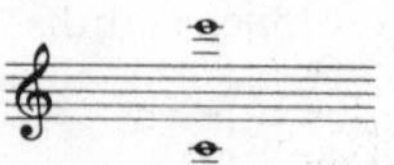
8′	note played (unison)		1-1/3′	Perfect 19th above	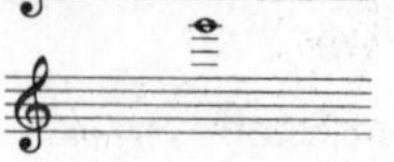

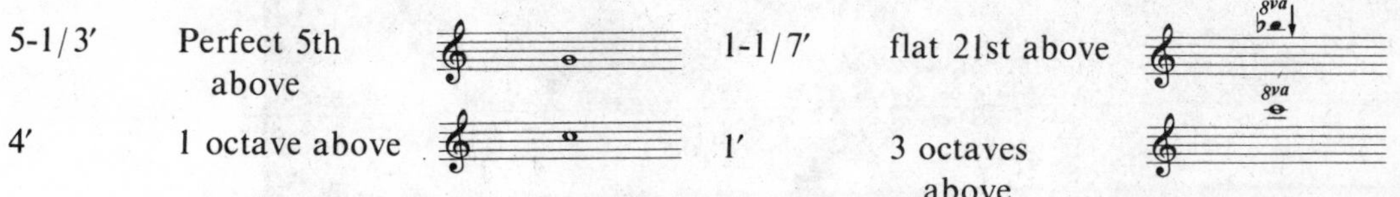

5-1/3′
Perfect 5th above
4′
1 octave above
1-1/7′
flat 21st above
8va
1′
3 octaves above
8va

The footages that include fractions are some of the normal pitches available on the organ. (There are others found, too, but not as often as those listed.) The stops that are tuned to these fractional footages are called *mutation* stops and, as the name implies, are used to alter the tone qualities of other stops. In traditional organ practice, a mutation stop is always used with one or more of the unison or octave-sounding stops. The practice of using various combinations of unison, octave, and mutation stops to synthesize tone colors is a very old organ technique. One traditional organ solo stop, the *Cornet* (pronounced kor̆-nā) consists of a 2-2/3′ stop plus a 1-3/5′ stop plus one or more 8′ and/or 4′ stop(s). The composite quality is quite distinguished and very nasal.

Mixtures

Mixtures are also found on the organ. These stops consist of several ranks of pipes that sound together when a single key is depressed. A mixture is made up of a combination of pipes of different footages, especially including pipes that sound one or more octaves above the key that is depressed as well as pipes that sound a fifth, a twelfth, a 19th or a 26th above the key depressed. The actual pitches and tone qualities making up a mixture stop vary, not only from mixture to mixture, but within a given mixture. Therefore, the relationship among the sounds heard when the low C key is depressed will not be the same as the relationship heard when middle C is depressed. Mixtures are not intended to be used by themselves but are designed to lighten the speech of the low-pitched bass pipes, reinforce the weaker high-pitched pipes, add clarity to the performance of complex contrapuntal figures, and to add brillance (but little mass) to the total organ sound. Adding high-pitched stops, mutations, and mixtures to the ensemble is the traditional way of achieving louder dynamics in organ performance, especially in literature of the Baroque and Classical periods.

Devices

In addition to all these stops and keyboards, the organist has other devices available to assist in the controlling of such a large instrument and to provide additional resources. Among these devices are the Swell box, the Crescendo, couplers, combinations, reversibles, and tremulents.

The Swell Box

This is a large box with one or two sides covered with movable shutters and the other sides sealed. Inside the box are all the pipes from one division of the organ (usually the Swell, hence the name; sometimes the Choir, Solo, or others, too.) The shutters are controlled by a foot pedal, called a *shoe,* located above the pedal keyboard and generally operated by the right foot. As the shoe is depressed, the shutters gradually open, allowing more sound out of the box.

FIGURE 29. An organ console. To the far left of the keyboards are the draw knobs for the Pedal Organ stops; next are the draw knobs for the Swell Organ stops. The small rectangular tabs centered over the upper keyboard control the couplers; the draw knobs to the right are first the Great stops and then the Positive stops. Below each keyboard are combination pistons; the three shoes centered over the Pedal Clavier are, from the left, Swell reeds, Swell flues, and Crescendo; The mushroom-shaped devices on either side of the shoes are toe studs that duplicate the functions of the combination pistons. The pipes visable in the foreground overhead are foundation pipes. (Photo by David Hruby)

The Crescendo

This device is operated by a shoe, like the Swell, but it mechanically adds the stops (as it is depressed) from the softest to the loudest, overriding whatever selection the organist has drawn.

Couplers

These are devices that mechanically connect the keys of one manual or the Pedal Clavier to the stops of another keyboard. For example, they make it possible to play any of the Swell Organ stops along with any of the Great Organ stops from the Great Organ manual. Typically the following couplers may be found: Swell to Choir, Swell to Great, Swell to Pedal, Choir to Great, Choir to Pedal, Great to Pedal, and others. An example of one of these, translated, is: *Choir* (the stops drawn on the Choir) *to* (will be played) *Great* (on the Great): Choir to Great. One often also finds footages on these controls, such as: Swell to Pedal 8′, or Great to Pedal 4′ (meaning that the Swell stops will be played on the Pedal and sound as though the corresponding keys were being depressed on the Swell; or that the Great stops will be played on the Pedal but will sound as though keys an octave higher were being depressed).

Combinations

These are mechanical devices to automatically draw a group of stops, selected ahead of time by the performer. The combinations are operated by buttons (pistons) located below the manuals or by foot (toe studs) located near the pedal clavier. With this device, very rapid and complex changes in registration (stop selection) can be made.

Reversibles

These are pistons and toe studs that turn special devices on or off, alternately. Among the devices controlled may be a particular coupler, a special stop, or, very commonly, a *sforzando* device. This latter device is a mechanical means of immediately turning on all the stops without having to draw each one by hand.

Tremulants

Tremulants are devices for shaking the wind supply to the pipes, producing an undulating effect like the human vocal vibrato. It can be overused, but it is not inappropriate when associated with certain solo stops. A more sophisticated undulation is achieved by the use of *Celeste* stops. These stops, usually of 8′ or 4′ pitch, consist of two pipes per key. One pipe is in tune, while the second is slightly out of tune—just enough to cause a rolling effect somewhat like a violin section playing together. Celeste stops usually are made of flute or string toned pipes.

Organ Design

It would not be appropriate to go deeply into the subject of organ design here. What the student needs to know is that organs differ according to size, installation, age, and builder. What is possible to do on an organ located in a concert hall may be totally impossible to do on even a very large church organ. The following digest of organ design characteristics may help.

Size. Larger organs have more stops, more keyboards, and more options than smaller organs. Small organs may have only two or three ranks of pipes used over and over again. The small organ may lack tonal balance and usually lacks reeds, mutations, and mixtures. However, just because an organ is large does not mean that it is well-designed. Also, it is the number of ranks, not the number of keyboards and buttons, that determines an organ's size.

Installation. The organ builder produces an instrument to suit the needs of his customers. If the customer is a church that needs an organ only for Sunday worship, the organ will be designed to perform hymns, preludes, and postludes, but may be almost useless for concert literature. Yet, some of the best concert organs *are* installed in larger churches. Concert hall organs, which *should* be better-equipped for performing organ music, may or may not be especially well-conceived musically.

Builders. Different builders have always had different conceptions of what is good organ tone and design. If one becomes very interested in organs and organ literature, it becomes important to listen to examples of work by a variety of organ builders in order to develop a concept of good organ tone qualities. Stops with the same name sound different on organs by different builders. (In order to truly comprehend and internalize the sound of a *gedeckt,* a lot of listening to various *gedeckts* is necessary.)

The Electronic Organs

There are basically two types of electronic organs: those that imitate pipe organs and those that do not. Electronic organs that do imitate pipe organs are close enough to pipe organs in both tone quality and design considerations that they need no further discussion here. Those that do not imitate the pipe organ provide other possibilities for the composer.

The manuals on electronic organs vary from 30 to 61 keys. Most electronic organs have two manuals. The pedal clavier on an electronic organ usually has only 12 to 13 keys. On larger instruments there may be as many as 24 to 32 keys on the pedal clavier. The sound on an electronic organ is usually produced in one of three ways:

1. *Electrostatic.* This involves revolving "gears" that interrupt an electromagnetic field at a certain frequency or pulse. These pulses are amplified and become the building blocks of tone, being added together to create timbres.
2. *Amplified reed.* Small reeds, blown by air and activated by the keys produce very faint sounds that are amplified and modified electronically to produce tones.
3. *Electronically generated.* These organs have electronic oscillators that generate complex waveforms which are filtered and altered electronically to produce a variety of tones.

There is no one best method. Each system produces certain types of tones and offers certain advantages and disadvantages. With the electrostatic organs, the performer has control over the mixing of the overtones to synthesize various timbres. Control consists of choosing to use or not use pure (sine wave) tones of 16′, 8′, 5-1/3′, 4′, 2-2/3′, 2′, 1-3/5′, 1-1/3′, and 1′ and control of the loudness of each component. Although these represent a wide variety of pitches and—

when mixed together—partials, they do not begin to encompass the partials usually heard by the human ear within most sounds. Thus, as imitators, these instruments are poor. As synthesizers of unique and new sounds, they are very valuable. A performer can create timbres for which there is absolutely no prototype. This is the sort of timbre control found on the classical Hammond organ.

The amplified reed organs generally try to imitate pipe organs but tend to sound more like amplified harmoniums. As a class of electronic organs, they probably provide the fewest unique sounds of any of the tone-generating designs.

The majority of the electronic organs available work on some variant of the electronic oscillator or generator design. Most of these systems, whether the source of frequency stability is a crystal-controlled oscillator or a tuned-resonance circuit, generate their various tone qualities through the filtering of complex wave forms. The main oscillators generate square, sawtooth, and/or triangular waves which are then fed through various electronic filters. The output of these filters is amplified and is the sound heard. The stop knobs on the console of the instrument turn the various filters on and off as desired.

Depending upon the sophistication and complexity of the instrument, the filters may be installed at the factory with no adjustment possible, may be modifiable from the console while playing, may be modifiable from the back of the console before performance, or may be computer programmable over a wide range of qualities. In addition, some instruments possess means of varying attack times and release (decay) characteristics. The more performer-variable controls over more aspects of the instrument's performance qualities, the more useful the instrument becomes to the composer.

Special effects often found on electronic organs include percussion effects (a form of attack and decay control), built-in rhythm (percussive sounds producing regular, but selectable pulses), and chords. The chord organ or chording attachment is simply a system that is designed so that when a single button is depressed (labeled D^7, for example) instead of the output from a single oscillator being amplified and heard, the outputs from four oscillators—D, F♯, A, and C—are amplified.

Other features of these instruments include variable vibrato (tremulant) and synthetic reverberation. The vibrato control may alter and control the speed of vibrato, the depth of vibrato, and the element subjected to vibrato: either pitch or loudness, or both. The *Leslie* speakers have two special qualities due to the rotation of the speakers. At slow rotation speeds the effect is one of sound dispersal over a large area, thereby minimizing the artificial speaker sound produced when all tone comes from a fixed location. At faster speeds of rotation, the moving of the speakers creates a pitch vibrato because of the Doppler effect. Electronic versions of the Leslie speakers have been developed.

Which of the above resources is available in any one electronic organ is impossible to say. Each model by each manufacturer will possess one or more of these characteristics, the specifics of which may vary yearly. It cannot be assumed, either, that the more costly instruments offer more interesting sound alternatives and possibilities to the composer.

ORGAN BIBLIOGRAPHY

Audsley, George A. *Organ Stops.* New York: The H.W. Gray Co., 1921.

Barnes, William H. *The Contemporary American Organ.* (5th edition. New York: J. Fischer and Brother, 1952.

Dorf, Richard H. *Electronic Musical Instruments.* Mineola, N. Y.: Radio Magazines, Inc., 1954.

Eby, Robert L. *Electronic Organs.* Wheaton, Ill.: Van Kampen Press, Inc., 1953.

Fesperman, John. *The Organ As Musical Medium.* New York: Coleman-Ross Company, 1962.

Niland, Austin. *Introduction to the Organ.* London: Faber and Faber, 1968.

THE FRETTED STRINGS

The Guitars

English	*French*	*German*	*Italian*
guitar	guitare	Gitarre	chitarra

The guitar is a very popular folk and classical instrument of ancient origin. A relative of the lute and the 'ud, the guitar is often used as an accompaniment for singing, as a rhythm instrument in jazz and rock bands, as a solo instrument, and as a member of an ensemble of mixed instruments.

A wide variety of guitars exist around the world and in various cultures. Within our own culture, several distinctly different styles and models of guitar can be found. All of them are related to the basic six-string, 19-fret guitar which has its strings tuned to the following written pitches:

EXAMPLE 236 Basic guitar tuning. The sound is one octave lower than notated.

Among the available guitars are:

1. Classical guitar.
2. Folk, country-and-western, western, or steel-string guitar
   (French: guitare de jazz; German: Schlaggitarre; Italian: chitarra battente).
3. f-hole guitar.
4. 12-string guitar.
5. Electric guitar
   (French: guitare électrique; German: elektrische Gitarre; Italian: chitarra elettrica).

FIGURE 30. (*top row, left to right*) f-hole guitar; hollow-bodied electric guitar; semi-solid-bodied electric guitar; solid-bodied electric guitar; (*bottom row, left to right*) 12-string western-style guitar; 6-string western-style guitar; 6-string classical-style guitar. (Photo by David Hruby.)

Classical Guitar and the Western or Folk Guitar

These guitars are generally tuned as indicated above. The western or folk guitar has a narrower neck than the classical guitar and the strings are generally made of steel rather than nylon. Traditionally the classical guitar is plucked with the fingernail, while the folk guitar is played with a pick or plectrum. (It is not unheard-of, however, for a pick to be called for in special works for the classical guitar.) These guitars have flat tops.

A special tuning, often used with the folk guitar in country-and-western music, is *high-G tuning.* In this tuning, the G string is replaced by a smaller string and tuned an octave higher than usual. This results in a more twangy, brighter sound and reduces the instrument's ability to play melodies. The high-G tuning is:

EXAMPLE 237 High-G tuning. (Sounds an octave lower than written.)

The f-hole Guitar

The f-hole guitar uses the same tuning as the classical guitar, but its strings are metal and the sound is much more incisive and bright. This guitar is often used, with or without amplification, in jazz bands and commercial music. It is a curved-top guitar.

The 12-String Guitar

This guitar has twice as many strings as other guitars. The strings are in six pairs, each pair corresponding to a single string of a 6-string guitar. The three highest pairs are each tuned in unison. The three lowest pairs are each tuned in octaves, with the additional string being pitched an octave above its mate.

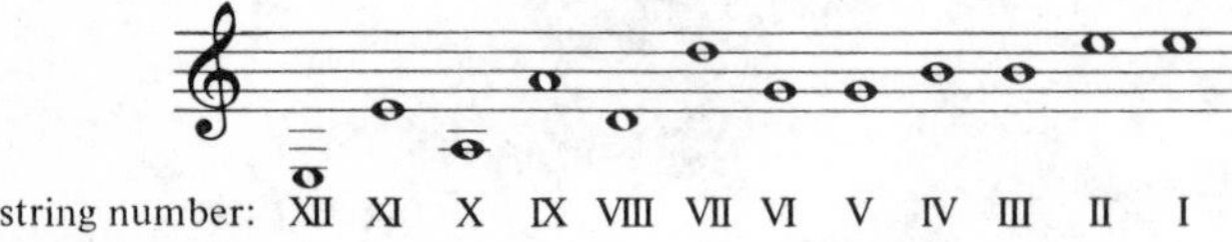

EXAMPLE 238 Tuning of a 12-string guitar. (Sounds an octave lower than written.)

Due to the extra strings to be stopped and the extra strength required, the 12-string guitar is a tiring instrument to play. The extra strings do provide additional resonance to the sound. Simple chords on the 6-string guitar become rich and warm-sounding on the 12-string. Complex sonorities on the 6-string can become hopelessly muddy on the 12-string. The instrument is well-suited for playing solos and is especially adept at filling in the middle harmonies and the bass lines in jazz and commercial music.

The Electric Guitar

There are three versions of the electric guitar, not including an amplified acoustical guitar which is, strictly speaking, not an electric guitar. The three types of electric guitars are:

1. Hollow-bodied.
2. Partially Hollow-bodied (semi-solid).
3. Solid-bodied.

The hollow-bodied electric guitars are very similar to the acoustical guitars with f-holes, except that they are especially adapted and equipped for an electric amplification.

The semi-solid-bodied guitar has a front and back the same size as traditional guitars, but not as metallic and bright as the solid-bodied guitar.

The solid-bodied guitar has almost no natural sound, being nearly inaudible when played without amplification. With amplification it is penetrating and nasal, capable of producing a wide variety of sounds. This is the guitar used in most rock bands.

The Range of the Guitar

As with other string instruments, the range of the guitar is actually the sum of the ranges of each of the six strings.

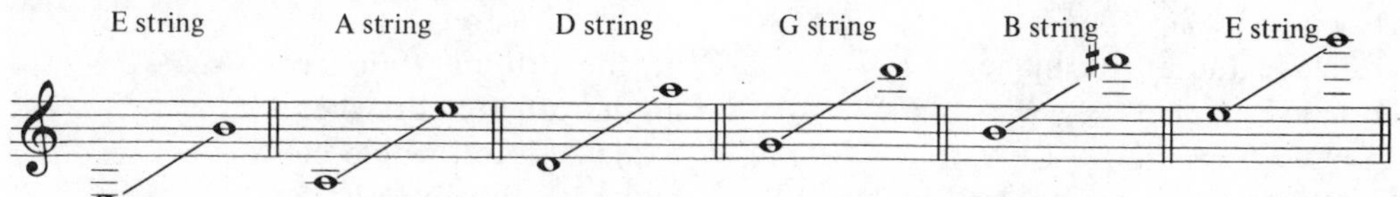

EXAMPLE 239 The written ranges of the strings for the normal tuning of the guitar. (Sound an octave lower than written.)

The upper limit of the range, given here as high B, is actually variable; some guitars can go up to C or a little above.

The Picks

Guitarists use either picks or the fingernails of their right hands to pluck or strum the strings. Picks come in a variety of sizes, shapes, and thicknesses and are made from rubber, tortoise shell, felt, celluloid, and plastics. For special effects other materials could be used. Felt picks work better on gut-stringed instruments while a medium-to-large, hard pick would be used if one were playing an acoustical guitar in a fairly loud ensemble, especially if the guitar part were highly rhythmic. Electric guitars usually require smaller, less stiff picks. Very light, flexible picks are sometimes used for tremolos and very rapid passages. The performer can change picks, but it requires time; allow at least four measures of a moderate $\frac{4}{4}$ tempo. As a guide to the effects of picks on the tone, remember that a thin pick will cause a small, twangy sound while a thick one will be dull and thumpy.

Thumb picks, which are worn on the right thumb of the player, are more often used by country-and-western and folk guitarists to allow use of all fingers and the thumb in plucking, and for special effects. Classical guitarists do not need these devices to facilitate techniques, since they have all of their fingernails available.

The direction of the movement of the right hand is important in its effect on the music. The symbol to indicate down-picking is: ⊓ . Up-picking is: ∨ . A tremolo is indicated this way: ≢ . And arpeggiation is shown as ⦚ with the ⊓ or ∨ added to show direction.

Harmonics

As with other string instruments, the guitar can play both natural and artificial harmonics. Natural harmonics are produced by touching the string lightly at one of the nodes with the left hand and plucking with the right. Artificial harmonics sounding an octave higher are produced by stopping the string to obtain a pitch with the left hand and touching the same string an octave higher with the first finger of the right hand while plucking with the right thumb or third (ring) finger. The artificial harmonic sounding two octaves higher is produced by the same procedure except that the string is touched a perfect fourth above the stopped note.

NATURAL HARMONICS

Sounds (relative to open string)	*Touched*
1 octave higher	at the 12th fret
1 octave and a fifth higher	at the 7th or 19th fret
2 octaves higher	at the 5th fret or where the 24th fret would be[8]
2 octaves and a major third higher	at the 4th, 9th, or 16th fret

ARTIFICIAL HARMONICS

Sounds (relative to pitch fingered in left hand.)	*Touched*
1 octave higher	12 frets above stopped note
2 octaves higher	5 frets above stopped note

Notation for guitar harmonics is not as standardized as for the orchestral strings. The small ° may be used for natural harmonics, but clarification as to the notation used, the sound to be produced, and the string to be played on is necessary. For artificial harmonics the normal practice is to simply state that the harmonics are artificial and should sound as written, or an octave higher. The recommended procedure for orchestral strings would be good for guitar, but not being standard, would require an explanation. (See Examples 42 and 43 on pages 33 and 34.)

EXAMPLE 240 a. Notation for four different natural harmonics, and the resulting concert pitches for each. b. Notation for two different artificial harmonics, and the resulting concert pitches for each.

[8]A few guitars have a fingerboard with 24 frets but not all are so equipped.

Vibrato

Vibrato is added to the acoustical guitar in one of two ways. The usual method is to vibrate the left-hand finger that is stopping the string back and forth on the fret. The speed of this motion and the distance covered will control the speed and depth (pitch range) of the vibrato. If one wishes to create the illusion of vibrato on an open note, it can be accomplished by playing the open string but moving the finger on another string that is stopped in unison with the string being played.

Bending the Tone

On electric guitars one often finds a *vibrato bar,* which is a lever that the performer may move to stretch all of the strings and thus bend the pitches upward. This may be used to add a small vibrato to the tone or may be used to create glissandos. A common technique among rock performers is to bend or stretch the string with a left-hand finger, producing bends and glissandos even when no vibrato bar is present.

The Capo or Barre

This device has been seen by most who have observed performances by guitarists playing Spanish, Mexican, folk, country-and-western, or rock-and-roll. It is a bar that clamps across the frets of the instrument, effectively shortening the strings. (It is often disdainfully called a *cheater bar,* but its use is not simply to assist guitarists who can only perform a few chords, although that is one of its uses.) The full name is *capotasto.*

In guitar playing, especially folk and Spanish, a characteristic timbre is produced by the use of many unstopped notes in the chords played. If the music is in a good key for the guitar, such as D major, many of the chords will naturally have open (unstopped) notes. If, though, it is necessary to perform a similar piece in a key such as A♭ major, many fewer unstopped strings will be used and the timbre will change. If the open string timbre is important, then the capo will improve the situation without requiring the performer to complétely retune the instrument.

The Grande Barre

This term refers to the use of the first finger on the left hand as a barre. The best way to facilitate the performance of certain chords is to place the first finger across the neck along a fret so that it really functions much as a capo although the sound is that of stopped strings. When the first finger is placed across the upper five, lower five, or all six strings, it is called a *grande barre.* Some performers have developed an *angled grande barre,* placing the finger across the frets at an angle other than 90 degrees. This is a difficult technique and requires skill to keep the tones of the strings clear.

The Electronic Options

The electric guitar and amplified guitar offer some other sound options to the performer and composer. Among these are reverberation or echo, the use of a fuzz box, and other electronic modifications of the tone. The pickup units on electric guitars are usually located under the strings both near the bridge and near the end of the fingerboard. The performer has the ability to select the output from the first pickup, the second pickup, or both, as the signal to be sent to the amplifier. The sounds picked up near the bridge tend to be thin and tight, while those from the end of the fingerboard are very rich and warm.

The use of an echo or reverberation unit on an electric guitar is very common. The amount of reverberation is often controllable by use of a foot pedal. Also controlled by foot pedal are various tone modifiers, the most common of which is the fuzz box, which electronically adds a degree of distortion to the tone by clipping the signal and mixing in against itself. The amount of "fuzz" may be varied from none to total distortion. Also available is an electronic vibrato built into the amplifier system. This vibrato is very mechanical-sounding, but it is an interesting effect.

Other Guitars

There is a bass guitar which is tuned an octave lower than the 6-string guitar but which reads the same pitches. There also exists in Europe a small descant guitar.

English	*French*	*German*	*Italian*
fret	sillet *or* frette	Bund	tasto
plectrum *or* pick	plectre	Plektrum	plettro
capo *or* capotasto *or* barre	barre *or* capodastre	Capotasto *or* Kapodaster, *or* Saitenfessel	capotasto

The Mandolin

English	*French*	*German*	*Italian*
mandolin	mandoline	Mandoline	mandolino

This is a fretted string instrument with a small pear-shaped body. It has eight strings tuned to four pitches. The strings are arranged in pairs of identical pitches.

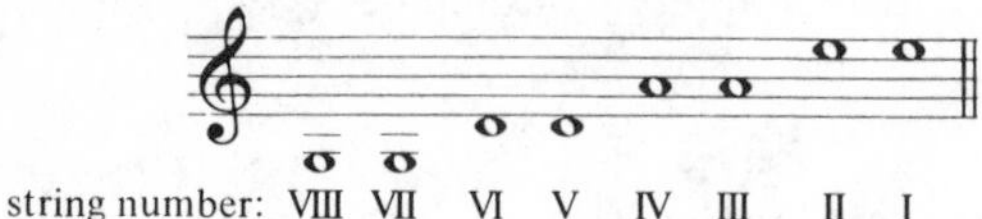

EXAMPLE 241 Tuning of the mandolin strings.

These are the same pitches to which the violin is tuned; and in many performance situations, where a trained mandolinist is not available, a violinist plays the instrument. The performance technique consists of the use of a shell or ivory pick or plectrum held in the performer's right hand and strummed rapidly between the two matched strings of each pair. It is basically a single-line instrument, but chords could be played following the cautions given for such writing on the violin.

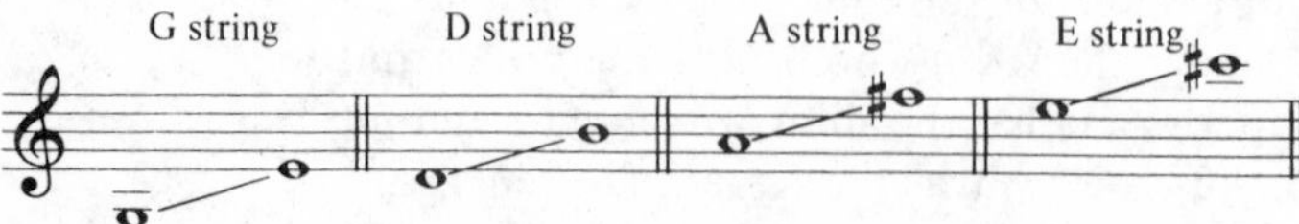

EXAMPLE 242 The ranges of the mandolin's four string pairs.

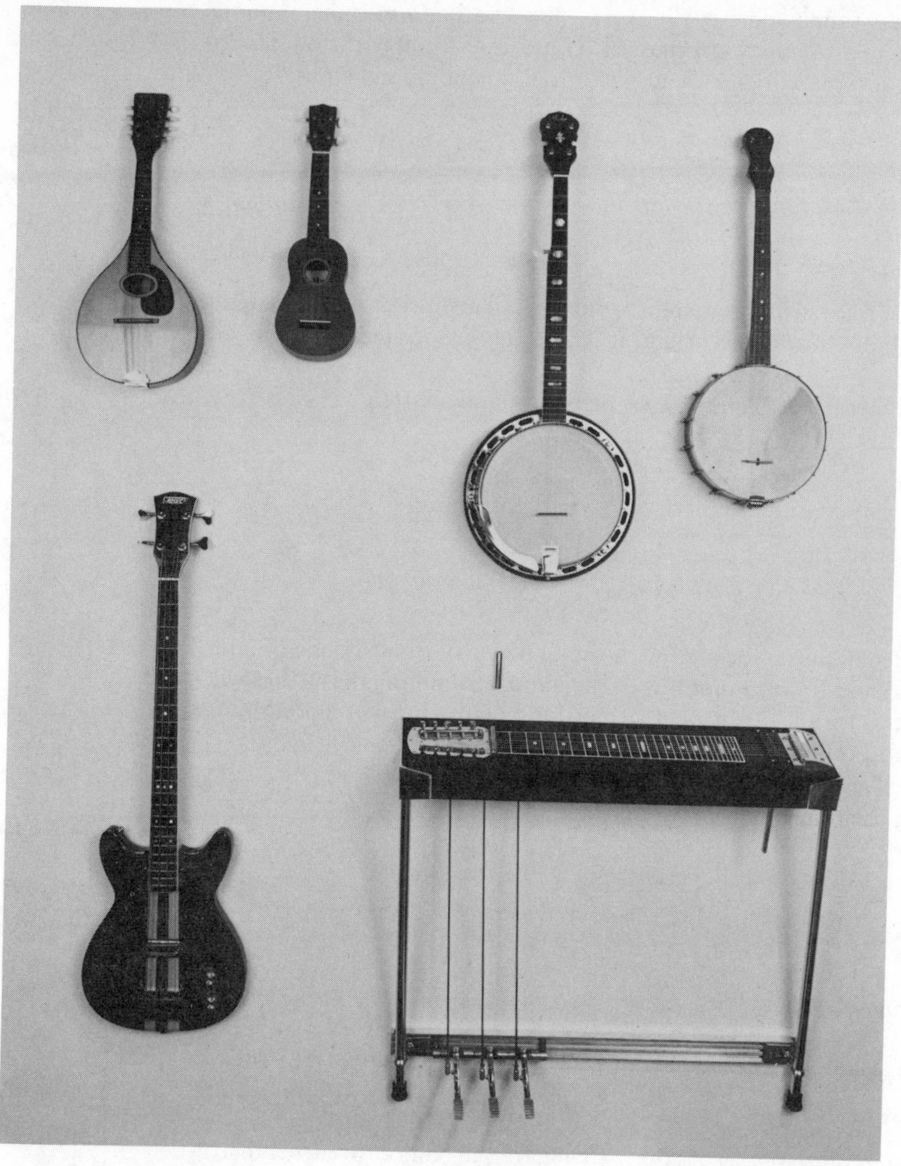

FIGURE 31. (*top, left to right*) mandolin, ukulele, 5-string banjo, and tenor banjo; (*bottom, left to right*) electric bass and pedal steel guitar. Above the latter is a steel. (Photo by David Hruby.)

The instrument has found some use in opera, for creating atmosphere, and is called for in contemporary pieces from time to time. Important parts for mandolin are written in several works of Anton Webern, including his Opus 26.

The Ukulele

English	French	German	Italian
ukulele	ukulélé	Ukulele	ukulele

The ukulele is a four-string fretted instrument designed primarily for playing chords. Although of Portuguese origin, it is strongly associated with Hawaii.

The strings are tuned to: , sounding as written.

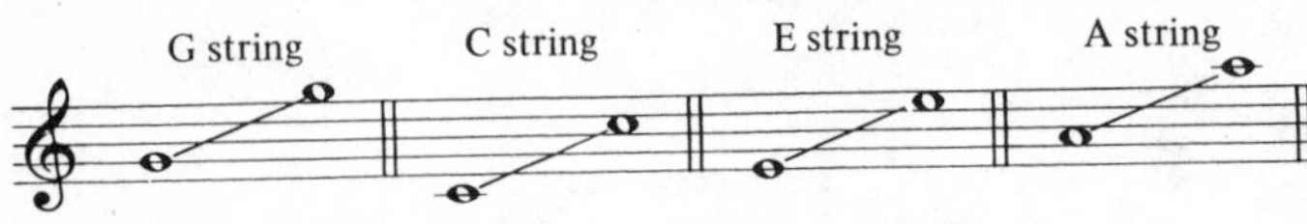

EXAMPLE 243 The ranges of the ukulele's strings.

The right-hand technique associated with the ukulele is primarily one of alternating downward and upward motions of the hand, strumming the strings with a felt pick or the fingernails. Most performers on the instrument read tablature rather than staff notation. (See pages 256-58.)

There is also a baritone ukulele with four strings tuned to: .

It has from 12 to 18 frets and is played much like the ukulele.

The Banjos

The Five-String Banjo

English	French	German	Italian
banjo	banjo	Banjo	banjo *or* bangio

The banjo that is normally seen is the 5-string, fretted banjo. An earlier instrument, not often found, is the 5-string, fretless banjo. The banjo is distinctive due to the shape of its body, which looks like a drum.

The banjo has over twenty different tunings. These are changed to suit the requirements of different music. Among the more common tunings are these:

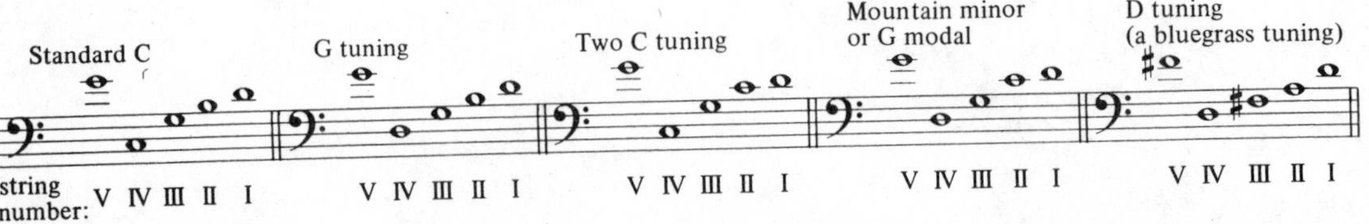

EXAMPLE 244 Five of the most common banjo tunings.

The four lowest-pitched strings are stopped by the fingers of the performer's left hand. The fifth (or thumb) string may be stopped by the left hand thumb, although it is more commonly left unstopped and treated as a drone.

One of the basic right-hand strokes is a *brush* that is achieved by the backs of the fingernails brushing the strings on a downward gesture. This usually occurs on a downbeat. The thumb is placed on its string and the string is plucked on the off beat as the hand returns to prepare for another brush stroke. *Hammering* is the sounding of a note by the striking of a string against the fingerboard by a left-hand finger. *Pulling* is what would be called a left-handed pizzacato in orchestral string technique. The right hand thumb is sometimes used to pluck a string other than the drone.

Other performance techniques for the banjo center around the use of one, two, or three right-hand fingers to pick one or several strings. The characteristic sound of banjo music comes from the constant and very rhythmic feeling that is created by regularly recurring attacks. Between the two hands alternating up-picking, down-picking, hammering, pulling, brushing, and the thumb string drone, the flavor of the banjo is captured. In banjo style, it is more important to keep this rhythmic pulse going than it is to always have the best-voiced chords. (Even a few "wrong" notes should not interfere with the rhythm.)

The ranges of the individual strings are a major ninth above the open string.

The tuning of the thumb string varies between  and  .

The Tenor Banjo

English	*French*	*German*	*Italian*
tenor banjo	banjo ténor	Tenorbanjo	banjo tenore *or* bangio tenore

This banjo has only four strings and is fretted. In many respects it is like the five-string banjo, but it does not possess the drone (or thumb) string. The tenor banjo is usually tuned to: 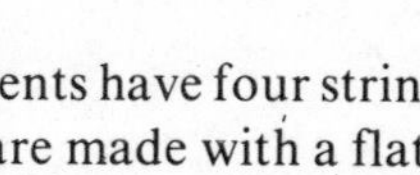

but is written an octave higher.

The Electric Bass

This instrument, not to be confused with an electrically amplified contrabass, exists in two styles. One style has frets and the other does not. The fretted style is more common.

These electronic instruments have four strings tuned to the same pitches as the contrabass. Most of them are made with a flat bridge, which makes bowing impossible. (A few are made with curved bridges and can be bowed.) The bowing is not totally missed, since most of these electric basses have reverberation units that provide electronic sustaining of notes. In addition, the use of fuzz boxes and other electronic tone modifiers allow for a wide variety of tone qualities and effects. (See Appendix II.)

Most parts for electric bass are improvised and require no notation, or are like jazz bass lines and consist simply of chord changes. However, if it is necessary to write specific parts for an electric bass, the notation is exactly like notation for the string bass. (See pages 61-66.)

Pedal Steel Guitar

English	*French*	*German*	*Italian*
pedal steel guitar *or* Hawaiian steel guitar	guitare hawaïenne	Hawaii-Gitarre	chitarra hawayana

This instrument, which is often heard in Hawaiian music and in country-and-western music, is characterized by the glissando and tremolo which are strongly associated with it. (It is sometimes called the Hawaiian guitar or the Hawaiian steel guitar.) Several tunings are used on this electronically amplified instrument. The most common tuning is the E^9 chromatic tuning.

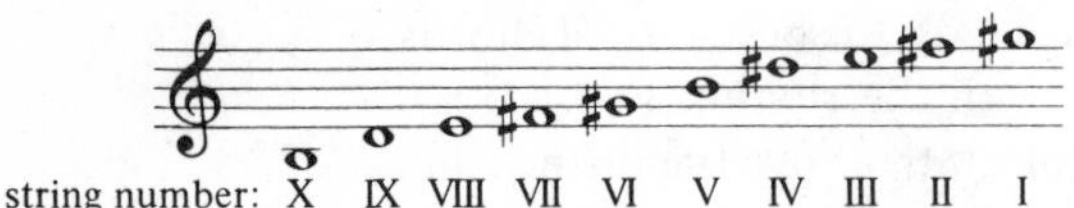

EXAMPLE 245 Pedal steel guitar's E^9 chromatic tuning. (Sounds two octaves lower than written.)

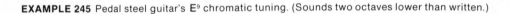

The instrument is placed horizontally so that the performer may slide a steel (bar) up and down the neck of the instrument, stopping the strings. The right hand is equipped with one or more picks to strum the strings. Chords and melodic lines are both idiomatic for the instrument.

A characteristic sound is the vibrato produced by moving the steel back and forth about an ⅛- to ¼-inch on either side of a fret. The other sound that is strongly associated with this instrument is that achieved by sliding the steel from one fret to another while the string(s) vibrate. Most professional instruments have three or more pedals and up to four knee levers. Moving the knee levers lowers the pitches of some of the strings, while depressing a pedal will raise the pitch of some strings. The mechanical connections are adjustable so that the performer can determine which strings will be affected by which pedal or lever according to his taste or needs, but these adjustments cannot be made quickly and must be completed well before the performance. The notation used is tablature.

Tablature

The association of fretted instruments with folk and popular music is clearly shown in the usual notation, called *tablature* (French: tablature; German: Tabulator; Italian: intavolatura). Of all the instruments discussed, only the mandolin and guitar have much literature in staff notation. Most music that is performed on all these fretted instruments is played by ear. When not played by ear, it is likely that the system of notation used is tablature, a very old form of notation for such instruments.[9] In tablature notation, a diagram is shown which tells the performer where to place his fingers.

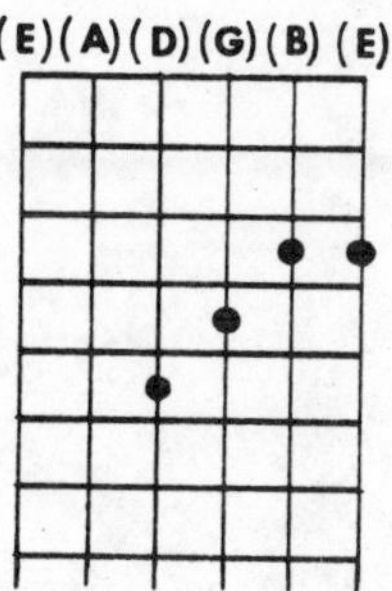

EXAMPLE 246 Guitar tablature.

The above symbol shows the player that he is to place his left hand in such a way as to stop the D string at the fifth fret above the nut, the G string at the fourth fret, and the B and E strings at the third fret. The two lowest strings, not being marked, are to be left unplayed. (A substitute notation indicating that a string is not to be played is an x.)

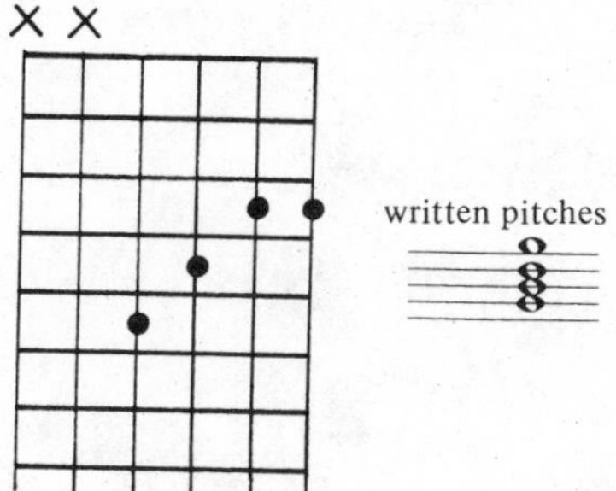

EXAMPLE 247 Tablature showing unplayed strings and the resulting chord.

The pitch obtained when a string is stopped at the first fret above the nut is a semitone higher than the open string pitch. Each successive fret raises the pitch another semitone. To determine the sounds represented by the tablature one counts semitones above the open string equal to the number of the fret at which the string is stopped. Thus, in Examples 246 and 247 the D string will produce G—five semitones above D, the G string will produce B—four semitones above G, the B string will produce D—three semitones above B, and the E string will produce G—three semitones above E.

If a string is to be played but left unstopped, the symbol o is used. Here is an example:

[9]Older tablature notations use different symbols to achieve similar results.

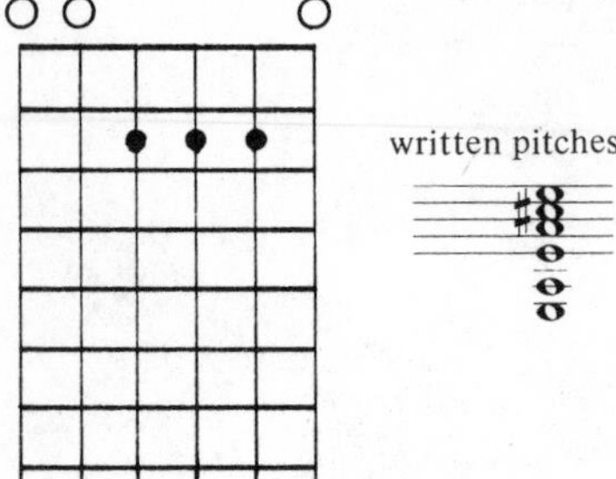

EXAMPLE 248 Tablature showing unstopped strings and the resulting chord.

In the tablature that one usually encounters, the line to the left is the last, lowest-pitched, or closest string. The line to the right is the first, highest-pitched, or furthest-away string.

FRETTED STRINGS BIBLIOGRAPHY

Bellow, Alexander. *The Illustrated History of the Guitar.* New York: Colombo Publications, 1970.

Brosnac, Donald. *The Electric Guitar: Its History and Construction.* San Francisco: Panjandrum Press, 1975.

Brosnac, Donald. *The Steel Guitar: Its Construction, Origin, and Design.* San Francisco: Panjandrum Press, 1977.

Burke, John. *John Burke's Book of Old Time Fiddle Tunes for the Banjo.* New York: Amsco Music Publishing Company, 1968.

Kealakai, Major. *The Ukulele and How to Play It.* Rev. ed. Los Angeles: Southern California Music Company, 1916.

Sharpe, A. P. *A Complete Guide to the Instruments of the Banjo Family.* London: Clifford Essex Music Company, 1966.

Stahl, William C. *Wm. C. Stahl's New Mandolin Method.* Rev. ed. Milwaukee: J. Flanner, 1900.

Turnbull, Harvey. *The Guitar from the Renaissance to the Present Day.* New York: C. Scribner's Sons, 1974.

Wheeler, Tom. *The Guitar Book.* New York: Harper and Row, 1974.

THE FREE REEDS

English	*French*	*German*	*Italian*
free reed	anche libre	Durchschlagzunge	ancia libera

The Accordion

English	*French*	*German*	*Italian*
accordion	accordéon	Akkordeon *or* Handharmonika *or* Ziehharmonika	fisarmonica
piano-accordion	accordéon à clavier	Piano-Akkordeon	piano-melodium

The accordion that is usually seen and heard is a *piano accordion,* so called because of its piano keyboard.

The Accordion Keyboard

The range of the right-hand keyboard varies from 25 to 41 keys. The typical range of a concert model spans 41 keys: Because of the position in which the instrument is held, the lower pitched notes are closer to the head of the performer. There are from 3 to 13 *treble shifts* which control the tone quality of the keyboard. These work by activating various combinations of the sets of treble reeds.

Every tone produced on the accordion is the result of one or more reeds being set into vibration by the air drawn into or pushed out of the bellows. On concert-model accordions, the keyboard is equipped with four sets of reeds. One set is tuned in unison or written pitch, another set of reeds is tuned an octave higher than the first, the third set is tuned an octave lower than the first, and the fourth set is tuned higher than unison, each pitch being a fraction of a semitone too high. This last set of reeds is known as *tremulant.*

The shifts that control the reed sets and combinations are labeled with various names which vary from one maker to another. To overcome this confusion of names, a symbol system has been developed to indicate the various voices or reed combinations:

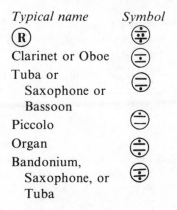

Reeds used	*Typical name*	*Symbol*
Master = All reeds sets on	Ⓡ	
Unison only (sometimes called *chorist*)	Clarinet or Oboe	
Octave Lower only	Tuba or Saxophone or Bassoon	
Octave Higher only	Piccolo	
Octave Higher and Octave Lower	Organ	
Unison and Octave Lower	Bandonium, Saxophone, or Tuba	

Unison and Octave Higher	Violin or Oboe
Unison and Tremulant	⊛ or Violin
Unison and Octave Higher and Octave Lower	Harmonium
Unison and Octave Higher and Tremulant	Musette
Unison and Octave Lower and Tremulant	Celeste or Accordion

Due to these various combinations of reeds and individual sets of reeds, the total range of the 41-note keyboard may become: 

. However, the use of the total range involves stopping to press a shift button. It does not take long, since the shift buttons are directly over the keys, but it does mean that a continuous passage from the lowest pitch to the highest is not possible.

The keys on the accordion are a little smaller than on the piano or the organ. Therefore, an interval of a tenth is playable.

The Bass Buttons

The performer's left hand plays the bass buttons. On the concert instruments there are 120 of these buttons and several bass shifts. The buttons are arranged in 6 rows of 20 buttons each. As the performer holds the instrument, the two rows that are the furthest from the performer, and therefore automatically under his fingertips, are the rows that provide the lowest pitches. The row furthest away is called the *counterbass* row (note: *not* contrabass!) and the next closest row is the *fundamental bass* row. These two rows each have a series of buttons, arranged in the circle of fifths for all twelve chromatic pitches. The counterbass row has exactly the same notes as the fundamental bass row. The difference is in the location of the buttons. Diagonally above each button of the fundamental bass row, in the counterbass row, is a button for the leading tone to the fundamental bass row's button.

The next row closer to the performer has major triad (chord) buttons; the next row has minor triad buttons; the next row has dominant seventh chord buttons; and the closest row has diminished seventh buttons. All of these chord buttons are designed to allow the performer to produce an appropriate chord simply by pressing one button. The mechanism automatically activates appropriate reeds.

The bass shifts vary from two to seven. One of the shifts is a master that activates all of the bass reed sets, which may number as many as five. The typical bass shifts work as follows:

Effect on Fundamental and/or Counterbass Buttons	*Effect on Chord Buttons* (approximately)[10]
Master-all Reeds on Unison and One Octave Lower, One Octave and Two Octaves Higher	Unison and Octave Higher and Two Octaves Higher

[10]The sets of reeds that produce the chords have a range of only an octave each. Therefore, as different chords are played, different inversions and different doublings will occur. Since these variations in chord voicings is typical of the accordion, it need not concern the orchestrator.

Two Octaves Higher	Two Octaves Higher
One Octave and Two Octaves Higher	One Octave and Two Octaves Higher
Unison and One Octave and Two Octaves Higher	One Octave and Two Octaves Higher
Unison and One Octave Lower	Unison and One Octave Higher
One Octave Lower and One Octave Higher and Two Octaves Higher	One Octave Higher and Two Octaves Higher
Unison and One Octave Higher	One Octave Higher

Not all of these shifts are available on all accordions, nor will the exact relationship between the effect upon the bass and the effect upon the chords be the same. In general, though, one can anticipate that the chord qualities will be higher and lighter than the bass qualities.

Bass Notation

The notation used in the bass clef is really a combination of notations, designed to provide three types of information: fundamental bass, counterbass, or chords. All pitches written on the middle line (D line) in the bass clef and below are to be played on the fundamental bass buttons or, if the note has a line under it, it will be played on a counterbass button.

EXAMPLE 249 Notation used to indicate fundamental bass and counterbass buttons.

Notes written in the third (E) space and above are chords and must be accompanied by an appropriate symbol: M for Major, m for minor, 7 for dominant seventh, or d (dim) for diminished. (The dominant seventh chords do not contain the fifth of the chord.)

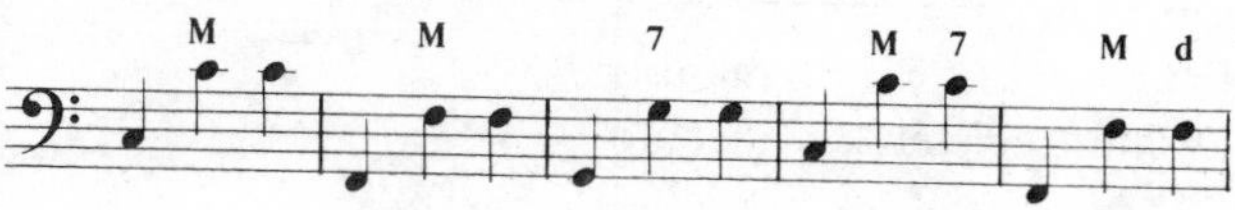

EXAMPLE 250 Notation for bass notes and chords.

The practice is that once the chord symbol (note and quality symbols) is given, repetition of the note alone indicates the repetition of the same chord. If the chord quality is to change, then a new symbol must be added.

The written range of the bass buttons is: . However, due to the various shifts the range may be as great as: .

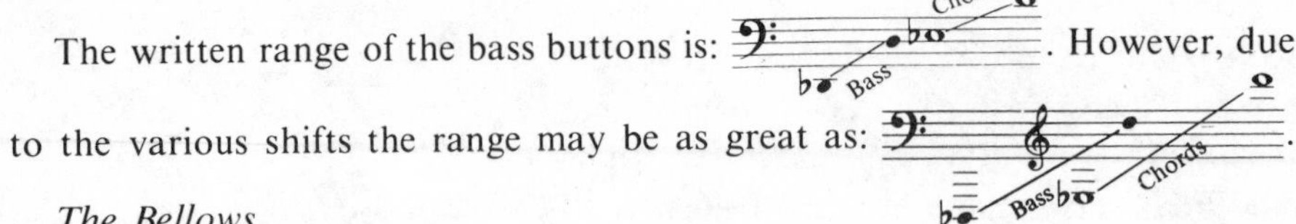

The Bellows

The bellows is the only means of providing wind for the reeds. Because of the basic efficiency of the free reed design, the accordion is capable of creating a large amount of sound with relatively little effort. At full loudness with full chords, the bellows can provide enough air while opening to sustain the sound for about four seconds. The same is true for the closing of the bellows. At softer dynamics or with very few pitches being played, the sustaining can be longer.

The operation of the bellows is somewhat like the bow on the string instruments. It is not possible, though, to change directions on the bellows without re-attacking the notes. (This is due to the design which requires each reed set to have separate reeds for the opening and the closing cycles of the bellows.) It is necessary therefore, to provide opportunities for the performer to change bellows directions. It is not customary to specifically mark the opening and closings, but phrase marks serve as guides to the performer in determining direction changes. When bellows markings are needed, these are used: open = ←—— close = · ——→.

Dynamics and accents are controlled by the bellows. Quicker opening or closing produces louder dynamics. Sudden increases in speed produce accents, called *bellows accents,* and shown by >. Diminuendos are produced by slowing up the movement of the bellows.

One special bellows effect is called the *bellows shake.* This is produced by alternating open and close motions rapidly. The notation for this is:

EXAMPLE 251 Notation used for bellows shake.

When the effect is no longer wanted, the indication is B.N. or *bellows normal.*

English	*French*	*German*	*Italian*
bellows	soufflet	Balg	mantice
treble shift	registre de la partie chantante	Diskantregister	piccolo
bass shift	registre des basses	Bassregister	registro basso

ACCORDION BIBLIOGRAPHY

Fortina, Carl. *The Accordion; As Written.* North Hollywood, Calif.: Holly-Pix Music Company, 1961.

The Harmonica

English	*French*	*German*	*Italian*
harmonica	harmonica à bouche	Mundharmonika	armonica a bocca

Harmonicas are made in various sizes and with a variety of ranges. The common tone qualities are called *single-reed, tremolo-tuned,* and *octave-tuned.* The typical styles are *diatonic* and *chromatic.*

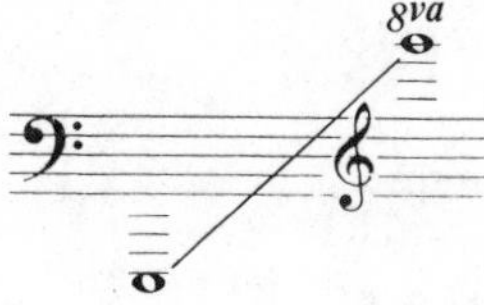

EXAMPLE 252 Overall range of all the harmonicas. (No one harmonica spans this range.)

English	*French*	*German*	*Italian*
diatonic	diatonique	diatonisch	diatonico
chromatic	chromatique	chromatisch	cromatico
blow	souffler	blasen	soffiare
draw	inspirer	einatmen	inspirare

Blow and Draw

The terms *blow* and *draw* are applied to the manner of producing the sound on the harmonica. When air is blown into one of the holes, a reed (or reeds) start(s) to vibrate, producing a pitch. When the performer inhales (draws) air through the harmonica, another reed (or reeds) vibrate(s), producing another pitch. The pitches produced on the draw may or may not be the same as the pitches produced on the blow.

Types of Harmonicas

Single-reed harmonicas have one reed for each hole that responds to blowing, and one reed for each hole that responds to drawing. The tremolo-tuned harmonicas have two reeds per hole that respond to blowing and another pair that respond to drawing. In these harmonicas, the second reed per hole is tuned slightly sharp, creating a tremolo, or, as called in organ design, celeste effect. The octave-tuned harmonicas also have two reeds per blow or draw per hole, but the second of these is tuned an octave above the others.

The diatonic harmonicas can produce only the diatonic pitches of the key in which they are built. Typical keys are A, D, G, C, and F major, but models are built in all keys. Harmonica soloists that play the diatonic instruments usually carry several tuned in a selection of keys with them. Typical ranges for these instruments are from middle C to the C 3 or 4 octaves above, or the equivalent starting and ending on another pitch.

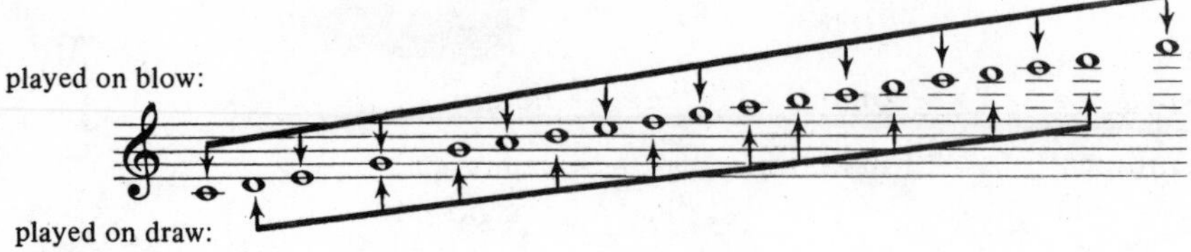

EXAMPLE 253 Diatonic harmonica in C (with 10 holes).

The chromatic harmonica is constructed with a lever on the right end. With the slide out, the instrument is a diatonic harmonica with a four-octave range. With the slide pressed in, the missing chromatic pitches are available.

EXAMPLE 254 A typical range showing the available pitches for a chromatic harmonica in C.

With the arrangement of the holes on the harmonica and the tuning of the reeds, it is possible to play some triads and altered seventh chords on most models simply by controlling the blow and the draw. Fluctuation of the air stream without changing direction can produce a type of breath vibrato. Often, especially in blues playing, the performer "bends and chokes" the tone, producing pitch inflections that are very characteristic of this style of music.

The Harmonium

English	*French*	*German*	*Italian*
harmonium	harmonium	Harmonium	armonio

Sometimes called a reed organ or a parlor organ, the harmonium exists in various sizes. One usually encounters an instrument of one manual, but two-manual models exist, as do models with pedal keyboards. The tone is produced by the vibration of metal reeds set into motion by an air supply that is provided by means of a bellows, pumped by the feel of the player or by an electric motor.

A typical range is: . As with the pipe organ (see pages 237-44), which to a limited extent the harmonium is intended to imitate, stops are available to alter the timbre. On larger instruments a variety of names may be found —"Gedeckt, Vox Humana, Celeste, Diapason," etc.—all of which appear similar to pipe organ tone qualities, but none of which sound like their namesakes. All stops on the harmonium have a characteristic, reedy quality. Nonetheless, the various stops do display different timbres and loudness.

In order to provide more variety in registration, many of the stops are divided with names such as "Treble Oboe" and "Bass Bassoon." In these stops, the reeds for the upper notes on the keyboard are controlled separately from the reeds for the lower notes on the keyboards. By drawing the "Treble Oboe" and the "Bass Flute," one can play a melody in the upper register and accompany it in the lower register, keeping the two areas aurally distinct due to the contrasting tone qualities. The dividing point between treble and bass stops varies from manufacturer to manufacturer but is usually between F (below middle C) and middle C.

Many harmoniums have stops at different pitch levels, the most common being 8′, 4′, and 16′. The number of stops and distribution of qualities and pitches vary, but a typical small harmonium has three or four treble stops and about the same number of bass stops.

Loudness is controlled by levers operated by the performer's knees. The performer pushes the knee lever toward the end of the keyboard and the tone gets louder. The dynamic range available through this process is not great, but is noticeable. On instruments with divided stops, the left knee controls the loudness of the bass range and the right knee controls the loudness of the treble range.

THE WHISTLE FLUTES

The Recorders

English	*French*	*German*	*Italian*
recorder	flûte à bec *or* flûte douce	Blockflöte	flauto dolce *or* flauto a becco

Recorders are end-blown whistle flutes. The modern family of recorders commonly consists of five sizes:

1. Alto recorder
   (French: flute a bec alto; German: Altblockflöte; Italian: flauto dolce contralto).
2. Soprano recorder
   (French: flûte à bec soprano; German: Sopranblockflöte; Italian: flauto dolce soprano).
3. Tenor recorder
   (French: flüte à bec ténor; German: Tenorblockflöte; Italian: flauto dolce tenore).
4. Sopranino recorder
   (French: flûte à bec sopranino; German: Sopraninoblockflöte; Italian: flauto dolce sopranino).
5. Bass recorder
   (French: flûte à bec basse; German: Bassblockflöte; Italian: flauto dolce basso).

These instruments have simple, fluty tone qualities that are shockingly soft for ears more accustomed to modern metal flutes. The typical range of a recorder is a little over two octaves.

The alto and the tenor recorders sound as written; all the others sound an octave higher than the notated pitch.

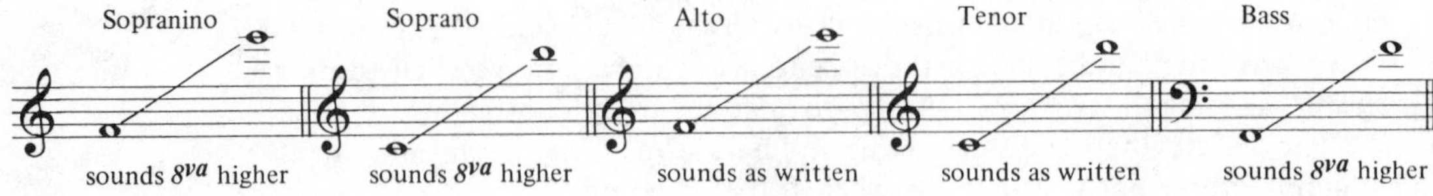

EXAMPLE 255 Recorder ranges.

Recorders are popular for performing music of historical interest and as folk instruments. The unique, breathy flute tone also has appeal for composers and orchestrators. Amplified, the tone quality becomes a good alternative to the orchestral flute.

Due to the simple fingering mechanism, complicated and intricate passages are not easily executed. The best effects tend to be longer, slower lines. The instrument is fully chromatic, but pitch sequences related to keys having one or two sharps or one flat are more natural to perform than other combinations.

It is possible to affect the attack by using different consonants and vowels. Singing and playing is also possible, and the addition of a vibrato is effective. All of these must be done in a most delicate manner, though, due to the simple response characteristics of the recorders.

The Ocarinas

English	*French*	*German*	*Italian*
ocarina	ocarina	Okarina	ocarina

The ocarina is a wind instrument, usually made out of terracotta or plastic, that is blown much like a whistle. The body is approximately teardrop-shaped with a short pipe equipped with the whistle that is blown by the performer. The shape of the instrument is somewhat like a "sweet potato"—hence the popular name for the ocarina.

The range of an ocarina is a little more than an octave, typically a ninth, and within this range it is chromatic. The most normal sizes with their ranges are given below:

EXAMPLE 256 Ranges of the various ocarinas.

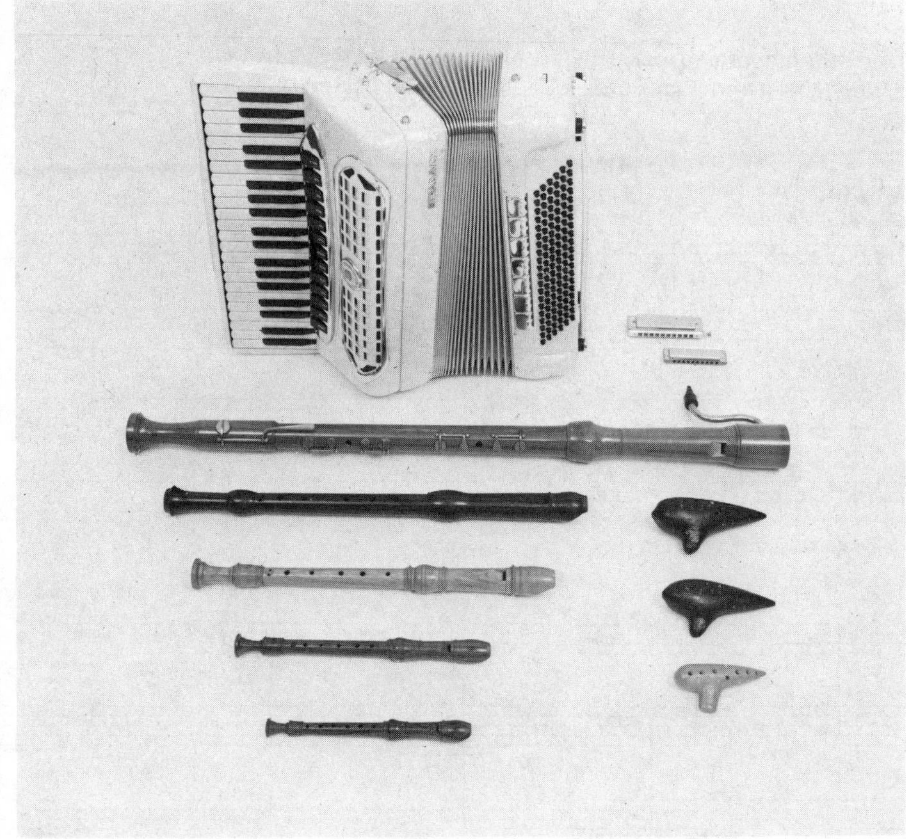

FIGURE 32. The free reeds and whistle flutes: (*rear, left to right*) piano accordion, chromatic harmonica, diatonic harmonica; (*bottom left, front to rear*) sopranino recorder, soprano recorder, alto recorder, tenor recorder, and bass recorder; (*bottom right, front to rear*) F soprano ocarina, C soprano ocarina, and B♭ soprano ocarina. (Photo by David Hruby.)

The higher-pitched ocarinas have soft, fluty sounds. The lower-pitched instruments possess a hollow, melancholy quality that is unique. The instrument is not capable of any significant dynamic change. Attempts to produce *crescendo*s actually bend the pitch upwards and *decrescendo*s do the opposite. These pitch inflections are typical of the instrument and are either specifically called for or added by the performer. A limited variety of tonguings is possible; but due to the very easy response of the instrument, only truly delicate tonguings are generally effective. There appears to be no standard notation for the instrument, due, in part, to its folk origins. Treating it as a transposing instrument with a written range from middle C upward would be convenient.

Problem Set No. 20

1. Using the Mozart string quartet excerpt given below, score the first line (through measure 4) for piano. Play your example or have it played.

2. Rescore your piano reduction from exercise 1, above, for a harpsichord with two manuals. Assume the upper keyboard to have a more brilliant sound. Place the second violin, viola, and cello parts in the left hand for the lower keyboard. Revoice the chords to accommodate the performer's hands if necessary.

3. Score the last 8 measures and pick-up of the Chopin Prelude in A Major from exercise 2 of Problem Set No. 6 (page 50) for harp. Indicate all pedal settings and changes. Have your version performed.

4. Score the Bach chorale harmonization of "Vater unser im Himmelreich" given in exercise 2 of Problem Set No. 10 (page 90) for organ. Assign the bass line to the pedals, the tenor and alto lines to the left hand and the soprano line to the right hand. When the result is performed, have the organist play it several times changing stop combinations for each playing.

5. Score the same passage from the Chopin prelude assigned in exercise 3, above, for two guitars. Assign one guitar to the top melodic line (to sound an octave lower than the piano version) and write out the chord symbols (or tablature) for the other guitar. (If tablature is used, be sure that it represents the chords of the original, inverted as required, an octave lower than the piano version.) Have two guitarists perform your version in class.

6. Score the same passage from the Chopin prelude assigned in exercises 3 and 5, above, for accordion. Write out the piano right hand parts for the accordion's keyboard and the left hand parts should be assigned to the bass and chord buttons. Have the result performed.

7. Score "In Four Parts" of Bartók, given in exercise 1 of Problem Set No. 6 (page 49) for soprano, alto, tenor, and bass recorders. Transpose the actual pitches up one octave to suit the ranges of the instruments better. Have the result performed in class.

7

INSTRUMENTATION: *The Voice*

THE VOCAL INSTRUMENT

English	*French*	*German*	*Italian*
voice	voix	Stimme	voce

Adult human voices can usually be placed into one of the following categories: soprano, mezzo-soprano, contralto (or alto), tenor, baritone, or bass. The first three categories are usually women's voices and the last three are usually male. However, male contraltos, called countertenors, do exist and many church or community choirs have a female "tenor." All of these voices and variations in voices occur naturally.

Vocal Mechanisms

Head Voice

The head tone, head voice, or head register is the name given to the voice quality produced when the female singer's vocal folds are stretched thin. (It is important to understand that thickening or stretching of the vocal folds—more commonly called vocal cords—are not the only means available to the singer for pitch modification. The spacing between the vocal folds, the speed of air rushing between the vocal folds, *and* the shape into which the vocal folds are arranged all contribute to pitch control.) When the vocal folds are stretched into a long, thin shape, the singer can produce a range of from one to two octaves. For example:

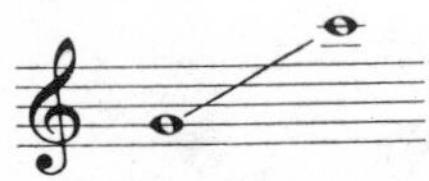

EXAMPLE 257 Typical head register range for a soprano voice.

In trained female singers, this "head register" or "light mechanism" is used for most of the range of the singer.

Chest Voice

When the shape of the vocal folds is modified to become thicker and fatter, the tone quality produced is called *chest voice,* chest tone, or chest register. In this position, the vocal folds of the singer may still produce a range of pitches of from one to two octaves. For example:

EXAMPLE 258 Typical chest register range for a soprano voice.

Both males and females possess a chest voice. One of the characteristics that separates the singing approaches of the trained female singer from the trained male singer is in the use of this chest voice. The male singer will produce most or all of his vocal sound by using this chest voice, while the trained female singer uses her chest voice for only about the lower third to fifth of her range. (Sopranos use less than mezzo-sopranos or altos.)

In contrast, many popular and untrained female singers will use the chest voice for as much as the lower octave and a half of their range, thereby producing the characteristically dark and somewhat foggy voice associated with the female "blues" singer. In female popular singers, one can often hear a complete change from the darker, richer quality of the heavier mechanism to the little-girl, smallish quality of the lighter mechanism. In singers trained in the concert hall or operatic traditions, this obvious change is avoided as much as possible by an attempt to develop the ability to mix the two registral qualities throughout the middle two-thirds of the vocal range.

Falsetto

The higher or lighter mechanism of the male voice is called *falsetto.* In truth, this is a misnomer since it is not at all false but is actually a very natural vocal mechanism. However, the contrast between the childlike quality of this register and the normal speaking and singing register is, for most males, so great as to preclude an intermixing of the two for most common-practice music. There are exceptions.

The lightest of the tenor voices possess a transparent quality that is very close to the quality of the falsetto register. This often enables the performer, especially in softer passages, to switch to the "falsetto" voice for extremely high notes. Well done, the effect is one of having achieved a very high note with no discernable change of timbre.

Another use of this falsetto register is in the case of the countertenor, who sings exclusively in this register. The tone quality is quite pure and transparent throughout the whole singing range (about the same range as a female contralto). This is the highest natural male voice; it occupies a female range but lacks the darkness of the lower female voices.

English	*French*	*German*	*Italian*
chest voice	voix de poitrine	Bruststimme	voce di petto
head voice	voix de tête	Kopfstimme	voce di testa
falsetto	voix de fausset *or* fausset	Falsett *or* Falsett-stimme, *or* Fistel-imme	falsetto
vocal cords *or* vocal folds	cordes vocales	Stimmbänder	corde vocali

Problems of Sound Production

A significant difference between male and female singers that is of importance for anyone writing for voices is the matter of the singability or lack of singability of certain vowel sounds on high notes. Female and unchanged treble voices have difficulty with the following phonemes: ee as in see, i as in sing, e in bed, and ay as in say. These "closed" vowels must be greatly modified in sound by all female voices in the higher range. When attempted by untrained females, the effect is to almost choke off the sound completely.

Except for ee, the adult male voices have no problems with the vowels listed above. However, open vowels—a as in palm, aw as in saw, and o as in go — are difficult for the mature male voice to sing on the higher pitches. An additional problem is oo as in moon, which shows a tendency to "break" into falsetto when sung high.

Neutral vowels like u in up seem to present no problems for either male or female singers. In the middle and lower registers of all voices, when the vocal folds are more relaxed there are no phonemes that produce particular vocalization problems.

Tessitura and Range

Tessitura is a term associated with instrumental and vocal usage but is especially important in performance decisions made by singers and choir directors. Tessitura refers to the area of the vocal range that is most used within a musical work or passage. These two passages have the same range, but different tessitura:

EXAMPLE 259 Two lines with the same range. The upper line has the higher tessitura.

In the following example, the range is greater than either of the two above, but the tessitura is lower:

EXAMPLE 260 Passage with a wider range than either line in Example 259, but with a lower tessitura.

One needs to remember that it is the highness of the tessitura that determines how fatiguing a vocal passage is.

Vocal Notation

Traditionally, vocal music has been notated a little differently than instrumental music. The main differences have had to do with the beaming of the notes and the placement of the dynamics. Modern practice has now started to change the beaming methods of vocal music, and it should now be beamed like instrumental music.

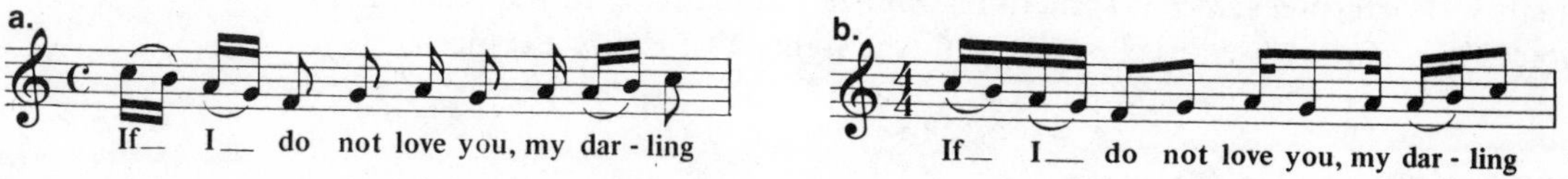

EXAMPLE 261 a. Traditional style of beaming. b. Recommended style.

Notice that the slur is now used to indicate two or more pitches to be used for the same syllable or phoneme. In the old tradition, both the beaming and the slurring were used to provide this information.

The location of dynamics above the staff in vocal music is required because of the placement of the text below the staff. This practice continues:

EXAMPLE 262 Showing location of dynamics above the staff and text below the staff.

Another notational concern is the text itself. The horizontal spacing of the notes should be determined by the rhythm of the music, not by the length of the words used. Therefore, it is important to allow enough horizontal space to avoid crowding or confusion. When a word has to be divided, one should be sure to indicate clearly what portion of the sound is associated with that pitch. Ultimate clarity can be obtained by the use of the International Phonetic Alphabet to indicate exactly which phoneme(s) is (are) to be associated with which pitch and will also clear up questions of pronunciation. Unfortunately, only those singers who have had a certain type of vocal training (or who sing a lot of contemporary music) are able and eager to deal with this sort of notation. (See Appendix VII.)

Vocal Qualities

Terms such as coloratura, lyric, and dramatic are often associated with voice qualities. The term *coloratura* refers to rapid scales, trills, arpeggios, and other effects of a virtuoso nature. Therefore, a coloratura voice is especially adept at performing such figurations. It is usually not very dynamic, but tends to be smallish and pure.

A *dramatic* voice is one of great power and dynamic contrast. It is able to be powerful and project throughout its range. A typical dramatic voice does not have the agility of the coloratura.

A *lyric* voice is lighter and more flexible than a dramatic voice, and more powerful and expressive than a coloratura voice.

Other terms encountered are acuto sfogato, soubrette, leggiero, spinto, and cantante. These descriptions of vocal qualities are not universally used, but may be encountered in certain literature. *Acuto sfogato* refers to the highest, lightest of all coloratura sopranos. *Soubrette* and *leggiero* are terms applied to progressively lower and heavier voices, but still of a coloratura quality. *Spinto* is a term sometimes used for a soprano or tenor that is between a lyric and dramatic in quality. The term *leggiero* is sometimes applied to the highest and lightest tenor voice. *Cantante* is used exclusively with the lightest of the bass voices.

SPECIAL VOCAL EFFECTS

The vocalist can produce a wide variety of sounds. Some of the vocal modifications and effects are listed below.

Timbre changes	*Pitch changes*	*Other vocal and non-vocal sounds*
sotto voce	vibrato	whistling
parlando	tremolo	laughing
speaking	trill	crying
whispering	repeated pitches (trillo)	coughing
Sprechgesang		belching
Sprechstimme	sub-tones	tongue clicks
humming	multiphonics	lip smacks
mouth open	yodelling	sighing
mouth partially open		aspiration
mouth closed		inhaling
mouth pursed		exhaling
falsetto		finger snaps
nasal sound		hand claps

In addition it is possible to ask for certain well-recognized styles of singing. Among these are:

scat singing
blues singing
brassy singing
jazz singing

The voice may be modified by many external means including electronics, singing into a can or barrel, into a piano, into a paper bag, or through a megaphone. (In *L's GA,* Salvatore Martirano has the vocalist wear a helium mask, causing the voice quality to become unnaturally high-pitched.) Possibilities are only limited by the composer's imagination.

Timbre Changes

The indication *sotto voce* is an instruction for the singer to sing at the dynamic level and with the tone quality of a whisper. Literally translated, the instruction is "beneath the voice," which should give some insight into the appropriate interpretation.

Parlando is an instruction meaning "in a speaking or recitative manner." In older music, the interpretation is often for the performer actually to speak the words, but in more contemporary usage, the understanding is that the line is to be sung, but with a speechlike quality of delivery. When actual speaking is desired, the appropriate instruction is *speak* or *spoken,* which may be delivered in rhythm or rhythmically free. Two other terms are products of the twentieth century; these are *Sprechgesang* and *Sprechstimme.* The meaning of the former is "songlike" while the latter means "speechlike." *Sprechgesang* may be pitched while *Sprechstimme* is only approximately pitched.

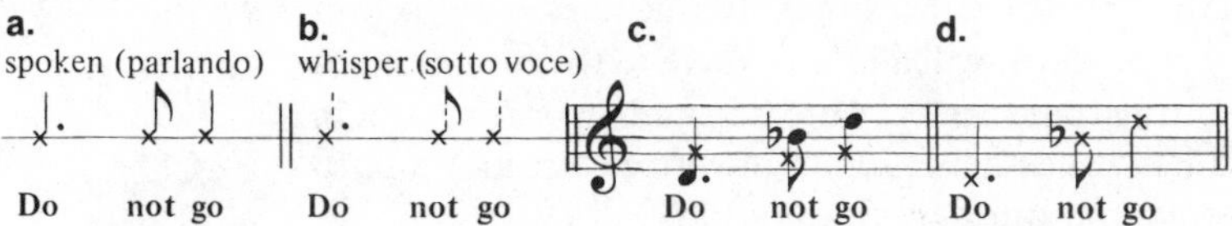

EXAMPLE 263 a. Notation for speaking. b. Notation for whispering. c. Notation for *Sprechgesang.* d. *Sprechstimme.*

Another effect often called for is *humming.* Humming may be on any sustainable (voiced) phoneme and may be done with the mouth closed, partially open, open, or pursed. To indicate humming, simply write the instruction *Hum,* give the appropriate phoneme, and indicate the mouth position. The symbols for the various mouth positions are:

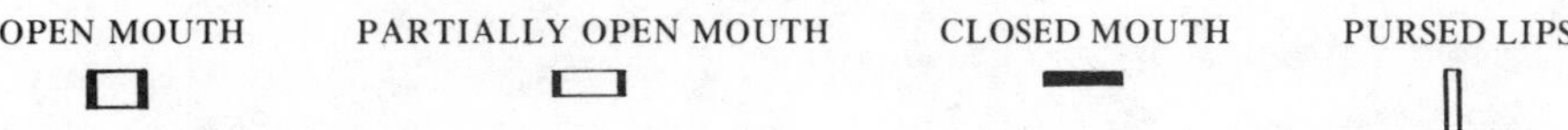

Most lower male voices and some female voices can easily switch to their lighter or higher registers and sing falsetto. The indication for falsetto singing is simply the instruction *falsetto* above the music.

It may be desirable to have the singer alter their tone quality by making the sound more nasal (with a "twang") indicated by △ .

Pitch Changes

Vibrato is the slow (about 6 to 10 vibrations per second) alteration between two pitches—one above and one below the pitch perceived to be sung. Thus, if one were singing an F, the actual pitch produced would vary between about E and G♭. To a limited extent, it is possible to speed up the vibrato; but it is easier to slow it down, and it is also possible to eliminate it altogether. The indications of these effects are:

1. N.V. = no vibrato
2. M.V. = molto vibrato
3. Norm. Vib. = normal vibrato

Tremolo is often confused with vibrato. It is not the same thing, and it is also not "bad vibrato." Tremolo is the pulsing, at a speed of around 4 to 8 times per second, of the *dynamic* level of the voice. The control of tremolo is possible. (But, since many trained singers have worked to "eliminate" this effect and otherwise have not been asked to learn to control the tremolo, difficulty may be encountered in the execution of tremolo control.)

The traditional *vocal trill* is merely a combination of vibrato and tremolo mechanisms, used in such a way as to produce the perceived alteration between the main pitch and an upper auxilary pitch (just like instrumental trills). An older form of trill, sometimes but not universally, called a *renaissance trillo,* or simply *trillo,* is a tremolo (i.e. a pulsing of the dynamic level) the speed of which is controlled and varied by the performer for expressive purposes.

Subtones or *resultant tones* can be produced by the voice. With the proper relaxation of the vocal apparatus and control of the air flow, the vocal folds can be made to vibrate at about half of their normal lowest frequencies. This technique, which takes time and effort to learn, will add an octave to the lower end of most vocalist's range. The resulting tones are very breathy and not strong, but in an appropriate, quiet environment (like a small room) or with electronic amplification, they become both usable and quite interesting.

Some vocalists have developed the ability to produce *multiphonics*— usually only two discernable pitches, but at times three or more— by producing multiple vibrations within the vocal folds. The effect is learnable by most persons, but few singers have developed it to any great extent.

A vocal technique acquired by many folk singers, but learnable by others, is the yodel. This is a controlled alternation between the chest voice and the head voice (usually) an octave higher. The phonemes selected for the yodel should be singable within the appropriate range of the vocal mechanism involved and should be voiced. There is no standard notation.

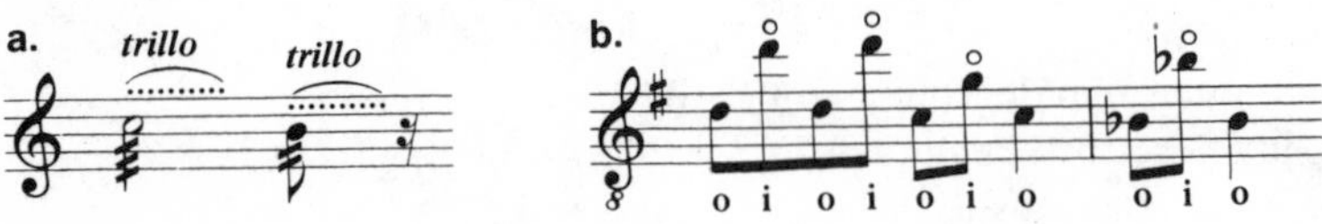

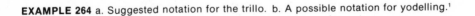

EXAMPLE 264 a. Suggested notation for the trillo. b. A possible notation for yodelling.[1]

[1] The use of a small circle, like a string instrument natural harmonic symbol, to indicate falsetto is not a standard usage, but is encountered. Its use in a yodelling passage would be especially valuable.

Other Vocal and Non-Vocal Sounds

Among these effects are some that have been used in older music, but which are not usually taught in the studio. Such effects as whistling, laughing, crying, coughing, sighing, finger snaps, and hand claps have been used in many pieces. The best notation for these depends upon the situation. Usually, if the effect is desired during a passage in which the performer is also called upon to produce specific pitches, the following notation is suggested:

EXAMPLE 265 Notation for pitchless sounds.

If the effect is voiced or pitched, then of course, specific pitches are written:

EXAMPLE 266 Notation for pitched sounds.

In addition to the above sounds, any sound producible by the human organism could be, and probably has been, used. Among these are belches, tongue clicks, lip smacks, and so on. Notation for these effects would follow the same principles as those given above. If an unpitched, non-vocal effect continues for a while, with no ongoing pitched events, the following notation is probably clearest:

EXAMPLE 267 Notation for extended passage of non-pitched sounds.

Other vocal effects sometimes specified in contemporary music—also used in the process of interpreting traditional music—are aspiration, inhaling, exhaling, and sighing. Aspiration is a breath accent, achieved by adding an unvoiced, but strong *h* to the attack of a sound, or by the addition of this sound to a sustained sound. The indication for aspiration is:

EXAMPLE 268 Notation for aspiration. The word *ordinary* (*Ord.*) removes the effect.

Normally the process of breathing is left up to the performer, or the point at which a breath may be taken is indicated by a comma: ❜. If the inhaling(s) and/or exhaling(s) are to be audible, these indications may be used:

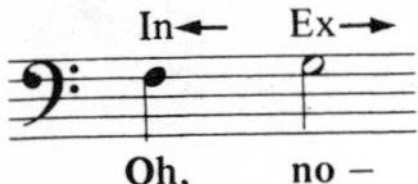

EXAMPLE 269 Inhaling and exhaling notations.

THE VOICES

The Sopranos

The soprano voices are the highest female or immature male voices. The most important of these are:

1. Coloratura.
2. Lyric.
3. Dramatic.
4. Child Soprano.
5. Choir Soprano.[2]

The coloratura soprano is the highest of all human voices. It is small, and very, very flexible. The lower portion of the range is not strong and is easily covered by any sort of accompaniment that is not transparent. In the highest portion of the range, the coloratura resembles a flute or bell in timbre.

The lyric sopranos have fuller voices. The flexibility is good, but not as amazing as that of a coloratura. In the middle and upper register the voice carries well, but the lowest register is not powerful. In contrast to the coloratura, though, the lyric soprano's lowest register is usable.

The dramatic soprano is the biggest and most powerful of all the high voices. It is darker than the lyric soprano and less agile, but it should not be considered to be either dark or sluggish. In this voice the lowest register is strong enough to require no special scoring approaches. This is the voice capable of keeping even with a full Wagnerian orchestra.

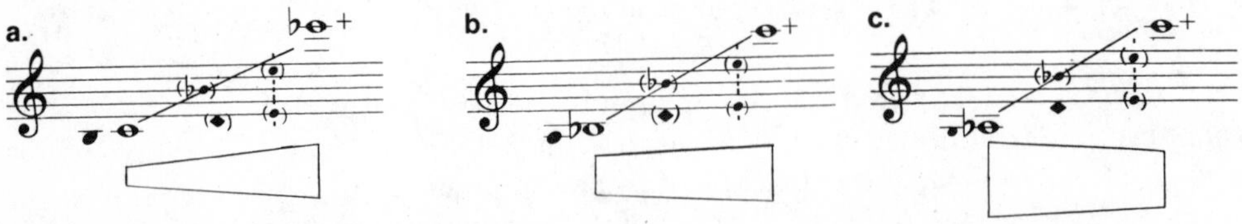

EXAMPLE 270 Typical ranges and dynamic curves for sopranos.[3] a. Coloratura soprano. b. Lyric soprano. c. Dramatic soprano.

[2]The term *choir soprano, choir alto,* etc. will be used for the typical untrained singers found in community and church choirs. In reality, these voices are probably trainable even as some other quality of voice, but, without such training, must be treated differently.

[3]The diamond-shaped notes represent typical speaking pitches; single notes in parentheses are the central pitches; breaks are indicated by vertical dotted lines connecting two notes in parentheses.

The unique voice of the child soprano has a great deal of appeal to composers. It is sometimes described as being clear and colorless. It is a very light and transparent voice, requiring careful scoring to avoid covering it up. There is little difference in quality between the high-register and the low-register notes. In writing for this soprano, special care should be exercised to avoid fatiguing the voice which, due to the limited air capacity and immature qualities, is quite delicate. Notes above the upper break should never be written for these voices unless the children have had some vocal training. Untrained children cannot sing effectively above D.

EXAMPLE 271 Typical range and dynamic curve for child soprano.

If a choir is composed of professionally trained singers, then the first sopranos will be a mixture of all types of sopranos (coloratura, lyric, and dramatic) and the second sopranos will be made up of lyric and dramatic sopranos, plus some mezzo-sopranos. In the case of a professional choir, the range and dynamic curves given for these voices should be the guide. But, in the case of the non-professional choir, the following ranges and dynamic curves should be used as the composer's guide:

a.

b.

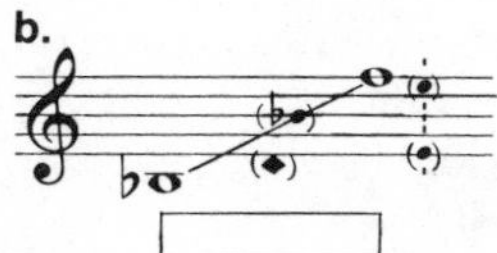

EXAMPLE 272 Ranges for non-professional choir. a. First sopranos. b. Second sopranos.

The Mezzo-Sopranos

These middle-range adult female voices are divided into four types:

1. Coloratura mezzo-soprano.
2. Lyric mezzo-soprano.
3. Dramatic mezzo-soprano.
4. Choir mezzo-soprano.

As a group the mezzo-sopranos differ from sopranos mainly in terms of voice quality. While no mezzo-sopranos can sing as high as the coloratura sopranos, the mezzo-sopranos have ranges that are typically only a whole tone or semitone less high than the dramatic sopranos. The distinction is in the darkness and power of the lower range. While the usual soprano is almost a purely head register voice, the mezzo-soprano voice is a balanced mixture of high- and low-register qualities. Therefore, the mezzo-soprano is both heavier and darker than the soprano, but may be more flexible.

The coloratura mezzo-soprano is the lightest of all mezzo-sopranos and has the type of flexibility and agility worthy of the name coloratura. The lyric mezzo-soprano bears the same relationship to the coloratura mezzo-soprano as the lyric soprano bears to the coloratura soprano: a little darker and less flexible. The unique feature of the dramatic mezzo-soprano is, of course, its darker quality and more powerful low register.

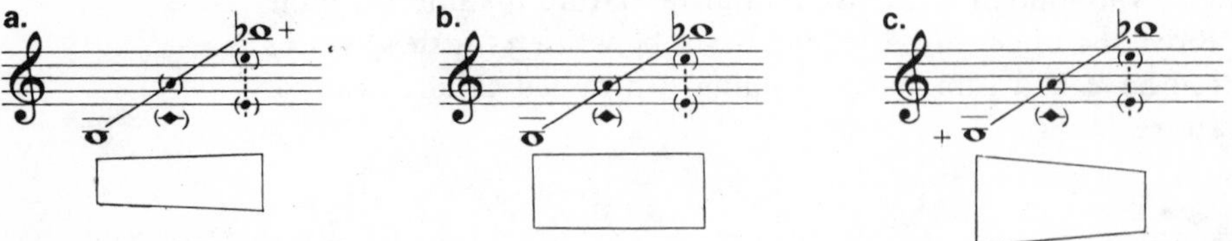

EXAMPLE 273 Typical ranges and dynamic curves for mezzo-sopranos. a. Coloratura mezzo-soprano. b. Lyric mezzo-soprano. c. Dramatic mezzo-soprano. Although all possess the same range, the dynamic curves differ.

The choir mezzo-soprano is defined much as the choir soprano was; a younger or less-trained mezzo-soprano voice. In a choir, these voices are used as second sopranos and as first altos, assisting the former with the lower portions of the range and the latter with the higher pitches.

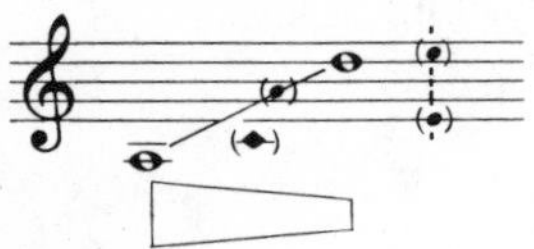

EXAMPLE 274 Range and dynamic curve for choir mezzo-soprano.

The Contraltos

These are the lowest of the female voices. The quality is dark and heavy. The lower portion of the contralto's range is very powerful. There are two types of contraltos (often called simply *altos*) to deal with:

1. Contralto.
2. Choir contralto.

The professional contralto voice is most valued for the lower half of its range, which is strong, heavy, and extremely dark-sounding as a result of the powerfully developed chest register. Agility is not one of the traits for which a contralto voice is admired, but the voice is more flexible than most literature written for it would indicate.

The choir contralto has a more limited range, with a noticeable lack of strength at the top of the range. In the choir, these voices are used as second altos. One should not be misled by the frequent amateur choir practice of using undeveloped soprano voices on the alto part simply because they can read music. These "leaders" of the alto section often have nothing but "breathy," inaudible low registers in spite of all good intentions. Ranges and dynamic curves for typical contraltos would be:

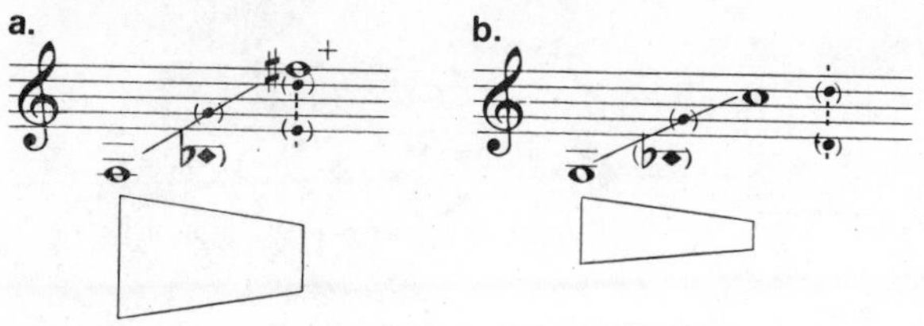

EXAMPLE 275 Typical ranges and dynamic curves for contraltos. a. Professional contralto. b. Choir contraltos.

It is not uncommon to find women with lower pitches available than those given in either of the above figures. Often in choirs these women are assigned to sing tenor parts; but they are not tenors, merely low contraltos. (Their use on the tenor line is easily understood, because the male tenor is the most difficult of all untrained voices to find.)

The Tenors

The tenors are the highest of the natural male voices. There are four basic types of tenor voices:

1. Countertenor.
2. Lyric tenor.
3. Dramatic tenor.
4. Choir tenor.

Typical of male voices, all (but the countertenor) use the chest or heavy register for most of their ranges. The lightest and highest of the lyric tenors, sometimes called *leggiero* tenors, can make a transition to the head register (falsetto) almost imperceptably. Other tenors may or may not have this ability.

The countertenors quite often have a very low speaking voice but have developed their head register for singing, providing a voice that is in the same range as the female contralto, but which is colorless and strangely pure. Long-ignored in common-practice music, although in the eighteenth and early nineteenth century it was much written for, the countertenor has recently made a comeback among pop and rock singers. The voice is still rare, but quite valuable. Its power is good and, as shown in the dynamic curve, uniform throughout its range.

The lyric tenor possesses a very light and supple instrument with coloratura properties. In its lightest form, like the Irish tenor, it may have great apparent range due to the singer's ability to go from lower register to head register very smoothly. This voice is not powerful at the top of the range (a lack that is mainly the consequence of its light quality) and is certainly not strong in the low portion.

The dramatic tenor does not have the extreme highs of the lyric tenor but possesses much power and is distinctly of a heavier quality. In its normal form, it is a good all-around tenor voice—enough highs to be exciting and enough power to carry through almost any context. It is interesting to note that the most popular of the lyric tenors also possess the power of the dramatic tenor.

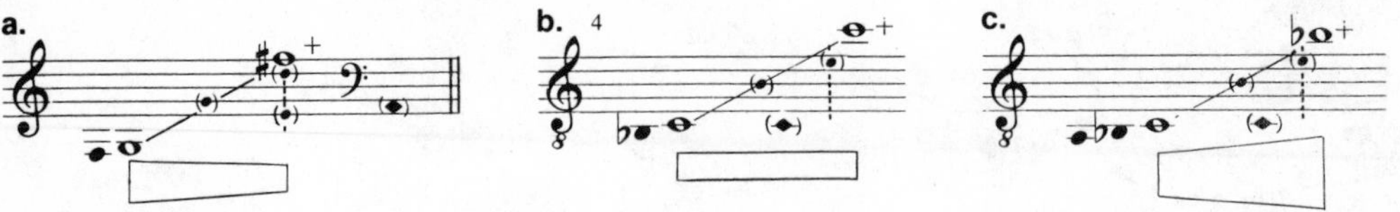

EXAMPLE 276 Typical ranges and dynamic curves for tenors. a. Countertenor. b. Lyric tenor. c. Dramatic tenor.

A special type of dramatic tenor is called the *Heldentenor*. This voice is simply a dramatic tenor of greater than normal power and endurance. In addition, as an operatic voice, the Heldentenor is usually a very big, powerfully built man; he looks like a hero.

The choir tenor is often a light baritone who strains for the higher notes. Indeed, the untrained tenor is very rare, and so the choir tenor is often not a possessor of a very high voice, nor is it likely to be especially powerful.

EXAMPLE 277 Typical range and dynamic curve for the choir tenor.

The Baritones

There are four types of baritone voices usually encountered. These are:

1. Lyric baritone.
2. Dramatic baritone.
3. Bass baritone.
4. Choir baritone.

The most frequently encountered male voice is undoubtedly the baritone.

The baritone voice is much darker and richer in tone color than the tenor. However, there is definitely less flexibility and suppleness to the voice. The lyric baritone has a lighter, more flexible upper register than other baritones.

The dramatic baritone has a range that is identical to the lyric baritone's but lacks the flexibility and light upper register. In return, the dramatic baritone possesses a larger, more powerful voice which maintains a very even distribution of its power throughout its range.

The bass baritone has most of the characteristics of the dramatic baritone, but a slightly lower range and a much darker tone quality. This voice can easily give the impression, like the mezzo-sopranos and contraltos, that it is producing lower pitches than it actually is. This is due to the heavy tone quality of the voice.

[4] The clef used here is often found in music for the tenor voice. It indicates that the pitch will sound one octave lower than written.

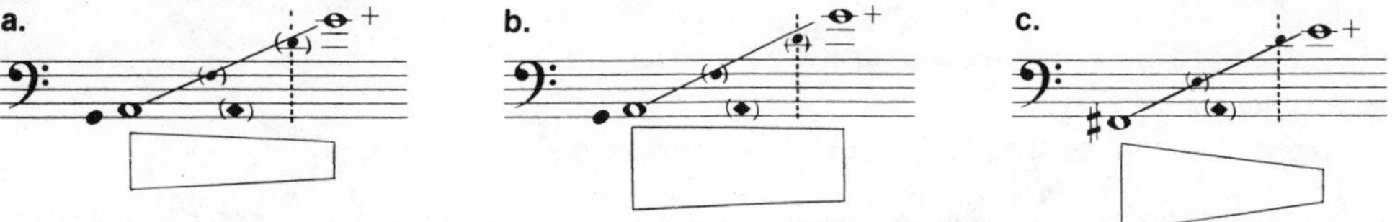

EXAMPLE 278 Typical ranges and dynamic curves for baritones. a. Lyric baritone. b. Dramatic baritone. c. Bass baritone.

The choir baritone is often an untrained tenor or untrained bass. One can write lower notes for this voice than for the normal (and trained) lyric or dramatic baritones, but the higher range is limited.

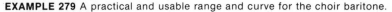

EXAMPLE 279 A practical and usable range and curve for the choir baritone.

The typical choir baritone is not as dark as the dramatic baritone, nor as flexible as the lyric. The tone quality is less interesting and lacks the character associated with the bass-baritone. It is usually a very neutral, but quite usable, voice quality.

The Basses

One usually considers three different bass qualities. These are:

1. Bass cantante.
2. Basso profundo.
3. Choir bass.

The basses do not come close to the flexibility and gracefulness of the higher voices. The bass voice could be described as being dark to very dark, with a perceptively heavy quality. The higher notes of the range are apt to be rough and to sound somewhat strained. Of all the basses, only the somewhat rare *cantante* possess any true agility; and this is limited. The tonal characteristic of the cantante is one of evenness from the lowest to the highest notes. (Basses that possess this range, but lack the flexibility of the cantante are usually called simply "basses.")

The *basso profundo* is a very low, powerful, dark, heavy, and inflexible voice. It has a low range in which slow movement is the most satisfying kind of motion. Displays of agility and attempts at coloratura usually sound ridiculous and are apt to reduce a well-trained performer into an inadvertant comic.

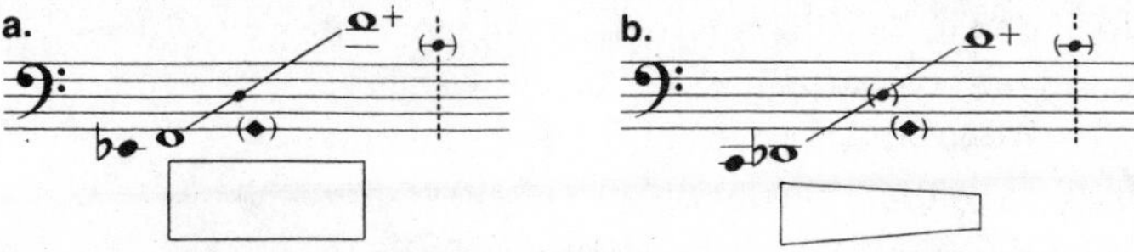

EXAMPLE 280 Typical ranges and dynamic curves for basses. a. Basso cantante. b. Basso profundo.

When a bass voice has a crispness to its tone quality, a clearness to its articulation, and is located in a body capable of the proper gestures and expression, one has the *bass buffo* or "comic bass." This operatic voice-character of some charm may have the range of either the cantante or the basso profundo, but due to other factors is not typical of either.

The choir bass is likely to be simply a naturally low untrained voice. Its quality may be good or gravelly and the range in which it actually possesses a bass darkness of tone is often limited to the lowest fourth or fifth of its tonal range. Mixed with the baritones, as described before, the combination provides a very suitable (and the most typical) "bass" for a church or community choir. As a solo voice, untrained examples are very rare.

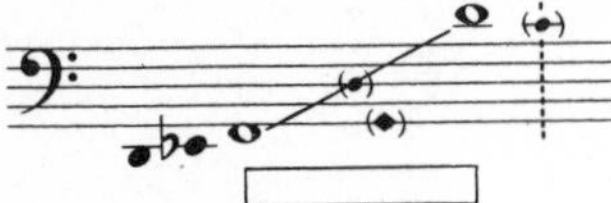

EXAMPLE 281 Typical range and dynamic curve for the choir bass.

Other Voices

In addition to the voices discussed above, there are other voices one encounters or hears about. Among these are:

1. The *castrati.*
2. The pop singer.
3. The contrabass (Russian bass).

The *castrati* were adult men who, prior to puberty, were castrated. This was done to excellent boy sopranos who, it is said, "agreed" to the operation since it might be a means of achieving fame and fortune for a boy born to poverty. The vocal ranges were those of the female sopranos discussed above, except it is doubtful that any coloratura sopranos existed. The voices had the unworldly quality of the boy soprano's voice, but with the power of an adult male singer. Many articles and comments from the period have raved about the greatness of these singers, but there is also some evidence that the voices were coarse and not polished; the possesser was willing to impress listeners with power over control and with uniqueness rather than taste.

The *pop singers* really can be placed into one of the six basic categories of singers discussed above. However, most popular artists choose, for the purpose of establishing their careers, to obtain a unique vocal timbre. The vocal sounds of all singers are distinctive, but this is not the only concern in the development of a concert or opera singer. On the other hand, the singer who wishes a popular singing career, and this includes jazz, rock, commercial, folk, and other popular vocalists, needs to develop a distinctive style *and* tone quality. For this reason, they are not as obviously classified as *tenor* or *mezzo-soprano* as are other vocalists. One may apply the information included in this chapter to these singers, but only in light of the specific qualities a certain vocalist possesses and wishes to project. To say that Frank Sinatra is a baritone, and then to check the comments about baritones above, is not enough to allow one to write music effectively for him. His style and unique qualities *must* be the point of departure. An opera composer often writes a part for a baritone; a pops composer writes a part for Sinatra. The difference is very important. Interestingly, many contemporary composers of non-pops music are also writing for specific vocalists rather than just for a voice quality.

One of the significant contributing factors to the development of these unique voices has been the use of electronics in the popular music field. With the advent of the microphone and amplifiers, voices that did not have the necessary power to make it in the concert halls or opera houses could, without the alterations of the voice quality necessary to provide the power needed to project, easily be heard just by holding the microphone close and turning up the volume. This made a whispery little voice usable with a large jazz band, and a very transparent, boyish baritone having no power or sound mass the equal of a full orchestra. Voices that had not been traditionally classified and named, because they were not (historically) capable of being used as voices, now have become commonplace.

An additional benefit of the advent of electronic amplification is the possibility of using electronic means to alter the voice quality, other than merely increasing the loudness. By the use of filters and mixers of various types, the singer can now create vocal timbres and effects that are not possible with just an acoustically projected voice.

The *contrabass,* sometimes called Russian bass, is the lowest and rarest of all voices. Its deep range gives it a very dark quality. Typically, this voice has been found only among choirs of the Russian orthodox church and, for obvious reasons, the numbers have been diminishing. However, in some folk groups and barbershop quartets, one will appear.

EXAMPLE 282 Typical range and dynamic curve for the contrabass voice.

TYPICAL VOCAL SCORING

This example from Benjamin Britten's "War Requiem" shows typical homophonic writing for choir. In spite of a more modern idiom than Bach chorale, the historical influence can be seen in the voice leading and the spacings employed.

EXAMPLE 283 An example of homophonic writing for chorus, beginning at rehearsal number 68 in the "Offertorium" of Britten's *War Requiem.*[5]

Later in the same work, Britten writes this contrapuntal passage for the chorus. Again the voice leading, range, and tessitura are typical of good choral writing as found in works since the Renaissance, no matter what style or period is considered. Both of these Britten excerpts are quite singable, even by untrained singers.

EXAMPLE 284 Beginning at rehearsal number 30 in the "Dies Irae" of Britten's *War Requiem* is this contrapuntal vocal passage.[6]

This famous passage from the Queen of the Night's aria "Der Hölle Rache kocht in meinem Herzen" from Mozart's *Die Zauberflöte (The Magic Flute)* is a classical illustration of coloratura writing. The aria is intended for the highest, lightest, and clearest of all soprano voices: the coloratura soprano. Note that the phoneme sung is derived from *mehr.*

[6]Copyright 1962 by Boosey & Hawkes Music Publishers Ltd. Reprinted by permission of Boosey & Hawkes, Inc.

EXAMPLE 285 From the famous Queen of the Night's aria for coloratura soprano by Mozart.

In Gounod's *Faust,* the character Valentine, a baritone, sings this famous aria. Note the wide range which is typical of writing for the trained voice. In contrast, one does not write many G's for a choir tenor, much less a baritone. However, in opera, trained voices are assumed. "Dio possente" shows the lyrical but not especially flexible writing usually given to the lower voices.

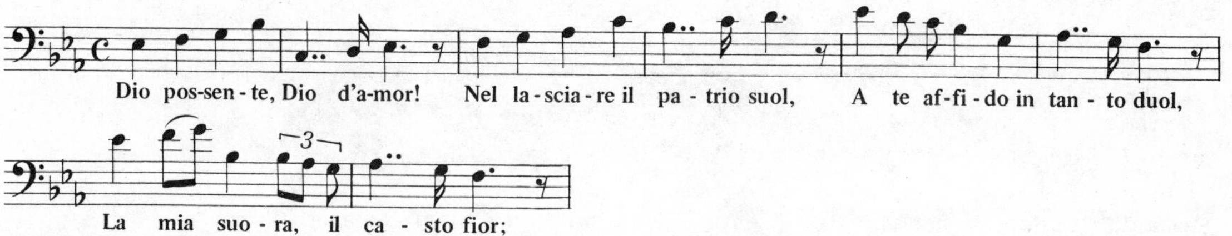

EXAMPLE 286 Typical operatic writing for lower voice: "Dio possente" from Act II of Gounod's *Faust.*

In his work for soprano, flute, and piano, Thomas Albert uses a proportional time notation. He is also very careful to notate longer and shorter syllable durations. Note, too, the use of an X for an unvoiced, separated consonant. The care demonstrated indicates that the composer is well aware of the potential and the properties of the voice.

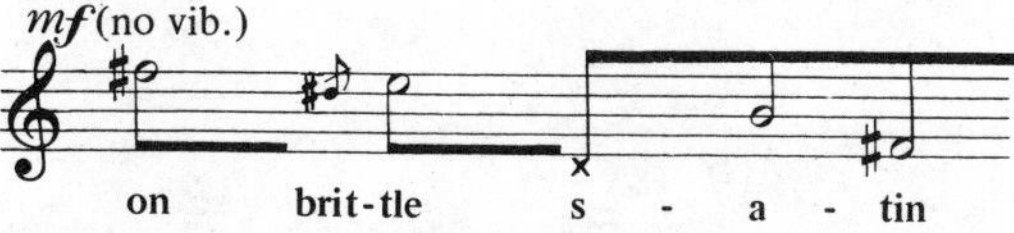

EXAMPLE 287 From *Winter Monarch* by Albert[7] (third system of the second page). Time is notated proportionally.

David Cope wrote for voice and percussion in his composition *Ashes.* This example shows Cope's symbol for open (o) and closed (+) mouth. The horizontal lines mean "gradually change to" and the term *blend* indicates that the singer should attempt to match the percussion tone quality. The use of lines extending from the note heads to show the contour of pitch inflections is commonly found in both vocal and instrumental music. The letters underneath the music are not from the International Phonetic Alphabet but are the symbols used in English dictionaries to show pronunciation without respelling the word.

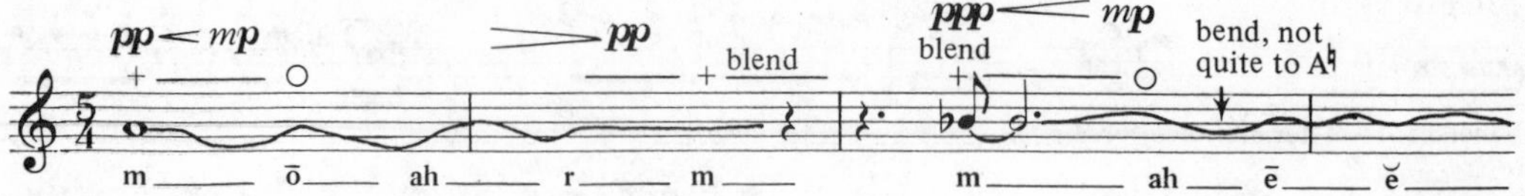

EXAMPLE 288 Excerpt from David Cope's *Ashes*[8] (measures 2-5).

A use of the International Phonetic Alphabet is shown in this line from Robert Newell's *Spirals* for tenor, soprano, and percussion. In this work the composer, who is himself an excellent tenor, calls for the singers to use megaphones and to cup their hands over their mouths while singing, producing, on the one hand, an amplification and, on the other, a muting effect.

EXAMPLE 289 Soprano line from page 4 of Newell's *Spirals.*[9] The symbol ◊ means "through a megaphone"; ◊ means "megaphone away."

In his chamber work *Ancient Voices of Children,* George Crumb instructs the soprano to sing *into* the piano at the beginning. The reverberation produced this way, which can be controlled by the piano pedals, produces an unusually effective, dramatic quality. The notation for the tongue click, shown as headless grace notes or sixteenth notes, is of special interest also.

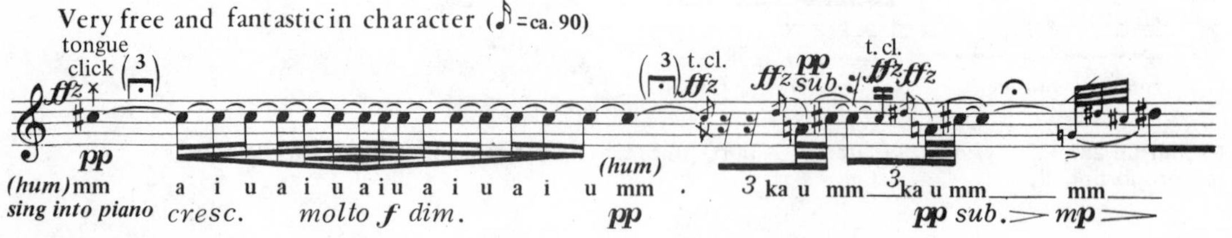

EXAMPLE 290 The opening of Crumb's *Ancient Voices of Children.*[10]

Problem Set No. 21

1. Score the Mendelssohn "Song Without Words" given below for a four-voice choir (SATB: soprano, alto, tenor, bass). Convert the music on the upper staff by beginning with the altos alone and then having the sopranos enter on the A in the second measure. Create a tenor line and a bass line out of the music on the lower staff by continuing in the manner shown in the sample measure below. Add phonemes to all of the lines and have the result performed in class. (Do only the first twelve measures.)

2. Rescore the music given in exercise 1, above, for solo voice and instrumental accompaniment. Change the key according to the range of the solo voice desired. Use instruments available to the class and have the result performed.

3. Score the following Bartók piece, "In Four Parts," for SATB choir and string quartet. Perform the result in class. Also, perform it with various vocal and instrumental combinations such as sopranos, altos, viola, and cello, etc. (If a string quartet is not available, use another agreed-upon combination of instruments.)

4. Select a nonsense poem, an appropriate text, or make up a text of your own and write an original piece of about 10 to 20 measures for a solo voice and an instrument of your choice. Use contemporary devices and effects in both the vocal and instrumental parts. Experiment with unusual sounds and avoid most "traditional" sounds. Have your work performed if possible.

VOCAL BIBLIOGRAPHY

Appelman, Dudley Ralph. *The Science of Vocal Pedagogy.* Bloomington, Ind.: Indiana University Press, 1967.

Van Riper, Charles Gage and John V. Irwin. *Voice and Articulation.* Englewood Cliffs, N. J.: Prentice-Hall, 1962.

Vennard, William. *Singing.* Rev. ed. Los Angeles: William Vennard, 1964.

Wilson, Harry Robert. *Choral Arranging.* New York: Robbins Music, 1949.

ORCHESTRATION: Scoring Musical Elements

MUSICAL LINES

Identification of Musical Lines

Line is the important element in a piece of music. It is true that students of music learn to identify and use chords, but most chords found in Western European art music are the result of several melodic lines being heard or identified in a vertical configuration. The majority of musical instruments, and the voice, are one-line instruments. When writing for the piano or organ, composers are careful to create most vertical structures out of several well-conceived lines. It is therefore important that the person who is orchestrating a composition be able to locate musical lines in the composition.

Consider the following excerpt.

EXAMPLE 291 From "Novellette", Op. 21, No. 6, by Robert Schumann.

Two lines stand out.

EXAMPLE 292 The two prominent lines identified from Example 291, shown in isolation.

However, the other notes also form lines.

EXAMPLE 293 The less prominent or subordinate lines remaining from Example 291.

Which are the prominent lines and which are subordinate? In a traditional view of the piece, the two lines isolated in Example 292, above, are prominent "melodies" while the Example 293 lines are subordinate or "accompanimental" in nature. Less traditional views may see other assignments for these elements, but at some point a separation into more and less prominent lines is inevitable.[1]

The Use of Instrumental Color

One of the chief goals of the orchestrator is to mix, blend, match, and contrast the instrumental and vocal colors at his disposal. As with any art, there is not just one correct method. Often the use of rather pale and uninteresting colors can serve as a perfect and desirable preparation or backdrop for more brilliant and exciting hues. In other situations, layer upon layer of the most colorful sounds at hand, vying for the listener's attention, may prove to be the most artistic solution to a musical problem.

In general, lines that are given the more colorful treatment are the musically more prominent lines while subordinate lines, often serving as accompaniment or background, are colored less vividly. The distinction between these two basic colorations will be maintained in the following sections, but the reversal of these obvious color assignments should be explored and considered by the serious orchestrator. One may draw attention by being different, not necessarily by always being more "colorful."

Colorful Versus Less Colorful

The words colorful and less colorful are being used here in a relative sense which can have meaning only within a context. Thus, although one may consider the sound of an oboe to be "colorful", in an ensemble of double reeds it is not especially colorful. Compared to these double reeds, a solo violin would be colorful, but contrasted to a string orchestra, the oboe would again seem colorful.

The orchestral unison, a combination of all the many tone qualities, is a powerful and effective sound. But, much as the mixing of many colored lights will produce a gray-white light, the orchestral unison may more rapidly lose its ability to sound fresh than will the sound of a single solo instrument. For the mass of mixed timbres presented by the full orchestra, in spite of its magnificence and grandeur which *capture* our attention, lacks the subtle nuances of the solo instrument or voice, which may *hold* our attention over very extended periods of time.

[1]Even in contrapuntal music, it is rare for all lines to be exactly equal in prominence.

Scoring Prominent Lines

From the above considerations, one can construct six basic procedures available for the scoring of prominent lines:

1. One instrument playing the line.
2. Two or more of the same instrument, playing the line in unison.
3. Two or more of the same instrument, playing the line in different octaves.
4. Two or more different instruments, playing the line in unison.
5. Two or more different instruments, playing the line in different octaves.
6. Several instruments playing the line with the intervals between the instruments being other than only unisons and octaves.

Procedure 1. This is the simplest and one of the most effective ways of scoring a line. It has the advantage of placing all the responsibility for intonation and musicianship in the hands of a single performer; thus, there are no ensemble problems. Lines scored in this manner can take advantage of the colorations available from the instrument selected, and will be perceived as being very clear and clean.

EXAMPLE 294 Procedure 1: One instrument per line.

Procedure 2. With two or more of the same instruments playing the line, additional warmth is added, but a small sacrifice in terms of purity of color or clarity of articulation may be made. In school organizations, this is more than made up for by improved security. Intonation, even in professional situations, becomes a problem for the performers if only two are assigned to the line. Assigning more than two performers minimizes intonation problems.

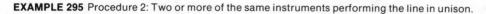

EXAMPLE 295 Procedure 2: Two or more of the same instruments performing the line in unison.

Procedure 3. Two or more of the same instruments in different octaves can produce interesting new tonal qualities. The intonation problem is not as serious between two performers as it is in unison writing. The effect is not so much one of greater sound mass, as is achieved by procedure two, but one of greater penetration. (If one wishes to also increase the sense of mass, then several instruments should be assigned to each octave.) The most interesting results with procedure 3 are obtained when the lower line is scored to be more prominent (louder) than the upper line(s). This causes the upper line(s) to be perceived as partials of a new timbre which has the lower line as its fundamental.

EXAMPLE 296 Procedure 3: Two of the same instruments doubling the line at the octave.

The doubling of a line at the octave or some multiple of an octave is usually more effective when the doubling is outward—that is, when the top line is doubled an octave or more above, and the bass line is doubled an octave or more below. This remains true regardless of whether the instruments involved are the same or different. One notable exception would be in trying to create an organ effect. Here the bass line is often doubled both above and below. The thickness created by this sort of doubling is a familiar organ sound.

Procedure 4. Two or more different instruments perform the line in unison, creating new, synthetic tone qualities. Even with only two performers involved, the listener is less likely to notice small deviations in intonation between two different instruments (although for the performer the actual tuning process may be more difficult). This procedure is especially good for generating and transforming various tone qualities through the additive properties of sounds.

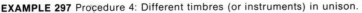

EXAMPLE 297 Procedure 4: Different timbres (or instruments) in unison.

Procedure 5. Two or more different instruments playing a line in different octaves is a very effective way to synthesize new timbres. One must define ("different instruments" here to include combinations like two clarinets which, in different octaves, possess totally distinctive tone qualities.) The more octaves between the instruments, the more the result will sound like separate instruments and not like one integrated tone. With imaginative selection of instruments, interesting and colorful new sounds are possible.

EXAMPLE 298 Procedure 5: Different instruments (or timbres) playing the same line in different octaves.

Procedure 6. This very interesting procedure uses several instruments in much the same manner as mutation stops are used on the pipe organ. By assigning several instruments of the same or different timbres to the line, but by doubling it at intervals other than just unisons or octaves, even greater synthetic possibilites are opened up. Typical relationships would be: one instrument on the melody, another on the melody an octave higher, a third instrument on the melody a perfect fifth above that, and another instrument on the melody a major sixth above that. This particular arrangement, which is very similar to the old organ solo voice known as a *cornet* is especially effective but the problem of intonation becomes great. (See pages 240-41 re: *mutation stops* and *cornet*.)

EXAMPLE 299 Procedure 6: Line doubled at the 12th and at the 17th.

In the context of other kinds of music, other combinations of intervals may be more appropriate.

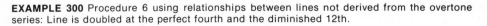

EXAMPLE 300 Procedure 6 using relationships between lines not derived from the overtone series: Line is doubled at the perfect fourth and the diminished 12th.

Scoring Subordinate Lines

Subordinate lines are usually perceived to be accompanimental in nature. As such, one generally does not wish to draw too much of the listener's attention to these lines. But, one also does not wish to have them "lost" in the texture. The desirable scoring would be one that locates all elements of these lines, or the figures the lines create, within a very playable and controllable range of the instruments assigned to the lines. (Thus, a line intended to be unobtrusive would not be given to three trumpets asked to play in the top fifth of their ranges, for example.) There are four basic procedures for scoring subordinate lines. These are listed here from least attention-getting to most attention-getting (that is, from most subordinate to least subordinate):

A. A *group* of very similar sounding instruments assigned to each element (line) in one or more octaves.

B. A *group* of dissimilar sounding instruments assigned to each element (line) in one or more octaves, each group possessing an unique sound.

C. A *single instrument* assigned to each element or line, all instruments possessing very similar sounds.

D. A *single instrument* assigned to each element or line, each instrument possessing an unique sound.

Procedure A. Perhaps the most traditional way of dealing with accompanimental lines is to assign all of these elements to the same or similar-toned instruments and to make sure that a group is playing each element. In the orchestra, this has led to the extensive use of the second violins, violas, and cellos for the performance of this material; in the band, the clarinets, alto clarinets, and bass clarinets have had the same roles. The use of an ensemble tends to "take the edge off" the articulations and will average out the individuality of the performers involved.

EXAMPLE 301 Procedure A: Groups of similar instruments assigned to each element. Note the use of second violins and violas for rhythmic figures and the use of cellos and contrabasses, in octaves, for the bass.

Procedure B. Again the massed forces idea of Procedure A is used, but now the groups are heterogeneous.

EXAMPLE 302 Procedure B: Each element Is played by several different instruments. The colorations and the octave doublings of the two elements differ.

Procedure C. The use of a single instrument per accompanimental line provides clarity. If all of the accompanimental lines are performed by instruments with similar tone qualities, these subordinate elements will blend and be generally less likely to call attention to themselves. If one does wish to make these elements more prominent, the use of more colorful timbres is appropriate. By scoring with only one player on a part, each performer becomes a soloist and, assuming skilled players and sensitive musicians, will cause each element to be heard as a fresh and vital part of the music.

EXAMPLE 303 Procedure C: Four individual instruments, all possessing similar tone qualities, perform the four elements of the accompaniment.

Procedure D. This procedure is the most difficult to make work, but the inherent challenge also makes it the most interesting. When one instrument is assigned to each accompanimental line, the cleanness of Procedure C is obtained. But, when the instruments involved possess dissimilar timbres, balance and blend become a problem. Using the characteristics of the instruments involved requires the careful assigning of a particular line to a particular instrument. One might match low-register flute to muted horn and throat tones of the clarinet to blend three unlike instruments into a balanced ensemble. One could also, when required, revoice this combination to take advantage of the differences between these instruments so that a certain figure or line could be emphasized or brought out.

EXAMPLE 304 Procedure D: Four different instruments each assigned to a different subordinate line.

Scoring and Voicing Isolated Chords

In many orchestrating situations, the orchestrator is faced with the problem of scoring chords which contain many octave doublings. One may need to score a simple C major triad for full band or orchestra. This will require the assigning of many C's, many E's, and many G's throughout the ensemble. One may well be concerned with how this can be done effectively. A very traditional answer is to use the overtone series as a model. (See Appendix VI.) From this model, one can generalize that larger intervals between the elements of the chord are found in the lowest registers, while smaller intervals are more common in the higher registers. In addition, one finds the root of the chord to be the most frequently assigned pitch in the lower registers, while in the upper registers all members of the chord are equally likely.

If the chord with which one is dealing is not a simple triad or seventh chord, then other criteria will become important in making decisions about voicing and doubling. Among these, one needs to consider which of the pitches are more significant to the structure of the composition. If a hierarchy of pitches, from most important to least important, can be established, then one can generalize the distribution of these pitches in this manner: The most important pitch should appear in many octaves and should be included as the lowest or nearly lowest pitch present; the least important pitch may not require doubling and will probably appear in the highest (or higher) octave(s). Also, the overtones of the more important pitch(es) will probably also be reinforced—especially the 3rd partial (a 12th above). Again, we have come close to defining the traditional overtone series model.

EXAMPLE 305 Four chords voiced according to the overtone series model.

If one always follows the overtone series model for voicing chords, one will always obtain a smooth-sounding, well-balanced chord. But it has never been the ideal of the composer or orchestrator to obtain nothing but smooth, well-balanced sounds. Indeed, much of the excitement of music, the tension, the liveliness, is a result of sounds that are not "perfect"; sonorities that are rough, not smooth; structures that are out-of-balance, not balanced. Therefore, consciously avoiding the overtone series model can provide an alternative method of scoring: the *less* the voicing of a chord follows the overtone series model, the more unique, unstable, attention-getting, coarse, or interesting the chord may sound.

EXAMPLE 306 Various chords voiced so as not to follow the overtone series model.

The final test as to whether a chord has been voiced like or unlike the overtone series (or any other) model is the *ear,* not the *eye,* of the orchestrator. If one is, for example, attempting to create a chord with an overtone series voicing, but assigns assertive or especially colórful voices to a unique assortment of pitches, then those pitches will be more audible and could thereby unexpectedly alter the final result. One would not usually wish to assign all of the brass instruments to the third of a final chord and evenly divide the strings among the remaining pitches. The strange balance the listener would hear is indicative of the sort of voicing problems one must always try to avoid.

Special Scoring Approaches

A tone or sound can be divided into three temporal aspects: the *attack,* the *steady-state,* and the *decay*—that is, roughly the beginning, the middle, and the end. Each musical instrument has a characteristic attack. Modification by the performer is often, but not always, possible. The same statements may be made about the steady-state and the decay. However, adding other instruments to the various portions of the tone can bring on greater changes than the individual performer is capable of. A *fortepiano* attack played by a muted trumpet can be significantly altered by adding unison string pizzicatos to each attack, as in the following:

EXAMPLE 307 Pizzicato strings added to trumpet attack to create a different attack envelope.

During a held oboe tone, the clarinet could enter much, much softer, crescendo up to match or exceed the oboe's loudness, and then decrescendo to nothing while the oboe tone remains unchanged:

EXAMPLE 308 The clarinet tone is used to modify the steady-state tone of the oboe.

A loud brass chord could be released, revealing the same chord, but played *pianissimo* by matched, muted brasses, still sounding. Then this softer chord diminuendos into silence:

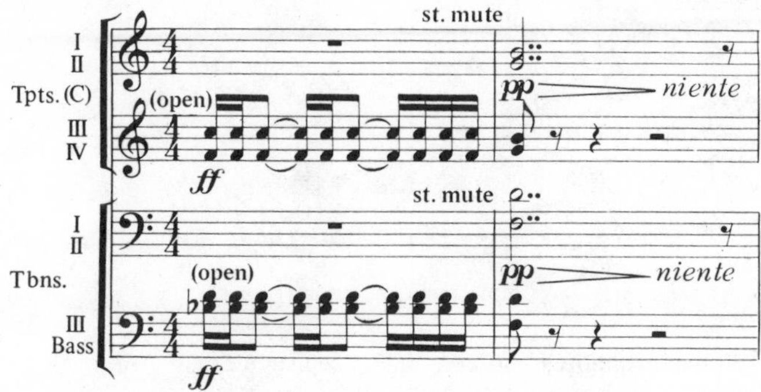

EXAMPLE 309 Brass decay being altered by the use of muted brasses.

By using a little imagination, one can discover a variety of ways of using one instrument to alter the sound of another instrument. The percussion section of the band or orchestra does itself suggest hundreds of new sound-shapes.

Klangfarbenmelodie

In many contemporary scores one finds the use of *Klangfarbenmelodie,* a term suggested by Schönberg for the use of timbre as a compositional element. Typically, in this type of scoring, the orchestration of a line changes timbre (and perhaps register) with every change in pitch, or after every few pitches. The effect may be achieved on a single pitch or superimposed upon a line of many pitches. One may choose to use an ordering of very similar timbres, creating the effect of a tone quality gradually evolving, or one may use startlingly different tone qualities on each pitch to heighten the pointillistic effect of this sort of scoring. All of the discussion in this section having to do with the relation between voicings and modifications of doublings, attack, steady-state, and decay may be applied to the individual timbres used in *Klangfarbenmelodie.*

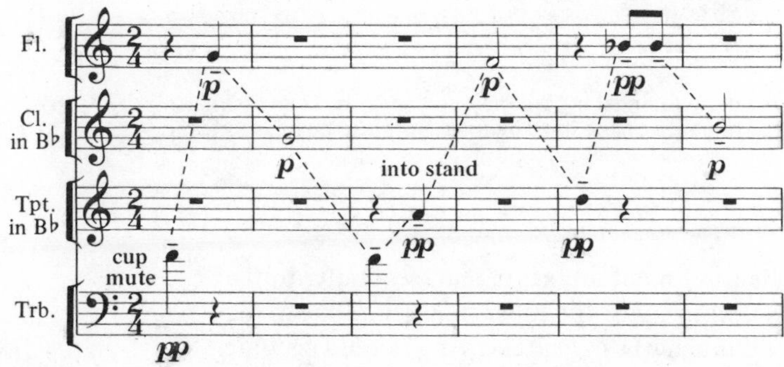

EXAMPLE 310 *Klangfarbenmelodie* using similar timbres and registers.

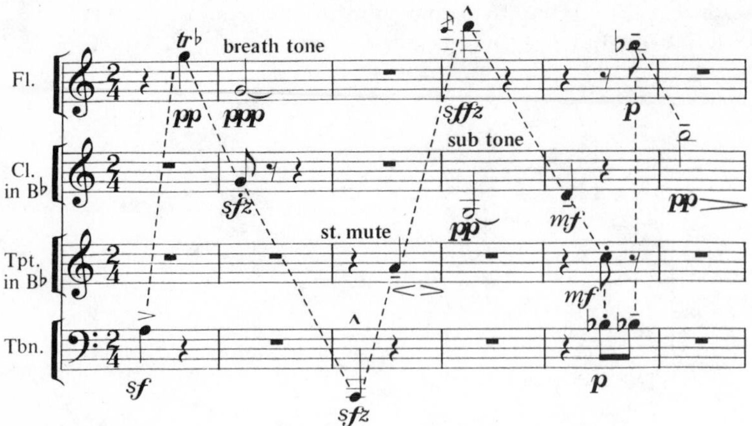

EXAMPLE 311 *Klangfarbenmelodie* in which dissimilar timbres and contrasting registers are stressed.

Connecting and Not Connecting Lines

When, for whatever reason, a continuing line is passed from one instrument or group of instruments to another and the orchestrator wishes to avoid a break in the line, the last note played by one instrument or group should be tied into the first note played by the group or instrument that takes up the line. Without this tie, a hole is likely to develop, since there is little agreement among musicians as to when any given duration is to be released.

Since the problem of deciding when a duration ends exists, a clear notation seems desirable for when one wishes to create a space in a line, or when one would like to have an ensemble release together. Such a system does not commonly exist, however. There is a notation sometimes encountered in jazz scoring which indicates that a note is to be released at a specific moment, such as on the fourth beat (symbolized by -4) or on the first beat (-1). Since this is not familiar to all musicians, an explanation would need to be included in the score if it were used.

EXAMPLE 312 a. No connection between the two lines; a hole may be heard. b. The two lines connect because of the tie. c. Note is to be released on the third beat. d. Note is to be released on the fourth beat.

Placement of Prominent Lines

Our ears are most sensitive to the top line of a texture and, secondly, to the bottom line. Thus, it always works well to place the most significant line in the top or bottom voice(s). However, too much of this "safe scoring" would become dull. It also would mean that the use of instruments such as horns and violas, or voices such as the baritone, as soloists would be nearly unheard of—a situation which is of course contrary to fact. However, simply assigning a prominent line to a middle voice does not automatically produce the desired results. When an important line is placed in a middle register position, there are two basic ways to assure its being heard: clear out the musical space around the important line, or assign an assertive voice to the line, a voice capable of cutting through the surrounding texture no matter how dense this texture is.

In the following example, the placement of the melody in the top voice assures that it will be heard.

EXAMPLE 313 Melody in the soprano voice.

By placing the melody in the bass voice, it is still easily heard.

EXAMPLE 314 Melody in the bass voice, also easily heard.

The placement of the melody in an inner line makes it almost impossible to hear. (However, if the rest of this example were played on the piano with a trombone on the melody, it would work fine.)

EXAMPLE 315 Melody in a middle voice. If all lines are equally weighted, the melody is difficult to hear.

If one places the melody in a middle voice but opens up, or clears out, the texture to give the melodic line room to breathe, even with all voices equal the prominent line is clearly audible.

EXAMPLE 316 Melody in middle voice, but with room to breathe. It is clearly heard.

EXAMPLES OF SCORING TECHNIQUES FROM THE LITERATURE

If one were to search through the orchestra, chamber music, band, and choral literature with which most of us are familiar, many examples of the various scoring techniques discussed above could be found. So that the student can see these procedures as they have been used by various composers throughout various styles and periods, here are some selected examples.

In the first example, from the Schubert *Octet,* we see a single instrument, the clarinet, assigned to the melodic line and three instruments with similar tone qualities assigned to the accompaniment lines—violins 1 and 2, and viola. (The excerpt is from the first movement, measures 116-120.)

EXAMPLE 317 An excerpt from Schubert's *Octet* showing the use of Procedures 1 and C.

In the Prelude to the Third Act of *Die Meistersinger* (measures 15-21), Wagner uses the following scoring, which features the altering of the attack and release of the chords by the addition of the brasses to the basic ensemble of two bassoons and four horns.

EXAMPLE 318 An excerpt from *Die Meistersinger* showing the altering of the attack and decay of tones.

At the beginning of the fourth movement of Berlioz's *Symphonie Fantastique,* the following voicing of the opening chords is used (remember, the contrabasses sound an octave lower than notated). The voicing does *not* follow the prototype of the overtone series.

EXAMPLE 319 An excerpt from Berlioz's *Symphonie Fantastique* showing a non-overtone series voicing of the chords (fourth movement, measures 1-5).

This example from Liszt's *Les Preludes* shows several procedures in use. The woodwind accompaniment is scored with several dissimilar instruments assigned to each element (Procedure B) while the string scoring of the prominent line uses several similar instruments in octaves (Procedure 3).

EXAMPLE 320 Excerpt from Liszt's *Les Preludes* (measures 19-21).

Wagner uses one clarinet, one bassoon, and two horns on the accompanimental figure in measures 50 and 52 of his *Siegfried Idyll.* This is an example of the use of Procedure D in scoring.

EXAMPLE 321 An excerpt from Wagner's *Siegfried Idyll* (measures 50-55).

The beginning of the second movement of Brahms's Fourth Symphony starts with two horns in unison (Procedure 2) to which are added two bassoons and two oboes in octaves, and then two flutes an octave above the oboes (Procedure 5.)

EXAMPLE 322 From Brahms's Fourth Symphony (second movement, measures 1-4).

Tchaikovsky has used what we have defined as Procedure A at the beginning of the second movement of his Fifth Symphony. Of course the horn solo writing is another example of Procedure 1.

EXAMPLE 323 The opening of the second movement of Tchaikovsky's Fifth Symphony (measures 1-9).

The scoring of the first and second violins in this passage from Debussy's *L'après-midi d'un faune* is an illustration of Procedure 3—that is, scoring prominent lines with two or more of the same instruments in octaves.

EXAMPLE 324 Excerpt from *L'après-midi d'un faune* by Debussy (beginning 2 measures after rehearsal number 5).

In Ravel's *Bolero,* the composer has scored the theme according to Procedure 6. Note the pitch relationship between the horn, celesta, and piccolos. The effect is most creative and very interesting. (This passage is from 2 measures after rehearsal number 8.)

EXAMPLE 325 From *Bolero* by Ravel.[2] The horn line is doubled by the celesta one and two octaves higher, by the second piccolo a 12th higher, and by the first piccolo a 17th higher.

[2]Copyright 1929 Durand et Cie. Used by permission of the publisher. Theodore Presser Company, Sole Representative U.S.A.

The following example from Elliott Carter's "Etude Number Seven" from *Eight Etudes and a Fantasy* for woodwind quartet shows a combination of *Klangfarbenmelodie* on a single pitch, as well as modifications of the attack, steady-state, and release of the tones.

EXAMPLE 326 The end of Elliott Carter's "Etude Number Seven" for woodwind quartet.[3] (measures 22-31).

Problem Set No. 22

1. Score "Tale" by Bartók for flute, oboe, clarinet in B♭, bassoon, 2 violins, viola, and violoncello. Use at least two of these procedures for the melodic line scoring: 1, 2, 3, 4, and 5. Use at least two of these procedures for the accompaniment: B, C, and D. On your score, label the procedures that you use.

TALE[4]

Béla Bartók

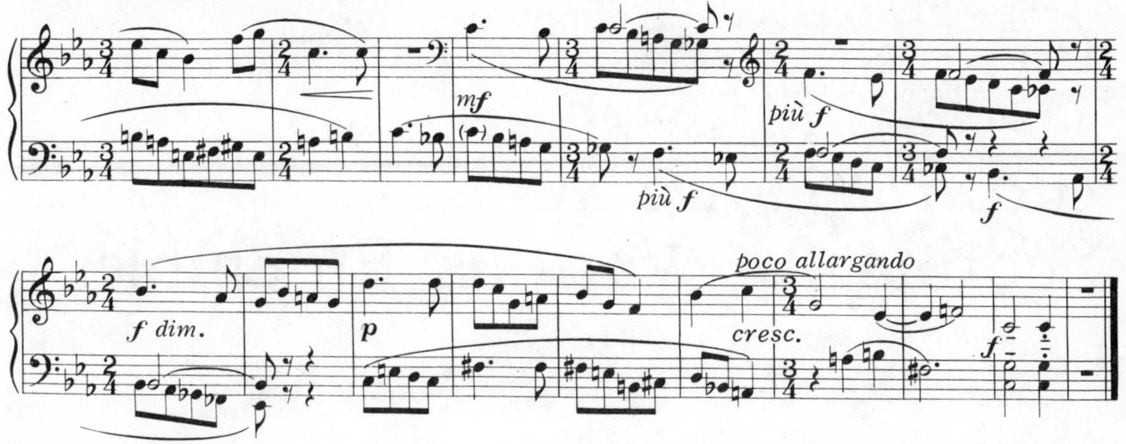

2. Given this instrumentation—2 flutes, 2 horns in F, 1 trumpet, 1 trombone, 1 violin, 1 contrabass—score the following line using *Klangfarbenmelodie:*

3. Given the chord sequence below, write out a four-voice version of the progression using open staves. You may change inversions, change octaves, double or omit pitches as needed. Just be sure that the lines created all demonstrate good voice leading. If desired, non-harmonic tones may be added, but the basic progression should remain unaltered.

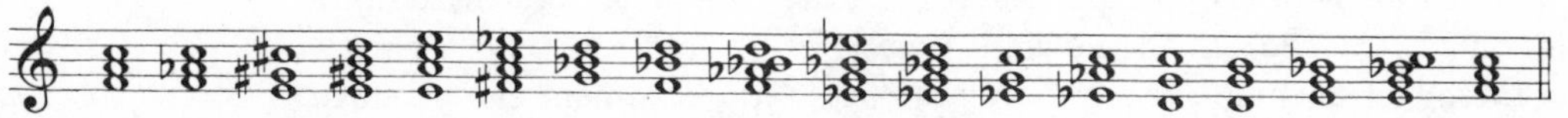

4. Score the lines extracted in exercise 3, above, for 2 flutes, 2 oboes, 2 B♭ clarinets, 2 bassoons, 2 violins, 2 violas, 2 cellos, and 2 basses. Illustrate all six procedures for voicing prominent lines and all four procedures for voicing subordinate lines in your example. Repeat the sequence enough times to provide all the required examples.

ORCHESTRATION: Scoring for Various Ensembles

WRITING FOR STRING ORCHESTRA AND STRING ENSEMBLES

For the novice orchestrator, the strings may well represent the easiest choir for which to write. In the hands of skilled performers, the orchestral strings are very forgiving of orchestrational errors within their own ensemble. Miscalculations of balance are correctable, usually without increasing the difficulty of performance.

In addition, the roles assigned to the various instruments in any of many possible string ensembles, from a string quartet to full string orchestra, are, with only a few limitations, exchangeable with the roles assigned to other instruments. Thus, the viola can present the melody, provide a counterpoint, play an accompanimental figure, be the bass, perform a descant, etc., and these same functions can be carried out by the violins or cellos or basses, too. The limitations on these role exchanges are purely practical. No instrument can produce pitches lower than its lowest string; double stop combinations are limited by the size of the human hand relative to the size of the instrument; and longer bows require less frequent bow changes than shorter bows.

One real strength of the strings is the ability to achieve blend and balance. The tone qualities are of a homogeneous nature. Thus, a simple series of chords, or a melody with accompaniment work well. However, the strings can just as easily produce the tonal differences necessary for clear articulation of complex, polyphonic structures by the use of subtle contrasts provided by string selection or bowings, or more obvious contrasts brought about by the juxtaposition of arco and pizzicato sounds.

Standard String Scorings

The most obvious method of scoring strings, assuming a SATB structure as a starting point, is to assign the soprano line to the first violin(s), the alto line to the second(s), the tenor line to the viola(s), and the bass to the cello(s), with the contrabasses doubling the bass an octave lower or omitted as desired. Since all strings make excellent solo voices, other common scorings would be soprano to viola, alto to first violin, tenor to second violin, etc., or soprano to cello, alto to first violin, tenor to second violin, and bass to viola. There are others, too.

However, it may not be literally possible to achieve these scorings due to range problems, etc. Note the following example:

EXAMPLE 327 First four measures of the Bach harmonization of "Freu' dich sehr, o meine Seele."

EXAMPLE 328 Scoring Example 327 for strings using obvious instrumental assignments.

If we wish to assign the soprano line to the viola, we obtain the following:

EXAMPLE 329 Soprano line assigned to viola; notes in parentheses are not playable.

With the soprano line assigned to the cello, this is the result:

EXAMPLE 330 Soprano line assigned to cello; notes in parentheses are not playable.

There are several solutions to the above situations. One solution would be to transpose the whole piece up a perfect fourth. Although this may seem ideal, it may not be possible if the string version has to be performed with voices which cannot sing a perfect fourth higher.

Another solution might be to omit the first (or second) violins in Example 329 and divide the violas, with one group of violas playing the melody and the remaining violas providing the tenor line; or divide the cellos, with the upper cellos playing the tenor while the lower cellos play the bass:

EXAMPLE 331 Soprano line assigned to upper violas.

EXAMPLE 332 Soprano line assigned to violas. Cellos divided, with upper cellos assigned to the tenor line and the lower cellos assigned to the bass line.

The usual size of the string section or string orchestra is 16 first violins, 14 second violins, 12 violas, 10 cellos, and 8 contrabasses; assuming two players per stand, this would be 8 stands of first violins, etc.[1] This proportioning of the instruments assures the orchestrator that he may assign a separate musical line to each of the five instrumental sections and the lines will be well-balanced.

If one needs to divide one or more of the sections into two separate parts, as was done in Examples 331 and 332, the string section balance is such that the two half-sections will still balance the other, undivided sections. But, when one or more sections are divided, unison doubling of two or more full sections can seriously upset the blend—not because of loudness, but because of great inequities in terms of mass and weight. It is for these reasons that one of the violin sections is omitted in Examples 331 and 332. The choice of which section to omit is left to the orchestrator.

Other solutions to the problems encountered in Examples 329 and 330 could be modeled on those used in Examples 331 and 332, but with the cellos playing the soprano line. Also, one could use octave doublings of some or all of the lines, as discussed in Chapter Eight, by calling upon the as yet unused contrabasses or by dividing several or all of the sections, or both. The identification of some of these solutions will be left to the student in Problem Set No. 23.

EXAMPLE 333 One method of scoring the chorale, with the soprano line in the cellos and by using doublings and the contrabasses.

For composers or orchestrators who are not string performers, it must be understood that divided passages (*divisi*) for string ensembles is not a substitute for double stops. The two sounds are quite different. A violin section of 14 performers playing a *divisi* passage would divide the pitches between the two

[1]For smaller string sections, the usual distribution may be found by taking the above numbers and subtracting an equal number of performers—say, 4—from each section. Thus, one may find that a small orchestra has a string section of 12 first violins, 10 second violins, 8 violas, 6 cellos, and 4 contrabasses.

players at each stand, the seven outside (right side of the stand) performers playing the upper pitches and seven inside (left side of the stand) performers playing the lower pitch; or, 7 instruments producing each pitch. If the same notes were performed *non divisi,* as double stops, then all fourteen performers would produce both pitches. Two pitches simultaneously produced by one performer on one instrument would of necessity be bowed alike; the performance of one of the pitches would affect the performance of the other. However, two pitches divided between two performers allow total independence of articulation, nuance, tuning, and character.

The choice between *divisi* and *non divisi* is usually made on the following basis: If the individuality of the lines is of primary importance, the situation calls for *divisi;* if the unity of the massed section is of prime importance, then *non divisi* is in order. (However, performability supercedes the above and may dictate the use of *divisi* because a certain double stop is impossible.) As is apparent from the previous discussions, the sound of a two-pitch *divisi* is not equal in strength to the sound of a double stop.

Other instructions for dividing a string section are: *half* (meaning that only half of the section, i.e., one player from each stand, is to play—usually only the outside player) and *divide by stands* (meaning that the upper line is to be played by the first and all other odd-numbered stands and the lower line is to be played by the second and all other even-numbered stands).

English	*French*	*German*	*Italian*
divided	divisé	geteilt	divisi
not divided *or* unison	unis *or* unisson	insieme *or* zusammen	unisono *or* insieme
half	la moitié	die Hälfte	la metà
all *or* tutti	tous *or* tutti	alle *or* tutti	tutti
divided by stand	divisé par pupitres	geteilt pultweise	divisi da leggïi

Scoring for Student Orchestras and Ensembles

All comments about string writing given above apply to writing for younger string performers of grade school through high school age, with these reservations:

1. There is often a significant difference in ability and technique between the first chair performer and the rest of the section.
2. The younger the ensemble, the less likely one is to find viola and contrabass performers, either in sufficient numbers or at all.
3. One should avoid writing music that is in the higher positions.

For music intended for general purpose usage, all major and technically demanding passages should be assigned to the first chair (principal) performer as a solo. If the ensemble effect is desired, then a simplified version should be provided for the rest of the section.

EXAMPLE 334 Line for concertmaster and the same line simplified for the rest of the first violins, for performance by a grade school ensemble.

In a high school ensemble, one can assume a strong principal first violin, principal cello, and (maybe) principal contrabass and principal viola. However, the difference in ability between the principal violinist and the principal violist may be great.

Because the contrabass and viola require a certain amount of physical size and musical maturity to perform, one often finds neither of these instruments in a grade school ensemble and few of them in many high school groups. To make up for the missing or weak violas, a third violin part is often provided that doubles in unison most or all of the viola line. One could also provide an upper cello line to accomplish the same end. Since no instrument can replace the contrabass, one should score the cellos so as to provide all of the bass necessary. The problem with both of these solutions is that they tend to produce "safe" and uninteresting viola and contrabass parts and, thus, fail to excite the would-be performers that must play them. This in turn convinces the student that playing the instrument is not especially worthwhile (i.e., not necessary) and the numbers again shrink.

When scoring music for grade school strings one should write all parts in first position, except for the concertmaster, who may be asked to play a few passages in third position. For high school musicians, one would limit the parts to third position notes as the upper limit, except for the concertmaster, who can be asked to play fifth position notes. (See Appendix III.) For literature intended for advanced high school performers, the section parts can go up to fifth position notes, while the parts for the principals can utilize professional ranges.

Problem Set No. 23

1. Score the four measures of Bach's harmonization of "Freu' dich sehr, o meine Seele" given in Example 327 for string orchestra in three different ways other than those illustrated in Examples 328, 331, 332 or 333.
2. Score "Wachet auf, ruft uns die Stimme" for grade school strings using first, second, and third violins, violas, cellos, and optional contrabasses.
3. Rescore "Wachet auf, ruft uns Stimme" for professional string orchestra consisting of 7 stands of first violins, 6 stands of seconds, 5 stands of violas, 4 stands of cellos and 3 stands of basses. Use divisi strings, solo strings, special effects, etc. as you choose.

WRITING FOR BAND AND ENSEMBLES OF WINDS

Approaches to Woodwind Scoring

These instruments possess some of the most interesting tone qualities available to the orchestrator. In contrast to the strings, which offer great timbral similarities, the woodwinds offer great diversity. For this reason it requires careful scoring on the part of the composer to produce a balanced, homogeneous blend from the woodwinds. On the other hand, woodwinds lend themselves to the delineation of several separate lines, as found in polyphonic music.

Achieving Balance and Blend

The most obvious means of guaranteeing blend and balance among the woodwinds is to use only instruments of the same family (i.e., all clarinets). When this instrument selection is made, the scoring problems are similar to those of the strings. Quite simply, balance and blend are not problems. In bands, where there are always large sections of clarinets (and often large sections of other woodwinds), the concepts of *divisi* and *half* of the section (as discussed above for strings) are also applicable.

When numerous different woodwinds are involved, one can achieve blend by grouping similar woodwinds and following the homogeneous scoring procedures discussed above for strings. Some of these similar groupings are oboes and bassoons, flutes and clarinets, and saxophones and double reeds.

Reference to the dynamic curves of the various woodwinds will assist the orchestrator in dealing with dissimilar woodwinds. If the various woodwinds being scored are all assigned pitches in their equivalent registers, the balance will be assured. Thus, one could obtain balance by using middle- and upper-register flutes with middle- and lower-register oboes or low- or middle-register flutes with high-register saxophones or bassoons.

Efforts to bring out an otherwise weak line by the use of two or more of the same instruments usually meet with some limited success, except for low-register flutes where the extra mass seems to also "take the edge" off of the sound and the result is actually *less* penetrating than a single flute in the same range.

An effective means of equalizing the lines when a mixed group of woodwinds is available is to intermix the tone qualities on each line so that each of the lines has an equivalent timbre. This is very workable even though this mixing of timbres often produces tonal sums that are less colorful than the component parts.

EXAMPLE 335 a. Balanced voicing of the lines using similar instruments. b. Balanced chords using dissimilar timbres but carefully selected ranges. c. Balanced lines created by mixing contrasting timbres.

The creation of balanced lines by the mixing of diverse timbres is somewhat akin to a type of chord voicing known as *interlocking voicing.* In this voicing each element of the chord is played by a unique combination of instruments. Thus, for example the root may be played by oboe and clarinet, the third by oboe and flute, and the fifth by clarinet and flute. The instruments assigned to any one element may be scored in unison with one another or at the octave or double octave, etc.

A contrasting voicing of chords would be to cover all elements with (as nearly as possible) one of each type of instrument, assigning each instrument family to a specific, and often exclusive, pitch region.

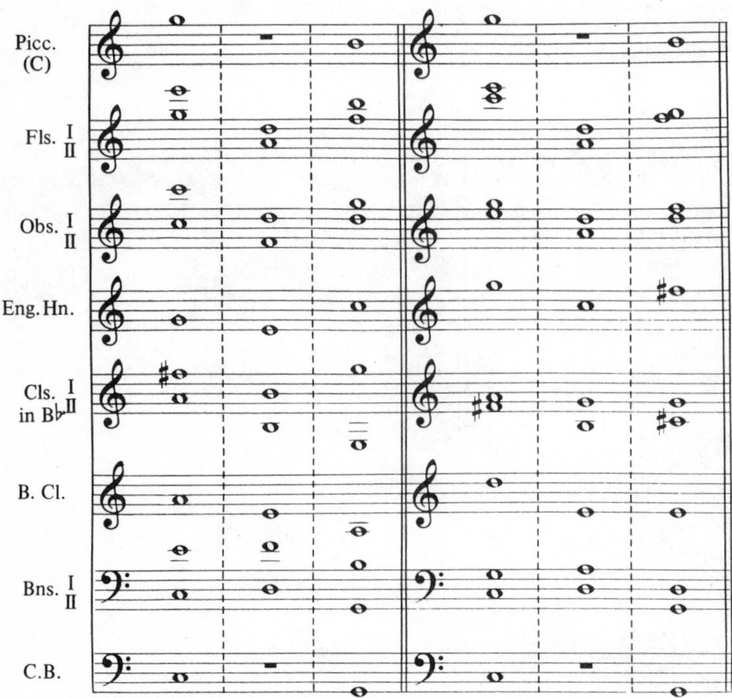

EXAMPLE 336 a. Voicing chords by the use of interlocking scoring. b. Voicing chords by family groups.

In its register of medium-to-strong dynamics, a single woodwind can match a section of strings on equal footing. In their weaker registers, the woodwinds are not quite equal to the string sections, but manage to do a good job of reinforcing the strings and can be used to offset some scoring disadvantages the strings may suffer. In the following example from Brahms' Symphony No. 4, the bassoon reinforces the violas who are in a weak tonal position due to the very intense sound of the high-register cellos within the same pitch area.

EXAMPLE 337 From the second movement of Brahms's Symphony No. 4 in E Minor, an example of the use of a middle range woodwind to reinforce a string line. (The excerpt begins at rehearsal letter C.)

Each of the scoring approaches discussed above can be further refined by using the suggestions in Chapter 8.

Approaches to Brass Scoring

Horns—open, muted, or stopped—and muted brasses can be treated much like the woodwinds just discussed. Unmuted brasses, not including horns, are different. Any single unmuted trumpet, trombone, or tuba can balance a whole orchestra and can almost balance a whole band. Thus, one should remember these balance guide lines for brasses:

1. Horns should be treated as woodwinds (see pages 320-23).
2. The other brasses never *need* doubling.
3. When other brasses are playing at a *mezzo-forte* or less, the horns can be assigned one to a part.
4. When other brasses are playing *forte,* the horns should be assigned two to a part.
5. When the other brasses are playing *fortissimo* or louder, the horns must be assigned four to a part.
6. Although very effective at louder dynamics, brasses can play effective *pianissimo*s like the other instruments. At these dynamics, balance with the rest of the ensemble presents no special problems.

Because of the homogeneous timbres of the brasses, at least in contrast to the woodwinds, the voicing of brasses can follow the guidelines offered for strings (pages 314-18). When muted, brasses come closer to blending and balancing like woodwinds. If a variety of different mutes are used, the coloration problems also become more like those of woodwind instruments.

Even though the second guideline above states that brasses (other than horns) never need doubling, they may be doubled to increase the mass or weight of the sound. (The doubling is not needed to increase the loudness; indeed, acoustical studies prove that doubling is an ineffective way to increase loudness.) The horn doublings referred to in points four through six above also serve only to increase mass so that the horn line can penetrate the brass sonorities.

EXAMPLE 338 a. Balancing of voicing in a soft brass passage. b. Balancing of voicing in a loud brass passage. c. Balancing of voicing in a very loud brass passage.

Scoring for Student Bands and Winds

When scoring for student groups consisting of woodwinds or brasses (or both together) the following points should be borne in mind:

1. There is usually a significant difference in ability between the first chair performer and those seated further down the section.
2. In younger ensembles, one will rarely find an oboist, bassoonist, bass clarinetist, or tubist. In older student ensembles, such as high school groups, the availability of an oboe performer or a bassoonist remains subject to chance.
3. Music for both woodwind performers and brass performers should avoid extremes of the range and should have a tessitura that approximates the lowest two octaves of the instrument's range. (For the horns, this would be the second and third octaves of the range.)
4. For brass players in elementary school, lines should primarily move by step, with only occasional motion by a third or fourth. For woodwind players in elementary school, one should avoid rapid changes of register of a repetitive nature.

The implications of point one for the orchestrator is that all difficult or important lines must be assigned to a strong (first chair) player. The lines assigned to the second and third parts should be well-doubled to insure confidence. In polyphonic music, each important line must be assigned to, among others, a principal player. (Thus, first line to 1st trumpet and 2nd clarinet, second line to 1st clarinet and 2nd flute, etc.)

In many student groups, or non-professional adult groups, one finds no oboe and/or no bassoon. For this reason, one should always cue important oboe solos in the first flute or first clarinet part and important bassoon passages in the bass clarinet, euphonium, or tenor or baritone saxophone parts. In elementary schools, one finds no bass clarinet, tuba, or baritone saxophone. Thus one needs to score music for this type of ensemble so that the bass line is provided by the tenor saxophone, trombone, and/or euphonium regardless of the availability of a tuba or other bass instrument.

When scoring for grade school musicians the most secure portion of the instrumentalists' ranges is the lowest octave and a half. Notes above this tend to be fatiguing or unplayable. As the performers mature, the usable (safely usable) portion of the range increases to about two octaves, but greatest endurance and accuracy remain in the middle of these two octaves for most brass players. Obtaining extended ranges is not so much a maturation problem with woodwind players, but one is still advised to view the lowest two octaves as a safe, rule-of-thumb range for typical student wind players.

In addition to the line-shaping suggestions given in point four above for brass players, octaves are usually easy to hear and, thus, easy to play, as are lines that follow the overtone series. Awkward-looking lines (involving augmented and diminished intervals and large leaps) should be avoided, or if unavoidable, assigned to a principal player.

Among young woodwind players, rapid alternation between a pitch in the upper register (with the octave or register key depressed) and a pitch in the lower register (without the use of the octave key) is difficult and should be avoided. At slow speeds it is no problem, and as the player grows and becomes more experienced it also ceases to cause difficulties at any speed.

Assigning Parts

When scoring for grade school and high school wind groups, the following chart can serve as a guide. One should not forget that this applies to a typical SATB distribution of lines. When contrapuntal writing is involved, the suggestion given above—to always assign a strong performer to each line together with weaker performers—is to be followed. The chart below applies regardless of specific octave assignments. It also works for reduced instrumentations (such as only woodwinds), but usually not without some adjustments in the exact distribution or the addition of some cues.

Instrumental Part	*Soprano*	*Alto*	*Tenor*	*Bass*
WOODWINDS				
1st Flute	x			
2nd Flute		x		
Oboe	x			
1st Clarinet	x			
2nd Clarinet		x		
3rd Clarinet			x	
Bass Clarinet				x
Bassoon				x
1st Alto Saxophone	x			
2nd Alto Saxophone		x		
Tenor Saxophone			x	
Baritone Saxophone				x
BRASSES				
1st Trumpet	x			
2nd Trumpet		x		
1st Horn		x		
2nd Horn			x	
1st Trombone			x	
2nd Trombone				x
Euphonium				x
Tuba				x

As a precaution, the orchestrator writing for the school ensemble should anticipate that some instruments—oboes and bassoon especially—may not be available, and that other parts—2nd horn or 3rd clarinet, for example—may be assigned to weaker players (or may not be played at all). Thus, one should be sure that the scoring is such that even without these parts or instruments available, the piece sounds complete. This is easiest to accomplish by careful use of doublings and cuing important passages.

The Marching Band

When scoring for the marching band, the orchestrator should remember these points:

1. There is no standard marching band instrumentation. Some bands are all brass, some are brass and saxophones, others are almost standard symphonic or concert bands.
2. Due to the need to compensate for the problems of playing out-of-doors, special scorings are often used for marching bands.
3. Some precautions are sometimes taken for bands that often play out-of-doors in freezing weather.

Because of its usual performance environment or (perhaps) tradition, a particular band may select a special instrumentation. Since there is no standard-sized marching band, one may find variations in size from 30 or 40 performers to over 300. Many college bands will use only piccolos and no flutes, but high school bands usually use a mixture. Oboes and bassoons are rarely used in marching bands and bass clarinets are also rare. However, some of the larger college bands do use bass clarinets and baritone saxophones. Horns may be replaced with alto horns or mellophoniums.

Typically, the backbone of the marching band will be trumpets (or cornets), trombones, euphoniums, tubas (Sousaphones), and percussion. To maximize the amount of sound that these instruments can produce, marching band scoring often takes advantage of much unison and octave scoring. An emphasis is made upon the melodic line, the bass line, a counterpoint (countermelody) line, and the percussion. A possible distribution of parts for a marching band might be as follows:

Piccolos (flutes)	Melody one or two octaves above 1st trumpets	
1st Clarinets	Melody one octave above 1st trumpets or high pitched countermelody	
2nd Clarinets	Melody in unison with 1st trumpets or high pitched countermelody in unison with 1st clarinets	
Alto Saxophones	Melody in unison with 1st trumpets or middle range countermelody	
Tenor Saxophones	Middle range counter melody or bass line	
Baritone Saxophones	Bass line	
1st Trumpets	Melody	} may divide at cadences
2nd Trumpets	Important harmony	} may divide at cadences

Horns	Secondary harmony or middle range countermelody
Trombones	Middle range countermelody, secondary harmony, Melody in unison with or down an octave from 1st trumpets, or bass line
Euphoniums	Bass line or middle range countermelody
Tubas	Bass line
Percussion	Rhythmic figuration.

For final chords and special effects, any of the sections may be divided; but during the march, divided parts are not encouraged. It is difficult to march and play all of the written notes, and thus some sound is always lost. In addition, for show marching, the band may often have personnel facing in two or more directions, thus weakening the sound heard from any given vantage point.

When very cold weather is expected, special arrangements may be prepared for the marching band. These arrangements are intended to compensate for the frozen valves and slides that occur on brass instruments below about −12° Celsius. The writer should plan for different performers to allow their instruments to become frozen with different valve combinations depressed or slide positions extended. (Note: As a practical matter, slides should be frozen in the first four positions only.) Thus, one trumpeter may have his valves all frozen in the non-depressed position. Another trumpeter will have his valves frozen with the first valve depressed.

The scoring then calls for each brass performer to produce only those pitches playable with the frozen valve or slide setting. Since woodwind pads also freeze, rendering those instruments unusable, at these cold temperatures the band is reduced to brasses and percussion only. (See Appendices V and VI.)

Problem Set No. 24

1. Score the chorale "Wachet auf, ruft uns die Stimme, given in exercise 2 of Problem Set No. 23 (page 320) for grade school woodwind players. The ensemble should consist of 2 flutes, 1st, 2nd, and 3rd clarinets, bass clarinet, 2 alto saxophones and a tenor saxophone.

2. Score the same chorale used in exercise 1, above, for a grade school brass group of 1st and 2nd trumpets, 1 horn, 2 trombones, 1 euphonium.

3. Score the same chorale used in the above two exercises for a professional wind group composed of 2 flutes and 1 piccolo, 2 oboes, 1 E♭ clarinet, 3 B♭ clarinets, 1 bass clarinet, 2 bassoons, 2 alto saxophones, 1 tenor and 1 baritone saxophone, 4 horns, 3 trumpets, 3 trombones, 1 euphonium, and 1 tuba. Illustrate various voicings discussed in this section including the use of similar instruments on all lines, the use of dissimilar but carefully selected tone qualities, the use of blended lines, vertical voicing by families and by interlocking. Use scoring procedures outlined in Chapter 8 and brass mutes as desired.

4. Score the following melody for marching band. Assign the melodic line to the flutes, 1st clarinets, 2nd clarinets, and alto saxophones as well as the 1st

trumpets. Assign the bass line to the tenor saxophones, trombones, euphoniums, and tubas. Assign important chord tones to the 2nd trumpets and horns. Write an appropriate drum part for bass drum, crash cymbals, snare drums, and tom-toms.

INSTRUMENTAL DOUBLING

Usually, when one writes for a violinist, a clarinetist, or a hornist, one intends the performer to play a violin, a clarinet, or a horn, respectively. But, there are times when one may wish the clarinetist, for example, to put down his clarinet and to pick up and play a bass clarinet. When a performer is asked to play two or more instruments within the same composition (or concert) he is said to *double.*

It should be clear to the orchestrator that a person cannot instantaneously change from clarinet to bass clarinet. The appropriate instrument must be placed to the side with care, the other instrument put into playing position and gotten ready—reed wetted, etc.—and then the performer can become the bass clarinetist. These movements take time and care. An orchestrator or composer must allow the performer sufficient time to make the change.

The process of switching instruments can make the orchestrator aware of something that he should never forget: One does not write for instruments; one writes for performers who play instruments. (This is especially true in the case of percussion writing.)

WRITING FOR PERCUSSION

Approaches to Percussion Scoring

The percussionist is a performer who often plays no specific instrument, but rather *may* play any of several instruments. In the case of the symphony orchestra's timpanist, the jazz or rock group's set drummer, or most drummers in a marching band, one does observe percussionists who play a single instrument, or a limited group of instruments to the exclusion of other instruments. But, all other percussionists represent potential instrument assignments, not specific assignments. Because of these facts, one must approach percussion writing a little differently than other scorings.

1. Percussion instruments may be struck, bowed, shaken, pulled, cranked, turned on and off, picked up, set down, dropped, rubbed, muffled, or blown; all of these actions require the use of a hand, a pair of hands, another device, or an extra pair of hands.
2. Some percussion instruments such as timpani, bass drums, and marimbas are very large and take up a large amount of space.
3. Some percussion instruments are noisy and cannot be moved both quickly and quietly; among these are maracas, wind chimes, and tubos.
4. In addition to instruments, percussionists must have available an assortment of mallets, beaters, scrapers, and other devices for causing the instruments to sound.

In writing for percussion instruments, it is not enough to indicate what instrument is to be struck by what performer. It is just as necessary for the composer-orchestrator to plan in advance how the performer is going to pick up the mallets and get to the instrument. (This may require that he plan for the performer to put down other mallets, cross from one location to another, pick up the correct mallets, press a pedal or turn on a switch, and *then* play the instrument.) Percussion music of any complexity requires choreography; the orchestrator is the choreographer.

The student of orchestration should become as familiar as possible with the percussion instruments. Some suggested activities include:

1. Lift and move the percussion instruments. How big is a 29″ timpano? How heavy are a pair of crash cymbals? How tall are the tubular chimes?
2. Under the guidance of a percussionist try various mallets, sticks, and beaters. How much bounce is there to a pair of snare drum sticks? To a pair of yarn mallets? Do these feel different when striking a tom-tom? A woodblock? Try to pick up and set down various pairs of mallets. How quickly can this be done without noise?
3. Walk around the percussion instruments. How close together can they be placed? Turn the snares on and off on the snare drum, turn the motor of the vibraphone on and off. How quickly and quietly can these actions be performed?
4. Become familiar with the mallet stands (tray stands). How much space do these require? How close to various instruments may these be placed? How close to the instruments can music stands be located? How large must the music be to be legible?

Without the above experiences, scoring for percussion could become a very inaccurate guessing game on the part of the orchestrator.

The Percussion Ensemble and Multi-percussion Writing

A percussion ensemble is a group of two or more performers. The performers may each be asked to play one instrument or several instruments. The percussion ensemble may be a totally complete performing group or may be used with other instruments as in the band and orchestra.

Multi-percussion is a term used by many contemporary percussionists to describe writing for one performer who plays many instruments. Thus, a multi-percussion solo would imply a solo performer who plays an assortment of percussion instruments. In the percussion ensemble a member may or may not be performing a multi-percussion part. As a matter of efficiency, multi-percussion writing is to be encourged. But, successful multi-percussion writing requires an especially knowledgeable and concerned orchestrator.

Instrument Scoring Versus Performer Scoring

In older styles of percussion writing, one often finds what may be called instrument scoring. In this approach, a separate staff is provided for each percussion instrument used in a composition. The parts provided to the performers often reflect this situation. Therefore, the percussion passage shown in example 339 might provide the performers with a timpani part, a triangle part, a woodblock part, a cymbal part, a snare drum part, and a bass drum part.

EXAMPLE 339 Organization of percussion score by instrument.

Although the score shown in example 339 is clear from composers' and conductors' points of view, the performers have several unanswered questions to deal with. Does the composition really require six different performers or could one performer play several instruments? It is clear that the snare drummer cannot also play bass drum, but could the triangle player also play woodblock? What combinations, if any, work? and how does one find these?

It should be obvious that to answer the above questions will take valuable time and that the answers are by no means clear from the music. A better scoring would call for the arrangement of the percussion parts as in example 340. Here, the orchestrator has determined that four performers can perform the music (one timpanist and three percussionists).

EXAMPLE 340 Organization of percussion score by performer.

Percussion parts such as in Example 340 in which all actions are assigned to specific performers do not come about by accident. Experienced orchestrators may be able to predict and plan the number of performers required and the specific instruments each performer must play even before they write a single note. Less experienced orchestrators will need to follow these steps:

1. As the piece is being written, write the ideal percussion part. Use as many staves as are available. Do not be concerned with how an action will be accomplished. Only be concerned with the sound qualities. Specify the instruments that are to be played, the mallets or beaters (etc.) that are to be used, the length of the sound, the shape of the sound, and the loudness of the sound.
2. When the ideal part is completed, list all instruments used. Note on the list all mallets required and in what order. Also indicate all instrumental combinations that occur together or in rapid succession.
3. On the basis of the information gathered in step 2, above, determine the maximum number of performers required. Be realistic about the use of manpower. If a performer can play two or more instruments together or in rapid succession, utilize this more efficient scoring. (Less experienced orchestrators who are not percussion performers usually overestimate the number of performers required.)
4. Whether the number of performers required seems to be reasonable or not, examine the percussion writing to see if the number of performers could be reduced by substituting instruments, changing (or not changing) mallets, having two or more performers share the same instrument(s), omitting an effect that may not be audible, etc. Obtaining the most efficient use of the performers will improve the percussion writing.
5. Rescore the percussion part using the number of performers that the above steps have determined to be the minimum necessary. Start by distributing the instruments among the performers so that the most complex passages will be performable. Work from the most complex passages toward the most simple passages. Keep the assigned instruments in the same part throughout unless it is clearly possible to move the instrument or the performer to another location during the course of the performance. Record all assignments and mallet selections in the part. Be very complete.

6. Based upon the arrived at distribution of instruments and an awareness of the performance situation, draw a plan that shows the location of instruments, mallet trays, music stands, and performers. This too should be very complete.
7. With the plan created in step 6 as a guide, think through each performer's part in tempo. Imagine or pantomime all motions and actions to see if it is possible. If problems arise, they must be solved now. Go back over steps 3 through 6 and make necessary changes until the parts work.

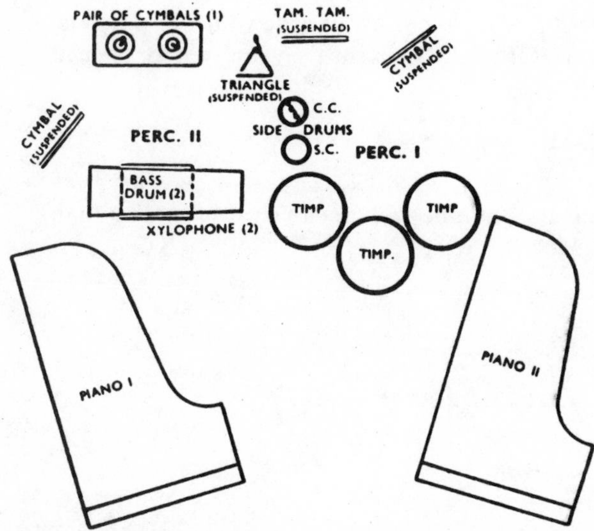

(1) The pair of Cymbals should be laid on cloth, when not in use, to prevent vibration.
(2) The Xylophone should be placed above or next to the Bass Drum.

NOTES.

The Bass Drum is to be played with a double-headed stick.

The Triangle is to be played (*a*) with the usual metal beater ; (*b*) with a thin wooden stick ; (*c*) with a short, but rather heavy, metal beater ; each according to the indications in the score.

The Cymbal is to be played (*a*) with an ordinary timpani stick ; (*b*) with the heavy end of a side drum stick (marked in the score " col legno " or " c.l.")—here the Cymbal should be struck either on the edge or, if indicated, on the dome in the centre ; (*c*) with a thin wooden stick ; (*d*) with the blade of a pocket-knife or some similar instrument. The sign " a2 " indicates that two Cymbals should be clashed.

The Side Drums, either with or without snares, are to be played with the usual sticks. If, however, the Side Drum with snares should sound too loud, thinner sticks may be used especially in mezzoforte, piano and pianissimo passages (the same as those mentioned above in (*c*) for the cymbal). The snares of the Side Drum should be released when the instrument is not in use, to prevent vibration.

Experience has proved that two skilled players are sufficient for the whole percussion part. Should this in some cases prove difficult, a third player may be employed for the Xylophone, which in this case should be placed either behind or in front of the other percussion instruments.

FIGURE 33 A typical plan with instructions showing locations of instruments and performers, from Bartók's *Sonata for Two Pianos and* [Two] *Percussion.*[2] The audience will be at the pianists' backs.

[2]Copyright 1942 by Hawkes & Son (London) Ltd. Renewed 1969. Reprinted by permission of Boosey & Hawkes, Inc.

Percussion Parts and Scores

Modern percussion parts are more and more becoming percussion scores. All of the percussion actions are recorded as shown above (according to performers.) These are then reproduced in sufficient quantities for all performers to have whatever number they require. The result is that all performers have the same music and can see each other's parts. This improves ensemble and speeds up sight reading as well as allowing the performers to cover for one another in an emergency.

The percussion score should consist of one or two staves for each player. One staff is often enough, but two is sometimes needed or helpful. More than two is almost always unnecessary. The staff should consist of as few lines as possible, never more than five. (The five-line staff is almost exclusively reserved for pitched percussion instruments.)

Writing for the Set Drummer

In writing scores for set drummers, one is best advised to write less rather than more. This would be a typical part:

EXAMPLE 341 Typical set drum part.

The notation above tells the drummer enough to allow him to provide the rhythmic support necessary. By not telling him too much, the performer will feel both an obligation to add more as well as the license to do so. If the part were to look like this:

EXAMPLE 342 A poor example of set drum writing: too detailed.

The drummer might feel that it was not intended for him to add or modify the written part. For this reason, set drum parts that have portions that are very explicit will require clear indications to the player whenever he is to improvise. Instructions like these would help: "Improvise upon given figure," or "Samba, ad lib." When the notated part is to be played literally with no improvisation, this instruction is needed: "As written."

It is not necessary, usually, to do more than give general information about the tempo, style, dynamics, and duration to the drummer unless something special is needed. One of the common special requirements is to reinforce (brass) accents. To show this, one would write the part this way:

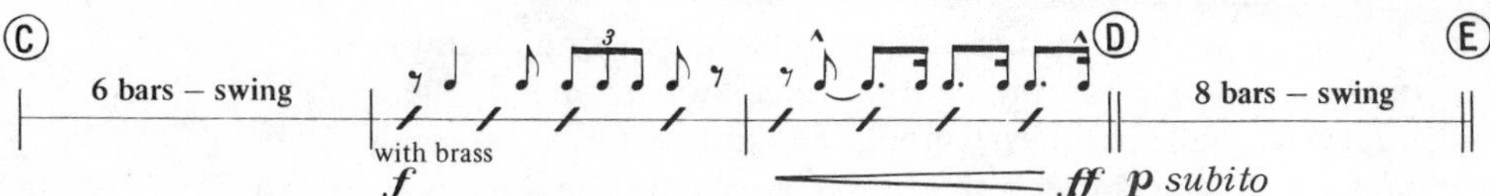

EXAMPLE 343 Set drum part showing accent cues.

If more explicit instructions are wanted, this could be written:

EXAMPLE 344 Set drum part with specific accents written in.

In some situations it might even be best to provide very complete cues for the drummer, along with either a very detailed part or with the instruction to improvise. The problem is always to maintain the balance between giving the drummer enough information to allow him to effectively back the group and not making the part any more complex or difficult to sightread accurately.

In set drum parts, notes with the stems pointing down are for the bass drum; those with the stems pointing up are for the snare drum and/or tom-toms; and note heads in the shape of an x and located in the upper part of the staff or above the staff are for cymbals, cowbells, or other metal sounds. Instructions as to specific instrument or mallets to be used are written (or abbreviated) as words. Pictograms are not usually used for set drum writing.

Scoring for Student Percussionists

Student percussionists are usually asked to perform only one instrument, or at most two, during the course of a single piece. Multi-percussion writing for student percussionists is the exception rather than the norm. An additional difference between the writing done for students and that done for professionals is in the use of definite-pitched percussion. The younger the students, the less likely it is that a timpanist or keyboard percussionist will be available. Thus, all timpani parts should be cued or doubled in commonly found indefinite-pitched percussion, such as bass drum or variously pitched tom-toms.

All keyboard percussion parts, xylophone, orchestral bells, vibraphone, should be assigned to a single performer, unless the parts are very simple (like two repeated pitches, etc.) Even so, if the pitches are important, they should be cued in some other part. Examples of workable cues are: orchestra bell notes in the piccolo; xylophone notes in high clarinets or cup-muted brasses; vibraphone notes in low flutes and horns. The effect of the material of the instrument may be obtained from indefinite-pitched percussion: Woodblocks or claves in place of xylophone; triangle or the crown or dome of the cymbal for orchestra bells are examples of possible substitutions. These indefinite-pitched colors may be added to the use of piccolos or clarinet or cup-muted brasses to produce almost a substitute for the original sounds.

Another limitation associated with student percussion writing is simply the availability of instruments. Among the definite-pitched instruments, these are usually found: orchestra bells, chimes, xylophone, and two or three timpani. Less commonly found are vibraphones, marimba, a fourth timpano, and roto-toms. All other instruments of definite pitch, including piccolo timpano and crotales, are rarely found in school situations.

The commonly available indefinite-pitched percussion are snare and field drums, bass drum, one or two tom-toms, tambourine, woodblock, claves, temple blocks, maracas, crash cymbals, suspended cymbal, triangle, and sand-paper blocks. Other less common instruments are bongo drums, castanets, guiro, cowbells, sleighbells, whip, ratchet, and various whistles. All other instruments are rarely found in school ensembles.

Problem Set No. 25

1. Below is an idealized (maybe not practical) percussion passage. Score it for two professional percussionists. Must anything be left out? What would you choose to omit? Draw a plan showing the arrangement of instruments and performers.

2. Score the passage above for student percussionists. How many performers would one need? Should one substitute for some of the instruments? If so, which ones and what substitutes suggest themselves?

WRITING FOR CHORUSES AND VOCAL ENSEMBLES

Setting a Text

There is no single correct way of setting a text for singing. A traditional concern is usually one of ease of performance and intelligibility of the text. These concerns are still appropriate in some contexts and in some styles of music. (It would be foolish to produce an impossibly difficult setting for an amateur choir.) Still, it is essential to strike a balance between the varying demands customarily placed upon a writer of vocal music.

If one chooses to strive for ease of performance ("good vocal writing") and textural clarity, the following guidelines should be of value.

1. Match the range and tessitura to the type and training of the voice(s) to be used.
2. Keep most melodic motion simple. Use seconds and thirds, which possess diatonic relationships, and a few perfect fourths and perfect fifths; avoid large leaps unless the second pitch is perceivable as tonic.
3. Except for special effects, allow the musical accents, (rhythmic, dynamic, agogic, tonic, or metric) to match and reinforce the *natural* accents of the text.

Guideline 1. This concern for the requirements demanded of the voice in terms of range and tessitura is of great importance. An amateur singer or typical church choir cannot execute music written for operatically trained voices. Attempts to perform such music by untrained singers is often amusing to hear but discouraging to perform. It can even be possibly damaging to the voices involved, if only temporarily. As a simple rule of thumb to use, keep most of the music (75 to 80 percent) within a perfect fifth on either side of the central pitch of a given voice range. Increase the percentage for younger, untrained voices. If one exceeds this range, be sure that the singers are at least trained and with some idea of how to use their vocal apparatus.

Guideline 2. The most traditional rules associated with four-voice part-writing are actually based to a great extent upon good vocal scoring practices. It may not be stylistically necessary to follow these principles, but to do so will help produce more singable lines. The use of diatonic relationships, even in a very atonal context is a good one to assist with singability. Other ways of helping the voice include doubling at the unison or octave with another instrument, especially an instrument with a fairly complex wave form (oboe, string) rather than a purer tone quality (flute, horn). Other easy-to-hear pitch relationships include the dominant, the leading tone and the supertonic. If the pitch to be sung is related to any easy-to-hear pitch in the context as a tonic, dominant, leading tone, or supertonic, the singer is more likely to be able to produce the required tone. Lines that involve wide leaps are usually considered less idiomatic for voice. However, when the second note of the skip is heard as tonic, the leap is much easier. Also, skips which are between two or more perceivable lines, each line of which contains a fairly clearly heard logical structure, are not that difficult for a trained voice.

Guideline 3. When setting a text, regardless of whether it is poetic or not, following and reinforcing in the music the natural accents of the language of the text improves intelligibility of the words. The rhythmic accent of the words is always the easiest to locate, and can be replicated in the rhythmic structures of the music.

The wall was high and slick and ston-y.

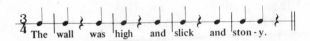

EXAMPLE 345 Use of natural rhythmic accents to determine the rhythm of the setting.

Concern for the communication of the meaning of the text could dictate the use of other accents such as dynamic accents.

. . . and so I said, "Shh!" "Stop!" he yelled.
mp *pp* *sfz* *mp*

EXAMPLE 346 Using dynamic accents to illuminate the text.

Agogic accents are often used to emphasize syllables of particular importance by extending the syllable and drawing attention to it.

I need your love

EXAMPLE 347 Use of an agogic accent to reinforce the text.

The use of higher or lower pitches to stress the meanings of some words is a common technique. Overdone, it is humorous.

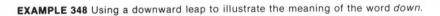

EXAMPLE 348 Using a downward leap to illustrate the meaning of the word *down*.

Using changing meters, so that one may take advantage of the natural accents within these meters, works well when setting free verse or prose.

EXAMPLE 349 The use of natural accents produced by changing meters.

Word Painting

Word painting is the illustrating in the musical dimension of information which is being conveyed by the verbal component. In certain styles or periods of music, word painting has been overdone to the point of becoming ludicrous. Still, a carefully used example can, when tastefully done, enhance the effectiveness of the communication of the text. The following are typical examples of word painting:

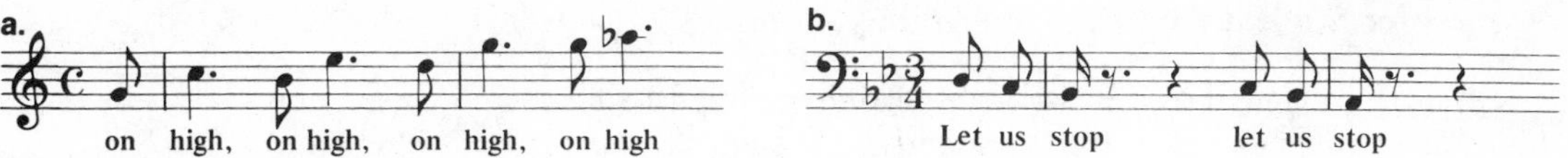

EXAMPLE 350 a. Word painting with pitches. b. Word painting with silences.

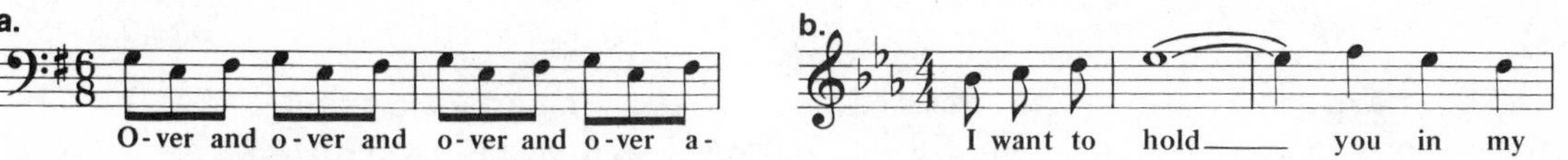

EXAMPLE 351 a. Word painting with repetition. b. Word painting with duration.

When writing for the voice, it is good to remember that a simple folksong is one of the most perfect examples of "good" vocal writing. The more a composed melody approaches this model, the easier it will be to sing and the more ideally suited for the voice it will sound. The more like a folksong in style and complexity a vocal line is, the easier it is for the untrained voice to sing. The less like a folksong, the more likely it is to require a trained performer. The concern expressed about trained versus untrained singers is not misplaced. It is of course possible to write extremely difficult and demanding vocal music for a solo singer or even for a quartet or chamber choir of singers and expect all of the performers to be well-trained and capable of mastering the demands of the music. It is almost impossible to write for a large choir (30 or more voices) and expect to have all performers be trained singers.

Scoring for Voices

If the student has studied Bach chorales, then he will be familiar with an effective approach to vocal writing. The contrapuntal-harmonic technique used to produce choral writings based upon the Bach prototypes is still to be favored for its ability to solve, successfully, problems of voice leading, vertical spacing, and performability in vocal music, especially in music intended for performance by amateur and semi-professional choirs.

Writing for solo voices in combination is more akin to woodwind writing in terms of having to deal with color mixes and balance; in these situations, the typical voice-leading practices assure clearly independent, contrapuntal lines. Writing for choirs is more similar to string writing, where the mix of different vocal timbres on each line provides a homogeneity of tone quality that assures excellent blend; in these circumstances, the usual voice-leading practices help assure at least a minimum amount of aural independence between the lines.

One very important point to remember when writing for voices is to keep the tessitura as low as possible. The less well-trained the singers, the more important this principle becomes. The fatigue encountered by the performers is directly related to the tessitura. Very high and extended writings produce quick fatigue. In a less-than-professional situation this could be disastrous, and even in professional situations it may limit performances.

Scoring for Student Choruses and Young Voices

All advice given above for writing for and voicing for singers and vocal combinations apply equally well to younger voices such as found in junior high and high schools. The additional cautions are these:

1. Keep the tessitura low.
2. Avoid the breaks in each voice part, especially in parts for adolescent boys.

The idea of a low tessitura was discussed above; it is very important in writing for younger singers. The voices are fragile, untrained, and immature. Fatigue and straining are their worst enemies.

Vocal breaks (see Chapter 7, the ranges for each voice category) are permanent problems for all singers, but only mature and trained voices can deal with the breaks; young and amateur voices cannot. Many knowledgeable choir directors avoid music that keeps moving around and across the vocal breaks when selecting music to be performed by a young or volunteer choir.

Problem Set No. 26

1. Using the following poems, show a variety of ways to use accents, durations, pitches, dynamics, etc., to illustrate the texts.
   a. "I have a friend who's fat and wide,
      He doesn't walk, he doesn't slide.
      He isn't much at running, but . . .
      He moves real well when in a rut."
   b. "Only when the night is dark and still; just then,
      As moonlight pours through the trees; and when,
      The insects, too, are still and calm; I know,
      That life's a mystery I cannot solve, oh, no."
2. Select one of the Bach chorale harmonizations given earlier in the book and discuss specifically how it illustrates good vocal writing. What changes would you make if you were to arrange this chorale for a high school choir? Would you change keys? Would you rescore the tenor line? If so, prepare a version of the chorale that would be appropriate for high school voices.

ADDITIONAL INFORMATION

Relative Loudness

Loudness is produced by the performer and not (usually) the instrument. Although one would expect ten trumpets to be louder than one trumpet, that need not be the case. It would take more trumpets than the average marching band has to produce twice as much sound as one trumpet. However, more than one of any instrument increases the mass and the broadness of the sound. The composer must remember that ten trumpets playing a true *pianissimo* can be easily dominated by one *fortissimo* cello. (But, extremely high or extremely low notes for some instruments may make true *pianissimo*s impossible to play.)

Relative High and Low

High does not necessarily mean at the right-hand end of the piano keyboard. Nor does *low* mean the left-hand end of the piano keyboard. High and low are merely relative.

Middle C is in the middle of the piano keyboard. With regard to the piano, it is neither a high nor a low pitch. However, for the tuba, middle C is a high note. And, for the flute, middle C is a low note. If one were to assign a melody that began on middle C to the tuba player, the reaction of the listener would be that the performer's part must be high, since it would be easy to hear the tension associated with playing (physically producing) a high note.

On the other hand, if a melody were assigned to the flute, and the melody began on middle C, the listener would perceive that the first note was breathy and low-sounding. No strain would be perceived, but rather a sense of trying to relax down to the pitch. This is an important point for the writer to remember. If, as in the above case, one wished to preserve the impression that the flute was high and the tuba low, it would be necessary to juxtapose the two instruments so that the inertia of the tuba's tone quality would contrast obviously with the responsiveness of the flute's tone quality. Since a certain ponderousness is also a hallmark of *low* and swiftness of articulation is characteristic of *high,* a side-by-side comparison of the tuba and the flute will convince us that the flute is indeed "higher" than the tuba.

Instrument Substitutions

The following list of instrument substitutions is by no means complete. The success of any of these substitutions requires an effort on the part of the performers to produce a good match. These suggestions are provided to stimulate the student's thinking. Other substitutions can be developed using more instruments, special voicings, dynamic controls, etc.

Instrument	*Replaced by this instrument*	*Replaced by this combination*
Piccolo (high)	violin harmonics	
Piccolo (low)	viola or cello harmonics; E♭ clarinet	
Flute (high)	violin; oboe; clarinet; viola harmonics	
Flute (low)	clarinet (throat tones); horn (open or stopped)	
Alto flute (high)	muted horn; E♭ clarinet (*sotto voce*)	
Alto flute (low)	clarinet; cup-muted trumpet; cup-muted trombone; stopped horn	
Oboe (high)	flute; E♭ clarinet; viola; violin	
Oboe (low)	straight-muted trumpet (or cornet)	

English horn (high)	soprano saxophone; harmon-muted trumpet (stem removed);	
English horn (low)	viola	clarinet with bassoon and muted horn
Clarinet (high)	piccolo; flute; violin (E string)	
Clarinet (throat)	breath tone on flute; muted horn; viola (*sul tasto*)	
Clarinet (low)	alto flute; cup-muted trombone; muted tuba	
Bass clarinet (high)	cello harmonics; harmon-muted trumpet (stem in)	
Bass clarinet (throat)	flute breath tones; stopped horn; string bass harmonics	
Bass clarinet (low)	cup-muted trombone; cello	bassoon with muted horn
Bassoon (high)		muted horn with oboe; clarinet with soprano saxophone
Bassoon (low)	horn (muted)	bass clarinet with cello
Contra bassoon (high)	viola or cello (*ponticello*)	
Contra bassoon (low)	muted tuba	trombone with string bass
Soprano saxophone (high)	clarinet; English horn; bassoon	
Soprano saxophone (low)	cup-muted trumpet; flugelhorn into hat	
Alto saxophone (high)	violin	violin with oboe; clarinet with flute
Alto saxophone (low)		horn with cello (or viola); clarinet with horn
Tenor saxophone (high)		muted horn with bassoon; cello with clarinet
Tenor saxophone (low)		tuba with cello; bassoon with horn (or trombone)
Baritone saxophone (high)		oboe with clarinet; viola with horn
Baritone saxophone (low)		tuba with string bass; trombone with cello
Bass saxophone (high)	string bass; cello (*ponticello*)	
Bass saxophone (low)	electric bass	tuba with string bass
Horn (high)	flugelhorn; trombone; trumpet with harmon mute (without stem); flute; alto flute	

Horn (low)	bassoon	cello with bassoon; (bass) clarinet with trombone
Stopped horn (high)		clarinet or flute with oboe and violin (*ponticello*)
Stopped horn (low)		bassoon with bass clarinet (or clarinet) and viola (or cello, *ponticello*)
Muted horn (high)	bassoon; clarinet (throat tones); flute (breath tones)	
Muted horn (low)	string bass (*sul tasto*)	cello with clarinet
Trumpet (high)		oboe with clarinet and flute
Trumpet (low)		horn with clarinet and flute
Cornet (high)	trumpet (into stand); flugelhorn	clarinet with oboe and flute
Cornet (low)	trumpet (into stand); flugelhorn	flute(s) with muted horn
Straight-Muted Trumpet (high)	oboe	soprano saxophone with flute
Straight-Muted Trumpet (low)		stopped horn with clarinet; stopped horn with flute and oboe
Trombone (high)	horn(s); muted horn(s)	clarinet with oboe, flute, and violin
Trombone (low)		cello with horn; cello with bassoon and clarinet
Straight-Muted Trombone (high)	viola (*ponticello*)	clarinet with English horn and flute
Straight-Muted Trombone (low)		muted horn with cello (*ponticello*)
Tuba (high)	euphonium	trombone with horn
Tuba (low)		bass saxophone with horn, bassoon, and bass clarinet
Muted Tuba (high)		muted horn with clarinet
Muted Tuba (low)		muted horn with bass clarinet (or bassoon or string bass)

Violin (high)		flute and E♭ clarinet
Violin (low)		flute with soprano or alto saxophone
Viola (high)		soprano saxophone with horn
Viola (low)		alto saxophone with horn
Cello (high)		alto saxophone with bassoon and clarinet
Cello (low)		tuba or horn with bassoon and bass clarinet; horn with baritone saxophone
String bass (high)		English horn with horn and saxophone
String bass (low)		baritone or bass saxophone with bassoon and horn
String harmonics	flute (or piccolo or clarinet or oboe) with or without muted horn	
Ponticello quality	add to selected combination: stopped horn or straight-muted brasses or double reed	
Tasto quality	add to selected combination: flute breath tone or clarinet throat tone and/or muted horn	

10
ORCHESTRATION: Techniques of Transcribing

For purposes of organizing the following material, a distinction will be made between transcribing and arranging. The more elementary process is that of transcribing: taking a composition written in one medium and rescoring it, almost note for note, into another medium. The only alterations made are those necessitated by the idiomatic differences between the two media. Arranging is a process that incorporates both transcribing and a certain amount of composition. In the arranging process, one usually begins with some musical material—perhaps a melody and a few rudimentary chords—and proceeds to supply all that is missing through a variety of creative means, such as writing introductions and endings, constructing transitional passages, adding counterpoint, creating a bass line, adding ornaments to the melody, and elaborating upon the harmonic structure. Neither of these processes should be viewed as mutually exclusive of the other, for in practice the blending of aspects of both is common.

TWO APPROACHES TO TRANSCRIBING

In making a transcription, one starts with a piece of music that exists in another medium, and often this original version is the composer's own. The transcriber is faced with taking one of two approaches to this task. On the one hand, the transcriber may try to recreate as nearly as possible in the new medium, the sound of the original piece. With the other approach, the transcriber views the original version as being only one of several possible realizations of the piece: a particular realization for a particular medium. The transcriber then reconceives the piece in a new medium, carefully examining all aspects of the original to ascertain those elements inherent to the musical conception, and those that are purely idiomatic to the medium in which it was set. The transcriber then recasts these elements so that they become idiomatic to the new medium.

The difference between the two approaches to transcription is one of philosophy, not a choice between the right way and the wrong way. If one transcribes a

Bach organ fugue for orchestra, one may desire to have the orchestra sound as much like, and to create the effect of, an organ as possible. If so, then the first approach would be used. If, on the other hand, one takes the Bach piece as a collection of musical ideas which were once scored for organ, and studies the piece from the point of view of writing it for orchestra, the final product will be different.

The First Approach. When using the first approach, these steps should be followed:

1. Become very familiar with the sound of the original. Determine which timbres can be duplicated in the new medium and for which timbres substitutions will be required.
2. Using a list, such as given in Chapter 9 (pages 341-44), or which the transcriber has prepared, plan the substitutions to be used.
3. Score the piece in the new medium. Assign passages scored in the original for available instruments to those instruments and those passages scored for unavailable instruments to close substitutions.

The Second Approach. When using the second approach, these steps should be followed:

1. Determine which characteristics of the original are the results of the medium in which it was cast and not inherent musical structures.
2. Determine which are the obvious characteristics (or those to be stressed) of the new medium.
3. Decide upon scorings and techniques to be used to eliminate elements associated with step 1 and to reinforce elements determined in step 2.
4. Score the piece in the new medium using approaches identified in step 3.

POINTS TO NOTE ABOUT TRANSCRIPTIONS

The transcriber should not necessarily assume that anything about the original is sacred. It is often wise to reconsider many aspects of the music in light of the situation into which the transcriber intends to place the piece. Among the aspects that should be studied carefully and about which conscious choices should be made are these:

Selection of Key

Traditionally, the choice of key has been guided by ease of performance. The assumption has been that wind instruments play better in flat keys and strings play better in sharp keys. To a limited extent, these generalizations are correct. However, there has been too much made of them. In orchestral situations wind players play in both sharp and flat keys and, (except for clarinetists) they do so on the same instruments. In contemporary music, pitch patterns more difficult than any one may encounter in a major-minor key system are played with ease.

The idea that strings play sharp keys well since they can use open strings is false. Orchestral string players often avoid open strings (except for special effects) whenever possible, due to the edgy, vibratoless sound and lack of intonation control. All this leads us to the conclusion that the selection of key has very *little* to do with ease of performance and much more to do with musical considerations. Such considerations include limit of range and control of tone quality.

The only time the argument that a key is primarily selected for ease of performance should be used is in writing music intended for use by young or very inexperienced players.

Two valid arguments for selecting one key rather than another are concerned with the matters of playable range and tone quality. One may select the key of E♭ for a particular transcription because the lowest instrument available is the bassoon and there is a passage where the bass line needs to drop down to the dominant and leap up to the tonic. Since this can be done using the lowest pitch B♭ on the bassoon, if the key selected is E♭ one therefore chooses this key. One would not choose D, because a low A (dominant) does not exist on the bassoon and so the whole passage under consideration would end up being a M7 higher than it would be in E♭. This may well seem too high because the bassoon would not be reedy enough in that range (tone quality choice).

Another reason to select a particular key would be to increase the available scoring options. In a certain key, it might be impossible to double the oboe at the octave with the flute because the flute part would become too high. Yet in another key the doubling could work. In other words, the following alternatives would exist:

1. Flute as written.
2. Oboe as written.
3. Flute an octave higher.
4. Oboe as written with the flute an octave higher.
5. Oboe as written with the flute as written.

However, in a higher key, only these options would be available:

1. Flute as written.
2. Oboe as written.
3. Flute as written with oboe as written.

If one wishes to follow the first approach to transcription, that of attempting to recreate the sound of one medium through another medium, it is usually wise to select a key that is as close to the key of the original as possible. (The same key is best.) Otherwise, many extra problems are created. If, for example, the original version had an important oboe solo, and an oboe will be available for the new version, the oboe solo could become so changed by a great shift in register due to a new key, or it may become unplayable by being moved out of the range of the instrument, as not to sound at all like the original, thereby reducing the possibility of capturing the original effect.

Meter Signature

No matter what the original meter signature (nor how "great" the composer is considered to be), it is very possible that a different meter signature would improve the likelihood of an accurate reading/ or performance. If the original is in a divided $\frac{2}{4}$ time, with lots of thirty-second notes, it may pay to notate the transcription in $\frac{4}{4}$ time with sixteenth notes as the smallest value. This is especially true for student groups, but it would not hurt to do it for the professionals either. In the latter situations it can save time and money and improve the ability of the performers and the conductor to comprehend the score.

Ornaments

In music, especially keyboard music of the Baroque and Classical periods, one finds many ornaments used. The interpretation of these ornaments is not necessarily agreed upon by the experts. To save time and avoid a lot of unnecessary discussion, write out the interpretation of the ornaments and do not even include the ornament symbols (trills are one of the very few exceptions, and here too, one could very well indicate clearly how the trill is to begin and end.) As the transcriber, you have time to look up the accepted interpretation of the various ornaments, and not have to expect the performers to automatically know how to play them. Remember too, saxophone or tuba players do not normally have to deal with Baroque ornaments, so one cannot expect them to be as prepared for such a task as a violinist would be.

When faced with writing a transcription, one needs to do the following:

1. Study the original medium.
2. Determine the approach to be adopted: to imitate the original, or to create another, different realization.
3. Identify the idiomatic differences.
4. Outline solutions available for the problems.

If at this point all seems promising, then the transcription should be done. However, not every conceivable transcription will work. It is sometimes necessary to decide that the best solution to some transcription problems is simply not to do the transcription for the medium available. Rather, one should find a more likely work.

SOURCES FOR TRANSCRIPTIONS

Different sources offer different advantages and problems to the transcriber. An examination of these should be helpful to the student who is planning his first transcription effort.

Piano Literature

If one needs to transcribe a piece of music from the piano, it is necessary that the transcriber know the piano as a musical medium. This is not the same as saying that the transcriber need to be able to play the piano, but the transcriber needs to be familiar with its characteristics, weaknesses, strengths, and clichés. (See pages 222-26).

In order to provide a feeling or sense of sustaining, several pianistic devices have been developed. Among these are the Alberti bass, rolled chords or tremolos, and the use of the damper and sustenuto pedals.

EXAMPLE 352 Excerpt from Mozart's Sonata in B♭ Major, K. 333 (measures 57-58) featuring an Alberti bass in the left hand.

To rescore this passage for a group of (basically) one-line instruments would require rewriting. Even though the Alberti bass could be played by another instrument, it may be awkward and not idiomatic. The specific details that Mozart has written for the keyboard are due to the construction of the instrument and the shape of the human hand. Therefore, an orchestrator is not merely being willful when he makes these changes; they are necessary in order to produce an effectively scored string orchestra piece.

a. Allegro
I Vns. II
(divisi) Vas.
Vcs,
pizz. Cbs.

b.
I Vns. II
Vas.
divisi Vcs.
(arco) Cbs.

EXAMPLE 353 a. Transcription of Mozart excerpt in a rather static rescoring for string orchestra. b. A more active rescoring.

Example 353-a is more static due to a great use of repeated pitches, while 353-b with the alternation of thirds is more active and captures the original effect rather well. The viola and cello parts in either example could be redistributed without significantly altering the result. Note the use of a simplified contrabass part. This is not technically necessary, but is very characteristic of classical scoring practices. The contrabass eighth notes in the second measure of 353-b have been added to increase the impetus toward the cadence.

As an alternative sustaining device on the piano, one often finds the use of rolled octaves. (This can be used to imitate thunder or drum rolls, too.)

EXAMPLE 354 Use of rolled octaves (tremolo) in the left hand of Beethoven's Sonata in C Minor (*Pathétique*) Opus 13 (measures 11-15).

To replace the piano's rolled octaves in an orchestral score, one could use the scoring given below:

EXAMPLE 355 Scoring of bassoons, timpani, violoncellos, and contrabasses to replace piano's octave tremolo.

The bassoons are in octaves; the cellos and basses are also in octaves, both sustained; while the repeated eighth notes in the timpani provide the rhythmic impulses. The bowing indication in the string parts means to change bows as necessary.

To create the effect of changes in timbre on the piano, devices such as register shifts, use of various pedals, and octave doublings are used.

EXAMPLE 356 From Brahms's Piano Sonata, Opus 2 (measures 154-157). The damper pedal is used to sustain the sound, and octave doublings provide timbral contrast and weight.

Example 357 shows a scoring of Example 356 made for brass quintet. Since there are more lines in the original than instruments in the brass quintet, it is necessary to selectively omit some lines. Notice that the tuba A in the second measure is written as a dotted half note to produce the effect achieved by the pedal indication in the original. It is also marked *crescendo.* There is no way the piano could produce a crescendo on this note, but rather the crescendo is achieved in the triplets. The tuba dynamic reinforces this effect. Also the piano triplets include an A which is omitted in the brasses since there are not enough instruments to play all the pitches and the tuba is supplying the A. (One would usually not omit the tuba note—that is, the bass note—because that would change the inversion of the chord, significantly altering the final sound.)

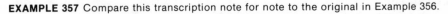

EXAMPLE 357 Compare this transcription note for note to the original in Example 356.

EXAMPLE 358 Excerpt from Beethoven's Piano Sonata, Opus 53 (*The Waldstein*) (measures 2-4) featuring a register shift which is orchestrationally a timbre change.

The change of register in the original (Example 358) is replaced by a change of instrument in the transcription (Example 359). Note, too, that the transcription is an octave higher than the original because none of the instruments of a woodwind quintet can provide the low G. It was thought best to keep the shape of the bass movement—down—and sacrifice the octave.

EXAMPLE 359 Transcription of Example 358 for woodwind quintet.

EXAMPLE 360 a. Original by Debussy—measure 19 of "Reflets dans l'eau," from *Images* for piano, Book I, featuring widely spread-out chords with middle unfilled in. b. Same passage scored for string orchestra.

Rescoring the Debussy excerpt (Example 360) presents other problems. The first chord would sound very hollow or empty if it were literally transcribed for instruments. Therefore, the version for string orchestra fills in the middle.

In order to create an effect similar to the original on the last beat of the measure, the string version uses a solo violin (solo to minimize ensemble problems) on the triplets, sustained eighth notes in the *tutti* first violins and cellos, and pizzicato, *non-divisi* chords, arpeggiated from low to high, to suggest the pyramiding effect. One could keep the octave of the original if the solo were assigned to the principal viola, but this limits the performance possibilities to only string orchestras of semi-professional quality or better.

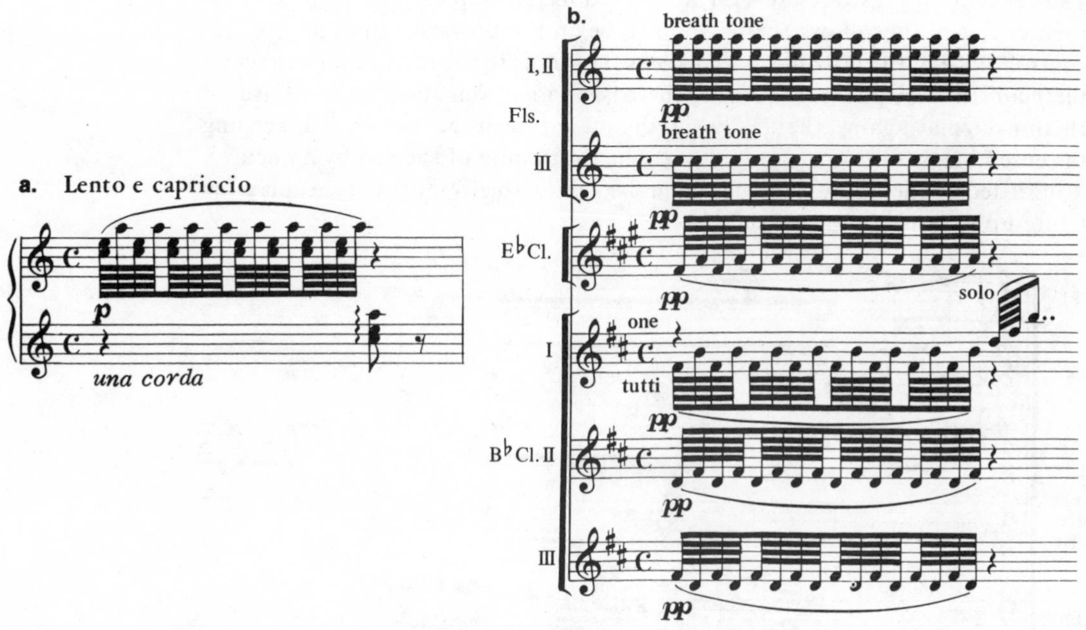

EXAMPLE 361 a. Brief passage from Liszt's Hungarian Rhapsody No. 11 (measure 1) featuring the use of *una corda.* b. Same passage scored for band.

Example 361 shows a possible scoring of the Liszt excerpt for concert band using only flutes, E♭ clarinet(s), and B♭ clarinets. The flute breath tones together with the clarinets' throat tones are selected to obtain an amount of the lack of focus associated with the *una corda* timbre of the original. (The B-natural for the *tutti* B♭ clarinets is available as a side key and this would be the preferred fingering in this passage.) The arpeggio is transformed into a solo figure, assigned to one performer for the same reason cited for Example 362.

Since the action of the piano allows the performer to produce many notes within a short span of time, it is often tempting to composers to write very rapid sequences of pitches. These will often cover three, four, or five octaves without a break and are commonly associated with virtuoso piano writing and performance.

EXAMPLE 362 A florid passage from Chopin's Etude in E Major, Op. 25, No. 7 (measure 53).

One possible method of dealing with a florid figure is shown in Example 363. Here, a woodwind quintet is given the Chopin passage above (Example 362). The realization illustrates several transcription techniques. First, the key has been changed; this allows the bassoon to begin the upward run in an easy-to-control range of the instrument and keeps the whole figure high enough to retain the pianistic transparency. Second, the bassoon is given specifically measured rhythms to play against the steady eighth notes of the upper voices, thus keeping the ensemble problems to a minimum. The shortening of the run by an octave, a third technique, allows the bassoonist a reasonable opportunity to play the figure up to tempo.

EXAMPLE 363 Portion of the Chopin etude scored for woodwind quintet.

Arpeggiated or broken chords are commonly found in piano writing. These are often used to facilitate the fingering of a passage but have become so commonplace that they now represent a common pianistic effect.

EXAMPLE 364 From the first of Three Romances by Robert Schumann, Opus 28, a passage featuring broken or arpeggiated chords.

A string orchestra version of Example 364 is given below (Example 365). All string sections are *divisi,* except the basses. The pedalling in the piano original produces a sustained quality which is provided in the string version by the cellos and string basses. The violas maintain the triplet impulses but do not literally play the original figure. The melody is doubled at the octave to provide additional bite and mass to the line so that it will not be covered by the rather thick middle and lower textures.

EXAMPLE 365 A string orchestra version of the Schumann Romance excerpt.

Problem Set No. 27

1. Score the first 12 measures of Brahms's Intermezzo in A Major, given below, for string orchestra.

INTERMEZZO IN A MAJOR, OP. 118, NO. 2

2. Score the same 12 measures of Brahms's Intermezzo in A, given above, for woodwind quintet. It will be necessary to change the key, due to the range; perhaps B♭ would work well.

3. Score the following D Major Sonata excerpt (measures 1-21) for 2 oboes, 2 clarinets, 2 horns, and 2 bassoons. (You may wish to listen to or examine the scores of some of the classical divertimenti for similar combinations before writing.)

Organ Literature

The organ represents an excellent source of material for possible transcription. Organs can sustain notes and chords well, offer a wide variety of tone colors, and, in music written for more modern instruments, it can be assumed that the organ has some ability to produce a crescendo on a single pitch or chord. A famous example of transcribing from organ to orchestra is William Schuman's transcription of Charles Ives's "Variations on America." (A good introductory project would be to listen to the original organ version, with music in hand, and then listen to the transcription, with the score.)

Pedal Parts

It would seem that the pedal parts in organ works should present very few scoring problems. But, pedal parts can be problems because:

1. The pedal line is *not* always the bass.
2. Even when it is the bass, it may not be in the octave notated.
3. The importance, weight, and function of the pedal part may not be clear from its notation.

In many pieces, the pedals are used to provide a slower-moving but not necessarily low-pitched chorale melody. In cases like these, the organist will draw a prominent 4′ or 2′ stop on the pedals and the line will sound in the middle of, or above, the general tessitura of the organ. If the pedal registration calls for a 4′ or 2′ "chorale bass" or "reed," or if the pedal part is marked "chorale melody" or even if it simply looks like a chorale melody, the chances are that the pedal line is not functioning as a bass line and should be treated as a melody. The true bass will be found in a manual part.

As a standard practice, pedal parts are normally understood to sound an octave lower than written. Because of this convention, it is especially important to ascertain whether it is applicable in the composition with which one is dealing or not. In the case cited above, it is not. A careful study of the registration given or usually used in the piece under consideration should reveal whether the pedal usage is an exception to the common practice or not.

Often it is not clear what role the pedal plays simply by looking at the notes. If one sees that the pedal registration is a soft 16′ stop coupled to one of the manuals, and the manual registration is soft stops, one can assume that the pedal is serving primarily as an extra finger. In this case, one would be better off treating the pedal and the manual that is coupled to the pedal as one group of instruments.

In contrast, the registration for the pedal may call for a loud solo reed or other prominent stop or for a loud manual, such as "full great," to be coupled to the pedal. If this is the case, and the pedal plays in passages that are not otherwise full organ passages, the pedal may be serving as a solo line.

In transcribing from organ literature, one should be sure to observe the following:

1. Registration:
   a. loudness.
   b. couplers.
   c. pitch-levels.
2. Changes of manual.
3. Role of the Pedal Organ:
   a. bass line.
   b. solo line.
   c. extra finger.
4. Changes of registration.
5. Unusual scorings:
   a. intended by the composer for a musical effect.
   b. unavoidable due to a limitation caused by the instrument or the performer.

Problem Set No. 28

1. Score "O Lamm Gottes, unschuldig," below, for string quartet. Compare the pedal part to the alto line. In what octave should one place the pedal line?

2. Score "Nun komm' der Heiden Heiland," below, for 2 violins, viola, violoncello, and contrabass. Compare the pedal line to that in exercise 1. Will the treatment be different?

String Literature

When transcribing string music for other instruments, the primary problems are created by contrasts in range, agility, and the use of pizzicato. One insidious problem can come from the number of pitches involved. An inexperienced transcriber may forget that to successfully transcribe a string quartet may require more than four instruments.

The strings are a homogeneous group of instruments. The effect of register is quite often more timbral contrast than any other device available. The next most significant change is that produced by moving from a group of instruments to a solo instrument, or the reverse. Changes in tone quality created by moving from one string to another on the same instrument are also significant. In contrast to brasses, the effect of mutes is very subtle.

Therefore, the transcriber must keep the following in mind:

1. Strings usually offer subtle timbral variety.
2. Pizzicato and special bowings are idiomatic to the instruments.

3. A direct substitute for the strings does not exist, but homogeneous ensembles are best.
4. It is necessary to have enough instruments available to cover all of the pitches that appear in the multiple stops, or be prepared to revoice and modify the chords.
5. Very agile string parts will need simplification in many situations; only very proficient woodwinds and keyboard players can execute passages as rapidly as strings.
6. Condensation of the range requirements may also be needed.

Problem Set No. 29

1. Score the first 35 measures of the Schubert Quintet, Opus 163, given below, for woodwind quintet. Examine the original carefully before beginning. Plan how all of the various pitches will be accounted for in your transcription.

QUINTET

2. Score the first 13 measures of the Mozart string quartet given in exercise 1 of Problem Set No. 20 (page 268) for brass quintet of 2 trumpets, horn, trombone, and tuba. Discuss the contrast in the problems created for the transcriber in the original assignment and this assignment.

Wind Literature

Wind literature is a good source of material for transcribing to any medium. (It is often difficult to score wind music for piano, due to the lack of sustaining power on the piano, but by the judicious use of rolled chords, rewritten and elaborated figures, and register changes, it can be done.)

Among the characteristics found in wind music which need to be considered by the transcriber are the following:

1. A wide variety of tone qualities are often used, including auxiliary instruments and devices such as mutes, etc. This means that compromises may have to be made in terms of tone quality variety. Changes of register or articulation may be used instead.
2. The agile instruments tend to be the sopranos of the choirs, leading to a tendency for more interesting parts to occur in the higher voices and duller parts in the tenor and bass voices. In another medium which does not possess the timbral diversities, this treble-dominated texture can soon become tiresome. It is important to reconceive some of the soprano lines as alto, tenor, or bass lines.
3. Special effects like flutter tonguing and double or triple tonguing will require a substitution of another solution: strings and percussion can do this, but keyboard instruments will present problems. Repeating octaves may help.
4. Accents and large crescendos and decrescendos are very idiomatic for winds. The other instruments probably cannot provide the amount of contrast available in the brass. (Percussion do provide a good dynamic contrast.)

Percussion Literature

Music with percussion parts, or music which is percussive in character, can present special problems. The piano may possess some of these characteristics, but in most cases, it is unable to imitate the kinds of sound that are typical of the percussion family:

1. Very large variety of timbres, dynamics, and attack-decay patterns. No other choir of instruments can even come close.
2. Traditional usage of the percussion for word-painting or graphic representation of some sort. The sound specified is uniquely percussion and simply no substitute exists.

A solution is simply to replace the percussion with percussion. In a band transcription, one often finds an orchestral timpani roll replaced with a bass drum or snare drum roll. A set drummer can do many of the things, that a percussion section can do, or substitutes for them. Remember, percussion is traditionally used to highlight or decorate an already existing musical idea. One can often substitute one type of decoration for another with very little loss. A passage using violins and xylophone together may become violins and flute double tonguing, or clarinets and cornet double tonguing; the flute or the cornet provides the highlight.

Problem Set No. 30

1. Score the 10 measures of Brahms's Minuet, given below, for string quartet. Will you choose to use pizzicato? Will you use all four strings? Discuss these questions in class.

2. Score the same Brahms Minuet excerpt for an available combination of five instruments, not including clarinets or a bassoon, and not including a string quartet.

Vocal Literature

In scoring from vocal music, it is wise to work with homogeneous sounds so that the blending can be as vocal in nature as possible. For these reasons, brass or string instruments suggest themselves immediately for transcriptions.

Woodwinds can be used in blended groups, such as clarinet choirs or clarinets plus flutes, as well as in unblended groups that feature all sorts of woodwinds in the most heterogeneous mix possible. In the latter situation, or any heterogeneous situation, the trick is to work with instrument combinations that, though made up of divergent sounds, possess a finished, integrated quality that can be gradually and subtly modified to obtain just exactly the right tone quality to bring out a line or to subjugate the line to another. When turning vocal music into instrumental music, it is wise to examine the words and the sounds of the words. The use of vowels and consonances to do more than convey the literal meaning is not uncommon. The consonances affect the attacks and releases, and the vowels affect the tonal quality. The effect of these elements can be recaptured in the tone quality selections made in the instrumental transcription.

Problem Set No. 31

1. Score Gesualdo's "Moro, Lasso, Al Mio Duolo," given below, for string orchestra. Assume an instrumentation of at least 12 first violins, 10 second violins, 8 violas, 6 violoncellos, and 4 contrabasses.

2. Score the same Gesualdo excerpt for the following woodwind ensemble: 2 flutes, 1 piccolo, 2 oboes, 2 clarinets, 1 bass clarinet, 2 bassoons. Discuss the problems encountered in exercise 1 versus the problems encountered in this assignment. What are some of the solutions that seem to work well?

ORCHESTRATION: Techniques of Arranging

ARRANGING TECHNIQUES

Arranging uses transcription skills and rudimentary compositional techniques. One usually begins with no full score. What one does have may be only a melody and a set of simple chords. It becomes the arranger's task to create all of the missing material: introductions, transitional passages, contermelodies, codas, etc.—all must be composed by the arranger.

To see how this might be done, let us assume that one is given the following melody:

EXAMPLE 366 "America the Beautiful"—a given melody.

If one examines Example 366 for rhythmic and melodic motives or gestures, among the many one might identify are these:

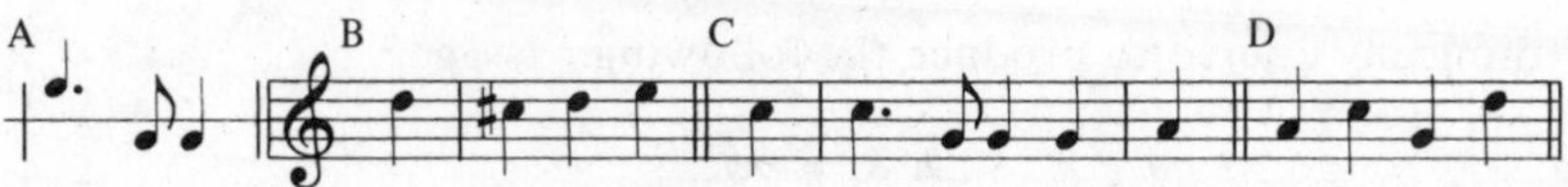

EXAMPLE 367 a. A high-to-low figure found in measures 1, 2, 5, 6, 10, 13, and 14. b. An interesting chromatic figure found uniquely in measures 6-7. c. A figure found in measures 13-15. d. A figure found in measure 15.

Characteristics of the motives or figures:

Motive (a): A high-to-low figure with dotted-quarter + eighth rhythm. The pitch of the eighth note is immediately repeated with a quarter note.

Motive (b): A chromatic lower neighbor on the downbeat—the only chromatic pitch in the melody.

Motive (c): A dotted quarter note preceded by an anticipation and followed by a leap to its dominant on an eighth with the repetition of this note as two quarter notes.

Motive (d): An upward melodic third that expands to an upward melodic fifth.

One may invert, retrograde, augment, diminish, transpose, repeat, and link together these motives to create fresh-sounding but related material to use in an arrangement.

EXAMPLE 368 An introductory type of passage made from motives (b) and (c).

Diminishing the durations and elaborating the (c) version gives:

EXAMPLE 369 Sequence produced by elaborating motive (c) and repeating the elaboration a step lower. The chromatic neighbor is suggested by motive (b).

Placing Example 369 into triple meter, the following figure is obtained; the relationship between motive (b) and the third beat of each measure is deliberate.

EXAMPLE 370 Example 369 in a new meter.

A fanfare type of passage developes from motive (c) very easily.

EXAMPLE 371 Fanfare derived from motive (c).

Example 370 could be rhythmically altered to produce the following passage:

EXAMPLE 372 A rhythmically altered version of Example 371.

Augmenting the durations of motive (c) produces this which resembles a very typical bass line:

EXAMPLE 373 A possible bass line derived from motive (c).

Using Example 368 as a starting point, a bass line suggested by Example 373, and some elaboration suggested by Example 369, this passage, which could serve as an introduction to an arrangement of "America the Beautiful" for high school band, is produced:

EXAMPLE 374 Introduction to "America the Beautiful" produced from motives derived from the melody itself.

The process is self-perpetuating, because each variation contains motives that may be developed into new variations, and so on. This means that if an interlude is needed in the arrangement, one can be derived from the material used for the introduction.

EXAMPLE 375 Interlude derived from soprano line in Example 374.

A $\frac{6}{8}$ meter interlude, different from the one above, can also be derived from Example 370.

EXAMPLE 376 Interlude derived from soprano line of Example 374. Lower neighbor borrowed from motive b.

In addition to this, these themes are also the raw material from which counter-melodies can be derived:

EXAMPLE 377 Countermelody derived from Example 374 with an obvious debt to motive (b).

and, from which descants can be fashioned:

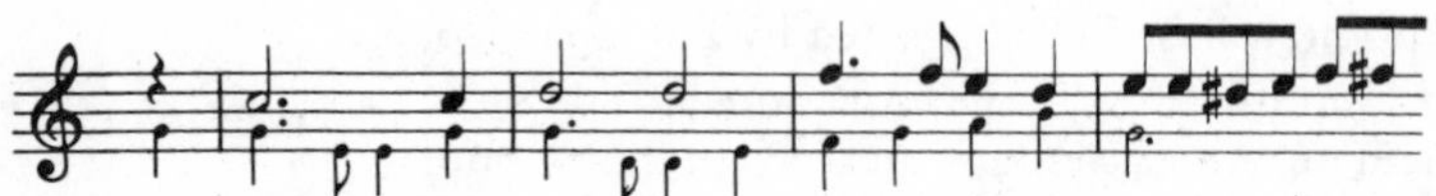

EXAMPLE 378 Descant related to Examples 374 and 375.

A slightly different bass line, derived from the motivic materials, can generate new harmonic structures and suggest new treble melodies composed especially for this bass.

EXAMPLE 379 Another possible bass that could be generated.

POSSIBLE VARIATIONS

Although this is not an exhaustive list of possible variations, it should provide a student with some valuable suggestions.

Rhythmic

By altering the rhythm, meter, and/or tempo of a melody, one can create a whole set of variations that are rhythmic recastings of the original.

Harmonic

By reharmonizing the given melodic material, even to the extent of changing a few melodic notes to make it work, it is possible to create a whole series of variations on a given melody.

Melodic

By changing the melodic contour, direction, or intervallic size, one may create a large number of variations on a given musical idea.

Setting

Modification of the setting in which a musical idea is cast can provide many variations in the finished product. Among some settings to be considered are:

1. *Contrapuntal.* Using the original material as one voice in a multi-voiced fugue, invention, or other contrapuntal work.
2. *Chorale.* Using the given material as a soprano, alto, tenor, or bass line in some sort of hymnlike (Bach chorale) setting.

3. *Bassline* or *Descant*. Using the given theme as a slow moving bass or descant over or under which totally different musical events are taking place.
4. *"Games."* A hidden line, not to be perceived by the listener, is created from the given material. Everything else that is happening disguises what is going on and seems on the surface to have no relationship to the original material.
5. *Change of Mode*. Typically from major to minor or minor to major, but change from minor to whole tone or major to pentatonic is always possible (as are the reverse).
6. *Change of Style*. Through the use of different styles of counterpoint, different harmonic language, different treatment of non-harmonic tones, different orchestrational colors and combinations, it is possible to score a particular musical element as though it were being treated by Bach, or Beethoven, or Babbitt, or Bartók.

Problem Set No. 32

1. From each of the following melodies, derive at least three motives. Then using one of these derived motives, create an introduction of two or three measures for string quartet.

2. Create two countermelodies to each of the following lines. Score each pair (line and countermelody) for two unlike instruments, such as oboe and violin, and perform in class.

3. Given the following chord progressions, write two different melodies for each progression. Base these melodies upon motives derived in Number 1.

a. I vi V/ii ii^7 V^7 I

b. I IV ii V vi ii I$^6_4$ V^7 I

4. Rewrite each of the following melodies in three ways as suggested below. Select your favorite resulting melody and harmonize it in each of the four ways cited below. From these, select your favorite and score it for a group of instruments and/or voices available. Have the results performed in class.

   A. Possible melodic alterations:
      (1). change meters.
      (2). change the location of the downbeats relative to the meter.
      (3). add additional pitches of shorter duration. (Do not simply add ornaments.)

   B. Possible harmonic alterations:
      (1). allow the harmony to be, at times, dissonant with the melody.
      (2). use only major (or only minor) chords.
      (3). use chords built on fourths or fifths.
      (4). have the harmony change at points within the measure other than when one would expect.

12

ORCHESTRATION: Some Final Thoughts

It is important that the orchestrator realize that he is writing for persons and not for instruments. The fact that he considers the needs and problems of the performer(s), including the conductor, should immediately assure more successful efforts. Additionally, the performer can be found in two rather contrasting roles—that of a soloist and that of a section member. An examination of the contrast between these roles is valuable.

CHAMBER MUSIC

Writing for the Chamber Music Performer

Each performer in a chamber music group is a soloist. A soloist in this context will be attempting to communicate the important nuances and subtle shadings of *his* instrument's line to the listener. The performance of accompaniment figures will be done with care and pride. The chamber music player knows that this note or that accent is very important and will play it with as much musicality as possible. Except where limited by doublings, each performer is free to contribute expressive rubatos and clear articulations to the performance with the satisfying feeling that it *does* matter. Each performer can be heard through the texture. The importance of the individual's contribution is often magnified in the individual's eyes. Writing for chamber music groups should take advantge of these performer attitudes.

Chamber music groups cannot produce the walls and waves of sound for which the symphony orchestras and concert bands are famous. It is much more difficult to achieve a gorgeous blur of sound with only a few players, and impossible to produce the volume needed for overwhelming acoustical climaxes.

Ensemble in chamber music is an exciting merging of very strong individual personalities, each one a soloist, each a virtuoso, and each cooperating with the others in an effort to make music. No one, in a good ensemble, can fail to contribute. In a well-balanced chamber group, each performer feels as though he has a vital and necessary role to play; the best of each person is needed and no one is unnecessary.

Instrumentation of Normal Chamber Music Groups

There are many standard chamber music ensembles. The instrumentations given below are typical. It is now more common than it once was to ask performers, especially of woodwind instruments, to play an auxiliary instrument.

Name of Ensemble	*Makeup*	*Name of Ensemble*	*Makeup*
String quartet	2 vlns, va, vc	Piano and woodwind quintet	ob, cl, bn, hn, piano
Piano trio	vln, vc, piano	Piano and woodwind quintet	fl, ob, cl, bn, piano
String trio	vln, va, vc	Brass quintet	2 tpts, hn, tmb, tu
String quintet	2 vlns, 2 vas, vc	Brass quintet	2 tpts, hn, tmb, bs. tmb
String quintet	2 vlns, va, 2 vcs	Brass sextet	2 tpts, hn, tmb, euph, tu
Piano quartet	vln, va, vc, piano	Brass trio	**tpt, hn, tmb**
Piano quintet	2 vlns, va, vc, piano	Brass quartet	**2 tpts, 2 tmbs**
(solo wind) quintet	2 vlns, va, vc, (solo wind)	Percussion ensemble	2 or more percussionists
Woodwind quintet	fl, ob, cl, bn, hn		
Woodwind quintet	fl, ob, cl, bn, bs. cl		
Woodwind quartet	fl, ob, cl, bn		

LARGE ENSEMBLES

Writing for the Large Ensemble Performer

The section member is not necessarily less skilled, less talented, or less musical than his soloist colleague. In fact, the violinist who is only one of sixteen first violinists in an orchestra may also be a very respected and skilled first violinist in a string quartet. However, a musician who must fill both roles has to be able to shift personality types. (A soloist attitude in the middle of the section can lead to disastrous musical problems.)

When scoring for a section of performers, whether in a band or orchestra, remember that the resulting sound from the section is the average of all of the performers' efforts. This implies that the central pitch of a line played by a section of several performers is not a single, focused pitch but rather a pitch band of some width. This pitch band produces a mass of sound that tends to obscure details. But this same pitch band is responsible for the overwhelming sound that can create the musical effects that have caused the large ensembles to satisfy the esthetic desires of concert goers. It is this sound mass that still causes composers and orchestrators to write for the band or orchestra.

Instrumentation of Large Ensembles

The typical composition of some of these groups is:

CONCERT BAND

Name of Part	*Number of Players*
Piccolo	1-2 (alt. with flute)
1st Flute	1-8
2nd Flute	1-8
1st Oboe	1-2
2nd Oboe	1-2
English horn	1(alt. with oboe)
E♭ Clarinet	1-2
1st B♭ Clarinet	6-10
2nd B♭ Clarinet	6-10
3rd B♭ Clarinet	6-10
E♭ Alto clarinet	1-4
B♭ Bass clarinet	2-6
E♭ Contra alto	0-3
B♭ Contrabass clarinet	0-2
1st Bassoon	1-3
2nd Bassoon	1-3
Contra bassoon	1(alt. with bassoon)
1st Alto saxophone	1-2
2nd Alto saxophone	1-2
Tenor saxophone	1-2
Baritone saxophone	1
Bass saxophone	0-1
1st Cornet	2-4
2nd Cornet	2-3
3rd Cornet	2-3
1st Trumpet	1-2
2nd Trumpet	1-2
1st Horn	2-4
2nd Horn	1-2
3rd Horn	2-3
4th Horn	1-2
1st Trombone	2-4
2nd Trombone	1-3
3rd Trombone	1-3
Euphoniums	2-6
Tubas	2-8
Timpani	1
Percussion	4-6
Harp	0-2
Keyboard	0-2

SYMPHONY ORCHESTRA

Name of Part	*Number of Players*
Piccolo	1(alt. with flute)
1st Flute	1-2
2nd Flute	1-2
1st Oboe	1-2
2nd Oboe	1-2
English horn	1(alt. with oboe)
E♭ Clarinet	1(alt. with clarinet)
1st Clarinet	1-2
2nd Clarinet	1-2
Bass clarinet	1(alt. with clarinet)
1st Bassoon	1-2
2nd Bassoon	1-2
Contra bassoon	1(alt. with bassoon)
1st Horn	2-3
2nd Horn	1
3rd Horn	1-2
4th Horn	1
1st Trumpet	1-2
2nd Trumpet	1
3rd Trumpet	1
1st Trombone	1-2
2nd Trombone	1
3rd Trombone	1
Tuba	1
Timpani	1
Percussion	3-6
1st Violins	12-18
2nd Violins	10-17
Violas	8-14
Violoncellos	6-12
Basses	5-10
Harps	1-2
Keyboard	1(alt. with another inst.)
Saxophone	1(alt. with another inst.)

WIND ENSEMBLE[1]

Name of Part	*Number of Players*
Piccolo	1
1st Flute	1
2nd Flute	1
1st Oboe	1
2nd Oboe	1
English horn	0-1
E♭ Clarinet	0-1
1st Clarinet	1
2nd Clarinet	1
Bass clarinet	0-1
1st Bassoon	1
2nd Bassoon	1
Contrabassoon	0-1
1st Horn	1-2
2nd Horn	1
3rd Horn	1
4th Horn	1
1st Trumpet	1
2nd Trumpet	1
3rd Trumpet	1
1st Trombone	1
2nd Trombone	1
Bass trombone	1
Euphonium	1
Tuba	1
Timpani	1
Percussion	3-4
Saxophones	0-4
Harp	0-1
Keyboard	0-1

JAZZ BAND[1]

Name of Part	*Number of Players*
1st Alto Sax	1
2nd Tenor Sax	1
3rd Alto Sax	1
4th Tenor Sax	1
5th Baritone Sax	1
1st Trumpet (lead)	1
2nd Trumpet (solo)	1
3rd Trumpet	1
4th Trumpet	1
1st Trombone	1
2nd Trombone	1
3rd Trombone	1
Bass Trombone	1
Piano	1
String bass	1
Guitar	1
(Set) Drums	1
Percussion	0-1
Horn	0-1
Tuba	0-1

[1] From this chart, one would assume that both the wind ensemble and the jazz band are chamber (one-on-a-part) groups and not large ensembles. However, both are large in the total number of players and therefore the sound masses produced are those of a large ensemble. Also, the jazz band traditionally uses a lot of unison scoring, creating a large ensemble effect.

CHAMBER ORCHESTRA

Name of Part	*Number of Players*	*Name of Part*	*Number of Players*
1st Flute	1	Trumpet	0-2
2nd Flute	0-1	Trombone	0-1
1st Oboe	1	Timpani	0-1
2nd Oboe	1	1st Violins	5-6
1st Clarinet	0-1	2nd Violins	4
2nd Clarinet	0-1	Violas	3
1st Bassoon	1	Violoncellos	3
2nd Bassoon	1	Basses	1
1st Horn	1	Keyboard	1
2nd Horn	1		

By looking at the listings given above for some typical groups, one can see that in the symphony orchestra most of the woodwinds and brass players have solo parts. The presence of two players on some of these parts implies the availability of an assistant who may double in louder passages and spell the principal player during less important sections of the concert.

In the chamber orchestra, everyone except the violins, violas, and violoncellos are soloists. But, the concert band is quite different. In most bands, even though the extra oboe player, for example, is intended to be an assistant, a large percentage of the music is performed with all players involved.

The use of so many performers per part, whether in a band or orchestra, creates a tendency toward inertia not unlike that which plagues performers of large, low-pitched instruments. To overcome this inertia, the composer may utilize soloists to lighten the effect. Also, pizzicato strings are more incisive than arco strings, and a band does not have pizzicato available to lighten and focus its attacks. Thus, some band leaders, aware of the problem, instruct their players to shorten all durations, especially on marches. This helps, but the orchestrator could do much to alleviate the problem simply by opening up more space between attacks.

SOME IDEAS FOR ORGANIZING RESOURCES

Consider the whole ensemble as composed of various groups of instruments which can be combined in many different ways. Here are some of the ways in which you might do this. Note that each combination has a commonly shared tone quality that somehow defines the group. To assist in remembering or imagining the sound of each group, adjective pairs have been used to describe the sound quality for each:

Dark and Smooth: all the clarinets (from the E♭ through the contrabasses), the string bass, and the marimba

Dark and Mellow: cornets, flugelhorns, horns, euphoniums, tubas, marimba, and vibraphone

Dark and Reedy: horns, euphoniums, tubas, saxophones (at softer dynamics), bassoons, marimba, vibraphone, and tam-tam

Dark and Full: all flutes in low register (no piccolo), English horn, bassoons, low-register clarinets, low-register saxophones, horns, muted trombones, bass drum, tom-toms, tam-tam, and timpani

Neutral and Full: all flutes in low register, clarinets, cornets, muted horns, euphoniums, and tubas

Bright and Smooth: all of the flutes, plus the clarinets *above the break,* the upper range of the saxophones, the muted horns, and the vibraphone

Bright and Clear: trumpets, trombones, tubas, triangles, glockenspiel, and timpani

Bright and Full: high-register flutes, high-register clarinets, oboes, high-register saxophones, trumpets, trombones, tubas, cymbals, triangles, snare drums, glockenspiel, xylophone, and chimes

Nasal and Bright: oboes, all saxophones, English horn, bassoons, chalumeau register of the clarinets, harmon-muted brasses, and stopped horns

Nasal and Dark: oboes, English horn, bassoons, saxophones, muted brasses, temple blocks, and string bass

Percussive: all percussion instruments, staccatos played on muted brasses and woodwinds, and pizzicato string bass

The names selected are fantasy; the groupings are very usable. These eleven sets of instrumental colors may be mixed, combined, or contrasted in a wide variety of ways. Obviously, other groupings could be assembled. In fact, an orchestrator might wish to define a new list of these groups for each orchestration project.

It is of course not necessary to employ *all* of the instruments from one group to suggest the sound associated with that group any more than it is necessary to have all pitches of a dominant seventh present to suggest the functioning of the chord. Thus, one can see that this approach to the utilization of instrumental qualities has an almost limitless number of possible variations inherent in its organization. Its only limit is the imagination of the orchestrator.

JUDGING YOUR WORK

A serious orchestrator is never really satisfied. Even if the sounds obtained are exactly those desired, one can always seek new and different tonal possibilities. And if the sounds obtained (no matter how acceptable) are *not* the sounds that were intended, one can then work to improve one's ability to create in sound that which is imagined in the mind. Some way to predict the scoring's potential for success would be helpful.

The most worthwhile suggestion that can be offered is to have the orchestrator read through each instrumentalist's part. Two items should be checked: playability and performer satisfaction. The former can be verified by referring to the appropriate sections in this book. The latter can be determined by the orchestrator asking himself, "Would I enjoy performing this part?" If the answer is yes, then the part is well written. If the answer is no, then a weakness may have been detected. If too many parts are found to be not interesting, the whole effort may be less well done than one would desire and revision should be seriously considered.

Problem Set No. 33

1. Transcribe Kuhlau's Sonatina in G Major, Op. 20, No. 2, for an orchestra of pairs of flutes, oboes, clarinets, bassoons, and horns plus strings.

2. From the following Sonata movement by Mozart, score the theme and first variation for band. The instrumentation of the band is 2 flutes, piccolo, oboe, bassoon, 1st, 2nd, and 3rd clarinets, bass clarinet, alto, tenor and baritone saxophones, 1st and 2nd cornets, 1st and 2nd horns, 1st and 2nd trombones, euphonium, tuba, bass drum, snare drum, crash cymbals, triangle, and 2 timpani.

VARIATION III

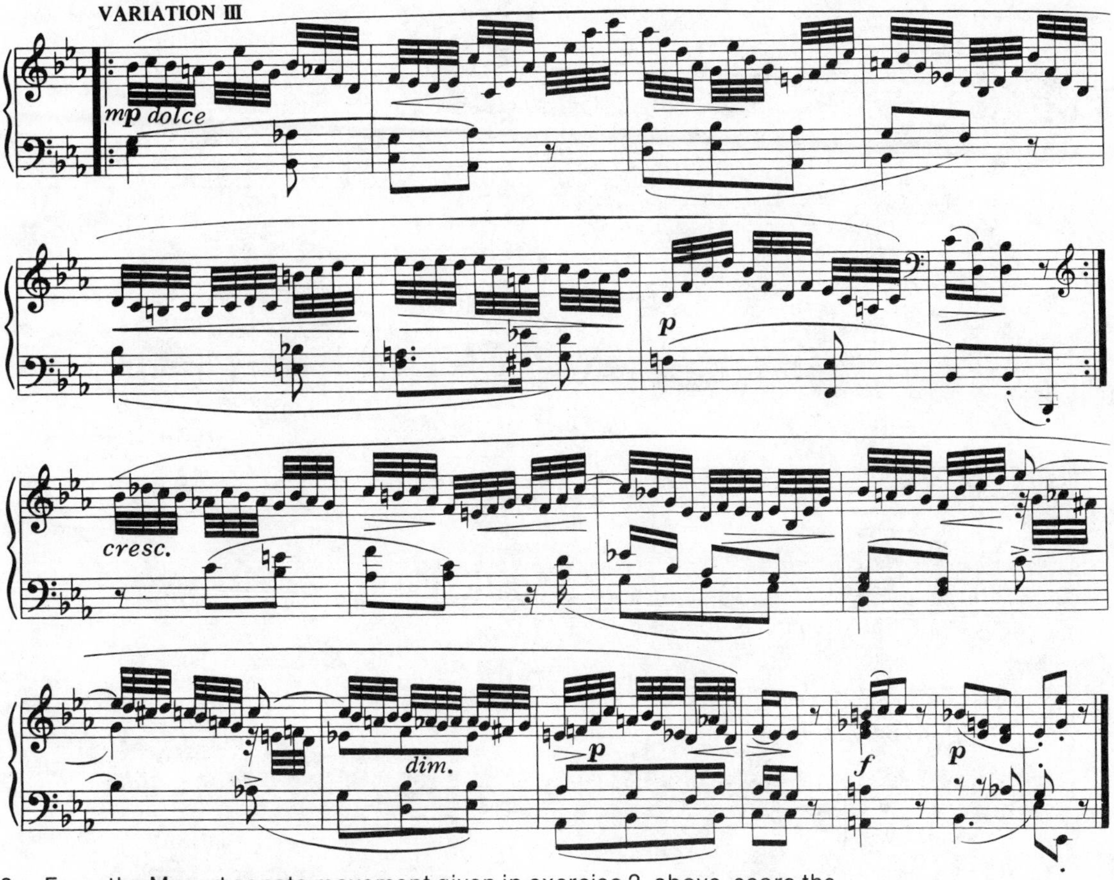

mp dolce

cresc.

dim.

3. From the Mozart sonata movement given in exercise 2, above, score the second and third variations for string quartet.

4. Score the following Scriabin Prelude for an orchestra, the instrumentation of which is your choice. Consider the use of extra woodwinds and percussion.

5. Score the following Mendelssohn "Song without Words" for a band, the instrumentation of which is your choice.

6. Select a folksong and prepare an arrangement of it for the instruments and voices available in class. Have it performed. (Limit your arrangement to about 32 measures.) Be sure to include an introduction and a coda derived from the melodic content of the folksong.

Appendixes

APPENDIX I

Transpositions of Instruments

Given a concert pitch, for example A, the correct notation for alto flute is given as P4 ↑, which means that the part is written a perfect fourth above the given pitch, thus: D. T = treble clef; B = bass clef; Tn = tenor clef.

Instrument	*Written*	*Clef*	*Instrument*	*Written*	*Clef*
Piccolo	8va ↓	T	B♭ soprano sax.	M2 ↑	T
Alto flute	P4 ↑	T	B♭ bass sax.	M16 ↑	T
Bass flute	8va ↑	T	E♭ sopranino sax.	m3 ↓	T
E♭ flute	m3 ↓	T	E♭ contrabass sax.	M20 ↑	T
English horn	P5 ↑	T	Horn in F	P5 ↑	T & B
Oboe d'amore	m3 ↑	T	B♭ Wagner tuba	M2 ↑	T
Baritone oboe	8va ↑	T	F Wagner tuba	P5 ↑	T & B
Heckelphone	8va ↑	T	B♭ trumpet	M2 ↑	T
B♭ clarinet	M2 ↑	T	D trumpet	M2 ↓	T
A clarinet	m3 ↑	T	E♭ trumpet	m3 ↓	T
B♭ bass clar.	M9 ↑	T	B♭ picc. tpt.	m7 ↓	T
E♭ alto clar.	M6 ↑	T	A picc. tpt.	M6 ↓	T
E♭ clarinet	m3 ↓	T	E♭ bass tpt.	M6 ↑	T
E♭ contra alto clar.	M13 ↑	T	B♭ bass tpt.	M9 ↑	T
B♭ contra bass clar.	M16 ↑	T	Euphonium (T.C.)	M9 ↑	T
Basset horn	P5 ↑	T	Orchestral bells	15ma ↓	T
A♭ sopranino clar.	m6 ↓	T	Crotales	15ma ↓	T
Contrabassoon	8va ↑	B & Tn	Celesta	8va ↓	T & B
E♭ alto sax.	M6 ↑	T	Xylophone	8va ↓	T & B
B♭ tenor sax.	M9 ↑	T	Guitar	8va ↑	T
E♭ baritone sax.	M13 ↑	T	Contrabass	8va ↑	B,Tn&T

APPENDIX II

Electronic Sound Modifications

Amplification

More correctly known as *sound reinforcement* or *sound enhancement,* the layman calls it *amplification.* This operation, the increasing in strength of a signal, is basic to the functioning of almost all other electronic devices. Amplification may be used to make a signal capable of being heard over an environment of noise or to allow an otherwise weak sound to balance normally loud sounds. Amplification allows the creation of audio balances not available in nature.

Filters

Low Pass Filters. These are electronic devices that allow lower frequencies to pass through them unaffected while higher frequencies are attenuated (made softer). The frequency above which attenuation takes place and the amount of attenuation are adjustable. These filters are sometimes called *band pass filters* since they allow a band of frequencies to pass through unaffected.

Notch Filters. These electronic devices allow only selected frequencies to pass through unaltered while other frequencies, above and below the selected frequency, are attenuated. The tuning and width of the unaffected frequencies are adjustable, as is the amount of attenuation. Used subtly, filters modify the sound. Used at more extreme settings, filters can provide a wide variety of distortions.

Flangers

These devices produce a very small time difference between one signal and another like or unlike signal. The time difference is usually less than one cycle and the effect is one of subtle timbral change. Greater time intervals, up to a second or more, can produce an echo or reverberation. Flangers are sometimes called *phase shifters.*

Frequency Dividers

These monitor the electronic signal and "count" the number of input pulses (cycles). They can be set to provide an output pulse for every so many input pulses. The typical ratio of input to output is 2 to 1, thus the frequency is divided in half. The signal from the frequency divider may be heard as a separate sound, an octave lower than the original, or it may be mixed together with the original to create a new sound.

Frequency Multipliers

These are the opposite of the frequency dividers. The electronic process is much more complex, but the result is simply a new signal that is at a higher frequency than the original. Addition of this signal to the original can produce new effects.

Fuzz Box

A *fuzz box* or *fuzz tone* changes the signal that is fed into it by exaggerating it and cutting off the extremes of the wave form. This resulting sound is added to the original to produce a distortion. Fuzz boxes are often used with rock guitar sounds.

Mixers

Two or more signals may be added together in a *mixer.* Mixers intended simply to make two separate sounds seem to exist together add the sounds without changing them. However, special effects can be obtained if the mixer causes the two sounds to affect each other. This commonly results in the production of summation and difference tones. One can even suppress the original tones, leaving, as a final output, only the distorted sounds. This latter effect is characteristic of a ring modulator.

Modification and Distortion

When an electrical signal is fed through an electronic device, the produced signal may or may not be an accurate reproduction of the original. If the original is greatly altered by any electronic device, especially in a way that causes some elements of the sound to be changed more than others, it is said to be *distorted.* Distortion may be used to create totally new sounds.

If the distortion is less pronounced, especially if it manages to alter an imperfect sound in a way that makes the result more ideal (such as replacing a missing bass component), it is referred to as *modification.*

Transducers

These are devices for converting acoustical energy to electrical energy. The most common of these are microphones. There are two types of microphones in common use: *contact microphones* and *air microphones.* The former do not pick up vibrations from the surrounding air but only from direct contact with the vibrating surface. The latter pick up vibrations from the air (or other fluid) surrounding them.

APPENDIX III

String Fingerings

The strings on a string instrument are stretched between the nut and the bridge. Given a certain length, tension, and diameter, a string will produce only one pitch. To produce other pitches, the performer must shorten the vibrating length of the string by pressing the string between his finger and the fingerboard. This is called *stopping the string.* The stopping process allows the performer to raise the pitch of the string.

Modern fingering techniques utilize all of the fingers on the left hand. The fingers are numbered in order from one to four with the index finger being designated number one. (On the violoncello and contrabass, the thumb is also used for higher pitches.)

The basic left-hand position for all string instruments is called *first position.* In this position the performer's hand is placed close to the nut so that the pitch immediately above the pitch of the open string can be produced by simply pressing down with his first finger. In this position, the performer can not only produce the first pitch above the open string, but a series of ascending pitches the highest of which is produced by the fourth finger.

The longer the string, the further apart are the semitones, and thus, the smaller the interval that the hand can span. Because of this, a violinist usually spans a fourth between first and fourth finger pitches, but a contrabassist can only span a second. The following offers a direct comparison:

Violin
Viola
Violoncello
Contrabass
Used with 4th finger for strength
In first position: open string | first finger | second finger | third finger | fourth finger

To obtain other pitches on the same string, the performer shifts his hand toward the bridge into another, higher position. When placed in a position so that the first finger plays the pitches formerly played by the second finger, the hand is said to be in *second position.* Another shift in the same direction, which places the first finger in position to play those pitches played by the third finger when the hand was in first position, will place the hand in *third position.* The pattern continues through as many as thirteen identifiable positions. Violin positions show these relationships:

open string	first finger	second finger	third finger	fourth finger			
2nd position		first finger	second finger	third finger	fourth finger		
3rd position			first finger	second finger	third finger	fourth finger	
4th position				first finger	second finger	third finger	fourth finger

Extensions

It is possible to extend the fourth finger toward the bridge without shifting the position of the hand, enabling the performer to play higher pitches in the same position. As the hand approaches the bridge, the physical locations of successively higher pitches are closer together. This makes it possible for a violinist to extend as much as an additional fourth or fifth.

Half Positions

Half positions can be identified between the positions described above. These are seldom discussed or needed on the violin, but become rather important in contrabass and violoncello technique. Other names are at times used to identify these positions, but this book will use the following: The position between first and second is called 1½; between second and third, 2½; etc. Because of its larger size, the viola uses more half positions and extensions than the violin, but less than the low strings.

Thumb Positions

In higher positions on the violoncello and contrabass, it is necessary for the performer to bring his thumb from behind the neck to on top of the fingerboard. This shift usually occurs above the seventh position. In these thumb positions, the performer's fourth finger almost ceases to be used for stopping the strings since the distance from the thumb to the third finger offers the greatest span. In fact, the thumb to third finger distance is greater than the first to fourth finger span used in the lower positions.

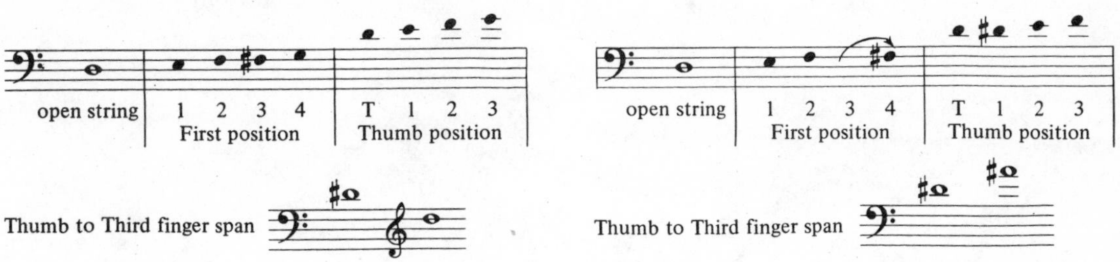

Shifting between thumb position notes and notes in the lower positions requires some time, but it is not always necessary. Violoncellists and contrabassists have developed the technique of reaching "back" up the neck with the thumb for lower pitches and thus avoiding shifts between thumb position and non-thumb position notes.

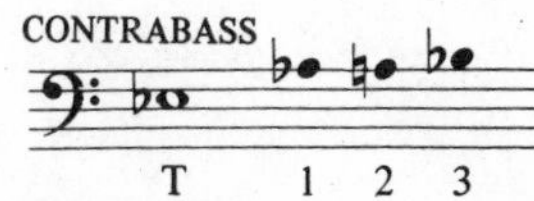

Natural Harmonics

Partial Number	*Pitch Obtained Relative to Opened String*	*Location Touched Relative to Opened String*
2	octave higher	octave above
3	12th higher	fifth above
4	15th (2 octaves)	fourth above
5	17th higher	major third above
6	19th higher	minor third above
7	flat 21st higher	flat minor third above*
8	22nd (3 octaves)	major second above*

*approximate locations

Fingering Charts

The following fingering charts show for each instrument the fingerboard and a typical hand span plus extension in correct proportion. The location of each of the basic hand positions is shown, and the nodes for natural harmonics (2nd through 8th partials) are shown with diamonds and labeled with the number of the partial.

To check the playability of multiple stops and broken chords, simply be sure that all pitches lie within one hand span or its extension.

In setting up the chart, enharmonic equivalents were assumed, so a B♭ will be played by the same finger as an A♯ or by the next finger, depending upon the passage, but will be at the same point on the string as the A♯.

Violin Fingerings

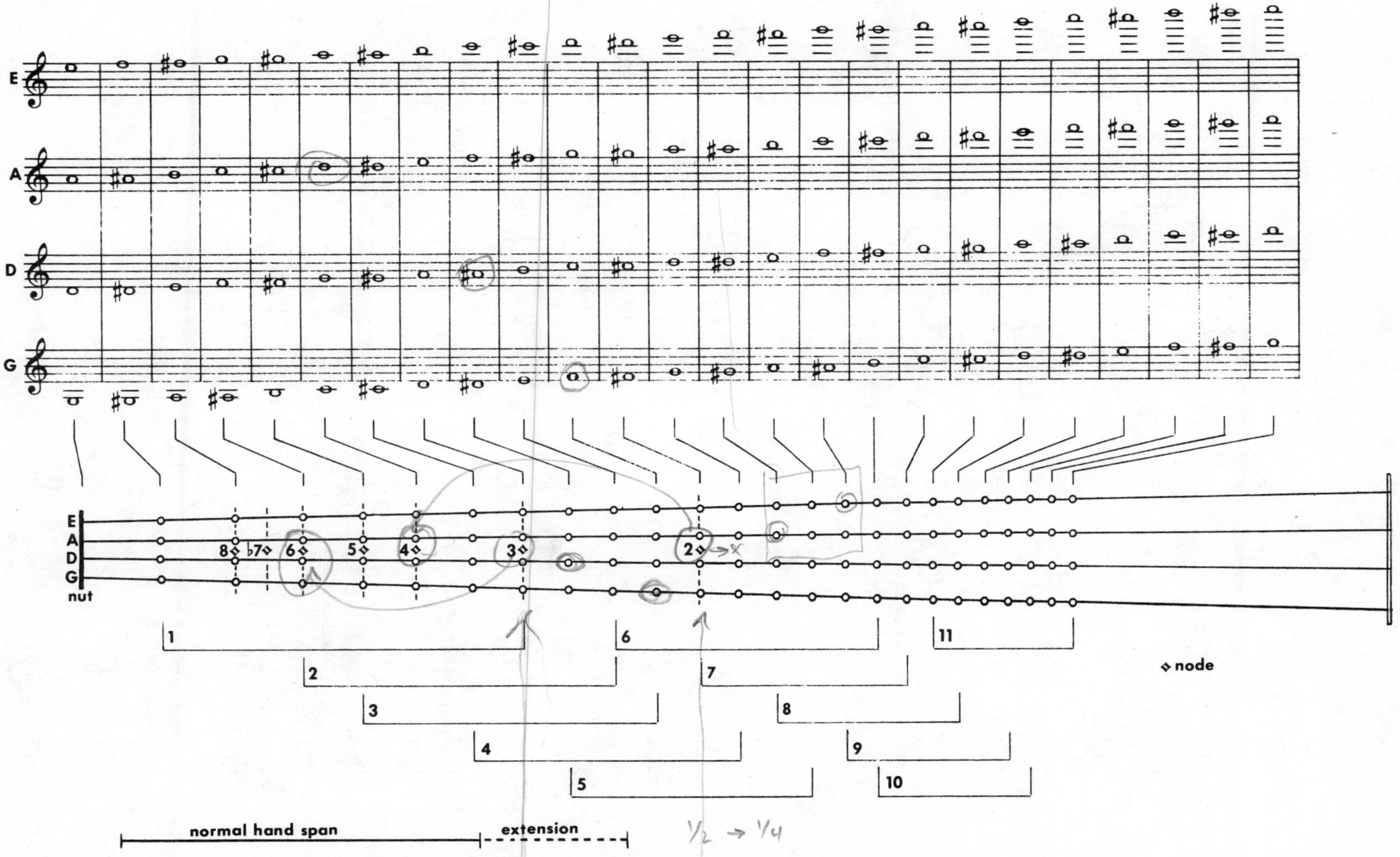

Viola Fingerings

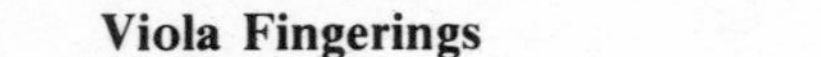

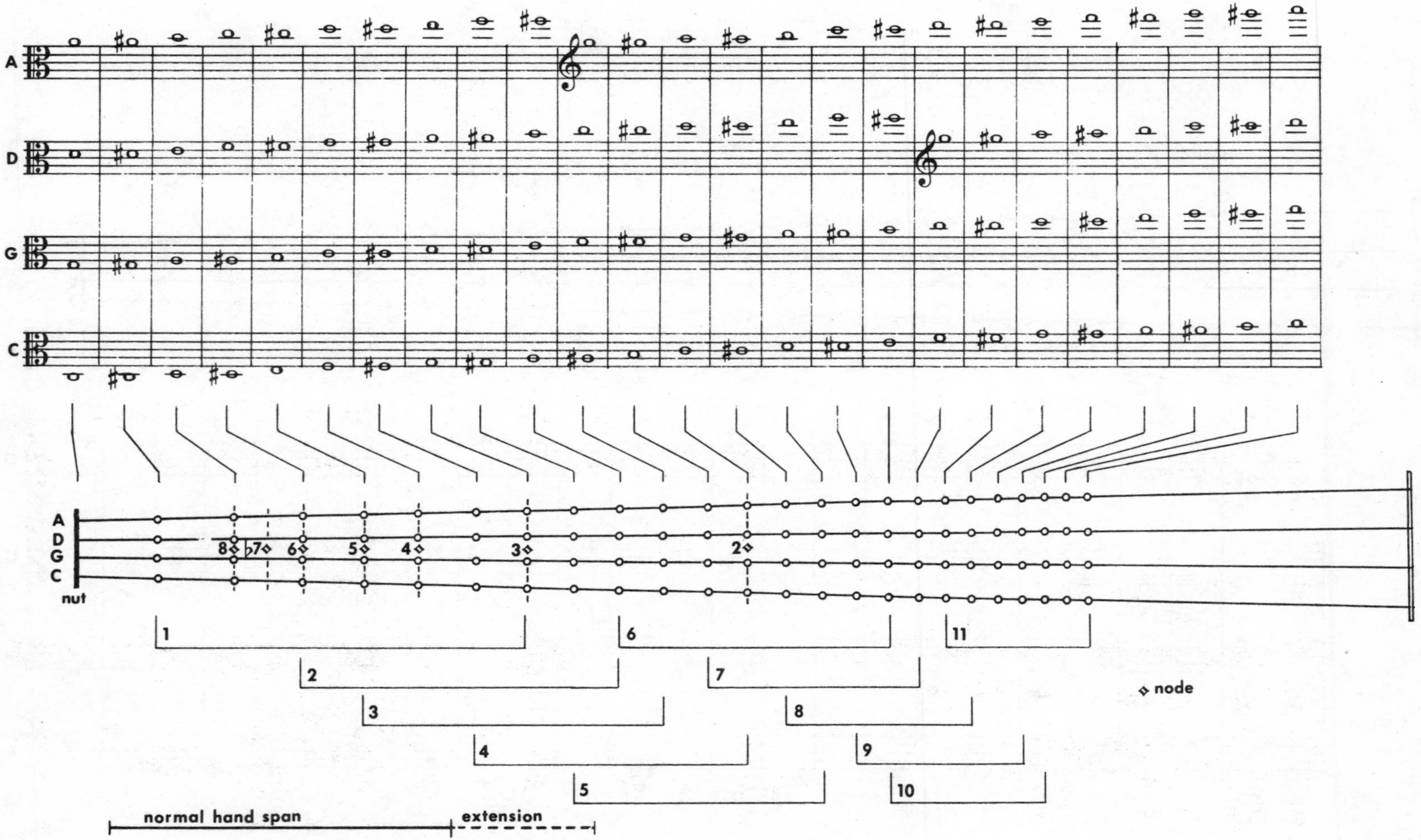

Violoncello Fingerings

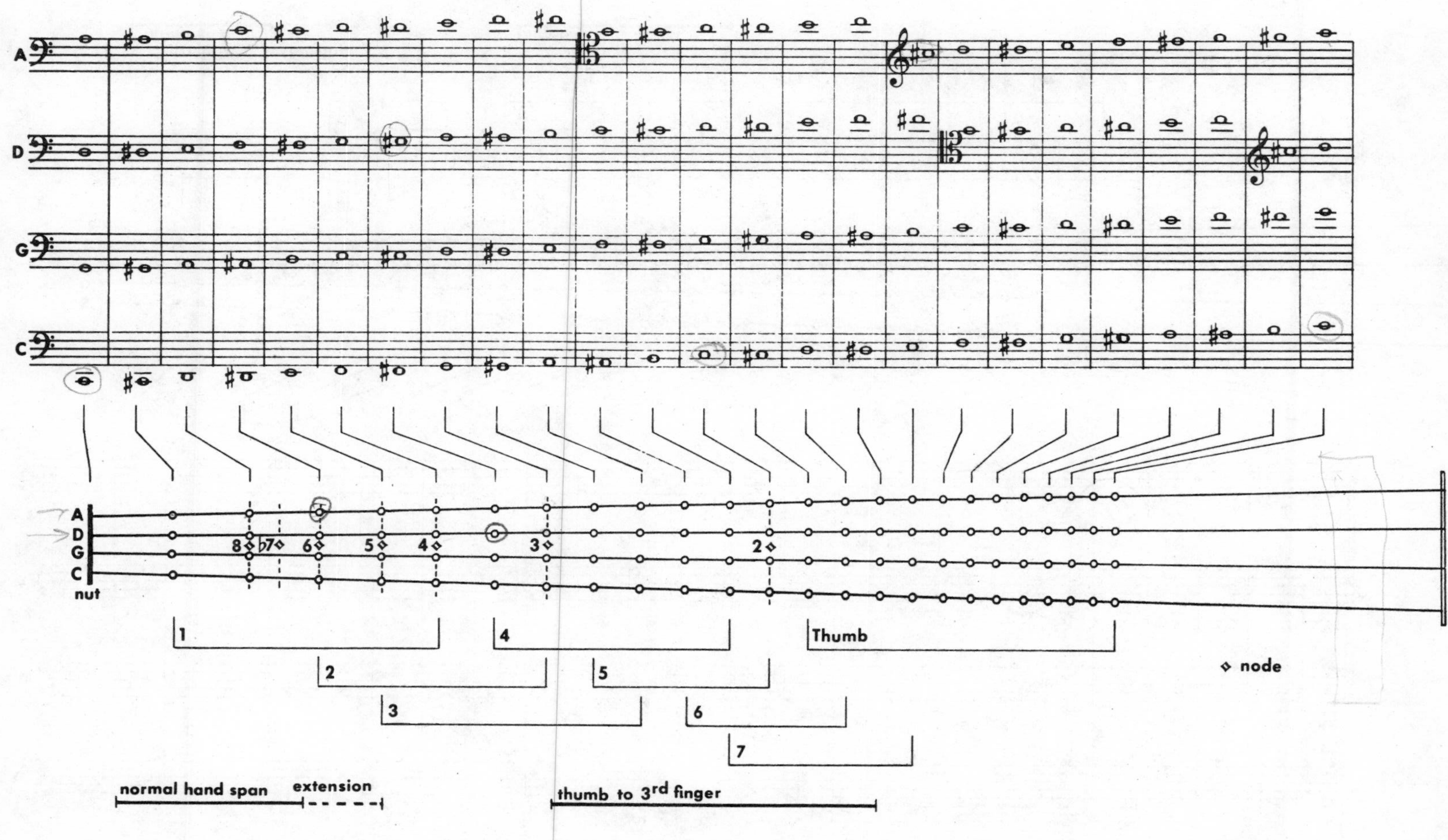

Contrabass Fingerings

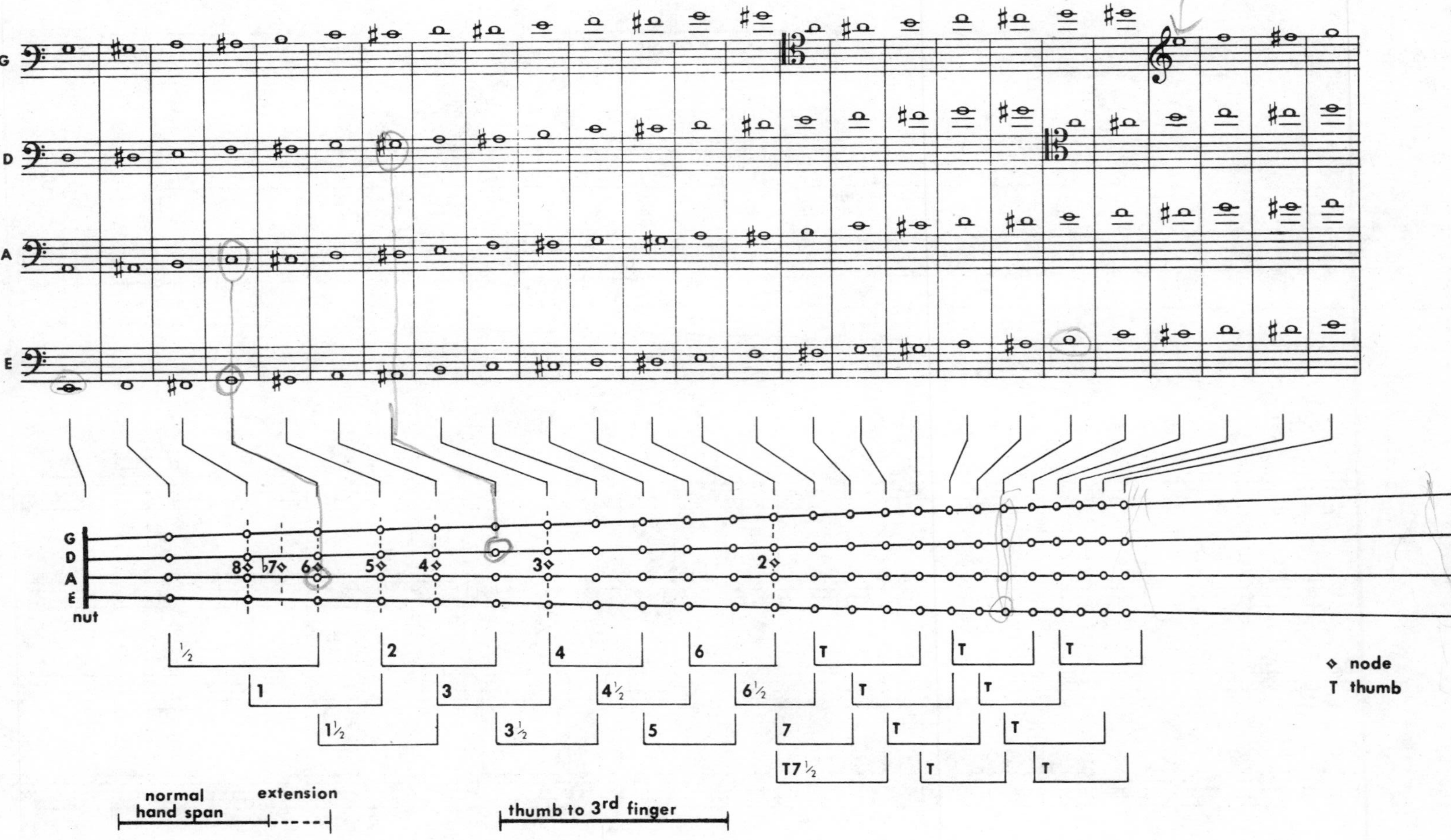

APPENDIX IV

Woodwind Fingerings

All woodwinds change pitch by utilizing the principle that the shorter the tube of vibrating air, the higher the pitch. All woodwinds consist of a tube into which holes have been drilled and which may be covered or uncovered by the performer.

The system works like this: If all holes are covered, the total length of the tube is used:

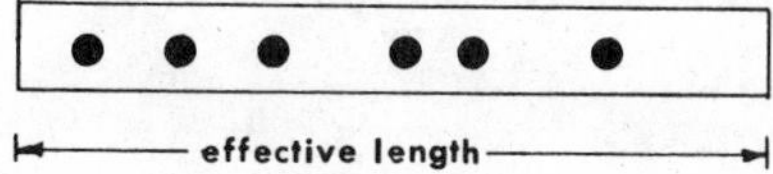

If the lowest hole is uncovered, the effective length of the pipe has been shortened:

As successive holes are uncovered, successively higher pitches are produced.

Simple instruments having 6 to 8 holes to be covered by the fingers are capable of performing diatonic scales. If an instrument has at least 7 properly spaced holes, a two-octave diatonic scale is producible.

The first octave is obtained this way:

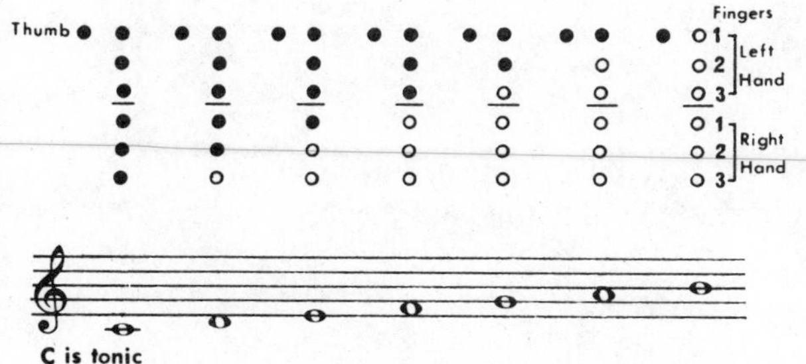

The second octave uses the principle of creating an overblown pipe or tube by the use of half-holing. To do this the performer will half uncover a hole, usually the thumb hole, which enables him to overblow the instrument, thus obtaining an octave above the fingered pitch:

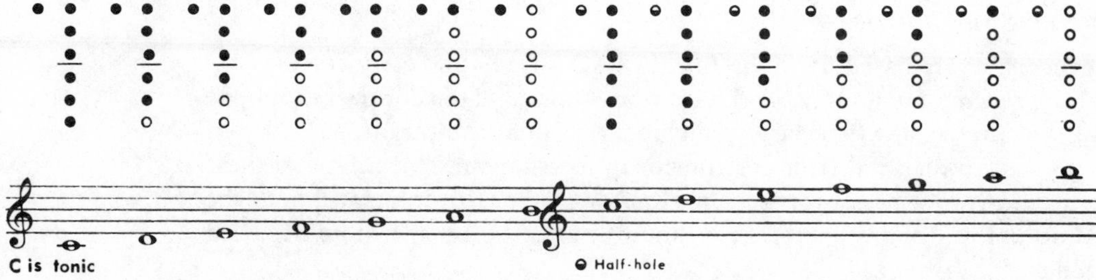

The second octave lacks the upper tonic, but uncovering the thumb should provide this note:

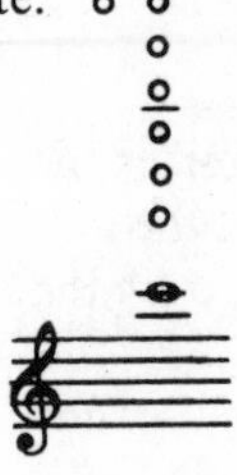

Three methods are used to obtain chromatic pitches. Half-holing can be used, as in this scale from tonic to dominant:

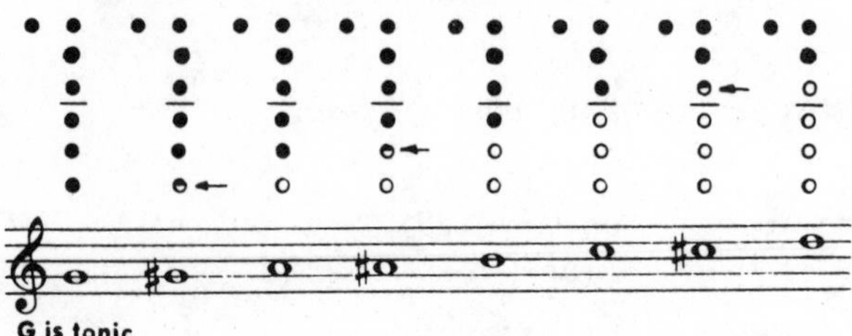

A second method, the use of forked fingerings, works this way: If one is fingering a pitch such as the dominant 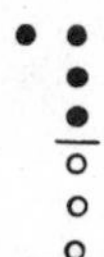 and adds the next lower finger, it is clear that one obtains the subdominant:

If one skips a finger, leaving the hole below the last covered hole open, but covering the hole below that, one has produced a fork in the fingering and the pitch will be the flatted dominant:

The third method calls for the drilling of extra holes at exactly the correct locations along the tube to produce chromatic pitches. Since these holes increase the total number of holes to more than the number of fingers available, this system requires additional mechanical devices to facilitate the operation.

The Fingering Charts

These charts are based upon the Boehm system flutes and clarinets, the conservatory system oboes, the Heckel system bassoons, and the normal saxophone keying system. In using the charts, remember that there are variations from performer to performer and from instrument to instrument. Thus, some of these fingerings will work better for some persons and other fingerings will not. The charts do not reflect any special keys that may exist on some custom-designed instruments.

Flute Fingerings

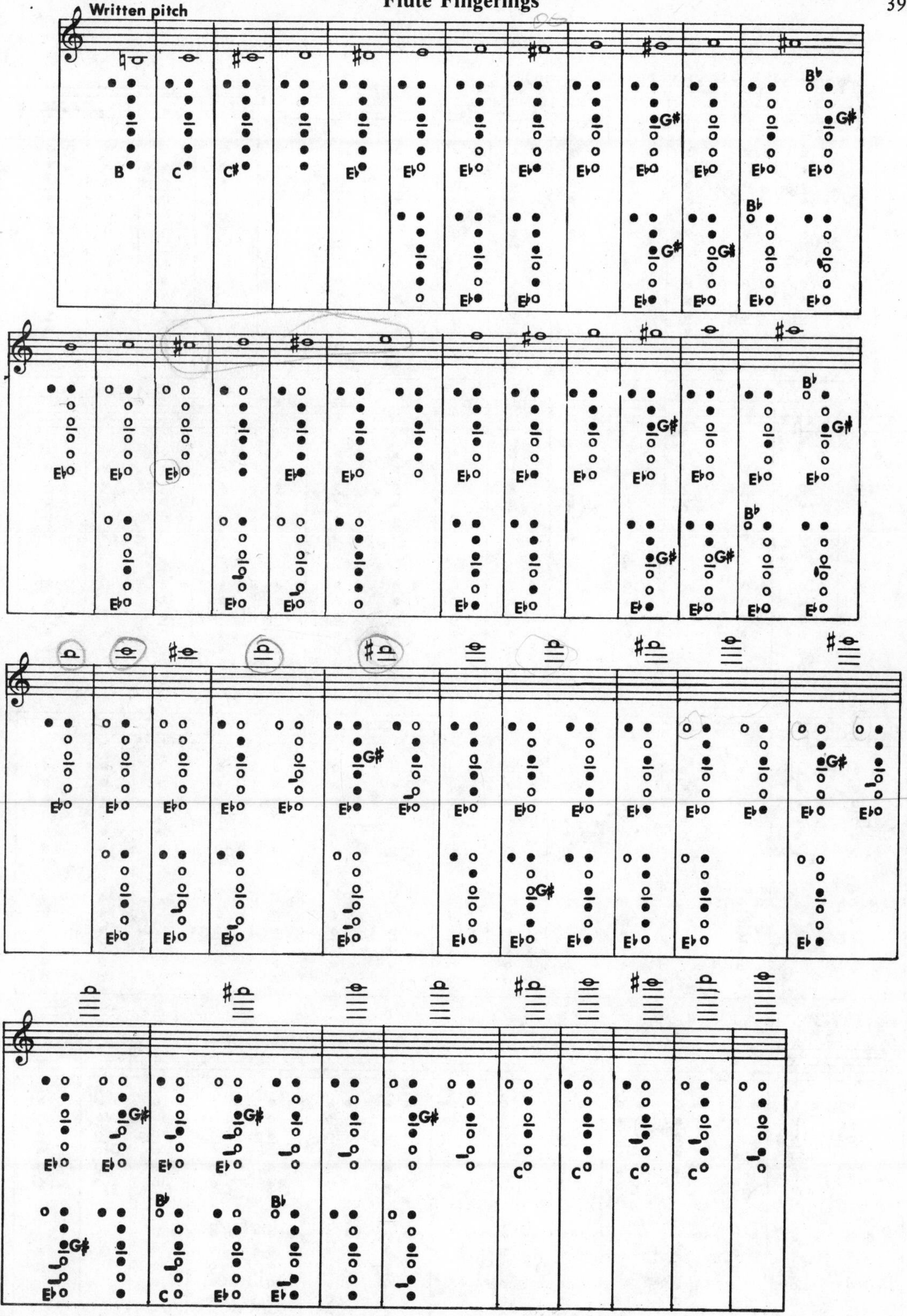

Written pitch

B C C♯ E♭ E♭ E♭ E♭ E♭ E♭ G♯ E♭ E♭ B♭ G♯ E♭

E♭ E♭ G♯ E♭ G♯ E♭ B♭ E♭ E♭

E♭ E♭ E♭ E♭ E♭ E♭ E♭ E♭ E♭ G♯ E♭ E♭ B♭ G♯ E♭

E♭ E♭ E♭ E♭ E♭ E♭ G♯ E♭ G♯ E♭ B♭ E♭ E♭

E♭ E♭ E♭ E♭ E♭ G♯ E♭ E♭ E♭ E♭ E♭ E♭ E♭ E♭ E♭ G♯ E♭ E♭

E♭ E♭ E♭ E♭ E♭ G♯ E♭ E♭ E♭ E♭ E♭ E♭

E♭ G♯ E♭ E♭ G♯ E♭ G♯ C C C C

G♯ E♭ B♭ C E♭ B♭ E♭

● Covered or depressed   ○ Uncovered or not depressed

Oboe Fingerings

Written pitch (*denotes harmonic fingering)

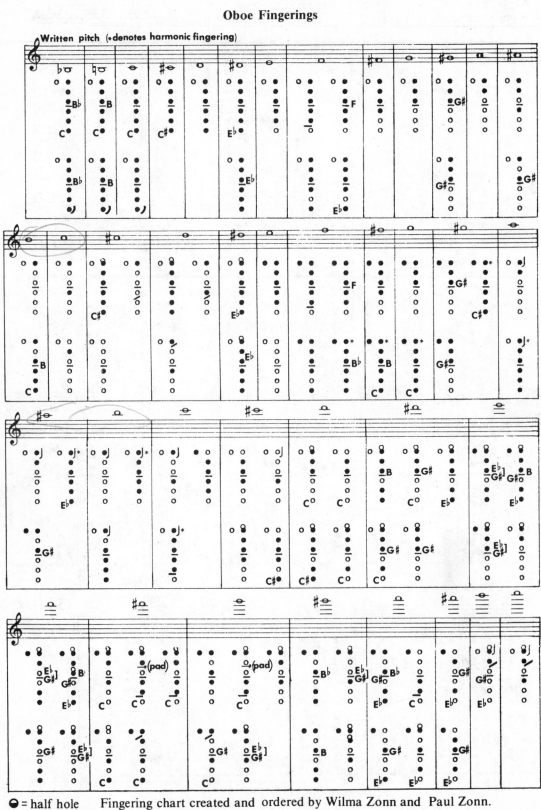

● = half hole   Fingering chart created and ordered by Wilma Zonn and Paul Zonn. Used by permission.

Clarinet Fingerings

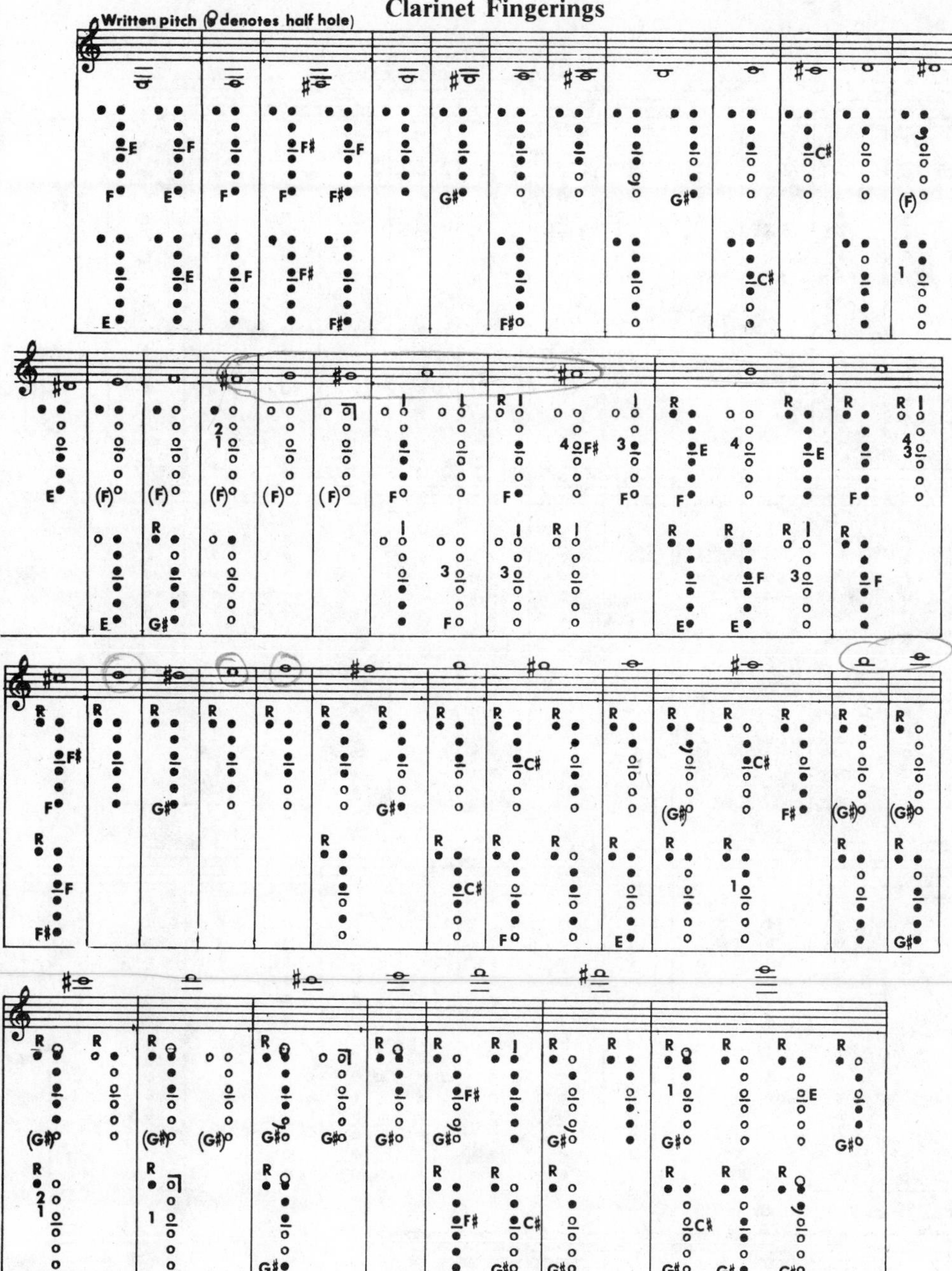

Sidekeys numbered from the bottom up
R = Register Key Depressed
◒ = Half hole

Fingering chart created and ordered by Paul Zonn. Used by permission.

Bassoon Fingerings

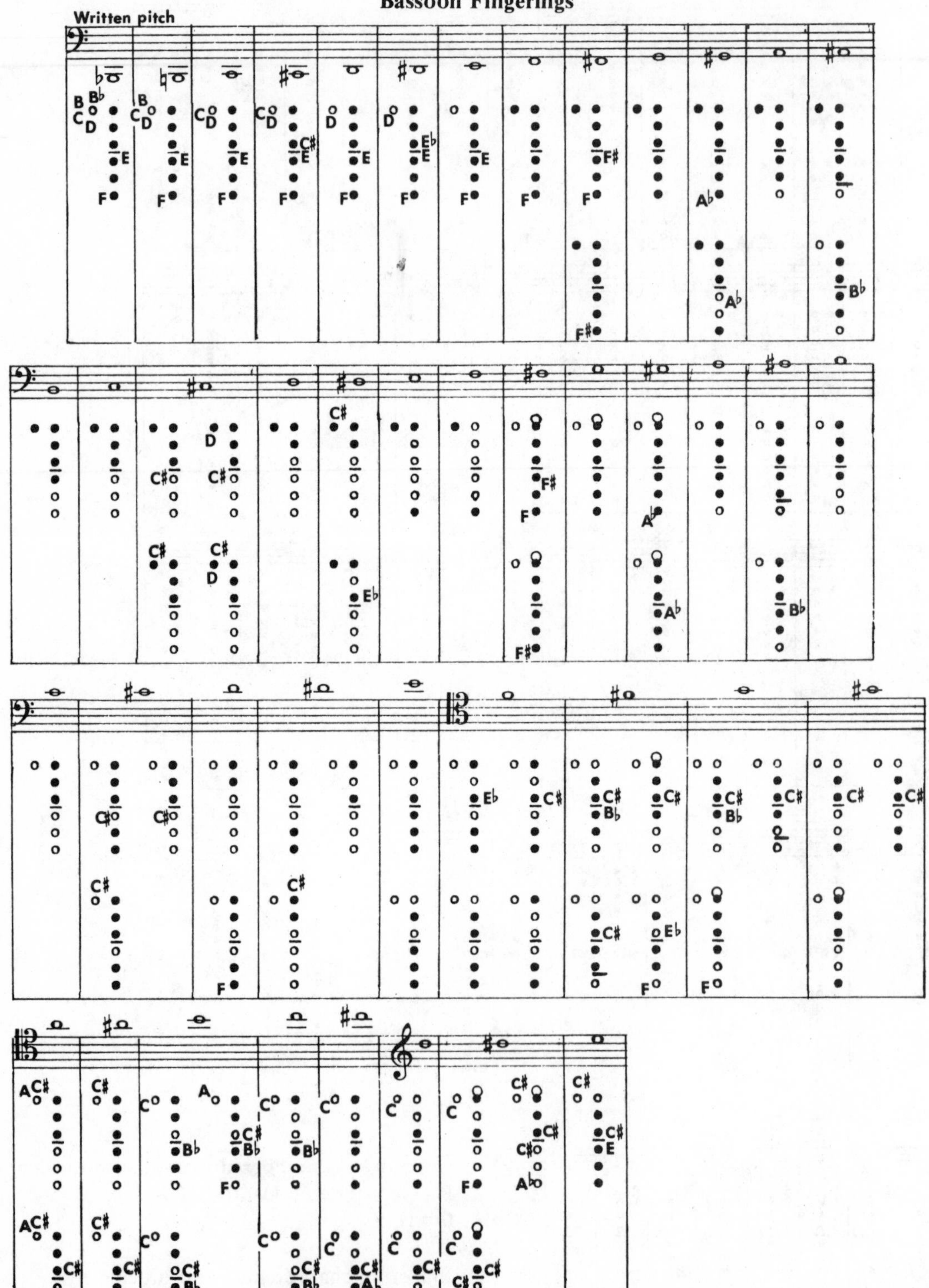

◓ = half hole

Saxophone Fingerings

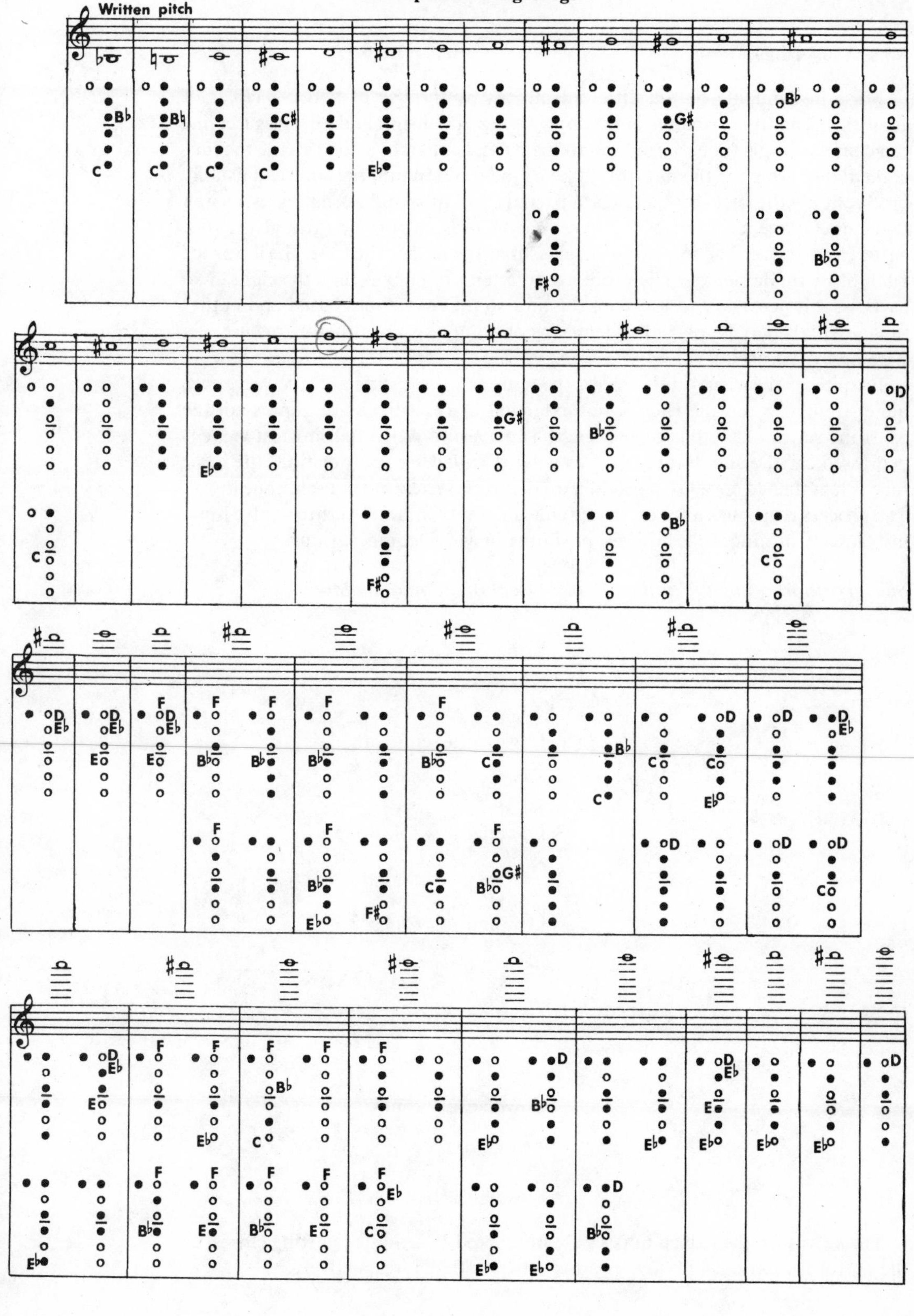

Written pitch

B♭ C B♮ C C C C♯ C E♭ G♯ B♭ B♭ F♯

C E♭ G♯ B♭ B♭ F♯ C D

D E♭ D E♭ F D E♭ F F F B♭ B♭ B♭ F B♭ C B♭ C C C E♭ D D D E♭ F F F B♭ E♭ F♯ C B♭ G♯ D D D D C

D E♭ F F F B♭ F F E♭ E♭ C E♭ B♭ D E♭ E♭ D E♭ E E♭ E♭ E♭ D

D E♭ F F F F F E♭ E♭ B♭ E E E♭ B♭ E C E♭ E♭ D B♭

APPENDIX V

Brass Fingerings

Brass instruments obtain different pitches by the use of two principles of acoustics. The first principle is that by varying lip tension and air pressure, one can cause a simple tube to produce all the partials of an overtone series, the fundamental of which is the natural sound of the tube. In practice, one can usually produce only the first through eighth partials, but tuba and horn players, as well as trumpet players who specialize in very high notes, can obtain through the 16th partial and above. The second principle is that the longer the tube, the lower the pitch of its fundamental. Therefore, to obtain more pitches than the eight or so partials, it is necessary to lengthen the tube so that overtones based upon other fundamentals may be played. The means of doing this are either by the use of a slide or by the use of valves.

In spite of the visual differences, the actions of the slide and the valves are quite similar. When the slide is not extended or the valves not depressed, the overtone series of the basic pipe length is playable. When the shortest valve is depressed, or the slide moved out to what is called second position, the basic tube is lengthened enough to produce an overtone series that is a semitone lower. The process continues and, on the standard tenor trombone or three-valve brass instrument, produces these seven positions or valve combinations:

Slide Position	*Valve Combination*	*Effect on Fundamental*
I	○ ○ ○	None
II	○ ● ○	Lowered a semi-tone
III	● ○ ○	Lowered a whole tone
IV	● ● ○ or ○ ○ ●	Lowered 1½ tones
V	○ ● ●	Lowered 2 tones
VI	● ○ ●	Lowered 2½ tones
VII	● ● ●	Lowered a tri-tone

The valves on the valved brasses are numbered 1, 2, and 3 (starting closest to the performer) and each valve produces these effects, respectively:

1st valve lowers the pitch a whole tone
2nd valve lowers the pitch a semitone
3rd valve lowers the pitch 1½ tones

Depressing two or more valves adds together the effects of each, producing a pitch lowering that is the sum of the depressed valves.

To increase range, flexibility, and ease of control, some brasses are built with more than three valves. Some trombones are constructed with one or two extra valves (triggers) that can be brought into play. These valves are useful but create an intonation or technical problem for the performer. This is most clearly seen on the trombone with an F attachment.

The longer the basic tube, the more tubing that one must add to lower the pitch a semitone. The F attachment adds enough tubing to lower the fundamental of the tenor trombone in first position a perfect fourth. But, when the slide is moved out to lower this new fundamental a semitone, it is found that second position is further from first position than before. In fact the use of the F attachment moves each position further out the slide and, since the slide is of a fixed length, eliminates seventh position altogether.

On valved brasses, the same acoustical properties exist when a fourth valve is brought into play, but there is no slide to compensate for the error and the pitch merely becomes too sharp to use. There are mechanisms produced to offset this problem, but, unless the instrument is equipped with one, a few of the lowest pitches which use almost all of the valves together will be useless.

A study of the overtone series of a pipe (see Appendix VI) will reveal that some of the partials, most notably the seventh, are flat. The difference between the tuning of the seventh partial and the equivalent pitch used in our Western European tuning system is enough to make it unusable—except for special effects—on all brasses but the trombones.

Because of the slide on the trombone, the seventh partial can be used in second through seventh positions by merely not putting the slide out as far as normal. When this is done, the slide is said to be in a sharp position, like #II or #V.

Brass Fingering Charts

The following charts are notated at written pitch. For the trombones, euphoniums, and tubas this is, of course, also concert pitch. The horn chart shows fingerings for the double horn in F. The upper set of fingerings, without the thumb valve depressed, are the single F horn fingerings (which has no thumb valve), while the lower set with the thumb valve depressed are also the fingerings for the single B♭ horn reading F horn parts. Of course, there is no thumb valve on the single B♭ horn. If no fingering is given, the written note is unplayable.

The fingering chart for the other valved brasses is divided into 3-valve combinations (upper set), which are available on all instruments; and 4-valve combinations (middle set) and 5-valve combinations, which are available only on some instruments.

The trombone position chart shows the slide positions available on an alto, single tenor, and contrabass trombone in the upper set; positions when the F attachment is in use in the middle set (remember there are only six positions); and positions when the E attachment is in use (again, only six positions).

Horn Fingerings

Horn in F Written Pitches

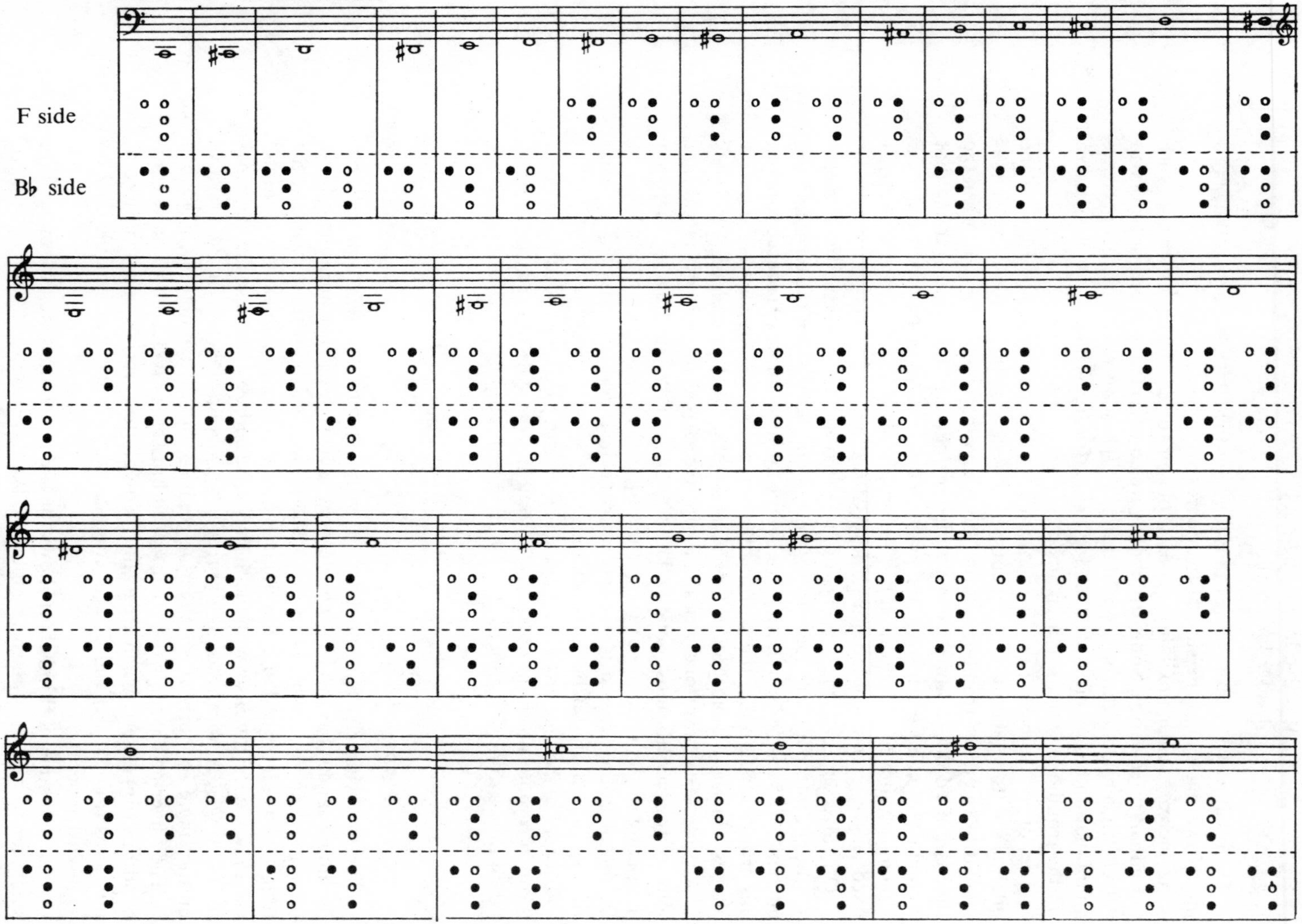

F side

B♭ side

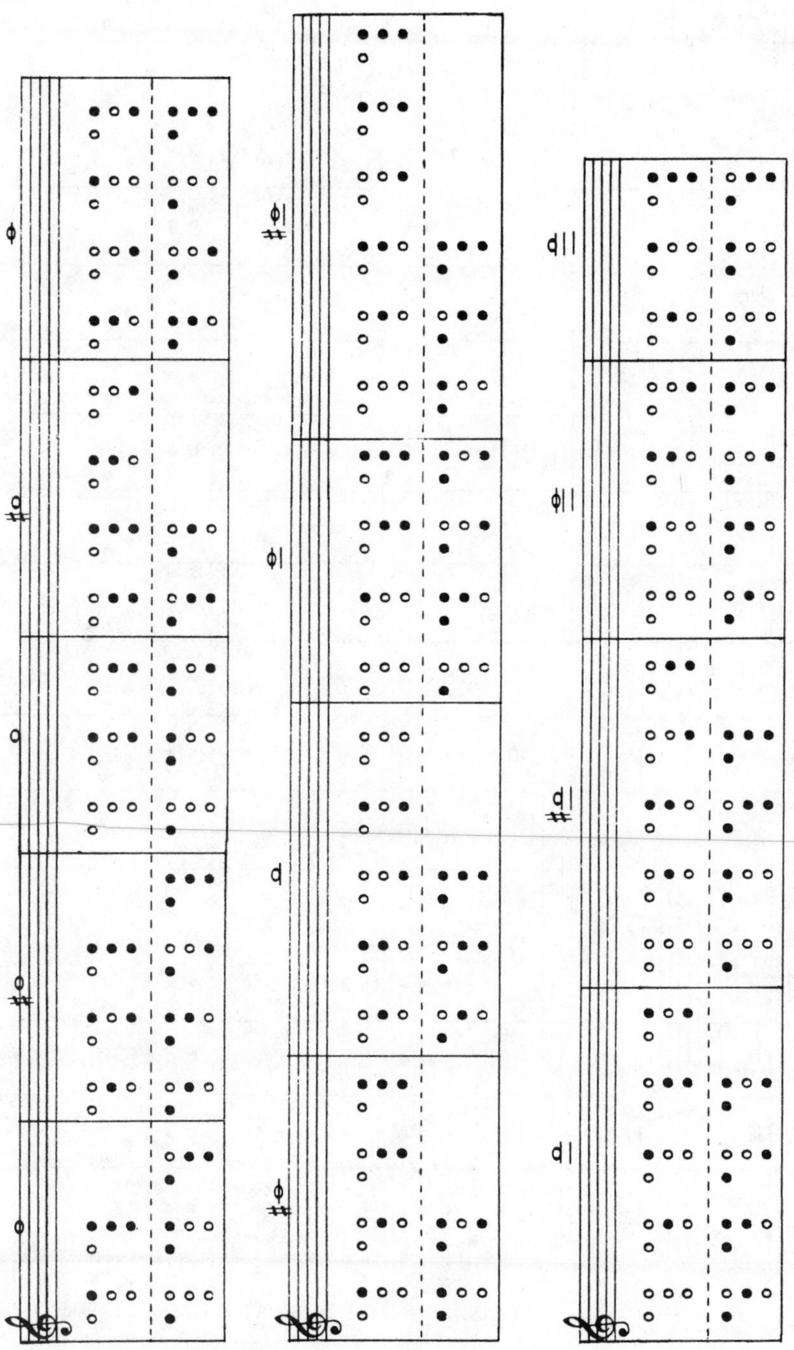

All Other Valved Brasses

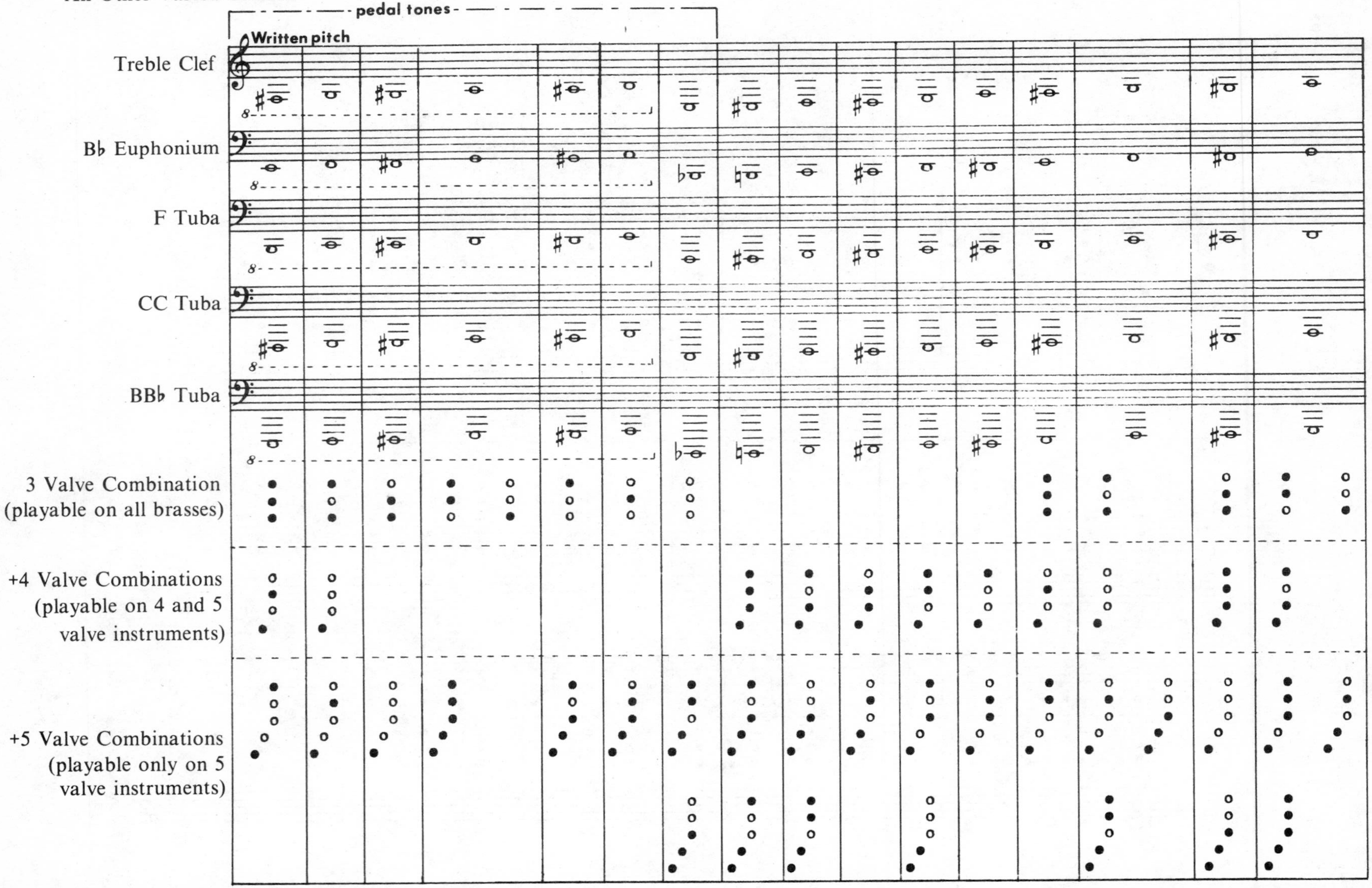

pedal tones

Written pitch

Treble Clef

B♭ Euphonium

F Tuba

CC Tuba

BB♭ Tuba

3 Valve Combination (playable on all brasses)

+4 Valve Combinations (playable on 4 and 5 valve instruments)

+5 Valve Combinations (playable only on 5 valve instruments)

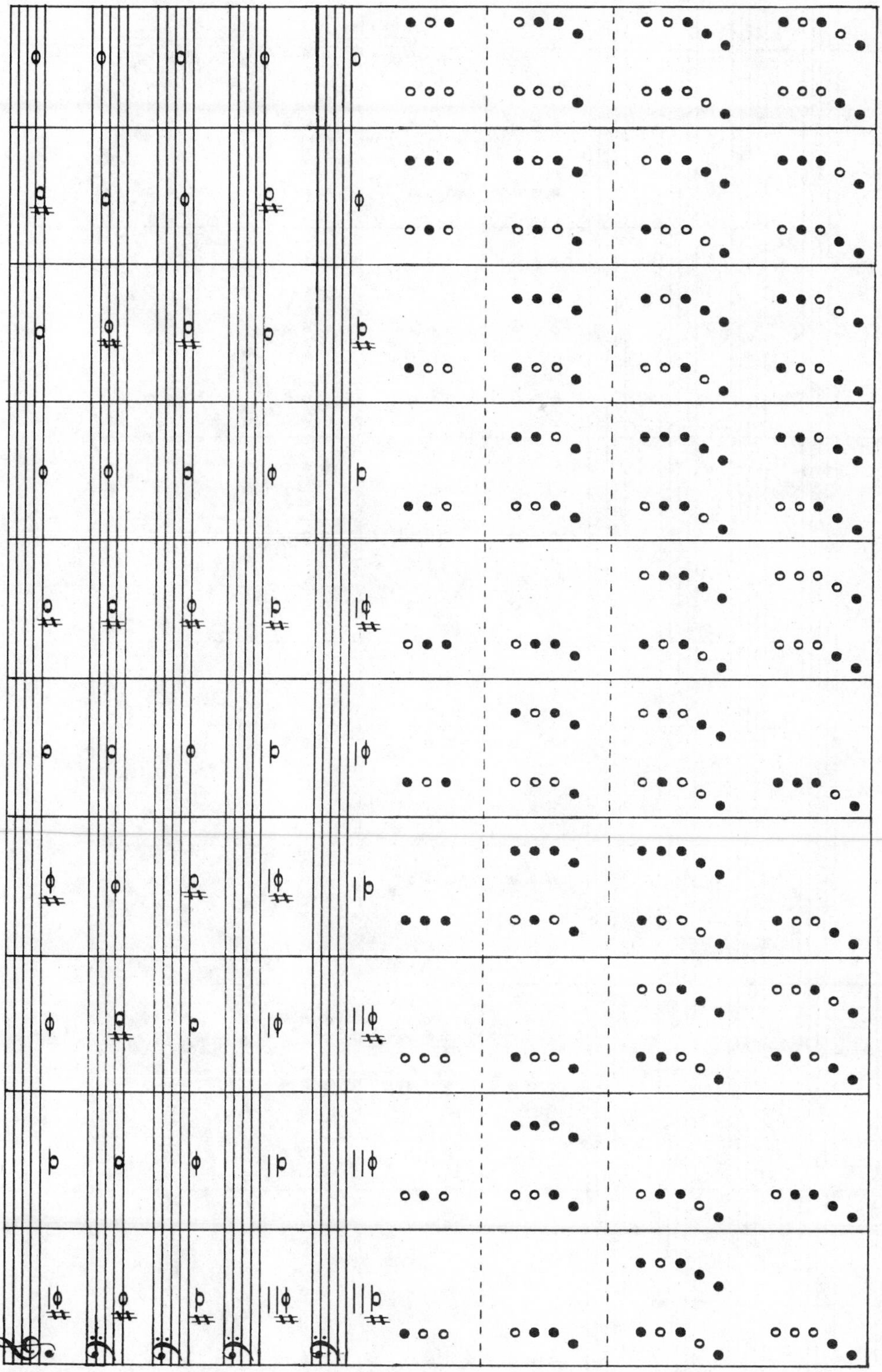

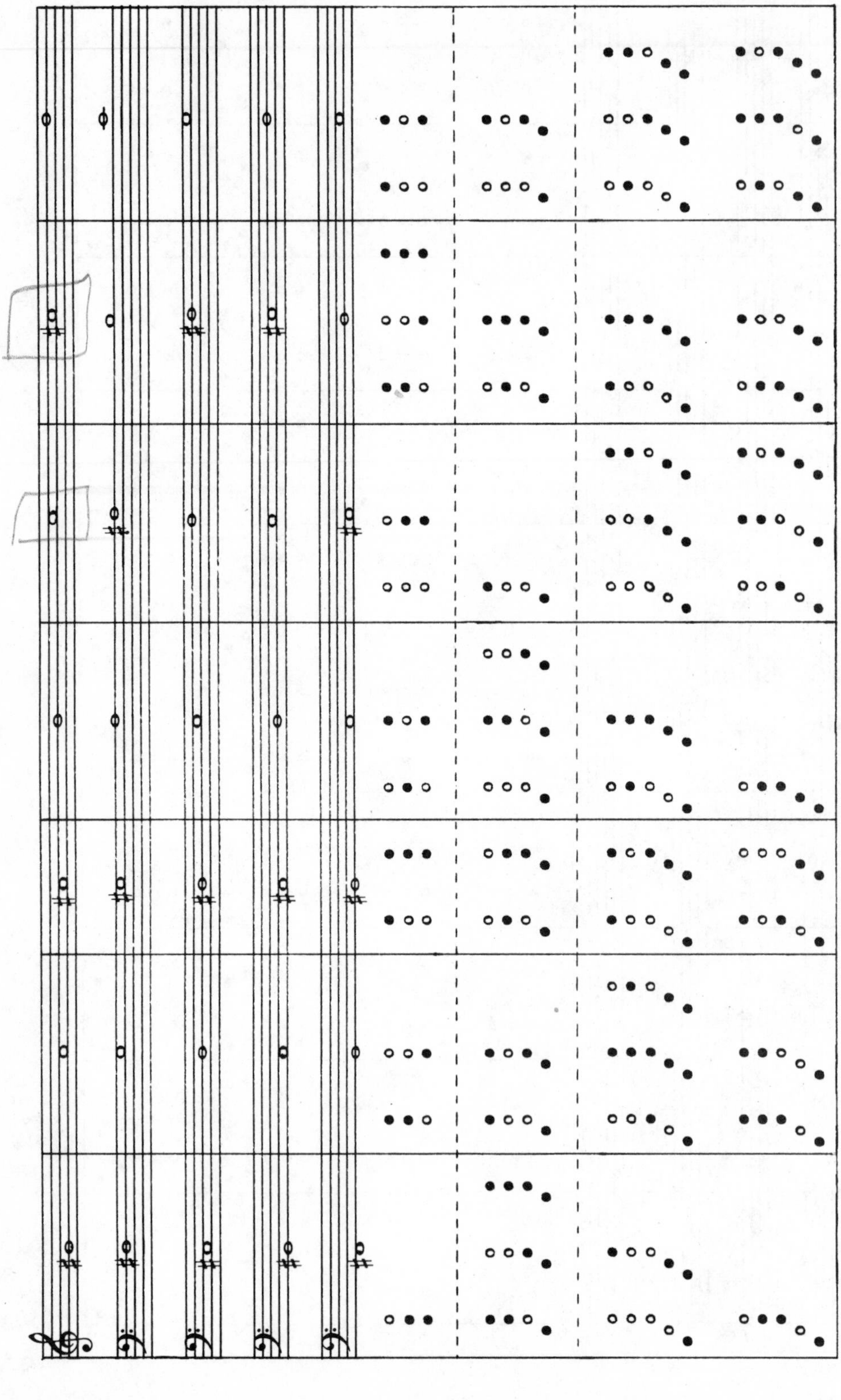

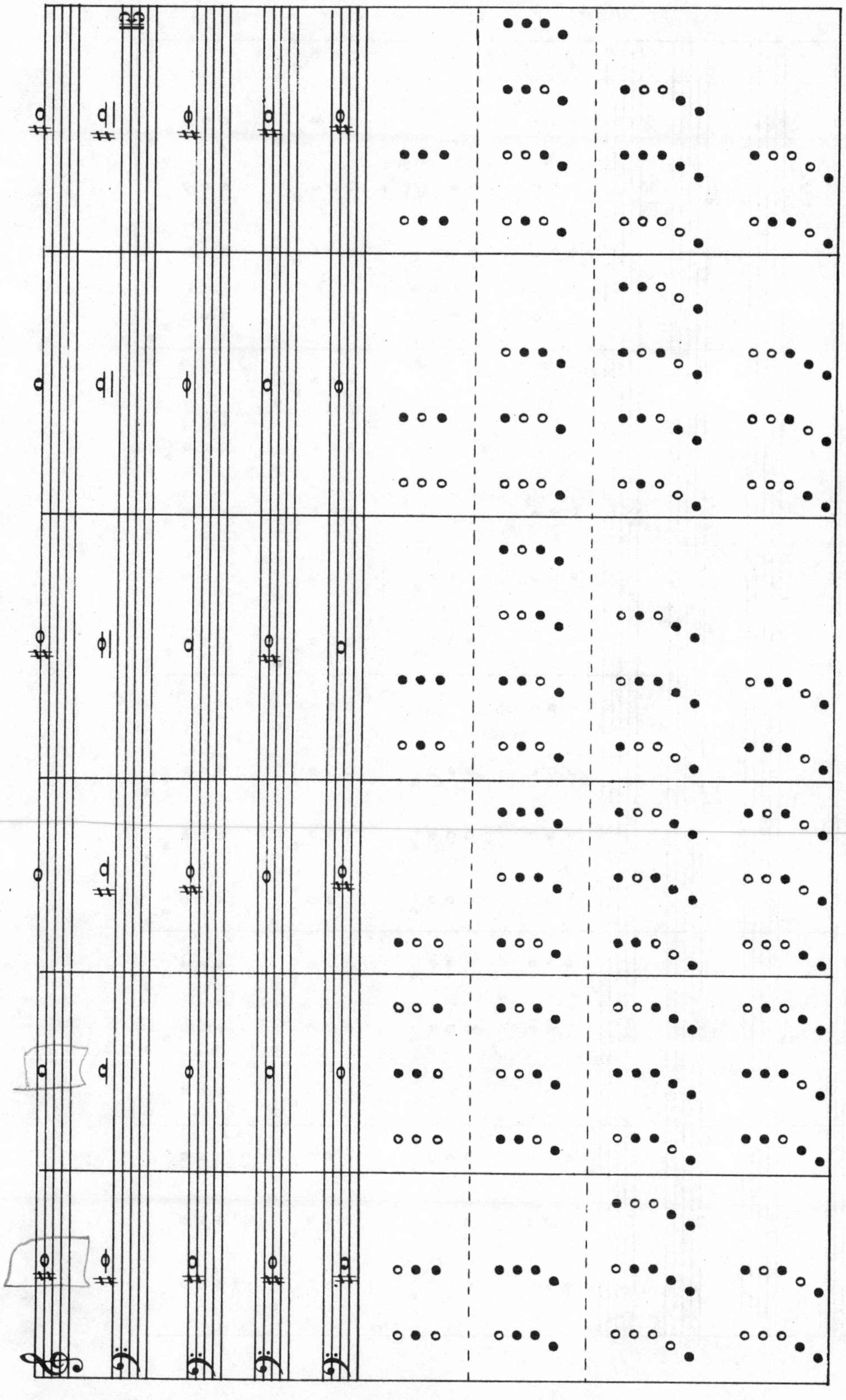

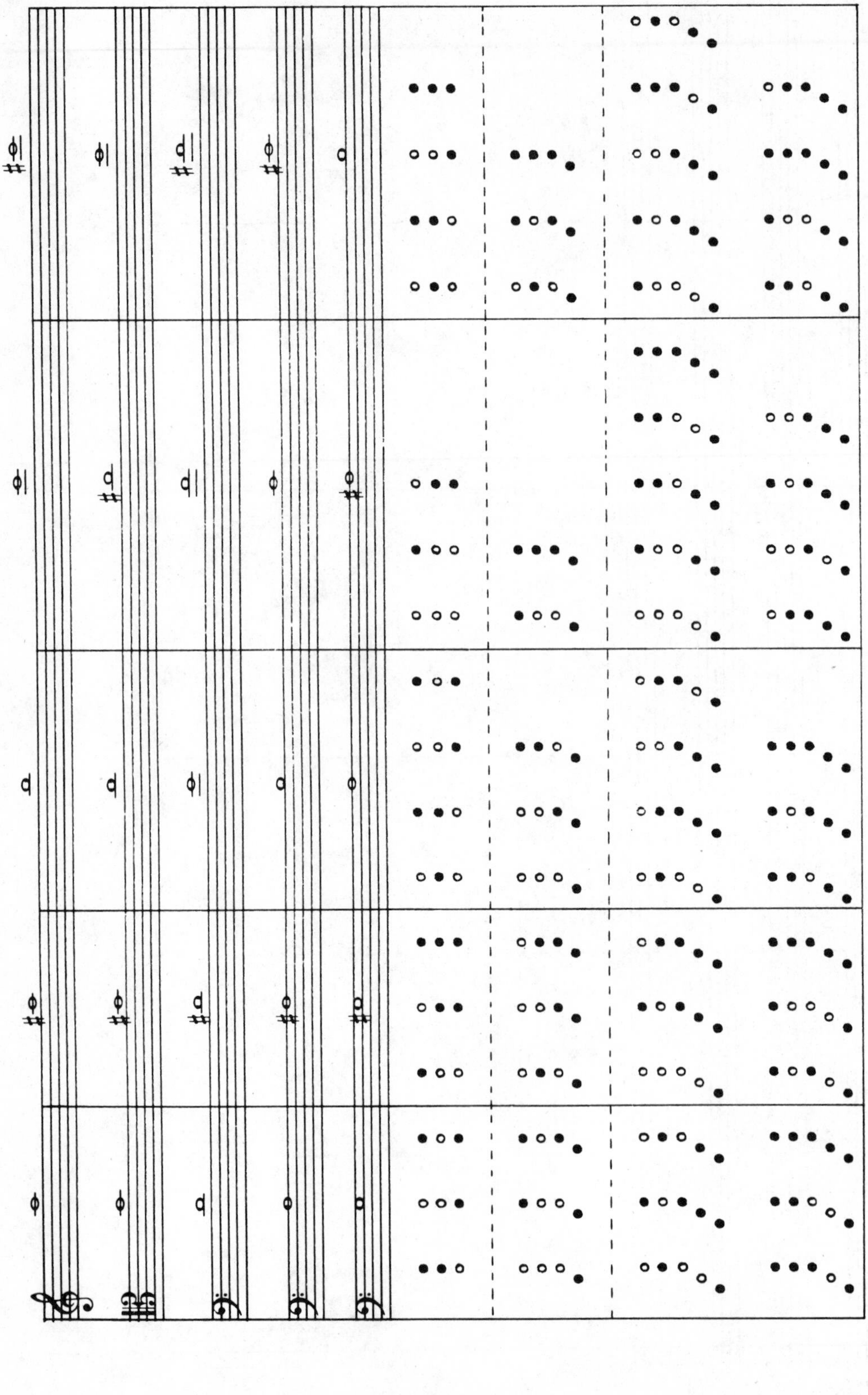

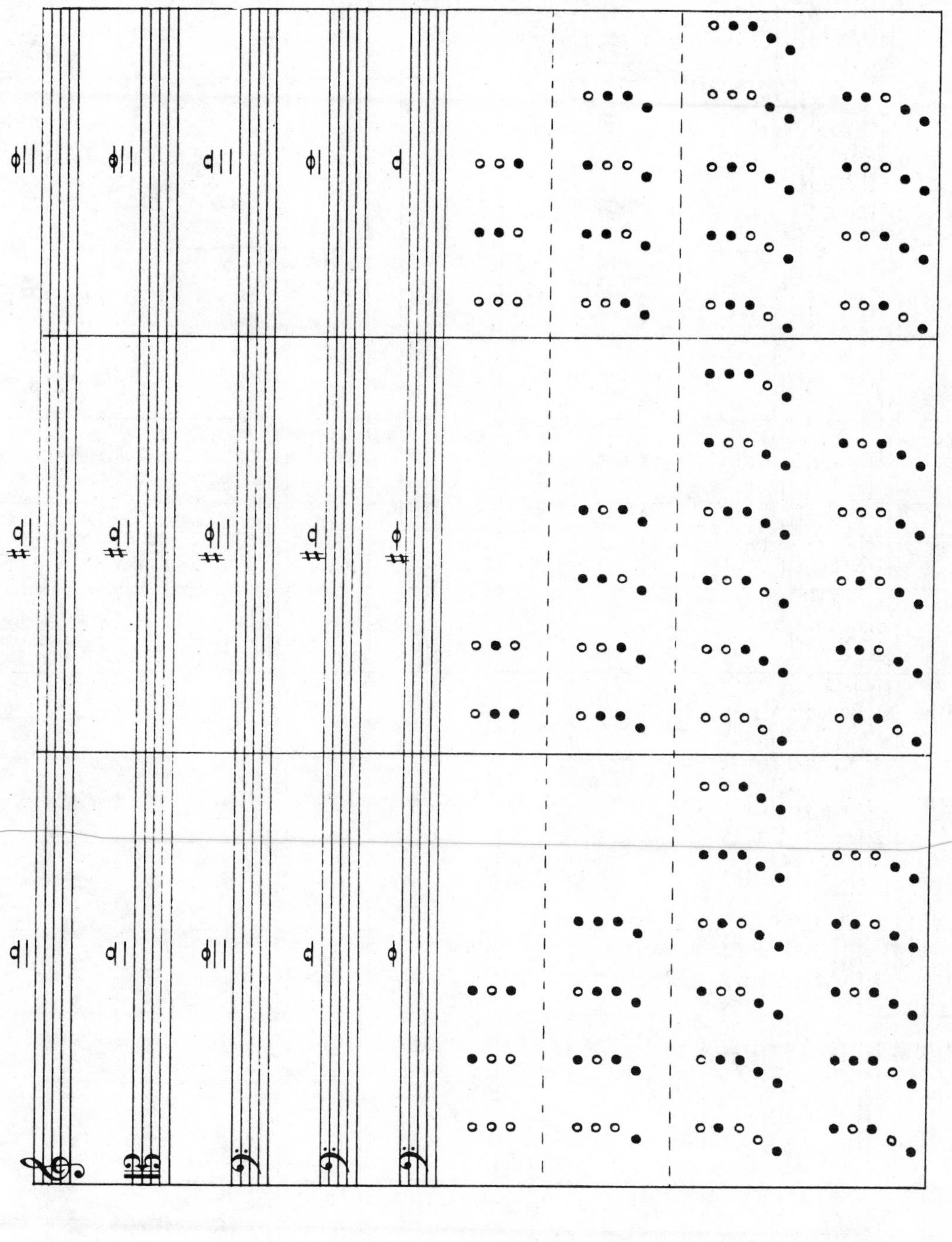

Trombone Slide Positions

Tenor and Bass / Alto / Contrabass (pedal tones at left)

with no attachments		VII	VI	V	IV	III	II	I						VII
with F attachment	III	II	I							VI	V	IV	III	II
with E attachment	II	I							VI	V	IV	III	II	I

with no attachments	VI	V	IV	III	II	I	VII	VI	V	IV	III	II VII	I VI	V	IV	III VII	II VI
with F attachment	I		VI	V	IV	III	II	I VI	V	IV	III	II VI	I V	IV	III VI	II V	I IV
with E attachment		VI	V	IV	III	II	I VI	V	IV	III	II VI	I V	IV	III VI	II V	I IV	III ♯VI

I V	IV VII	III VI	II V	I IV ♯VII	III ♯VI	II VII ♯V	I VI ♯IV	V VII ♯III	IV VI ♯II	III V VII	II IV VI	I III V ♯VII	II IV VII ♯VI	I III VI ♯V	II V ♯IV ♯VII	I IV ♯III ♯VI ♯VII
III ♯VI	II ♯V	I VI ♯IV	V ♯III	IV VI ♯II	III V	II IV VI	I III V	II IV ♯VI	I III VI ♯V	II V ♯IV	I IV ♯III ♯VI	III ♯II ♯V ♯VI	II VI ♯IV ♯V	I V VI ♯III ♯IV	IV V VI ♯II ♯III	III IV V ♯II
II ♯V	I VI ♯IV	V ♯III	IV VI ♯II	III V	II IV VI	I III V	II IV ♯VI	I III VI ♯V	II V ♯IV	I IV ♯III ♯VI	III II ♯V ♯VI	II VI ♯IV ♯V	I V VI ♯III ♯IV	IV V VI ♯II ♯III	III IV V VI ♯II	II III IV V

APPENDIX VI

The Overtone Series

Fundamental, first partial, through the 16th partial. All of the black notes represent the approximate pitch of the flat (out-of-tune) partials.

APPENDIX VII

The International Phonetic Alphabet

Symbols that are used in English are given English equivalents. If the symbol has no use in English, then an example from another language is used.

Front Vowels

[i] ee as in seed
[ɪ] i as in slid
[e] a as in spade
[ɛ] e as in sled
[æ] a as in had
[a] a as in lamb

Back Vowels

[ɑ] a as in palm
[ɒ] o as in hot
[ɔ] aw as in paw
[o] o as in float
[ʊ] oo as in look
[u] oo as in boot

The Nasals

[m] m as in mow
[n] n as in no
[ŋ] ng as in sing

Other Signs

[:] lengthen preceding sound
[˜] nasalize the sound below
[ˇ] trill the sound below
[ʔ] glottal stop; found in substandard English substituted for other plosives

Dipthongs

[ou] o as in no
[au] ou as in pound
[eɪ] ai as in pail
[aɪ] i as in pile
[ɔɪ] oy as in toy

Central Vowels

[ɜ] ir as in bird (stressed)
[ə] er as in brother (unstressed)
[ʌ] u as in mud
[ɜ] ir as in British bird (stressed)
[ə] er as in British brother (unstressed)

The Semi-Vowels

[w] w as in witch
[ʍ] wh as in which
[j] y as in you
[l] l as in law
[r] r as in raw

Non-English Consonants

[ç] ch as in German ich
[x] ch as in German Ach
[ʀ] r as in German rein
[ɡ] g as in German Wagen
[ɾ] r as in French sur
[ʎ] ll as in Castillian calle
[β] b as in Spanish abogado

Stop-plosives

[t] t as in to
[p] p as in pat
[b] b as in bat
[d] d as in do
[g] g as in gone
[k] c as in cast

Continuant Fricatives

[f] f as in fife
[v] v as in five
[ð] th as in thy
[θ] th as in bath
[h] h as in hat
[s] s as in sue
[ʃ] ss as in mission
[ʒ] s as in vision
[z] z as in zip

Combinations

[tʃ] ch as in church
[ʃt] shed as in rushed
[dʒ] j as in judge

Non-English Vowels

[y] uh as in German fühlen
[ʏ] u as in German Mutter
[ø] oe as in Göthe (German)
[œ] o as in German öffnen

It is important to understand that these phonetic symbols stand for the sound produced and have no particular relationship to the spelling, especially in English. Therefore, [i] represents the sound of e in he, of ee in free, of ea in pea, of ie in cookie, and of i in pot-pourri.

The consonants are often referred to as being *labial*: formed with the lips, or *lingual*: formed with the tongue. An example of the former is [b] b as in bed while an example of the latter is [θ] th as in thigh. Another classification used is *voiced* as opposed to *unvoiced*. An example of unvoiced sound is the sound [f] f as in fair. On the other hand [v] v as in very is voiced. In other words, consonants that consist of only oral noises, without the use of the vocal folds, are unvoiced, while the utilization of the vocal folds will produce a voiced consonant.

Orchestration Bibliography

Baker, Mickey. *Complete Handbook for the Music Arranger.* New York: Amsco, 1970.

Bennett, Robert Russell. *Instrumentally Speaking.* Melville, N. Y.: Belwin-Mills, 1975.

Berlioz, Hector. *Treatise on Instrumentation.* Enlarged and revised by Richard Strauss. Transl. Theodore Front. New York: E. F. Kalmus, 1948.

Betton, Matt. "Standardized Stage Band Articulations," *Selmer Bandwagon* (September 1961), p. 20.

Cacavas, John. *Music Arranging and Orchestration.* Melville, N. Y.: Belwin-Mills, 1975.

Casella, Alfredo. *La Tecnica dell'orchestra contemporanea.* Rev. Ed. Milan: Ricordi, 1974.

Erpf, Hermann Robert. *Lehrbuch der Instrumentation und Instrumentenkunde.* Mainz: B. Schott's Söhne, 1959.

Forsyth, Cecil. *Orchestration.* 2nd ed. New York: Macmillan, 1942.

Heacox, Arthur. *Project Lessons in Orchestration.* Boston: Oliver Ditson, 1928.

Jacob, Gordon. *The Elements of Orchestration.* New York: October House, 1962.

______. *Orchestral Technique.* London: Oxford University Press, 1940.

Keller, Hermann. *Phrasing and Articulation.* (Trans. Leigh Gerdine). New York: W.W. Norton and Company, Inc., 1965.

Kennan, Kent. *The Technique of Orchestration.* 2nd ed. Englewood Cliffs, N. J.: Prentice-Hall, 1970.

Kohut, Daniel L. *Instrumental Music Pedagogy.* Englewood Cliffs, N. J.: Prentice-Hall, Inc., 1973.

Lang, Philip J. *Scoring for the Band.* New York: Mills, 1950.

Leibowitz, Rene and Jan Maguire. *Thinking for Orchestra.* New York: Schirmer, 1960.

McKay, George F. *Creative Orchestration.* 2nd ed. Boston: Allyn and Bacon, 1969.

Mancini, Henry. *Sounds and Scores.* Northridge, Calif.: Northridge Music, 1962.

Piston, Walter. *Orchestration.* New York: W.W. Norton, 1955.

Read, Gardner. *Thesaurus of Orchestral Devices.* New York: Pitman, 1953.

Rimski-Korsakov, Nikolai. *Principles of Orchestration.* Ed. Maximilian Steinberg. Transl. Edward Agate. New York: Dover Publications, 1964.

Rogers, Bernard. *The Art of Orchestration.* New York: Appleton-Century-Crofts, 1951.

Sebesky, Don. *The Contemporary Arranger.* New York: Alfred, 1975.

Wagner, Joseph F. *Orchestration.* New York: McGraw-Hill, 1959.

Index